"I've long admired Leo Biga's journalism and prose portraiture for its honesty, thoughtfulness, and accuracy. On a personal note, throughout many years of being interviewed, I find Mr. Biga's articles about me to be the most complete and perceptive of any journalist's anywhere. They ring true to me—even in critique—in a way that reveals the depth of his talent in observation, understanding, and expression."

—Alexander Payne

Praise for *Alexander Payne His Journey in Film*

"Alexander Payne is one of American cinema's leading lights. How fortunate we are that Leo Biga has chronicled his rise to success so thoroughly."

— **Leonard Maltin**
Film Critic, Indiewire.com

"Alexander is a master. Many say the art of filmmaking comes from experience and grows with age and wisdom but, in truth, he was a master on day one of his first feature. Leo has beautifully captured Alexander's incredible journey in film for us all to savor."

— **Laura Dern**
Actor

"I'd be an Alexander Payne fan even if we didn't share a Nebraska upbringing; he is a masterly, menschy, singular storyteller whose movies are both serious and unpretentious, delightfully funny and deeply moving. And he's fortunate indeed to have such a thoughtful and insightful chronicler as Leo Biga."

— **Kurt Andersen**
NY Times Bestselling Author of *True Believers* and *Heyday*
Host of *Studio 360*

"Leo Biga, through his extraordinary talent with words, brings us a fascinating, comprehensive, insightful portrait of the work and artistry of Alexander Payne. Mr. Biga's collection of essays document the evolution and growth of this significant American filmmaker, and he includes relevant historical context of the old Hollywood and the new. His keen reporter's eye gives the reader an exciting journey into the art of telling stories on film."

— **Ron Hull**
Senior Advisor to Nebraska Educational Television
Professor Emeritus of Broadcasting, University of Nebraska
Author of *Backstage*

"Last night I finished your wonderful new book and I enjoyed it so much! Alexander Payne is such a terrific director and I loved reading about his films in detail. Congratulations.

– **Joan Micklin Silver**
Filmmaker (*Hester Street, Crossing Delancey*)

"Alexander Payne richly deserves this astute book about his work by Leo Biga. I say this as a fan of both of theirs; and would be one even if I weren't from Nebraska."

– *Dick Cavett*
TV legend

ALEXANDER PAYNE

PAYNE

HIS JOURNEY IN FILM

LEO ADAM BIGA

RIVER JUNCTION PRESS LLC
Omaha, Nebraska

ISBN 9780997266702
Second edition

Contact Leo Adam Biga:
www.leoadambiga.com
leo32158@cox.net

River Junction Press LLC
www.riverjunctionpress.com

Distributed by Independent Publishers Group
www.ipgbook.com

Printed in the United States of America

Publisher's Cataloging-In-Publication Data
(Prepared by The Donohue Group, Inc.)

Names: Biga, Leo Adam.
Title: Alexander Payne : his journey in film / Leo Adam Biga.
Description: Second edition. | Omaha, Nebraska : River Junction Press
    LLC, [2016] | Originally published: Omaha, Neb. : Inside Stories, ©2013.
    | "Downsizing, Nebraska, The Descendants, Sideways, About Schmidt,
    Election, Citizen Ruth"--Cover. | Interest age level: 14 and up. | Includes a
    discussion guide with index.
Identifiers: ISBN 978-0-9972667-0-2 | ISBN 978-0-9850178-8-0 (mobi) |
    ISBN 978-0-9850178-9-7 (ibook) | ISBN 978-0-9850178-7-3 (ePub)
Subjects: LCSH: Payne, Alexander, 1961---Criticism and interpretation. |
    Motion picture producers and directors--United States. | Film criticism.
Classification: LCC PN1998.3.P39 B54 2016 (print) | LCC PN1998.3.P39
    (ebook) | DDC 791.43/0233/092--dc23

Contents

Alexander Payne's Omaha: a quixotic appreciation

Foreword by Timothy Schaffert

"I'm from Omaha," Rosemary Woodhouse (mother of Satan) says in *Rosemary's Baby*, but one wonders if this frail flower with the finishing-school lilt and mod minis has ever taken one step west of Peyton Place. But no more representative of Omahans is the serviceman in *Fail-Safe*, who tells Henry Fonda, "I've lived in Omaha awwwl ma laf," with the hayseed twang of an inbred corn-shucker.

Omaha—and every other inch of the Nebraska landscape for that matter—has no real cinematic presence outside of the films of Alexander Payne. Though some iconic cinematic figures spent formative years in the state (Fonda, Marlon Brando, Harold Lloyd, Darryl F. Zanuck), and many movies have been filmed and set in Nebraska, few filmmakers have brought the Midwestern experience to the screen in any literal and consistent sense. Payne's Omaha, meanwhile, is both a funhouse-mirror image of his hometown and a sublime literary invention. It's a place where you probably don't want to live, and yet it's also one you don't want to leave—his characters' various slants on life are endlessly entertaining. Perhaps his characters' most redeeming quality is their indifference to fashion.

Payne's films create an intriguing conundrum for the city's cheerleaders. His Omaha films have coincided with a turn-of-the-century publicity blitz by Omaha leaders eager to promote the city as a place of progress, sophistication, and creative ingenuity. And while Payne's films give Omaha the nod of Hollywood that fits with glamorous big-city schemes, Payne's characters are decidedly unmoved by any gestures of cultural revolution. They are fiercely domesticated, too preoccupied with the troubles under their own roofs to worry about city improvements. Even Schmidt's correspondence with the orphan Ndugu in *About Schmidt* is sweetly buoyed by Schmidt's provincialism, and Schmidt and Ndugu's moment of connection late in the film, via the child's illustration, provides one of 21st-century film's most profoundly moving images.

Payne's Omaha is home to mild, befuddled, and charmingly unworldly insurance agents and school teachers (Jack Nicholson's Schmidt, Matthew Broderick's Mr. McAllister in *Election*) incapable of fathoming the depths of their own heartache. And Payne doesn't go easy on the city's undesirables, such as the anti-abortion activists and back-alley glue huffers of *Citizen Ruth* and perhaps his most enjoyable character, *Election*'s springy-curled sociopath Tracy Flick.

A few of Payne's films have been set in locales far more exotic (the Hawaii of *The Descendants* and the California wine country of *Sideways*), but those too demonstrate what's so thrilling about the Midwestern films—a masterly balance of connection and discord between character and place. As the characters seek either upheaval or stability, we learn how closely they identify themselves with their domestic trappings, and how their habits and routines—or their abandoning of those habits and routines—distract them from their fears.

We see this most succinctly in Payne's short film *14e arrondissement*. Carol, a Midwestern woman who has spent six days in Paris, opens her heart to her French class in a monotone recitation. She speaks of recent losses and disappointments, of love and death, but assures, "I am not a sad person." And as she recalls a walk through the city's side streets, she imagines a different life, one lived in Paris but much like the one she lives in Denver, as a mail carrier: simply meeting the people of the foreign city that has so moved her. "I am sure they are very nice," she tells us in perfectly flawed French.

Timothy Schaffert: The Nebraska native and Omaha resident is the author of several novels including *The Coffins of Little Hope* and *The Swan Gondola* set at the 1898 Omaha World's Fair. He is an assistant professor of English at the University of Nebraska–Lincoln and the founder-director of the (downtown) Omaha Lit Fest. Schaffert is a former editor of the alternative weeklies *The Reader* and *Omaha Pulp*.

Alexander Payne's Indiewood: an essay

Foreword by Thomas Schatz

Anyone from Omaha with a keen interest in movies is bound to be aware of the talent the city has bred—a phenomenon that dates back to early Hollywood and has continued steadily for close to a century. Alexander Payne is a rather distinctive member of this group for several reasons. One is that, unlike the majority of these movie notables, he is not an actor or a star but a filmmaker. Another is that, as an independent writer-director, Payne has chosen not only to situate many of his films in Omaha, but to shoot them there as well. And like Scorsese's Little Italy and Barry Levinson's Baltimore, Alex Payne's Omaha is not just a setting or a location but a sense of place and a sensibility.

A third reason is for me more personal. Like Alex Payne (but over a decade earlier) I grew up in the Dundee neighborhood, attended Creighton Prep, cut my eye teeth as a moviegoer in the Dundee Theater, and wound up with a career in film—primarily as a film professor, although I've produced a few independent features and written pretty extensively about the movie industry. In fact, Alex Payne figures prominently in my current book project, a history of contemporary Hollywood, as one of the chief architects of the indie film movement and so-called Indiewood phenomenon of the past two decades. Indeed, Payne's most successful films—*About Schmidt*, *Sideways*, and *The Descendants*—are quintessentially Indiewood: inventive, quirky pictures that flout Hollywood convention in terms of story and style, with just the right mix of star power, compelling characterization, and oddball affirmation of the human condition to engage a wider audience and crack the all-important $100-million box-office barrier.

Enabling this burgeoning indie movement were companies like Miramax, Sony Classics, and Fox Searchlight, quasi-autonomous subsidiaries of the mammoth media conglomerates that came to rule the industry in the 1990s. Dealing with indie outfits could be a challenge, as Payne learned early on. He started his career butting heads with Harvey Weinstein after Miramax picked up *Citizen Ruth*, then titled *The Demon Within*, prior to its debut at Sundance in January 1996. Weinstein pressed Payne to change the title (which he did) and to change the film's ending (which he did not), and then sat on the film for nearly a year before releasing it in December, just weeks after *The English Patient* and *Sling Blade*. Those other two films were a preoccupation for Miramax, to say the least, and *Citizen Ruth* received nowhere near the attention—and the marketing push—that it deserved.

Payne's second film, *Election*, fared better on all counts. Produced and distributed by MTV Films, an indie subsidiary of Viacom (parent company of Paramount Pictures), *Election* was a solid critical and commercial success, putting Payne on the industry map in a year (1999) that saw an astonishing run of Indiewood hits: Kimberly Pierce's *Boys Don't Cry*, Spike Jonze's (and Charlie Kaufman's) *Being John Malkovich*, Paul Thomas Anderson's *Magnolia*, David O. Russell's *Three Kings*, Sofia Coppola's *The Virgin Suicides*, David Fincher's *Fight Club*, and Sam Mendes's *American Beauty*. A few of those were major studio pictures, signaling mainstream Hollywood's investment in the indie film movement, and Payne himself edged a bit closer to the belly of the beast with his next film, *About Schmidt*—a $30-million production with a major star for a "mini-major" studio, New Line (then in its *Lord of the Rings* phase). That 2002 film was an even bigger hit and made Payne a serious Hollywood player, but he opted to return for his next film, *Sideways*, to the safe haven of the indie subsidiary Fox Searchlight, which limited his resources but ensured both his sanity and his creative freedom.

Sideways was of course a phenomenal success, not only critically and commercially but as an award-season triumph as well, bringing a flood of accolades highlighted by five Oscar nominations (and a win for Best Adapted Screenplay) and a sweep of the Independent Spirit Awards (including wins for best picture, director, actor, supporting actor, and screenplay). Alexander Payne clearly was at the very top of his game after that career-defining hit in late 2004, and thus one of the most baffling developments in recent Hollywood history was the seven-year hiatus before his next film.

There are many reasons for that break, including personal and professional travails that Alex discusses with Leo Biga elsewhere in this volume. But others worth noting here involve the American movie industry at large—particularly the rapid unraveling of the indie movement and Hollywood's increasing disdain for filmmakers unwilling to pursue more "commercial" projects.

Payne saw this coming; in fact he went on record to that effect in September 2004, just weeks before the release of *Sideways*, in a provocative piece he wrote for *Variety*'s "First Person" column. Under the headline "Declaration of independents," Payne bemoaned "the cleft between what we consider studio movies and independent movies," and condemned Hollywood's growing penchant for "starving the small and medium films in order to feed the increasingly mercurial 'tentpole' beast." Payne called for "a cinema that is intelligent, uplifting, and human," rather than the "consumer-oriented projections" and "glorified cartoons" that had come to dominate Hollywood filmmaking. "For some 25 years we've had American movies but not movies about Americans."

"Most likely things are going to get worse before they improve," Payne concluded. Indeed they did, and not even a film like *Sideways* could stem the tide—although many critics hoped that it might. Todd McCarthy in his rave review in *Variety* (just days after Payne's broadside) proclaimed that "Alexander Payne has single-handedly restored humanism as a force in American films in *Sideways*." And Manohla Dargis in her equally rapturous *New York Times* review of *Sideways* wrote: "Since the late 1970s we have been under the spell of the blockbuster imperative, with its infallible heroes and comic-book morality, a spell that the independent film has done little to break. In this light, the emergence of Mr. Payne into the front ranks of American filmmakers isn't just a cause for celebration; it's a reason for hope."

No pressure, Mr. Payne.

From all indications, Payne kept busy in the months and years after *Sideways*, but one project after another came undone as the independent sector went into free fall and Indiewood seriously retrenched. With the studios' tentpole beasts—*Harry Potter*, *Spider-Man*, *Shrek*, and the rest—ruling the global marketplace, the conglomerates could no longer rationalize their risky indie divisions. One after another was either folded into the parent company's major studio (Miramax into Disney, New Line into Warner Bros.) or shut down altogether. From 2004 to 2008, the number of conglomerate-owned indie divisions fell from 15 to just three: Sony Classics, Focus, and Fox Searchlight. And eventually the only profitable companies among the scores of true independents, Lions Gate and Summit, would merge to consolidate their own tentpole interests, i.e., the *Twilight*, *Hunger Games*, and torture porn franchises. Things were certainly getting worse.

All of which makes the success of *The Descendants* that much sweeter. Defying the odds and market trends, Payne came storming back on his own terms and in his own inimitable style. Modestly budgeted and deftly handled by Fox Searchlight, *The Descendants* was by far Payne's biggest commercial hit and another critical success, reasserting both his leverage and his stature in the dwindling ranks of indie auteurs. But most importantly, the film reminds us of what Alex Payne—and the American cinema—is capable of creating.

Like his earlier masterworks, *The Descendants* is a dark, disturbing comedy that veers into satire and slapstick and wrenching family drama. It's another compelling portrait of girls with gumption and restless middle-aged men dealing with loss and disappointment. Again Payne shines in terms of casting and his work with actors—not only the delightfully off-cast George Clooney but also Shailene Woodley in a breakout performance on a par with Reese Witherspoon's in *Election*. And again he employs a style of poetic realism that is utterly distinctive among contemporary American filmmakers (although Terry Malick comes close).

Essential to that style is a sense of place. In his early work, of course, that place was Omaha and the sensibility was ineffably Midwestern—stoic yet anxious city folk lost in the heartland and looking for a way out. *Citizen Ruth* bolting down that alley at film's end said it all. Payne too had an impulse to "light out for the Territory," in Twain's memorable phrase, and so we find his restless protagonists further and further West—Denver, then California, then Hawaii. But the Midwestern values persist as his characters are displaced, with family and community and the land itself growing more important in each of Payne's films. And weaving through them all is the essential humanism that McCarthy noted, a storyteller's capacity to create characters that actually matter to us and whose lives evoke the world we live in.

Payne reversed that westward direction but stayed firmly on course with *Nebraska*, a return to his native land and his arthouse roots. He first announced the project in 2003 after wrapping up production on *Sideways*, and his ensuing career hiatus was attributable in part to Payne's fierce determination to make a film that went so blatantly against the Hollywood grain—a character study, shot in black and white and without big-name stars, of an alcoholic old coot and his estranged son on the road in the desolate flatlands of Nebraska. But Payne's patience and persistence clearly paid off, and his distinctive style and vision continued to evolve. Nebraska gives us another tragi-comic road trip and another unlikely buddy film, which in the sure hands and poetic vision of this utterly singular auteur becomes a profound and moving story of life and loss, of forgetting and forgiveness. The generational motif operates on another level as well, with Bruce Dern's gritty, grizzled codger harkening back to his daughter Laura Dern's title character in *Citizen Ruth*—the first in Payne's gallery of homespun eccentrics, all of whom convey the essential humanism that McCarthy noted. Against all odds and with uncompromising artistry, Alex Payne continues to make "movies about Americans," creating characters whose lives actually matter to us and who cut to the very heart—and the heartland—of the world we live in.

Thomas Schatz is a professor (and former chairman) in the Radio-Television-Film Department at the University of Texas and the founding director of the UT Film Institute, which trains students in feature-length narrative filmmaking. He has executive produced five independent features through UTFI and its commercial partner, Burnt Orange Productions (which he also founded). Schatz has written four books about the American film industry, including *The Genius of the System: Hollywood Filmmaking in the Studio Era* and *Boom and Bust: American Cinema in the 1940s.* His writing on film has appeared in the *New York Times,* the *Los Angeles Times, Premiere, The Nation, Film Comment, Film Quarterly,* and many other publications. Schatz is currently writing a history of contemporary, conglomerate-controlled Hollywood.

Introduction

❦

As a career freelance writer in Omaha, Nebraska, I cover a multitude of subjects. I am the classic case of not being an expert in any one thing, but knowing enough about a whole lot of things to write reasonably intelligent articles and books about them. Film is a particular interest of mine.

The term film buff definitely applies to me. I actually used to program or curate films for public exhibition. As a journalist, I look for any opportunity I can find to write about cinema. In the course of following my nose for film news I began covering Omaha native Alexander Payne soon after his feature debut in 1996. I have not stopped since. *Citizen Ruth* came out the first quarter of that year, I first met Payne in the fall of '97, and my first story about him appeared at the start of '98. Though I have covered many other filmmakers and film projects since then, my body of Payne work remains unique for its duration, scope, and depth. Early on, I recognized in him an important cinema figure and the fruits of my cultivating that relationship are the stories that comprise this book.

I also saw in Payne an opportunity to write about one of the most significant Nebraskans in film to come along in a while. Many from the state have made major contributions to the film industry either by the prominence or quality or volume of their work. Lest you doubt me, try this list on for size:

Darryl Zanuck, Harold Lloyd, Hoot Gibson, Fred Astaire, Robert Taylor, Ward Bond, Ann Ronell, Henry Fonda, Dorothy McGuire, Montgomery Clift, Marlon Brando, Lynn Stalmaster, Donald Thorin, James Coburn, David Janssen, Inga Swenson, Sandy Dennis, David Doyle, Lew Hunter, Irene Worth, Joan Micklin Silver, Nick Nolte, Swoosy Kurtz, Paul Williams, Steve Lustgarten, Marg Helgenberger, Stephanie Kurtzuba, Lori Petty, Mike Hill, Gail Levin, Sandy Veneziano, Alexander Payne, John Jackson, Hillary Swank, Jon Bokenkamp, Jaime King, Dan Mirvish, Dana Altman, John Beasley, Kevin Kennedy, Patrick Coyle, Gabrielle Union, Monty Ross, Yolonda Ross, Nicholas D'Agosto, Chris Klein, Nik Fackler, Tom Elkins. If you allow me to stretch the "In Film" barometer a bit, I can add Johnny Carson and Dick Cavett to the list for good measure.

The names include mega-moguls, directors, producers, screen-writers, songwriters, editors, cinematographers, actors, actresses, casting directors. Their influence extends from the silent era through the Golden Age of Hollywood to the indie movement and right on up to today. There are Oscar winners both behind and in front of the camera, industry stalwarts and mavericks, household names, and lesser known but no less important figures.

I would have given anything to have interviewed Zanuck, Lloyd, Astaire, Fonda, McGuire, Clift, Brando, et al. I have interviewed several of the contemporary figures, including Hunter, Silver, Kurtz, Helgenberger, Kurtzuba, Cavett, Hill, Levin, Beasley, Bokenkamp, Union, the Rosses–Monty and Yolonda (no relation), and Fackler. I still hope to get around to Nolte.

Payne is the preeminent filmmaker among them all. When all is said and done, his legend may, if not supplant, then certainly equal that of the legends of the past. Until preparing the book I had not revisited my early Alexander Payne articles for some years. In reviewing those stories I made the usual spectrum of discoveries one makes when returning to long unseen work: from cringing at misspelled words or incorrect titles to feeling satisfaction about just how deeply and consistently I mine Payne's creative process. Some of the fondest memories I retain from my professional life are the lively, engaging, one-on-one sessions I enjoy with Payne. They are as much conversations and explorations between two film guys as they are interviews between subject and journalist.

Payne, as you would expect, is a superb interview. Highly literate. Thoughtful. Composed. He is rarely less than frank. He can be both profane and flat out funny. He is only politically correct and circumspect when it serves a project. He generally knows what you are looking for but does not necessarily hand it to you on a silver platter, which is to say he will only give as good as he gets. He does so much press now that he does sometimes repeat quotable nuggets or tag lines from interview to interview. The strategic part of him has shown more as his career has exploded. Who can blame him?

Oh, I have my scripted questions at the ready all right, because I always feel I have to be extra prepared, not to mention be on my mental toes with him, certainly more than with most subjects. He is so damned smart that it can be a bit intimidating even now, twenty years into our relationship. I make sure to do my homework when possible. But I am also comfortable enough to go off script and wing it on occasion and to let him take these interludes wherever he wants to go with them. The best material often comes from these asides or addenda anyway, and so I am not about to curtail his digressions or flights of fancy. Or my own for that matter.

But the extent to which my stories go into his creative process, from script to pre-production, to production, and right on through editing, surprised me because I think I began to take it for granted. I was also pleasantly surprised by the amount of analysis and interpretation I did. What re-reading these articles did was to remind me of the rather comprehensive Payne archive I have been able to compile as a result of doing so many interviews with him over two decades that roughly covers his entire feature filmmaking career. It is an archive that no other journalist or author has been in a position to acquire. This body of work has accrued because I have persisted in covering him and cultivating our relationship and because he has responded by consistently granting me great access. The often exclusive interviews and unfettered access continue.

Until he postponed the project, I was to have spent much of one spring on the set of his feature *Nebraska* to inform a book about the making of that film. Then he seemingly changed course and spoke about filming graphic novelist Daniel Clowes' *Wilson* in California. I expected to make my way onto its set and to catch up with the *Nebraska* production whenever it filmed. Well, as these things go in Hollywood, *Wilson* was abandoned and *Nebraska* got back on the docket. I visited the set. The making-of book has not happened yet, but it is still on the table. We just need to find the right project for it.

Through *Sideways* and for a few years afterward, our interviews were generally longer than they are today. Where a single session would go a full hour or sometimes two in the past, his more time-pressed life today allows for maybe half that when really busy; though there are exceptions when he still accommodates an hour or two, such as when he first got back to the mainland after completing *The Descendants*, his much feted movie shot in Hawaii.

Whatever time I get with him, I appreciate. If anything, my gratitude for his generous spirit has only grown. I know how privileged I am to gain the insider access he gives. After all, there is no reason he should be as loyal to me as he is other than my dogged reporting.

The interviews I have done with him—that is until this book—have fed into stories published in small newspapers, one of which no longer exists and mid-sized magazines. The stories also appeared on my blog. Not exactly formidable outlets with large, taste-maker-type audiences. No matter, he has continued making himself available through it all—his Oscars, Golden Globes, and Independent Spirit Awards, his critical accolades, and his growing stature. That is because there is not a careerist bone in his body. Therefore, I look at what he and I have as a stand-alone opportunity that I must nurture and honor.

Some who know about my long-tenured coverage of Payne assume that he and I are friends or buddies. Not exactly. I mean, we are certainly friendly with each other. But we do not hang out together. Ours is definitely a closer relationship than most journalists have with a subject, but it is by no means a rare or unprecedented one. We never speak about it, but my sense is that he and I feel the same in that while it is fine we have this thing together, we do not push it so far that it compels him to meddle in my work or tempts me to compromise my journalistic integrity.

In other words, we do not cross certain lines. That includes not probing too deeply into our personal lives. I only rarely mention his life away from film in my stories. He has no financial stake in or editorial control over this book. He never interferes with what I write, just as I never think about censoring my work to please him. We both want it this way. It's the right thing to do and it avoids weird conflicts of interest.

Because I am in the unique position of having covered him for so long and in such an in-depth manner, this book uses the interviews and stories I have done to chart the arc of his filmmaking career.

On a story-by-story basis, starting with the aftermath of *Citizen Ruth* and the making of *Election*, through *About Schmidt, Sideways, The Descendants, Nebraska*, and a peek at his latest, *Downsizing*. you will follow the development of Payne as an auteur. His incremental progress and growing confidence become apparent from the early stories to the later stories, though he was always mature beyond his years as well as always articulate and insightful in discussing his work. His journey as a filmmaker and the increased traction he and his work enjoy among critics and audiences alike are revealed in these pages in roughly the chronology in which these things unfolded.

You will read, too, about some detours along the way: directing his installment for the *Paris, I Love You* omnibus project; acting in Wes Craven's own *Paris* installment; doing for-hire rewrite jobs with longtime screenwriting partner Jim Taylor on several commercial features; directing the pilot for HBO's *Hung*; and producing a handful of films directed by others.

Then there is the production company Ad Hominem Enterprises, which he formed with Taylor and *Election* and *Descendants* co-producer Jim Burke. Not to be ignored are the projects he wanted to make but didn't, most notably *Downsizing*, though after years of being put on hold he finally got around to making it. That formerly aborted feature came in the midst of a several year interval between *Sideways* premiering and *The Descendants* shooting. There was a picture he talked about making that I completely forgot about until reading a reference to it in one of these stories: an adaptation of *The Picture of Dorian Gray* set in Hollywood.

At one point he began research on a Spanish-language film examining the lives of Hispanic migrants in sometimes hostile small towns whose packing plants draw the newcomers and pump much-needed revenue into rural coffers even as some locals work to limit the migrants' rights and to make life miserable for them.

He has pined to make a Western for a long time, though until recently I had not heard him talk about it for a while. And from time to time he has floated the idea of making films in Greece and Spain, countries he has deep ties to by virtue of heritage and scholarship, respectively. He's traveled to each numerous times.

He has also expressed other inclinations or plans that never came to fruition, such as at one point being hell-bent on moving to New York. From the start of his filmmaking career the artist has been professionally based in the L.A. area, though always keeping a home both on the West Coast and in Omaha. Also, you may notice apparent inconsistencies, such as a reference to Payne planning to write *Sideways* alone when in fact he and Taylor co-scripted the project. Circumstances change, that's all.

You will also note some repetition throughout the text. This is a function of the book being a compendium of stories that look at Payne and his work. Sometimes several stories focus on the same project or on a particular aspect of his work. Because I wish to present these stories as close to how they appeared when first published. I have left the repetitive bits in, though I think you will find in these reverbs I do use a number of different ways to describe him and his work, just as I approach the subject from a number of different angles. The end result, I trust, is a fuller appreciation for the who, what, where, when, why, and how.

Most of the stories gathered here originally appeared in *The Reader* (www.thereader.com), an Omaha alternative news weekly published by John Heaston I have long contributed to. Another segment of the work appeared in a short-lived paper, the *Omaha Weekly*, whose publisher was also Heaston. A few stray pieces appeared elsewhere.

The Payne I first met in 1997 is the same man today. A little wiser, a little more gray. But remarkably unaffected by his steady rise to celebrated international filmmaker. Strip away all the artifice and fame around him and he is the same decent, humble person he has always been. He embodies the best of us. I am proud to call him a fellow creative and Nebraskan.

The book's title, *Alexander Payne: His Journey in Film*, speaks to him assiduously refining and expressing a particular cinema sensibility and to still being in the prime of his career. There is presumably much more to come from him, and therefore this or any other work about him at this point in time is far from the final or definitive word about him. The title deliberately refers to his being on a path that is, by its very nature, progressive.

Like many artists, his ambitious subject matter is nothing less than the human condition. Viewed at a micro level, he is concerned with what people do when by choice or circumstance they find themselves at a crossroads—morally, emotionally, intellectually, spiritually. Once committed to go one way or the other, there is no turning back. They tumble past the tipping point, and gravity or momentum hurtles them down the rabbit hole. As the storyteller, Payne has us go through the ensuing crucible with the poor bastard.

But what makes Payne's work so rich and full is that the landscape his protagonists tread is never all black or white, instead various shades of gray. Yes, decisions are made and actions taken, and they may bear unpleasant consequences, but very little in his world is completely irrevocable or unsalvageable, just as his characters are never unredeemable. Not that he even implies his characters need saving. They are who they are, warts and all. No excuses or apologies necessary. No judgments made. Indeed, he finds a certain beauty and strength in their flaws. The good, the bad, the ugly are all one and the same. Because all these qualities reside and intermingle in the same space, in the same heart and soul, in the same mind and life, they cannot be separated or parsed out. He wouldn't want to anyway.

This combination holistic, realistic, poetic look at how life works and how people behave is his essential gift to the film canon. He is a truth-seeker of the first order. He is not the first to tread this terrain and he is not necessarily the best, but the consistency and precision with which he does look at the most mundane, moving, and mendacious human traits is notable. The fact that he makes his characters at once funny, poignant, revealing, lovable, and revolting is a rare thing. His films touch raw nerves and deep currents in us all. They are the most unerringly human of films, and therefore the most timeless, even as they perfectly capture the nuances of the times in which they are made and set.

Informing Payne's humanist world view, too, I suspect is the ever-seeking and compassionate Jesuit philosophies he was imbued with at Omaha Creighton Preparatory School, better known as Creighton Prep. Like most Society of Jesus-run educational institutions, the all-male school has taken as its motto the Jesuit mantra of "educating men for others" or variously calling each student to be "a man for others."

One can witness this merciful, graceful, inclusive attitude in his work, where he extends a loving embrace to virtually all his characters, even when they screw up and don't necessarily deserve it. That forgiving and generous attitude, I can attest, extends to how he conducts himself on and off the set, treating people with dignity and respect, once even giving me the coat off his back.

Talent and persistence only take one so far in any industry. Therefore, I have to believe Payne got to where he is and more so stays there as much for how he relates to people as for how brilliant and dogged he is. As his collaborators are quick to point out, he makes the work joyful. As all good directors must be, he is a charismatic leader in all the small ways and large ways that getting a picture mounted and finished requires. He is also the consummate professional who very much leads by example.

There is another often overlooked aspect that attends sustained success: hard work. Payne once told me that when he and Jim Taylor were starting out in the industry and trying to make something happen for themselves they never asked anyone for favors. True to the Midwest ethos he was raised in, Payne believes that your own honest labors will get you rewarded if you just continue to show up, improve your craft, and treat people with respect.

He grew up the son of an industrious Greek American restauranteur. A legend has grown that as a boy Payne bussed tables and washed dishes at the family's popular, open-24-hours-a-day Virginia Cafe in the heart of downtown Omaha. He, in fact, did not do that but he did gain an appreciation for the sweat equity his father and other members of the family put into the endeavor that earned the place legions of loyal customers and helped pay AP's way through prestigious and pricey Omaha private elementary and secondary schools. Payne has learned well to pay the price. He often said he detests writing but he puts himself through its unpleasant rigors anyway in order to create scripts he wants to direct. Likewise, I am sure there were parts of running the Virginia Cafe that his late father George Payne could have done without, but he did them anyway because it was a practical and expedient means to an end – in that case providing a comfortable living for the family. In the son's case, it is giving us films he wishes to make and that he trusts will add to cinema culture. After the Virginia Cafe was lost to a fire, Payne's father reinvented his career and became successful all over again, working well into his 90s. He loved his work and he loved people. He exuded joy and gratitude. All of these same qualities are apparent in the son and so it would not surprise me if he is still directing well into his 80s or 90s should he be blessed to live that long.

In his preceding essay, film historian Thomas Schatz rightly credits Payne with being a leader in the Indiewood movement. This movement finds a few gifted filmmakers staying true to their independent, auteurist instincts while working and thriving within the Hollywood system. In this sense, Payne is a leader to whom other film artists and film lovers look for inspiration. It's why so many of his peers desire working with him. It's why his work draws such attention and anticipation.

Novelist Timothy Schaffert in his appreciation creatively appraises Payne's use of his Midwest roots as the ballast for his characters and stories. Whether set in Nebraska or far afield from there, the core of Payne's work remains fixed in the benevolent yet acerbic Midwestern sensibilities he knows so well. Payne is a Nebraska neo-realist about whom it might be said, You can take him out of Nebraska, but you can't take Nebraska from him.

Because Payne is that seeker personality who delves ever deeper and wider into the human experience, his cinema journey promises to remain intensely personal and intimate even as he inevitably explores different, perhaps larger terrains. His long stated goal of making genre films should not change him; indeed it should only fix his interests in interesting new contexts. I, for one, look forward to the ride.

1

Election and Citizen Ruth

❧

Introduction

A couple things worked to my advantage when I first approached Alexander Payne for an interview in 1997. For starters, I made sure he knew I had not only seen his 1991 UCLA thesis film, *The Passion of Martin*, but that I had also screened it at an Omaha art house I was involved with in the early 1990s called the New Cinema Cooperative. My programming actually extended to two additional venues: the University of Nebraska at Omaha, where I ran a rather large film series for several years; and the Joslyn Art Museum, where I was public relations director and organized occasional film events on the side.

I had become aware of Payne through an item I read about him in the local daily, *The Omaha World-Herald*. Since I did programming and publicity for the now defunct New Cinema, I filed away his name and the title of his film and when the time was right I prevailed upon my fellow cineastes to allow *The Passion of Martin* on the schedule.

I cannot recall what kind of audience the film by the then-obscure young filmmaker drew. But it's a good bet no more than a few dozen souls saw it at our makeshift downtown theater in a former storefront we renovated ourselves. If memory serves, the site was once part of the Omaha Film Exchange and included a forbidding walk-in vault where the canisters containing nitrate stock features and short subjects were stored in an earlier era.

I was highly motivated to do a first-rate interview-profile of Payne for *The Reader*. When he made his first feature, *Citizen Ruth*, in our shared hometown of Omaha in 1995 I was neither covering arts-culture stories on a regular basis nor yet contributing to *The Reader*.

I was mainly freelancing for other publications when a former local television news anchor profiled Payne in *The Reader.* I thought the piece unworthy of a filmmaker of Payne's talent. By that time I had seen *Citizen Ruth* and in my eyes that film more than fulfilled the promise *The Passion of Martin* heralded.

Still, I seem to recall having to pitch hard to convince *The Reader's* editors they should turn me, by then only a fledgling contributor, loose on an extensive cover piece about a still somewhat unproven filmmaker they had profiled only two years earlier. My passionate conviction that Payne was a world-class artist-in-the-making got me the green light I sought and I tackled the assignment with vigor.

As a film buff I felt I could connect with Payne, and in a sense speak his language. By that I do not mean talking shop, as I am not a filmmaker and I do not pretend to know its technical side. Rather, I felt my aesthetic appreciation for cinema and my fairly good grounding in cinema history would resonate with him. Indeed, that is exactly what he responded to, along with, I suspect, the genuine enthusiasm I expressed for his work and, hopefully, the considered questions I asked and observations I made during our two-hour talk.

I think he may have also respected me for holding strong opinions about certain films and filmmakers and for not being afraid to challenge some of his own opinions. My having been a film programmer also helped because his own early discovery of cinema had been informed by film programs just like the ones I worked on. In fact, he has often referenced in interviews the film series he frequented at the Joslyn Art Museum (before I was there) and the art film screenings he attended at the Admiral and Dundee theaters, both within walking distance of the mid-town home he grew up in.

That first interview I did with him took place within days of his concluding pre-production on *Election* and starting to shoot the film. As the production got under way I did have one opportunity to visit the set but I was not able to make it. I did do a follow-up interview with Payne by phone, and I also did phoners with one of the producers, Albert Berger, and with the film's star, Matthew Broderick.

My object with the piece was to take the measure of the up-and-coming writer-director in a serious profile worthy of *The New Yorker* or *The New York Times.* I do not claim to have attained that goal, I will leave that for you the reader to discern, but I was satisfied with the results. I do not recall Payne's specific response to the article but let's just say he appreciated the effort that went into it, and from the time it was published in early 1998 until now he's accorded me interview after interview and, in some cases, exclusive access to his sets.

The profile that follows is by no means comprehensive. However, I believe it was the most in-depth piece done on him up to that time and it forms the foundation upon which I have built all the Payne stories I have filed since. So, as seen in this light, you will be gleaning my strongest first impressions of a filmmaker whom I pegged to be a major force in world cinema and whom I felt confident I would be covering for the rest of my journalistic career.

A final note before releasing you to read the piece: If there is one thing I do in covering Payne and that perhaps I used to do more of then than now, it is providing a certain context in which to better understand him and his work. The context I refer to will become clearer as you read more of my Payne work and learn about the influences, themes, concerns, obsessions, and compulsions that permeate his methodology and mise-en-scène. As the stories that appear in this tome are presented roughly in the order in which I wrote them, they form a progressive prism for looking at his filmography. It is my hope that this Alexander Payne primer reveals more than the sum of its parts in schooling you about the filmmaker and his work.

Alexander Payne: portrait of a young filmmaker

Published in a 1998 issue of *The Reader*

Alexander Payne

Groundings

Darryl Zanuck. Fred Astaire. Henry Fonda. Dorothy McGuire. Montgomery Clift. Marlon Brando. Sandy Dennis. Nick Nolte. Enduring film icons and Nebraskans all. Now add the name of thirty-six-year-old writer-director Alexander Payne to this list of native sons and daughters who have made their mark in cinema. Born and raised in Omaha, Payne made an impressive feature debut with the funky 1996 abortion comedy, *Citizen Ruth*, and is sure to make waves again with his second feature, *Election*, which wrapped shooting in Omaha December 15 and is slated for a summer release.

The made-in-Omaha *Citizen Ruth* netted wide critical praise for its satiric take on the pro-life–pro-choice debate, revealing Payne to be a keen social observer with an ironic sensibility. Payne, who is single and lives in Los Angeles, is a gifted artist. He's smart, witty, confident, yet refreshingly grounded. He knows exactly what he's after and how to get it. He's also brash and passionate enough to make delightfully subversive films far outside the Hollywood mainstream. Those who know him admire his agile mind, his unmannered sincerity, his barbed humor.

He has the cachet to make films anywhere, but continues coming back here to shoot his quirky independent pictures. Indeed, he remains fiercely loyal to his hometown, whose currents reverberate deeply within him. "I feel so strongly about shooting in Omaha," he said. "In nursing and nudging *Election* along, I made it clear I wanted to shoot here, and the producers said, 'Well, you can shoot this anywhere.' But I don't want to fake it. It's not the same thing. There's an atmosphere I want to get and be faithful to—about how people are. I want it to be real, I want it to be where I'm comfortable and where deep buttons in me are pressed."

Election co-producer Albert Berger feels Payne is well attuned to Omaha's zeitgeist. "I had never been in Omaha before, but interestingly enough I sensed an attitude that was very much Alexander's," Berger said. "There's a sort of courteous, formal presentation or exterior of normality, with a bizarre, eccentric, biting humor just beneath it, and I saw that time and time again ... so I'm not surprised Alexander came from Omaha and he's making the type of movies he is there. I feel he is very much of that place."

Payne agrees, but can't quite pinpoint the source of his sardonic streak other than to speculate: "Maybe historically, the fact the weather is so cruel on the Plains that for survival there's bred a sense of humor about it all." If nothing else, his humor is informed by Omaha's small town–big city schizophrenia. "There's always this tight-assed onservative element here that's very irritating," he said, "that doesn't think anything is funny except *Marmaduke* and *Family Circus*. But then there's this whole other Omaha I grew up with of really smart, funny, caustic people."

His cutting humor has no shortage of targets. In *Citizen Ruth* he lampooned the hypocrisy of pro-life–pro-choice extremists. In *Election* he exposes the hollowness of School-Suburbia USA rituals.

The role of satirist seems to fit Payne well, but he feels his career is too young to assign him a signature style just yet: "I don't like to analyze it too closely," he said, "because so far this type of stuff is just what comes naturally to me. And I almost fear that analyzing it too much will make me too self-conscious or make me think there's no rules. You know? I'm still just figuring it out."

The comedy of imperfection

Election, which Payne and his *Citizen Ruth* writing collaborator, Jim Taylor, adapted from the soon-to-be-published novel of the same name by Boston writer Tom Perrotta, promises to be Payne's breakthrough film. Why? Because the material retains the mordant, mercurial sensibility of his debut feature, but is neither likely to be as difficult for its studio (MTV Films, Paramount Pictures) to market nor as hard for audiences to stomach as the earlier film was, with its raw-nerve subject matter. Plus, *Election* stars two young, appealing crossover actors in Matthew Broderick and Reese Witherspoon who should attract the very demographic the film will surely target (ages 18 to 34).

The film, like the book, revolves around a high school teacher, Jim McAllister (Broderick), who, in the midst of a mid-life crisis, acts rashly and rigs a student election, setting in motion a series of seriocomic events that change the lives of everyone involved. Broderick should have just the right innocent deadpan persona (like his idol Buster Keaton) for the part. Much of the script's sly humor stems from normally upstanding folks behaving badly under pressure.

As Payne puts it, "All these horrible, pathetic things happen, but it's not as though any of the characters is bad, they're just doing it all for the first time. They just don't know any better."

For all its strengths, *Citizen Ruth* never quite fleshed-out the title character, Ruth Stoops. Payne and Taylor used her more as a siphon and symbol to comment on the absurd lengths pro-life–pro-choice activists go to, rather than develop her as a person with complex emotional shadings. Her escape at the end makes a strong statement, but tells us nothing we don't already know. While it's hard to believe anyone with a sense of humor could be offended by *Citizen Ruth*, the film surely put off some viewers who strongly identify with one side or the other of the abortion issue.

With *Election*, Payne isn't shying away from skewering more sacred cows, but is mining a richer vein of Americana than he attempted before. Where *Citizen Ruth* often settled for broad sketches, *Election* promises to probe more deeply into the lives of characters and the milieu they inhabit. And, at least as scripted, the new film allows room for its protagonists to grow somewhat through their ordeal.

Payne feels *Election*, with its fuller palette of colors, should prove to be "a much stronger film" than his first feature. "*Citizen Ruth* is particular in its having fun with stereotypes," he said. "It's funny and interesting, but this is a richer piece of material. It's got a more complex, nuanced human canvas. There's nothing schematic about it. I mean, once you figure out what's going on in *Citizen Ruth* you still might enjoy the film, but you kind of know where it's heading. This one, you don't really know what's going to happen next."

Ask him what *Election* is all about and he sighs, wearily weighing your question with one of his own: "How to articulate it? I don't know

... It's very human and it's very real, it's about life. It's like life—I can't sum it up. I hope always to make movies that can't be easily summed up."

Payne doesn't pander to audiences. His leading characters don't neatly conform to post-modern Hollywood's idea of winning protagonists. Instead, they're whimsically, tragically, unpredictably human. And because they're so authentic they engage us in ways "nice" characters often don't. Ruth Stoops is a pregnant inhalant addict who's made a mess of her life and is unrepentant about it. She's also street-smart and disarmingly honest. Jim McAllister is a philandering hypocrite who takes his hurt out on one of his students. He's also hard-working and surprisingly vulnerable.

Broderick wanted to do *Election* because it offered a chance to play "a complicated person, and not a terribly charming one," he said, adding: "I loved the script. For one thing, it was very literate. A lot of scripts are very hard to get through, but this was a very easy read. It was funny and sad. It made me want to know what was going to happen next. Alexander's very original, I think. He's a very careful, detailed director. He's very intelligent. He's funny, too."

He also liked Payne's handling of the material, which in lesser hands could easily have been superficial: "He's sympathetic to the characters, even when they do stupid things. He doesn't look down on the characters from some kind of higher moral ground. They're all very human. He doesn't categorize people. People aren't either perfect or evil, smart or stupid, they're all a mix of things."

But as Payne well knows, some stodgier segments of Omaha don't appreciate his irreverent humor. Omaha Public School officials were wary enough to deny him the use of Burke High School for *Election*. The film's Neo–*Peyton Place* school scenes were eventually shot (during normal school hours) at Papillion–La Vista High School [serving the Papillion and La Vista suburbs bordering southwest Omaha]. Payne resists any suggestion his comic sensibility is vulgar: "I think, for example, that *Citizen Ruth* has an amoral protagonist, yet it's a very moral film. The same thing now with *Election*. There's a lot of irresponsible and immoral behavior in the film, but I believe strongly that it's a very responsible and moral film."

Influences

A Hollywood outsider, despite still living in L.A. and getting his financing there (he plans on moving to New York City by year's end), Payne dislikes much of today's *nouveau hip* American cinema. "Hollywood, in the last few years, has produced films which take the attitude, 'Oh, isn't this cool, we have amoral characters,'" he said. "But in completely unredeeming, nihilistic films that simply anticipate moments of violence, rather than being about people in complex ways, I don't get much out of nihilism."

He finds most contemporary comedies wanting too. "I'm bored with most American comedies because they're about nothing. The attitude is, 'Oh, it's comedy, it's just fluff.' But, in fact, comedy should be about something. It's just another form of communication about experience and emotion."

Although Payne is generations removed from legendary filmmaker Billy Wilder, with whom he's been compared, he greatly admires the writer-director's acerbic, irony-laced style. In preparation for *Citizen Ruth* Payne screened Wilder's *Ace in the Hole* (about an unscrupulous reporter exploiting a human tragedy). One of his favorite Wilder films is the 1960 Best Picture Oscar winner, *The Apartment*, whose story of deceit in the bedrooms and boardrooms of middle-class America echoes that of *Election*, only Payne is substituting schoolrooms for boardrooms.

"I think *The Apartment* is sooooo good," he said. "People remember it as a cute film about a guy (Jack Lemmon) giving his apartment to his bosses for their afternoon liaisons, but you see it again and you have to take a shower afterwards. It's genuinely depressing. People see Billy Wilder's work as cynical and dark and all that, but it's really at the same time loving and playful with people."

It's precisely the same balance Payne tries striking. In Jim McAllister, Payne gives us an Everyman on the verge of a nervous breakdown. A man mired in a rut and desperate for a change. Payne describes him this way: "He's a very American protagonist, somehow. Optimistic. Boyish. Idealistic. Naïve. And tragic, because he's in denial about real things going on in his life and how he really feels about things, and it kind of leads to his downfall."

He could be describing Jack Lemmon's character in *The Apartment*, so alike are the two figures. How appropriate then that Broderick, who shares Lemmon's intuitive grasp of tragic-comic roles, and Payne, who shares Wilder's penchant for subversive satire, should collaborate on a film resonating so strongly with the Lemmon-Wilder canon.

Adaptation

Payne, along with Taylor, found a kindred spirit in Perrotta as well. "We found in his novel a starting place, a springboard for what we do best as writers together. It's very, very close to us. And also there's a certain sadness about the novel, and Jim and I like to extract comedy from sadness and pain," Payne said, laughing devilishly. "What I also liked about the novel, and I think this was maybe true of *Citizen Ruth* too, is that people compromise themselves through really, really good intentions. They all think they're doing the right thing, and they end up getting very, very compromised morally. One other thing it has in common thematically with *Citizen Ruth* . . . is that idea of people's personal-psycho-sexual situations being worked out in a public arena, especially a political arena."

He said one of the ways the movie differs from the book is its humor. "It's a lot funnier than the novel. The novel has a lot of humor in it, but it's kind of more ruminative. Jim and I always go for the laughs." In adapting the book, he and Taylor, who lives in New York City, ended up "dramatizing things Perrotta only mentioned in passing. We ended up writing a ton of new stuff. We changed his characters' names. We took a lot of liberties. When you go to adapt a novel you have to forget the novel. You owe nothing to the novel, yet you remain entirely faithful to it somehow in spirit," Payne said.

Perrotta, whose book is due out in March from Putnam Publishing, said of the adaptation, "I think they translated my work into this other medium in just a brilliant way." Of Payne, whom he had a chance to observe on the set during a late November visit to Omaha, he said, "He's incredibly smart. He seems to have an encyclopedic knowledge of literature and film that he carries around quite gracefully. He's so focused and sharp. I think he's one of these people who really knows what he wants."

Election, while still in manuscript form, was brought to Payne and Taylor in 1996 by Berger and his producing partner Ron Yerxa. Berger had had his eye on Payne since seeing the filmmaker's 1991 UCLA thesis film, *The Passion of Martin*. After agreeing to adapt *Election*, Payne said he and Taylor read the book several more times, noting lines, characters and incidents they wanted to keep or expand. The pair worked on the script throughout '96 and completed their final draft last spring.

"By the end, as we're doing more and more rewrites," Payne said, "the novel didn't even exist for us anymore because it (the story) became ours. We can't even remember anymore what's in the novel and what we made up." An important structural element Payne and Taylor kept is the book's multiple first-person narration (it's worth noting Wilder used narration to great effect in his films). Much of the film is told from the shifting perspective of four characters (aided by diabolically funny voice-overs), each of whom has a different take on their interwoven imbroglios.

Perrotta is delighted the multiple narrative survived the novel-to-screen adaptation: "I was pretty sure when the book got optioned that that particular quality would get lost. But amazingly these guys were able to do this very daring screenplay where they have the voice-overs of different characters that in a way mimics the structure of the book. I think they pulled off a pretty amazing technical feat . . . and were deeply faithful to the book."

For Payne, co-opting the novel's narrative motif "offered a very interesting and fun challenge." He adds, "The film is covered with voice-over (recorded at Omaha recording studio Pisaurus Productions). I love voice-over in films, and there's kind of a stigma against it." That stigma is an artificial one imposed by film executives and by "script experts" like Syd Field. Payne disdains the Syd Field cookie-cutter school of screenwriting: "He's an idiot. I'm still waiting for that first blockbuster Syd Field film script."

Making it real

Ever one to follow his own drummer, Payne dismisses the notion films must look or sound a certain way. It's why he insisted on making his first two features far away from La-La Land. For *Election*, he wanted a high school as it really looks, not as Hollywood envisions it.

"The high school movies I've seen have all been shot in California. They have Venetian blinds on the windows and really beautiful rays of sunlight coming and all the teachers have really good haircuts and all the students are bright, cheery-faced and look like actors out of Central Casting, and it's hideous. It's just fake. In *Election* all the extras are real students and teachers, even some of the leads. The classrooms, unlike ones in those California-filmed movies, are windowless foundation-blocks with fluorescent light overhead. That's what schools are and that's what I wanted to capture—the real thing."

Berger said, "Alexander was sort of relentless in his desire for a truthful, accurate portrayal of high school and of people, with no Hollywood *Beverly Hills 90210* bullshit. And he definitely got what he wanted." *Election* production designer Jane Stewart (she also designed *Citizen Ruth*) said Payne was equally exacting in creating visual cues for each character. To express McAllister's stuck-in-neutral life, she said, a Dundee-area house was turned into his home. "We tried to reflect older values and an oppressive feeling through things like colors and objects."

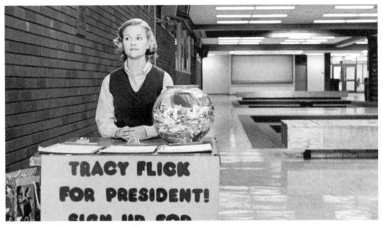
Reese Witherspoon in *Election*

Payne's search for verisimilitude informs his filmmaking. It's why he doesn't adhere to trends. "I take cues from reality, from observation," he said, "and not from other movies, even though I watch a lot of movies and I'm a film buff and all that. You have to feel inspired about what you write and what you want to commit to film. When it comes to shoot, all your ideas and what you're trying to capture has to come from observation. And it becomes a little bit like a fun reportage in that way."

On *Election* he immersed himself in the rhythms of Papillion–LaVista High School (Carver High in the film). "After the initial couple of weeks, the teachers and students felt very comfortable seeing us around and we felt very comfortable being there," he said.

A journey to cinema

He loves how filmmaking permits him to explore other realities. "What's fun about that is that you become like a spy and a witness to all sorts of worlds. Suddenly, you have this excuse to visit a place, but really visit it and really hear people talk about what they do. And if you're curious about the world and about people, it's just the greatest job to have."

Long before becoming a filmmaker, his curiosity led him to Stanford University, where his love for languages spurred an interest in Spanish literature and Latin American history. His studies took him to Spain and Colombia. He's since returned to Spain again and again. He still keeps in touch with friends he made there in the 1980s. After *Election* wrapped he vacationed with family in Florida before heading to Spain to "bum around."

Obsessed with cinema since childhood, Payne collected 8 millimeter prints of old movies and shot several short films with a used Super 8 camera [In some accounts the camera was a gift from Kraft Foods to his restaurateur father, George Payne.]. He recalls *One Flew Over the Cuckoo's Nest* as a seminal film in his teens and ironically notes it would probably be difficult to get that picture made today. It was, in fact, a difficult sell then, too. However, Payne didn't touch a camera again until he was at UCLA, which he attended after graduating from Stanford in 1984. Despite harboring a dream to pursue filmmaking, he didn't take a single film class at Stanford because he looked upon his undergraduate years as a time "to get an education."

Once he decided to study film, he considered both UCLA and USC, the West Coast's two most prestigious film schools. The story of why, after visiting each campus, he chose UCLA is classic Payne: "What I found was that USC was extremely Hollywood-oriented. It's a private institution and structured very much as a Hollywood feeder school. You have to compete for the privilege of making an advanced film. I saw a batch of those advanced films when I was down there, and they were extremely formulaic and banal. Extremely well-crafted and very watchable, like Hollywood films, but they were about nothing.

"I went to UCLA, and found it much more wild there. It's a public school. It seemed like a place to be freer and just explore and do what you want. Most of their student films are pretty experimental and unwatchable, but there's the attitude that it's one person, one film. At UCLA they popped a Super 8 camera in your hands and said, 'Go shoot something. We'll teach you technique later, but now, go fuck-up and just shoot from your gut.' And you work harder, of course, than you ever worked in your life, like you always do in films.

"They know there's many people like me who haven't had access to filmmaking before, and they just want you to come with ideas and experiences. That's the important thing. It's such a neat philosophy, but it's changed since then. Everything has gone to the right in our country, including film school."

There he came under the influence of top-flight editor Richard Marks (whose credits include the current James L. Brooks film *As Good As It Gets*). "My editing teacher and in a large degree my film mentor was Richard Marks. He's someone who taught me a lot about filmmaking and with whom I still keep in contact."

Payne's intense 50-minute UCLA thesis film, *The Passion of Martin*, played festivals and pegged him as a real "comer" in the industry. It led to a Universal development deal that eventually fizzled. Later, he teamed with Taylor and together they wrote short films for cable TV. Then they hit upon the idea for *Citizen Ruth* in '92 and, after surviving one dead-end producer, they finally saw the project to fruition. *Election* should once again prove Payne has delivered on his early promise.

Refining and progressing

Payne is currently in L.A. working with editor Kevin Tent on *Election*. He's also supervising some fantasy sequences (involving pictures in a yearbook coming to life) being filmed by a West Coast animation firm. MTV Films, which is co-producing *Election* with Berger and Yerxa's Bona Fide Films and independent producer Keith Samples, has been lobbying Payne with music suggestions. Payne is adamant about not bowing to MTV pressure. "I've been telling them, 'Wait till we get into the editing before you make any record deals.' I have a lot of ideas. I don't want to just put hit songs in there. I don't want this film to be a commercial for hit tunes. I think that's really terrible and actually dates the film."

Payne insists on creative control and has largely gotten it thus far. He feels the reason he's escaped studio meddling is because film executives consider comedy somewhat mysterious—"that it has to be a certain way or there's some magic to it." Then too his budgets have been small enough so as to keep his films "under the radar" of prying producers. Although the *Election* budget (under $10 million) surpassed that of his first feature, Payne said, "My stuff is still considered risky enough that even though *Citizen Ruth* was a critical success, I'm still not at the point where I'm demanding anything approaching a big budget."

He's at an enviable place now in his career. But even as his reputation grows and his projects increase in scale, he remains close to his by-the-seat-of-his-pants roots. "Every film I've made has been bigger than the one before," he said. "But I'm always surprised at how similar it (the process) is from film to film. You encounter the same basic filmmaker problems: How to get the actors to do what you want them to do. How to bring out their best with the camera. Hoping it doesn't rain. Hoping it does rain. Hoping it cuts together. Hoping the music works with it.

"I've taken a step-by-step progression and I feel a sense of apprentice-ship to the craft. I'm learning little by little. And I think as a filmmaker it's important to somehow keep in mind that even with all those trucks and all those technicians and all that money being spent, that it's you with a Super 8 camera. And to keep always an intimate relationship between yourself and what you're shooting. Don't let any of that other stuff bother you. The moment before saying, 'Action,' look around the set, see where the camera is, and just ask yourself in a split second, Is this really, exactly what I want, even if I'm wrong? Yes. 'Action.'"

Cut. Print It. That's a wrap.

Alexander Payne's emergence as a rising filmmaker

Published in 2000 in the *Inet Library*

Film director Alexander Payne (*Citizen Ruth* and *Election*), whose screenplay for *Election* earned him and co-scenarist Jim Taylor their first Oscar nominations (for Best Adapted Screenplay) cannot recall a time when the movies did not hold him enthralled. Like many contemporary film directors, Payne can trace his beginnings behind the camera to his youth, when he shot his own Super 8 millimeter films while growing up in Omaha, Nebraska.

When Payne was coming of age in the late 1970s, the Midwest was hardly a nurturing environment for an aspiring filmmaker, however. Hollywood was a long ways off. No film schools were nearby. The independent film scene had not yet exploded. A grassroots film culture was still more an ideal than a reality. So, he put his cinema dreams on hold, packed up and left home to study Latin American history and Spanish literature at Stanford University.

But the itch to pursue filmmaking never left him and after returning from a sojourn to Spain he entered the graduate film program at UCLA in the late 1980s. And it was there he found his calling. His 1991 thesis film, *The Passion of Martin*, was shown at film festivals and led to industry contacts that eventually landed him a studio deal, an agent and a gig writing for TV in Los Angeles. Meanwhile, he and a roommate from his UCLA days, Jim Taylor, became writing partners. After false starts, they hit upon the idea for an original screenplay and the resulting script became Payne's feature directorial debut, *Citizen Ruth*, which he shot in and around his hometown of Omaha.

The well-reviewed 1996 satire about the abortion debate starred Laura Dern in the darkly comic role of Ruth Stoops, a single, loopy, unrepentant drug addict long ago estranged from her family. When the pregnant Ruth is arrested, the future of her unborn fetus becomes the latest flashpoint for the pro-choice and pro-life camps (the pro-choice side represented by Swoosie Kurtz and Tippi Hedren and the pro-life side encapsulated by Mary Kay Place and Burt Reynolds), each of which goes to extremes in making Ruth the symbol for their opposing positions.

With Ruth caught in the middle and a media circus being made of her personal decision, nature intervenes and decides for her. She

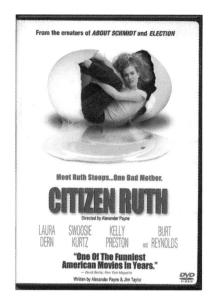

From the creators of *ABOUT SCHMIDT* and *ELECTION*

Meet Ruth Stoops...One Bad Mother.

CITIZEN RUTH

Directed by Alexander Payne

LAURA   SWOOSIE   KELLY   BURT
DERN   KURTZ   PRESTON and REYNOLDS

"One Of The Funniest
American Movies In Years."
— David Denby, New York Magazine

Written by Alexander Payne & Jim Taylor

DVD
VIDEO

returns to her life of oblivion while the debate rages on. It is an ambiguous but liberating ending for a woman who is no hero or symbol, but rather a survivor getting by the only way she knows how. In the end, she goes her own way—unswayed by any ideology but her own need for a fix.

A brave film that took on the excesses of both sides in the abortion controversy, *Citizen Ruth* never did find its audience at the box office, perhaps because the issue it skewered was simply too contentious and raw to make it attractive enough for moviegoers. For his part, Payne never set out to make cheap comedic capital out of the whole abortion conflict. Instead, he and Taylor simply saw in it fertile ground for exploring the extremes well-meaning people go to in pursuing their own version of the truth.

From a social commentary perspective, Payne said, he felt compelled to portray how people "compromise themselves through really, really good intentions. They all think they're doing the right thing and they end up getting very, very compromised morally." He was also attracted by the spectacle "of people's personal-psycho-sexual situations being worked out in a public arena, especially a political arena." Finally, he said, he was drawn to such serious subject matter in a comedy because the material touches people's lives in a deep way and he feels the best comedy addresses the most potent issues. "I'm bored with most American comedies because they're about nothing. The attitude, is,

'Oh, it's comedy, it's just fluff.' But, in fact, comedy should be about something. It's another form of communication about experience and emotion."

For his second film, 1999's *Election*, Payne trained his jaundiced eye on that most American of institutions—the suburban public high school—and that most hallowed of democratic tenets—the free election—to find the mendacity and hypocrisy lurking just beneath the surface. Payne, who once again collaborated with Taylor on the script, adapted the screenplay from the novel *Election* by Boston author Tom Perrotta. The book, while still in manuscript form, was brought to Payne and Taylor by producers Albert Berger and Ron Yerxa. The filmmakers immediately responded to it.

"We found in Tom Perrotta's novel a starting place, a springboard, for what we do best as writers together," Payne said. "It's very, very close to us. We took a lot of liberties though. When you go to adapt a novel you have to forget the novel because the story becomes ours ... yet you remain entirely faithful to it somehow in spirit."

Perrotta is pleased with the adaptation, "I think they translated my work into this other medium in just a brilliant way." He is particularly impressed how Payne and Taylor adapted a stylistic technique from his book— multiple first-person narration—to the film: "I was pretty sure when the book got optioned that that particular quality would get lost. But amazingly these guys were able to do this very daring screenplay where they have the voice-overs of different characters that in a way mimics the structure of the book. I think they pulled off a pretty amazing technical feat ... and were deeply faithful to the book." Like *Citizen Ruth*, *Election* explores the absurd lengths desperate people go to in defending their turf. The two protagonists are the seemingly stalwart high school history teacher Jim McAllister, played by Matthew Broderick, and his seemingly sweet over-achieving student Tracy Flick, played by Reese Witherspoon.

Behind their sunny façades, however, simmers a raging angst. Each is embroiled in an intrigue that intersects their lives and gives them a reason to secretly resent the other. As Tracy launches her sure-fire bid for the student council presidency, Jim encourages a popular jock to oppose her. Soon, teacher and pupil become openly bitter enemies. Eventually, Jim rigs the election to defeat Tracy. Before all the fireworks are done, he is left disgraced while she, as usual, has prevailed. In an interview during the making of the film (it was mainly shot in and around Omaha) Payne said *Election* is not so much an indictment of cherished foundations as it is an allegory of how even well-meaning people can undermine those same institutions under pressure. "All these horrible, pathetic things happen, but it's not as though any of the characters is bad—they're just doing it for the first time. They just don't know any better. It's funny, sad, human."

For his latest project, Payne, along with writing partner Taylor, is adapting author Louis Begley's acclaimed novel, *About Schmidt*, into a movie script Payne plans shooting in Omaha. *About Schmidt* is, like Payne's previous movies, concerned with a strong-willed individual (Warren Schmidt) at a moral and intellectual crossroads in his life. Unlike the earlier films, however, the protagonist here is a well-to-do older person with years of regret, guilt, accomplishment and failure behind him and now given to examining himself for perhaps the first time.

The story follows what happens when Schmidt leaves the cold comfort of his old life behind to stake-out a new life. Payne was drawn to the material because, like the other stories he's filmed, "It's very human and it's very real. It's about life. It's like life, I can't sum it up. I hope always to make movies that can't be easily summed up."

2

About Schmidt

❧

Introduction

This next set of stories focuses on *About Schmidt*. My most intense early coverage of Alexander Payne centered on that 2002 project because I determined it represented a leap forward for him in the industry before he ever shot a second of film. Why?

For starters, it marked a significant upgrade in budget and in star power attached to his work. I am not suggesting that good work is dependent on either a big budget or a mega name, but in this case Payne had three times the budget to work with that he had on *Citizen Ruth* and *Election*, and in Jack Nicholson he landed, to use that most overused word, an icon. What I am saying is that by securing these things Payne had arrived at a point where he could get almost anything he wanted, within reason.

As always, none of that matters unless you execute. No matter how you feel about the finished film, I think you have to acknowledge the film worked well enough with critics to receive glowing reviews and coveted festival slots. You also have to concede it resonated with enough industry insiders and theatergoers to reel in lots of award nominations and a healthy box-office take.

Yes, it's true *Citizen Ruth* got Payne noticed right out of the box in some quarters as a talent to be watched, and *Election* made him a critical darling and rising industry player. While neither of those films did much business initially, and Payne was not altogether happy with how they were marketed, particularly *Election*, both did go on to become cult discoveries. In fact, Payne often remarks that of all his films *Election* is the one that people most bring up as memorable or affecting. Given the overwhelmingly warm response to *The Descendants*, I have to think that film will now supplant the earlier one as the movie people most reference when talking with him.

Even in the early stages of his career Payne was already branded as a consummate satirist, though perhaps too prickly or wise-ass for some people's tastes. *Schmidt* was in some ways a different kind of film than his first two in its existential nihilism and melancholia, but it shared enough in common with them tonally that it served to only strengthen Payne's brand, not dilute it.

Also, where Payne was something of an enigma through *Election,* even though Oscar-nominated, he did so much press for *Schmidt* that he became much more of a known commodity. Even though *Schmidt* fizzled at the Oscars, everything was set up for Payne to capitalize on the momentum behind it, and, as a later batch of stories explores, he more than capitalized with the film that followed—*Sideways.* His wine country comedy certified and solidified the exalted position *Schmidt* originally put him in. That is why I regard the Jack Nicholson vehicle as Payne's real breakthrough picture, even though I think *Sideways* a more fully realized picture. There was more on the line with the earlier film. That is the one he had to really prove himself on, and he did so in a resounding manner.

By the time the *Schmidt* project rolled around, I was well ensconced with Payne. Curiously, I was also still the only Nebraska journalist that I am aware of, at least, who seemingly understood the significance of the filmmaker and his work. By the time *Schmidt* wrapped production, I had published several depth pieces; whereas, the local daily had assiduously ignored or marginalized Payne and his work. The daily finally did a feature on Payne but it was almost perfunctory at that point.

Yet as entrenched and committed as I was, I did not visit the *Schmidt* set. In the case of *Election,* I missed my one chance. In the case of *Schmidt,* I never got a chance because it was a closed set. Payne and the producers made it a priority to keep Jack happy and to minimize distractions. As it worked out, the first set of Payne's I stepped foot on was *Sideways,* shot halfway across the country. That's right, it took him leaving Omaha, where he shot his first three features, before I actually saw him work. It was worth the wait.

Alexander Payne discusses his new feature starring Jack Nicholson, working with the star, past projects and future plans

Published in a 2001 issue of the *Omaha Weekly*

Arriving at a new project

Citizen Ruth announced him as someone to watch on the independent film scene. *Election* netted him and his writing partner, Jim Taylor, an Oscar nomination for Best Adapted Screenplay. The commercial success of *Meet the Parents*, whose script he and Taylor contributed to, led to another high profile hired gun job—a rewrite of *Jurassic Park III*.

Now, with *About Schmidt*, which began filming in his hometown of Omaha this week, filmmaker Alexander Payne finds himself playing in a $30 million sandbox in his own backyard and sharing the fun with one of the biggest movie stars ever—Jack Nicholson. It is the culmination of Payne's steady climb up the Hollywood film ladder the past seven years. It has been quite a journey already for this amiable writer-director with the sharp wit and the killer good looks. And the best still appears ahead of him.

During an exclusive interview he granted to the *Omaha Weekly* at La Buvette [a restaurant] one recent Sunday afternoon in the Old Market (fresh from seeing off his girlfriend actress Sandra Oh at the airport) Payne discussed the genesis and the theme of his new film, his collaboration with Jack, his take on being a rising young filmmaker, his insider views on working in the American movie industry, and his past and future projects.

Although *About Schmidt* gets its title from the 1997 Louis Begley novel, it turns out Payne's film is only partly inspired by the book and is actually more closely adapted from an earlier, unproduced Payne screenplay called *The Coward*. As he explained, "When I first got out of film school ten years ago I wrote a script for Universal that had the exact same themes as *About Schmidt*...a guy retiring from a professional career and facing a crisis of alienation and emptiness. Universal didn't want to make it. I was going to rewrite it and come back to Omaha and try and get it made, and then Jim Taylor and I stumbled on the idea of *Citizen Ruth*, so I pursued that and put this on the back burner. Then, about three years ago, producers Harry Gittes and Michael Besman sent me the Begley book, which has similar themes, although set in a very different milieu."

Nicholson, who had read the book, was already interested. Payne first commissioned another writer to adapt the novel but that didn't pan out. "I didn't relate very much ultimately to the adaptation and then I turned to Jim Taylor and said, 'You know that thing I was writing ten years ago? How would you like to rewrite that with me under the guise of an adaptation for this thing?'" Taylor agreed, and the film *About Schmidt* was set in motion, with Gittes and Besman as producers.

Man in distress

Taking elements from both the earlier script and the Begley book, the character of Schmidt is now a retired Woodmen of the World actuary struggling to come to terms with the death of his longtime wife, the uneasy gulf he feels with his daughter, his dislike of her fiancé, and the sense that everything he's built his life around is somehow false. Full of regret and disillusionment, he sees that perhaps life has passed him by. To try and get his head straight, he embarks on a road trip across Nebraska that becomes a funny, existential journey of self-discovery. A kind of *Five Easy Pieces* meets a geriatric *Easy Rider*.

"What interested me originally was the idea of taking all of the man's institutions away from him," Payne said. "Career. Marriage. Daughter. It's about him realizing his mistakes and not being able to do anything about them and also seeing his structures stripped away. It's about suddenly learning that everything you believe is wrong, everything. It asks, 'Who is a man? Who are we, really?'"

Typical of Payne, he doesn't offer easy resolutions to the dilemmas and questions he poses, but instead uses these devices (as he used abortion politics and improper student-teacher activities in his first two films) as springboards to thoughtfully and, hopefully, humorously explore issues. "I don't even have the answers to that stuff, nor does the film really, at least ostensibly. But, oh, it's a total comedy. I hope . . . you know?"

Playing with Jack

For Payne, who derives much of his aesthetic from the gutsy, electric cinema of the 1970s, having Nicholson, whose work dominated that decade, anchor the film is priceless. "One thing I like about him appearing in this film is that part of his voice in the '70s kind of captured alienation in a way. And this is very much using that icon of alienation, but not as someone who is by nature a rebel, but rather now someone who has played by the rules and is now questioning whether he should have. So, for me, it's using that iconography of alienation, which is really cool."

Beyond the cantankerous image he brings, Nicholson bears a larger-than-life mystique born of his dominant position in American cinema these past thirty-odd years. "He has done a body of film work," Payne said. "Certainly, his work in the '70s is as cohesive a body of work as any film director's. He's been lucky enough to have been offered and been smart enough to have chosen roles that allow him to express his voice as a human being and as an artist. He's always been attracted to risky parts where he has to expose certain vulnerabilities."

Then there's the whole star power thing. The clout Nicholson wields. The Player label he wears. The attention he commands. Payne is savvy enough to know that having Nicholson on the project boosts the prestige and the pressure that goes with it. That's why this production is a little more all-business and a little less laid back than Payne's previous two. For example, the filmmaker is, for the time being anyway, giving no interviews (outside this one) and the set is closed to reporters.

This limited access all gets back to the Nicholson factor. It means catering to him and shielding him. Or, as Payne put, "We have a big fish on this one. Everyone knows him. Most everyone is a fan of his. Plus, there's the pop stuff of his winning three Academy Awards and having been in very many popular and artistic films. So, he's a big presence in American culture. And all of us, certainly from me down to the crew, want him to be impressed. We want him to feel protected and supported. We want to feel that we have his approval. And, as director, I'm really bending over backwards to make sure he feels comfortable enough so he will expose vulnerabilities and really dive into the part. So, just because of his stature there is a heightened will among the film company and crew to do a good job."

Making no bones about what a fan he is of Nicholson, Payne said his star has thus far been a filmmaker's dream. "Sometimes you think about a movie star as being more star than actor, kind of playing some version of themselves. That's not the case with Mr. Nicholson. He's all about the character. He really dives into who is that person. He's a consummate actor. I've been really impressed with what I've seen so far. And I think watching the character unfold through him is going to be really amazing."

Instead of full-blown rehearsal periods for the film, Payne, Nicholson and the film's other name actors, who include Hope Davis as the daughter, Dermot Mulroney as the future son-in-law, and Oscar-winner Kathy Bates as the future in-law, have held script readings. According to Payne, Nicholson is not throwing his weight around, as one might expect, but rather acting as a colleague and collaborator.

"My experience so far is that he expresses his opinions as he sees them and he tries to be helpful to me and to the process. He seems to respect the filmmaker. So far, it's been a really interesting collaboration. And I also think I have much to learn from him, so I welcome his input."

Into focus

Nicholson became attached to the project through the kind of old-boy networking Hollywood thrives on. The actor was given Begley's book by his old friend, producer Harry Gittes (whose name Nicholson appropriated for the private eye he played in *Chinatown*). Then, Payne came on board, writing the script with Taylor and being assigned directorial chores as well. All Payne knew was that Nicholson would read the finished script first.

"And, oh, thank God he liked and agreed to do it," he added. On a practical level, Nicholson's participation has meant a much bigger budget than Payne has worked with before. "It's around thirty million. Mr. Nicholson's getting a salary which is larger than actors have gotten in my previous movies. Another factor is that this is a union movie, where my previous two were non-union, so there's a little added cost there. "Thirty is actually quite modest—it's hard to believe, I know—by Hollywood standards. And it's really amazing this script is getting made with this caliber of star at that budget level, because there's no gimmicks, no special effects, no guns. It's just a guy in crisis."

Despite the hike in budget, the presence of a superstar and the imposition of union realities, Payne insists the film, which is being made for New Line, remains closer to his first two intimate independent features than to overblown mainstream Hollywood pics. "The scale of filmmaking is, for me, not that much different than my previous two. A lot of directors, as they get older or have more films under their belt or have more success or whatever, they consistently make bigger, more impersonal films. I am conscious of wanting to make increasingly more personal films."

Still, he said the nature of this new one, which is somewhat of a freewheeling road show, is a step up for him in terms of pure logistics.

"Just on a nuts-and-bolts level, it's a slightly more complex movie than my other two. Lots of locations. We have scenes in Omaha and scenes across Nebraska. We're shooting at the Kearney Arch and at Pioneer Village and at various locations around Omaha. We have a couple drive-bys in Denver."

An independent spirit

In Payne's view, a film's cost or backing has little to do with whether it is a truly independent work. Independent cinema, as he sees it, comes from a passionate spirit and a singular, overriding vision. "Martin Scorsese is an independent director making studio movies that cost fifty–sixty million dollars and then we have (so-called) indie filmmakers making movies for two million dollars that are put together by financiers and the message clearly is, Hire me to make a commercial studio film. So, I don't think it's the budget or where the film comes from or who finances it.

"Basically, I just think it's the presence of a clear vision that comes from one person. The presence of an authorial voice, as in other works of art. Now, I don't expect all films to have it, just as I don't expect best-selling books to be literature. In books, we clearly distinguish between literature and best sellers. It's a similar case with film. We have some that we know will make a whole lot of money and that, to some degree, correspond to formula. But then we have other films made by directors who are trying to say something or get across a genuinely humanist point of view or whatever it is, and that can do so unfettered."

Working as a maverick within the studio system is a long Hollywood tradition. Meddling executives in suits is another tradition. Payne has had his share of battles and compromises, but he has thus far maintained his integrity. He said with his first two films he had to "fight for things" with Miramax (*Citizen Ruth*) and Paramount (*Election*) executives.

"In *Citizen Ruth* they wanted an ending which was decidedly happy in a way that would have been very forced, and I was able to have that not be the case. And in *Election* we shot a new ending, and there was no question there should be a new ending, but exactly what that ending was going to be was a little bit of a battle. But it turned out fine. I know other filmmakers have had it much worse in many other circumstances." He said New Line has so far "been great" to work with. "They've given me remarkable faith and freedom to make the film as I see it."

In recent years Payne has been critical of the American film community for its timidity, its gargantuan appetites and its over-reliance on formula over character. He still is, but he softens that a bit now with the realization that he is living proof of how some filmmakers can work within the system and still produce original, edgy, character-driven features.

"I grew up in the '70s with all those great movies, and those movies, which were the commercial Hollywood movies, were also strongly authorial and humanistic and artistic and realistic. Then we hit the '80s and '90s, where a lot of American cinema was dominated by a lot of formula, grossly commercial concerns. And it's true I don't see many current American films. I continue to watch old movies and to go see foreign films. I nourish myself that way.

"But, look, if this film *About Schmidt* can be made right now for thirty million with a very big star and I can have final cut on it, then I'm hopeful. I can't be anything but hopeful. I know I am making the kinds of films I want to make, and I see some other young directors doing the same, like David O. Russell and Sofia Coppola and Spike Jonze and Paul Thomas Anderson."

Closer to home, Payne keeps tabs on Nebraska's growing film culture and sees promise in the recent crop of in-state features made by Shawn Prouse and Mike Meehan (*Shakespeare's Coffee*) and Dana Altman (*The Private Public*) and in the film production company begun by Mark Hoeger and partners. He says Nebraska will continue to have to nurture its own filmmakers because luring Hollywood here is still a hard act to sell, particularly in the absence of major tax incentives (the Nebraska Legislature is considering such initiatives). "I think a lot of the filmmaking is going to have to come from me and these other guys who are from here because it's just too tough to try and attract Hollywood films here, other than maybe once every five years."

Each time he shoots here, he not only reaffirms his stated commitment to do so but also contributes to the development of the area's filmmaking infrastructure, providing jobs to actors, grips, gaffers, gofers, and the like. As loyal as he is to the state, he is also itching to venture away and appease his sense of wanderlust elsewhere. Therefore, his next project, *Sideways*, which he is writing alone and directing, will be made in California.

The film, based on a novel by Rex Pickett, tells the story of, as Payne puts it, "Two loser guys from San Diego who go wine tasting in Santa Barbara the week before one of them is to be married. It's going to be a really fun, small film. While I'm finishing editing *About Schmidt* I'm going to be writing that one." As for his own restlessness, he said, "I'm anxious to get out of Nebraska for a little while. Just to move on. Just to explore other worlds. I like to travel and to explore other themes and cultures. I'd like to shoot in other countries." He pledges he will one day return to shoot here.

Work for hire

Payne's desire to spread his wings and to branch out was already evident in the rewrite jobs he and Taylor took after *Election*. Contributing to the final shooting scripts of one current hit (*Meet the Parents*) and one anticipated hit (*Jurassic Park III*, which opens this summer) has made Payne and Taylor viable, hotly sought-after commodities. It's also made them a lot of money. And it's exposed them to the manic, crap shoot, blockbuster side of Hollywood they usually steer clear of.

For each project, Payne and Taylor were brought in as part of a series of screenwriters, some working individually and some in teams, which is the norm on big-budget pics. "It's really high paying, and a lot of Hollywood screenwriters make a great living doing that, but I'm not really in it for that," he said. "I'm in it to work on my own stuff, basically. But the thing is, I haven't made that much money from my own films, so it's been a nice little booster and it gives Jim and me a chance to hang out together. We could do this stuff all the time. We've turned down a ton of them. But we would never take one of those jobs unless it were right and one we really thought we could do something with and give them their money's worth."

He said being part of an assembly line of writers whose work may or may not end up on the screen, much less earn a credit, is not a problem.

"We're fine with that. That's how it works. It's not the time to be an artiste. We were paid guns to come in. Fortunately, what we bring is our sensibility to it, and that's what they're paying us for, which worked well with *Meet the Parents* and maybe so-so with *Jurassic Park*. We got the feeling the producers of *Jurassic Park* wanted us for our character and our humor and then we gave them character and humor and they went, 'Yeah, but where's the action?' And we said, 'Well, that's your department.' I think we did a really good job, but from their perspective maybe it wasn't a perfect fit. I mean, what do we know from dinosaurs?"

Besides the vagaries of the screenwriting-for-hire trade, it is intense work. On *Meet the Parents* Payne and Taylor sweated out two and a half weeks right before shooting began. On *Jurassic Park*, the pair rewrote the entire screenplay, except for some large action set pieces, in four weeks. "It was a hard job," Payne said.

These experiences have given Payne new insight into the high-stakes Hollywood moviemaking apparatus, and they've left him reeling. "What's interesting and kind of appalling is that these huge Hollywood movies get so close to production without a shooting script, and then they have to pay through the nose for writers to come in and rewrite them in a high pressure week or two. It's really wild."

He may make satiric thrift of those experiences, as well as his Oscar night hobnobbing among the stars, on a future project slated to follow *Sideways*. It is an adaptation of *The Picture of Dorian Gray* set in, appropriately enough, Hollywood—the land where false beauty is both a religion and a commodity.

For someone who came on the Hollywood scene a relatively short time ago, Payne has come a long way. He is now well-positioned to make the leap into the upper ranks of filmmakers. What does he think of his success and where does he go from here?

"I mean, I'm really happy and grateful, and also it's exactly what I've been working toward for years and years. When you work for something that long, you never really believe on some level it's going to happen. On the other hand, I haven't worked with lightning speed. My films have taken a while to get off the ground. Even this one (*About Schmidt*). I finished the script last May and it will be almost a year before I start shooting. Just to get the financing in place. To get the actors.

"It's always a battle. In some ways it gets harder. More pressure. But I just like movies so much. I would like now though to start making films a bit more one-after-the-other-after-the-other. Not forever. But for a while. It'd be nice to just shoot."

Shooting on *About Schmidt* continues through June 1.

Being Jack Nicholson

Published in a 2001 issue of the *Omaha Weekly*

Alexander Payne and Jack Nicholson

Bigger than life

With filming proceeding in earnest on Alexander Payne's latest made-in-Omaha film, *About Schmidt*, real and imagined sightings of its world-famous lead actor, Jack Nicholson, are no doubt filtering in from star-struck citizenry. Not since Sean Penn stirred things up here with his directorial debut, *The Indian Runner*, largely shot in and around Plattsmouth, Nebraska, have locals been as frenzied about catching a glimpse of some celebrity.

The fuss is well-merited this time. For as great an actor as Penn is, Nicholson is a star on the order of the old-time greats. A genuine Hollywood legend. From his trademark shades to his romantic intrigues to his public indiscretions to his classic rebellious roles to his three Oscars, he is everything we want in a star. Cool. Sexy. Enigmatic. Independent. Well-respected. Justly rewarded. With greatness in our midst, now is as good a time as any to consider just why he looms so large in our collective movie consciousness.

The mere mention of Jack's name conjures a portrait in rascality. From the devil-may-care glint in the eye to the sardonic smile to the sarcastic voice, he is the lovable scoundrel of our imagination, saying and doing things we only wish we could. He is, like the best screen actors, a romantic projection of our liberated inner selves. The sly, shrewd man on the make. The ageless rebel. The unreformed rake. The eternal carouser. The agitator who stirs things up. The sharp-tongued wit cutting people down to size. The volatile time-bomb ready to explode.

In an amazing display of durability he has gone from being the embodiment of the rebellious 1960s and 1970s to essaying the angst of that same generation now grown old and disillusioned in the wake of chasing love and money and happiness in all the wrong places. At a pudgy 63, he shows the wear-and-tear of a sometimes hedonistic life. After all, he came to fame and fortune just as America entered the indulgent 1970s, emerging from the limbo of the B movie fringe to the heights and perks of major Hollywood screen stardom on the strength of remarkable performances in a string of fine films made between 1969–1975.

Nicholson was launched from obscurity into the front ranks of the industry with his scene-stealing turn in 1969's *Easy Rider* as a conventional Southern lawyer gone-to-seed and turned-on to the counter culture by hippie bikers Dennis Hopper and Peter Fonda. More memorable roles soon followed. Think of the best films of the 1970s and '80s and Nicholson appears in an inordinate number of them: *Five Easy Pieces*; *Carnal Knowledge*; *The Last Detail*; *Chinatown*; *One Flew Over the Cuckoo's Nest*; *The Missouri Breaks*; *The Shining*; *Reds*; *Terms of Endearment*; *Prizzi's Honor.*

As disparate as these films and their stories are, the characters Nicholson creates are largely variations on a theme, namely, a man fighting alone to protect his identity or independence in the face of forces he cannot hope to defeat. In one way or another he is playing the existential modern man trying to save himself amid the complex crush of the system or society or fate or nature.

Unlike many contemporary actors, Nicholson, even in his early groundbreaking work, brings a weight to his performances only gained from years of working at his craft and from living a full life away from film sets. Like the great actors of Hollywood's Golden Age (Tracy, March, Cagney, Bogart, Gable, Mitchum, Lancaster, Douglas) with Nicholson you get the sense he has been around the block a few times. That he is not merely an actor, but a complex human being with a rich personal history behind him. Besides technique, it's what lends his performances a certain credence and gravity you don't find very often these days outside warhorses like him, Nick Nolte, Gene Hackman, James Caan, Sean Connery, Morgan Freeman, and a few others.

Nicholson captures our fancy with the combination of his snake oil charm, angry defiance, and fierce intelligence. Behind that leering smile lurks something wild and dangerous and mysterious. It helps account for his appeal with both men and women. In classic rebel tradition he is the iconoclast or nonconformist at odds with the world, raging against the tide. He is the master of the slow burn and of the sudden violent outburst.

Signature '70s roles

Each of his signature roles from the '70s features scenes in which he acts out a full-blooded tantrum, from his famous table-clearing tirade at the truck stop cafe in *Five Easy Pieces* to his confrontation with a bartender in *The Last Detail* to his brutal interrogation of his lover in *Chinatown* to his fighting back against brutal guards in *One Flew Over the Cuckoo's Nest*. His star-making turns in the '70s found him working on the very edge of his craft, daring to go for deep emotional truths and idiosyncratic behaviors that reveal vital shades and nuances of his complex characters.

In Bob Rafelson's 1970 *Five Easy Pieces* Nicholson is frustrated former concert pianist Bobby Dupea, a man weighed down by the burden of expectation from his well-heeled family. He finds relief from the pressure of conformity by running away from the classical music world to work in the oil fields, where he is just another hand looking for a paycheck and a good lay. Ironically, his constant flight from his past leads him right back to where he started—to a family he can neither ever quite measure up to nor escape.

The 1971 Mike Nichols–directed and Jules Feiffer–penned *Carnal Knowledge* finds Nicholson as the callow Jonathan, who tries negotiating the attitudes, mores, and politics at work in the male-female dynamic during the dawn of the sexual liberation and feminist movement. No matter how the times and the terms of engagement change, he is still a predator and women are still his prey. The finer points of relationships seem to bore him. Emotions scare him. For men like him, love, commitment, and communication are mere decorative foreplay for making it.

In Hal Ashby's 1974 *The Last Detail* Nicholson stars as foul-mouthed, free-spirited Everyman Billy "Bad Ass" Buddusky, one of two career sailors reluctantly escorting a fellow sailor to prison. What is supposed to be an uneventful transfer over to authorities turns into a wild romp when Buddusky and his mate grow fond of the young, naïve prisoner (Randy Quaid) and decide to show him a good time en route. Nicholson's tragic-comic performance never misses a beat.

In the Roman Polanski–directed and William Goldman–scripted *Chinatown* (1974) Nicholson lends his interpretation to the classic private eye with a stunning evocation of Jake Gittes, a cocky and seedy

PI haunted by a love gone bad. When he stumbles onto a new case with giant implications for arid Depression-era Los Angeles, he finds himself sucked into a whirlpool of deceit by a femme fatale (Faye Dunaway) he can't resist. By the time the chips fall where they may, Gittes is a broken man undone in the same *Chinatown* district that undid him once before.

Forever cementing his rebel image, Nicholson plays Randall P. McMurphy with the sensitive brio of an underdog beaten down by an uncaring system in Milos Forman's 1975 adaptation of Ken Kesey's counterculture novel *One Flew Over the Cuckoo's Nest*. It is the kind of martyr role that all of the great screen rebels—from Cagney, Bogart, and Garfield to Brando, Clift, and Dean to Newman and McQueen—have portrayed.

Later work

Nicholson achieves a tour de force in Stanley Kubrick's 1980 version of Stephen King's *The Shining* by brilliantly detailing the mental breakdown of writer Jack Torrance, a tortured man caught in the grip of some awful supernatural force compelling him to kill his family in the eerie isolation of the Overlook Hotel. In a performance that is by-turns finely controlled and manic ("Here's . . . Johnny"), Jack displays astonishing range and courage by essaying a madman you loathe but pity too.

Terms of Endearment casts Nicholson as retired astronaut Garrett Breedlove, a man used to having his way with the ladies. Playing his age for a change, he strikes just the right note as an aging Lothario who meets his match in the figure of neighbor Aurora Greenway (Shirley MacLaine), whom he eventually beds, but not without making a commitment to her. Both Nicholson and MacLaine won well-deserved Oscars for their strong supporting performances.

Besides these stand-the-test-of-time roles, Jack's given compelling performances in otherwise flawed films like *The Fortune*, *The Last Tycoon*, *The Postman Always Rings Twice*, *The Border*, and *Heartburn*. By the time he reached icon status as the guy with the wink in his eye, he parlayed his legendary façade into some made-to-order parts where he hammed things up, including a horny Lucifer in *The Witches of Eastwick*, a pompous Joker in *Batman*, an egomaniacal colonel in *A Few Good Men*, and a bigoted curmudgeon in *As Good as It Gets*.

His recent collaborations with actor-director Sean Penn have seen a new, more mature and darker Nicholson emerge. In both *The Crossing Guard* and the current *The Pledge* he plays damaged older men seeking catharsis in extreme circumstances but instead finding only more pain. Gone is the impish and ironic persona of the younger Jack and in its place is a restless, brooding character that could very well be Bobby Dupea or Jake Gittes twenty five years later.

Jack as Everyman Warren Schmidt

Now, *About Schmidt* offers Nicholson yet another chance to play out the secret anxieties, regrets, and desires of a man his own age. The character of Schmidt is a bitter Woodmen of the World actuary retiree undergoing a crisis of conscience in the aftermath of his longtime wife's death. As the façade of his well-ordered world crumbles around him, the repressed Schmidt must confront some uneasy truths about himself. His struggle to make meaning of his life propels him on a road trip across Nebraska during which he comes into contact with an odd assortment of characters. With his feelings reawakened, life becomes an adventure again rather than a burden.

The passive title role of the Alexander Payne–Jim Taylor penned script they adapted from the Louis Begley novel and from an early, unproduced Payne screenplay appears in some ways a departure for Nicholson. But the implosion of his character is actually in line with the roles he's played for Penn.

As usual, Payne will try to extract the humor from what promises to be a sharply observed story of loss, loneliness, introspection, and discovery. The vulnerable figure of Schmidt offers a ripe and fitting part for Nicholson at this stage in his career. However the film turns out, Nicholson is sure to deliver the goods under the direction of Payne, who is known for eliciting strong performances from his leads.

About *About Schmidt*: the shoot, editing, working with Jack and the film after the cutting room floor

Published in a 2001 issue of the *Omaha Weekly*

Behind closed doors

Ever since Omaha native Alexander Payne wrapped shooting on *About Schmidt*, the hometown movie whose star, Jack Nicholson, caused a summer sensation, the filmmaker has been editing the New Line Cinema pic in obscurity back in Los Angeles.

That's the way Hollywood works. During production, a movie is a glitzy traveling circus causing heads to turn wherever its caravan of trailers and trucks goes and its parade of headliners pitch their tents to perform their magic. It's the Greatest Show on Earth. Then, once the show disbands, the performers pack up and the circus slips silently out of town. Meanwhile, the ringmaster, a.k.a. the director, holes himself up in an editing suite out of sight to begin the long, unglamorous process of piecing the film together from all the high-wire moments captured on celluloid to try and create a dramatically coherent whole.

Whether *Schmidt* is the breakout film that elevates Payne into the upper echelon of American directors remains to be seen, but it is clearly a project with the requisite star power, studio backing, and artistic pedigree to position him into the bigtime.

An indication of the prestige with which New Line execs regard the movie is their anticipated submission of it to the Cannes Film Festival. Coming fast on the heels of *Election*, Payne's critically acclaimed 1999 film that earned him and writing partner Jim Taylor Oscar nominations for Best Adapted Screenplay, *Schmidt* will be closely watched by Hollywood insiders to see how the director has fared with a bona fide superstar and a mid-major budget at his disposal.

Regardless of what happens, Payne's unrepentant iconoclasm will probably keep him on the fringe of major studio moviemaking, where he feels more secure anyway. As editing continues on *Schmidt*, slated for a September 2002 release, Payne is nearing his final cut. The film has already been test previewed on the coast and now it's just a matter of trimming for time and impact.

While in town over Thanksgiving, Payne discussed what kind of film is emerging, his approach to cutting, the shooting process, working with Nicholson, and other matters during a conversation at a mid-town coffeehouse, Caffeine Dreams. He arrived fashionably late, out of breath, and damp after running eight blocks in a steady drizzle from the brownstone apartment he keeps year-round.

He and editor Kevin Tent, who has cut all of Payne's features, have been editing since June. They and a small staff work out of a converted house in back of a dentist's office on Larchmont Street in Los Angeles. Payne and Tent work ten-hour days, six days a week.

"As with any good creative relationship we have a basic shared sensibility," Payne said of the collaboration, "but we're not afraid to disagree, and there's no ego involved in a disagreement. We're like partners in the editing phase. He'll urge me to let go of stuff and to be disciplined."

By now, Payne has gone over individual takes, scenes, and sequences hundreds of times, making successive cuts along the way. What has emerged is essentially the film he set out to make, only with different tempos and tones than he first imagined.

"Rhythmically, it's come out a little slower than I would have wanted it," he said. "I think it's been something hard for me and for those I work with to accept that because of its subject matter and for whatever ineffable reason this is a very different film in pacing and feel than the very kinetic and funny *Election*, which got so much praise. It has, I think, the same sensibility and humor as *Election*, but it's slower and it lets the drama and emotion play more often than going for the laugh. I think it just called for that. With this one, we don't go for the snappy edit."

Even before *Schmidt*, Payne eschewed the kind of MTV-style of extreme cutting that can detract from story, mood, performance. "Things are over-covered and over-edited these days for my tastes. There's many exceptions, of course, but the norm seems to be to cut even though you don't need to. And, in fact, not only don't filmmakers need to, their cuts are disruptive to watching performance and getting the story. I like watching performance. My stuff is about getting performance. I like holding within a take as long as possible until you have to cut."

Payne said this story, like any, took on a new life once it went from the printed page to being realized before the cameras and, finally, being pulled together in the editing stage. As different as the film is from the script, he said the essence of the story remains intact. "Even as much as the shot and edited film is like a bastard child of the script, somewhat related but different and kind of maimed, once you see the film coming together, it reminds you of the initial impulses you had writing it and, in a way, the screenplay which has been on vacation comes back.

"Writing the screenplay is one thing, but then while directing it's just all those trucks and all those people and all those affairs and all those politics and, you know, waging war. Then, when editing, it's whatever challenges that holds. But then, as the film starts to come together, you're reminded of the screenplay, and in the case of this film I made the discovery it's the most personal of my films."

Melancholia

The film's title character, Warren Schmidt, is a man adrift in a late-life crisis where the underpinnings of his safe world come unhinged, sending him reeling into an on-the-road oblivion that becomes a search for redemption. Because the story is really about a man's inner journey or state of mind, the film is not so much driven by traditional narrative as it is subtext.

"This film isn't so much about the story because there isn't really much of a story. It's about a man and kind of about a way of life," Payne said. "And it's a way of life I kind of witnessed in Omaha. Not that it doesn't exist elsewhere and not that many different lives don't exist in Omaha. But, from time to time, it has a whiff of something that's very genuine. It's just a feeling, and I'd be hard-pressed to describe it beyond that."

As an artist, Payne does not like limiting himself to expository narrative. He understands how seemingly whimsical, quirky or incidental elements, like the moon serenade in *Citizen Ruth* or the lesbian romance in *Election*, have value too.

"One thing Hollywood filmmaking urges you always to do is tell the story. If it's not germane to the story, then leave it out. And I kind of disagree with that," he said. "I mean, I like stories. I like seeing movies that tell stories. I like my movies to tell stories. But films don't operate only on a story level. There's a quote I like that says, 'A story exists only as an excuse to enter into the realm of the cinema.' Films operate on emotions, moods, sub-themes and maybe even poetry, if you're lucky enough to have a bit of mystery and poetry in your film."

If the screenplay is any guide, then reading it reveals Schmidt as a man who has built his life around convention and conformity but who, along the way, has lost touch with what he really is and wants. The things in his well-ordered life have become his identity. His actuarial job with Woodmen of the World Life Insurance. His office. His home.

His routine. His marriage. When, in short order, he retires, his wife dies, and his estranged daughter prepares to marry a man he does not like, he realizes he is alone, at odds, angry, and restless to find answers to why his supposedly full life seems so empty.

What makes Schmidt's dilemma more complex is that he is not a wholly likable man. He is a square, a miser, a malcontent. Payne is drawn to such richly shaded and often unsympathetic characters because they are more interesting, more real, more truthful. Just think of inhalant-addict mother-to-be Ruth Stoops in *Citizen Ruth* or arrogant, spiteful teacher Jim McAllister in *Election*. Neither is totally a shit, though. Stoops is brave, outspoken, independent. McAllister is sincere, caring, dedicated. And, so, Schmidt is solicitous, careful, reflective. As he begins defining a new life for himself without a job or wife, he begins behaving in ways that defy family-societal expectations.

In this way, the film is an indictment of the prefabricated mold people are expected to fit. With Schmidt, Nicholson mutely echoes the alienated character (Bobby Dupea) he essayed in 1970's *Five Easy Pieces*. Just as Dupea turns his back on his classical piano career and blue-blood roots to work the oil fields, Schmidt shucks his constraints to embark on a road trip that is as much escape as quest.

If reaction to the film by preview audiences is any gauge, then Payne may be striking the right chords with this gray, introspective story. He said test cards consistently use words like "real," "true-to-life," "genuine," "naturalistic," and "not funny" to describe it.

"And that's been kind of nice," said Payne, whose aesthetic is informed by the European and American cinema of the last Golden Age (the 1960s and '70s) when the best films were about real life. Payne said the September 11 terrorist attacks "helped cement more than ever my already existing desire to make human films—films which are about people."

Working with Jack

By design, Nicholson carries the film. He is in virtually every scene. That Payne got him to play the lead in the first place was a coup. That he worked with an artist he's long admired was cool. In an interview Payne gave the *Omaha Weekly* only days before shooting began, he said the actor was accommodating in every way, immersing himself in the part and making himself available to the entire process during script readings.

Now months removed from the shoot, Payne said Nicholson

remained a pro throughout the production, and his extraordinary talent provided him as a director with endless choices.

"I had a very excellent experience working with him. He was extremely professional and committed to his part. Jack Nicholson is a movie star and an icon and that's fine, but in the moment of doing it and really who he is in his heart he's an actor who gets nervous like other actors and wants to do a good job like other actors and hopes he got it right like other actors and needs reassurance like other actors.

"What was great about directing him was that unlike many situations where you give the direction and hope to God the actor can do it just the way you'd like him to or you hope you've thought of the right words that will trigger the right response, with Nicholson I had to be careful with what I told him because not only would he do it, he could do it. He just has an excellent instrument. Sometimes, when I'd impose blocking or I wanted a certain scene a certain way, I'd say, 'Is that all right with you?' and he'd go, 'Well, anything you come up with I can find a way to justify it to myself, so, what do you want?' I was like, 'Ohhhh ...' He makes every possible choice doable."

Nicholson's presence netted a bigger budget (thirty million) than Payne ever had before, which meant New Line insisted he use sound stages and multiple cameras as safeguards against cost overruns caused by shooting delays. "Because it's not a terribly commercial film and because it's somewhat costly, I was urged to not go over budget. I had to make all my days, so in order to do that I shot more on sound stages and I sometimes threw up two or three cameras. I'd used sound stages on a limited basis before because, one, we didn't have the budget to build sets and, two, I don't really trust it, I trust what exists. But practical locations, as they're called, are difficult. They're tight. You wreck people's front lawns.

"Building sets and shooting on them poses its own logistical problems, but it also solves a lot of problems. And rather than shoot from one angle and then move in closer, I tried to get both at once. I like doing it precisely for the reason of not wearing out the actors and saving time." In the end, Payne did meet his sixty-two day schedule. The crowds of fans that followed the *Schmidt* traveling all-star band from location to location have long dispersed.

The edit

Since June, the film has entered that most solitary and time-consuming art and craft—editing, an unseen and unappreciated but core part of the filmmaking process. Indeed, Payne said, "Film is all about editing.

Kurosawa used to say, 'The only reason I write and direct is to get things to edit.' That's where you make a movie. You go through all the takes and get a general sense of putting each scene together. You watch it and then go through it again and watch it and then go through it again ... and each time you go through it, it gets a little bit shorter and you start becoming more sure.

"A first or second cut is, by nature, quite long because you're still giving every possible moment its day in court. You're making sure all the moments are there—moment to moment. In editing, an emotion can change by the addition or subtraction of two frames, a twelfth of a second. It's quite extraordinary. Later, you're looking at how the film is working cumulatively, its effect as a whole. You get a sense that maybe the first part of the film feels too long or the relationship between so-and-so and so-and-so isn't strong enough or you're not making that connection between this action here and that action there, or whatever. So the whittling and the shaping begin. "

He said it's important to remember that "it's no sin to cut things," adding, "You kind of cover yourself, unconsciously, in writing. That's why scripts are always longer and have more scenes than finished films. The visual medium just has a different language from a screenplay because of the images. So points which you had to make verbally become redundant and unnecessary. One thing you do is cut out redundancies while editing. The most painful part of editing comes in not only taking out parts that don't work, but taking out parts that do work and work well. You have to be disciplined enough to go, 'No, the film is better without them.'"

He said editing can be a maddening affair because the filmmaker can always find things that could have been improved and therefore the temptation is to want to drag it on endlessly. "Most of the time I'm disappointed and thought it could have been better," he said. "But that's okay. I think a lot of the creative act is like that. And then other times you're elated because it came out better than you thought. In the middle of editing I start to have little idea of what the film is. I liken it to one of those big tapestries you see in Europe. I'm there like with my loop sewing knot by knot but then every once in a while you have to stand back and look at it and go, 'Oh, that's not working over there.' So, you need to get an overview and that's where a preview can help.

"The only way you know what your film is is by showing it to an audience." He said it is an occupational hazard to never feel a film has been perfected. "There's an old saying, 'Films are never finished, they're merely abandoned,' which is to say you could keep whittling away forever. I caught *Election* the other night on TV and just saw a bunch of stuff I wanted to change."

Once he has the final cut of *Schmidt* completed, he and Jim Taylor plan to write an adaptation of author Rex Pickett's novel *Sideways*, a comedy about the mishaps that occur when a guy who is to be married goes on a Santa Barbara wine-tasting tour with a buddy. The film, which Payne will also direct, will be his first feature made outside Nebraska. As research, Payne and Pickett went on a wine-tasting junket to the very sites the story describes.

On the back burner is Payne's remake of *The Picture of Dorian Gray*. Otherwise, he has no other projects in sight and likes it that way. "It's nice to have nothing in front of you at all and to just be able to think and respond to what's going on around you. I don't like locking myself into things. I don't know what I'm going to feel like doing in three, four, five years. I'd like to come back here (Omaha) and shoot, but I need to go away for awhile."

Meanwhile, Payne is content, but not complacent with where he is as a filmmaker. "I know I do feel more confident in insisting on certain things and in trusting certain things. But I'll always be a film student. I'm always asking questions rather than feeling I have the answers or really know what I'm doing. Even after three films I still have questions. They may change in sophistication, but I always have them."

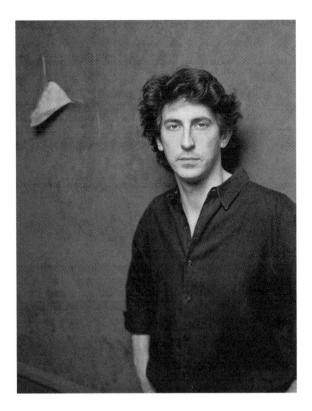

Payne at the midtown Omaha apartment he used to keep. My then-girlfriend and I visited him there around the time he was preparing to move out, and I remember commenting on an abstract rendering applied directly to one interior wall. He told us he painted it and he furthermore volunteered that he sometimes liked to paint in the nude in the middle of the night. I also recall an old piece of movie equipment he displayed on a table like an objet d'art. It might have been an ancient editing machine. I seem to recall seeing the same device in his new downtown Omaha place some years later. (photo courtesy of Bryce Bridges)

Conquering Cannes, Omaha native
Alexander Payne's triumphant Cannes debut

Published in a 2002 issue of the *Omaha Weekly*

Phantasmagorical

Press accounts of Alexander Payne's conquest of the Cannes Film Festival, where his new film *About Schmidt* created a buzz in the main competition, have largely focused on the film losing out on any awards or on the critical hosannas directed toward him and his star, Jack Nicholson.

But, as Payne noted during a recent Omaha visit, Cannes is a phantasmagorical orgy of the senses that cannot be reduced to mere prizes or plaudits. It is at once an adoring celebration of cinema, a crass commercial venue, and a sophisticated cultural showcase. It is where the French bacchanal and bistro sensibilities converge in one grand gesture for that most democratic art form—the movies. Only a satirist like Payne can take the full, surreal measure of Cannes and expose it for all its profundity and profanity.

"I likened it to the body of super model Gisel (Bundchen)," he said, "which is extraordinarily beautiful and draped in the most elegant clothes on the planet, yet, also possesses ... bile and all sorts of fetid humors inside of it. The festival is all of those things. I mean, one thing is the elegance, the red carpet, the beautiful tuxes and gowns, the fabulous beach parties and all that stuff. Another thing is the best filmmakers in the world showing work there.

"And still another side is the marketplace, which is like a bazaar, with people talking about how many videocassette units your film's going to sell in Indonesia. It's that kind of sordid marketplace that gives cinema its vitality. And you can't have the cinema body without all of it. So it's really like a beautiful woman. It's extraordinary to look at from the outside, but once you cut it and look inside, you could throw up."

He said the confluence of glitz, glamour, and garishness reminded him of Las Vegas. "It's all kind of Vegasy. You see really elegant things and you see really tacky things, which I liked. I was in such a good mood, that I just loved everything."

So what do you do for an encore when your third feature film makes a splash at the mecca of world cinema? Well, if you're riding a wave of success like Alexander Payne, your hot new film is next chosen to open the New York Film Festival (NYFF), September 27 through October 13, at Lincoln Center. "It's an honor," he said regarding *Schmidt*'s recently announced selection to open the Big Apple event. "That will keep the awareness of the film afloat. A lot of the New York press and international press and kind of the tastemaker-types will see it, I'm told."

To be accepted as an opening night feature there, a film must be making its North American premiere, which forced New Line Cinema to decline invitations for *Schmidt* to play other major festivals on the continent, including those in Toronto and Telluride. No matter. The word-of-mouth momentum attached to *Schmidt* from its Cannes screenings is so strong that early industry patter is already positioning the film as an award-contending late fall release.

For the filmmaker, Cannes (May 15–26) marked a milestone in a still young career whose sky-is-the-limit ceiling has his work being compared to and his name being mentioned with the most celebrated cinema artists in the world today. An indication of his growing stature is the fact that during a recent Omaha visit he was shadowed by a *New York Times* reporter preparing a major profile on him. He fully recognizes, too, what Cannes means for his reputation, although the sardonic Payne points out the absurdity attending such puffery.

"It was a huge honor just to be there . . . and it's a nice stepping-stone," he said. "As far as I'm concerned, it's bigger than being nominated for an Oscar (he and writing partner Jim Taylor earned Best Adapted Screenplay nods for *Election*) because it's international. It's also really political and full of bullshit to some degree, but what isn't? But given that reality of the world, it's still about pure love of cinema, not Hollywood people slapping each other on the back and awarding movies like *A Beautiful Mind*. Ugh."

Getting his due

Payne, who emerged as a serious player on the independent film scene with his first two features, *Citizen Ruth* and *Election*, is now routinely being referred to as one of America's leading young directors. By the time the NYFF rolls around, Oscar talk should be swirling around *Schmidt*'s principals, including Payne, lauded for his direction and writing (he co-wrote the script with Taylor), Nicholson, whose dour performance as an imploding Everyman is considered among his best, and co-star Kathy Bates, whose small but showy turn as a man-eater complements Jack.

The public highlight of Cannes for Payne was striding the red carpet with Nicholson, paparazzi fluttering away, for the gala May 22 evening screening of *Schmidt* at the opulent Palais Theater. "It was the big official screening where everyone wears tuxedos and evening gowns and they stand up as you enter and they stand up at the end of the film and applaud. The Palais seats 2,300 people. It has beautiful projection and sound. It's really great."

Making the moment even more special for Payne was the presence of a coterie of friends and associates, including his fiancé, actress Sandra Oh, a co-star on HBO's long-running comedy series *Arli$$* and a rising young film star (*Double Happiness, Dancing at the Blue Iguana, The Princess Diaries*). Also on hand were his editor Kevin Tent, his composer Rolfe Kent, as well as his agent, lawyer, producers, and old chums from London, Paris, and Brazil.

Describing the whole experience as "out of body," he said his emotions were running so high that night that details are hazy. "It's too much. You're trying to absorb it but it's kind of impossible to absorb. And, actually, I think being from Omaha debilitates you in that setting because you're supposed to downplay things, you know, when in fact that's the moment when you really want to have your mind grow big enough to take it in."

The comedy of melancholia

To his delight, *Schmidt* went over well with the cosmopolitan crowd. "Basically, the jokes played very well. Some jokes, which are very American, went over like lead balloons." But, as anyone familiar with the acerbic Payne will tell you, his humor is not so much sunny-funny-bright as dark-stark-desolate. "When people tell me the film is really sad, I take it as a compliment. Americans want so much to laugh at things. It is kind of a perverse idea that we should always be laughing, that things should always be funny. I mean, I'm happy to make people laugh. I think that's fantastic. But my comedy is based on a very melancholy sense of life, at least in this particular film, and if they come away with that, then that's nice."

A key to understanding what Payne is after in his work is revealed in something the *Times* reporter told him about the wedding reception scene at the end of *Schmidt*. "He said to me, 'It rang so true that I felt for a moment I was watching a well-shot documentary.'" That, Payne said, "was a very nice articulation of something that maybe I've been trying to achieve, which is a well-shot documentary. I mean, that's great when there's little difference between what exists around a spectator

Tragic Comic masks of Ancient Greek theatre represented in the Hadrian's Villa mosaic. (Wikipedia Commons)

and what's on the screen. It's nice when movies ring really true. Not related to something true, but kind of actually true."

In a variation of what Omaha native author Ron Hansen calls "in hot pursuit of the real," Payne has tried capturing the essence of his hometown in all three of his features, each of which has been shot here. Regarding *Schmidt*, Payne said, "If Omahans can see and smell Omaha in it, I would be happy, because somehow capturing Omaha is a very elusive thing. *Citizen Ruth* doesn't have it at all. It's kind of more of a generic Anytown-USA sort of a feel. That's a failure of the film. *Election* has a little bit more. This (*Schmidt*) has it even more."

While conceding "it's even elusive to talk about it," he tried putting into words what it is about the Omaha zeitgeist he seeks to portray. "You know, when you're in someone's house and there's the carpet and the feel of the air in that house, and you look out the window—it's maybe about five thirty in the afternoon and humid—and you hear the crickets going and you think this moment could kind of last forever? It's something about that."

Distilling that languid side of Omaha into a single shot or scene is hard enough, he said, but it's even harder being true to a city when "we're so many different people doing different things here. I mean, Omaha's very diverse. You stop at the intersection of 72nd and Dodge and on one side you have some very well made-up West O housewife and her Ak-Sar-Ben princess daughter. And on the other side there's some guy with very fat arms and a tattoo in a rusted-out Mazda and his bitch next to him with their muffler rattling and their AM radio blasting. They're both very Omaha to me."

Then, referring to Omahans' wry sensibility, which informs his films and his musings, he said, "I think there's a certain earthiness to the sense of humor here, which may have its roots in the pioneer experience, I don't know. It's something about looking at the world as it is, with a twinkle in the eye, and saying something borderline callous about it, but still getting a good laugh out of it."

Riding the whirlwind

Making the most of what was his first time at Cannes, he arrived for the start of the festival and stayed through its conclusion. "I was there from the beginning to the end," he said, "because I hadn't seen movies for a year. When you're making a movie, you don't see movies, and so I had a thirst for cinema. As a director there you get a free pass to see anything and, so, I saw about twenty movies, sometimes four in one day. And it's funny because I thought a lot of directors would do the same, yet I was told that I was one of the few directors who actually went to see movies while there."

He saw several small films he feels deserve wide acclaim and patronage if and when they ever find general release—never a sure thing with non-commercial work. He said, "There's an American film coming out next year called *Long Way Home*, a first feature by a recent film school grad named Peter Sollett, and it's just a sweet, sweet love story set among teenage Dominicans on the Lower East Side of New York. You don't see a gun in it. It's all done with non-professional actors. It's beautifully shot and edited. The guy's a real filmmaker. I saw a Thai movie called *Blissfully Yours* that was really strange and really alive.

"Cinema is such a funny thing. You can see really polished stuff by professionals, and you respect it, and then you see something kind of crude but it really knocks you out. I liked Paul Thomas Anderson's (*Magnolia*) new film, *Punch-Drunk Love*. It's very strange, but I thought it was pretty disciplined and cinematic. Very good. I also saw retrospectives. Big film festivals like Cannes are good places to see old movies too because they get great prints. There was a newly restored print of a 1961 Italian film called *Il Posto*, by Ermanno Olmi (*Tree of the Wooden Clogs*), from the Bologna Cinematheque (Cineteca Bologna), which was amazing."

Although he would have preferred seeing movies to schmoozing, Payne gladly acquiesced to studio requests that he press the flesh with journalists and foreign sales reps. He didn't mind the dog-and-pony because he felt obliged to New Line for the commitment it's shown him and *Schmidt*. Besides, he said, it only makes sense to "do a little meet-and-greet" if it boosts the film.

"Publicity is basically free marketing and so it's to the studio's benefit to have me do press interviews. The interviews were held in a hotel suite. Important print people got like fifteen minutes one-on-one with me. Less important print people sat around a table, ten at a time, and got like twenty minutes between them. TV reporters got five minutes each. I tried to make it fresh with everyone, because otherwise I felt stupid trotting out the same dog-eared mental file cards.

"Another big thing about Cannes, from the studio's point of view, is drumming up enthusiasm among the foreign distributors, so that they feel good for having pre-bought the film. So I went to the international sales office from time to time to shake hands with the international distributors. That makes everyone feel good and included, apparently. I was very cooperative with all that. Look, I'm grateful to them (New Line) for making a non-commercial film for thirty two million bucks. And, also, I got first-class treatment. First-class tickets on Air France for me and Sandra and a nice room at a swanky hotel (the Majestic). I ate a lot of good food, I drank a lot of good wine, I saw lots of pretty girls. It was like a phenomenal experience in life."

Name dropping

There was also time left over to meet an idol, Martin Scorsese, who in addition to presiding over the festival's short films jury had, in exhibition there, a trailer of extracts from his much-anticipated new film *Gangs of New York*. Payne said, "At the closing night party I made a point of getting myself introduced to him. He said, 'You're Alexander Payne?' And I said, 'Yes.' And he said, 'I've seen *Election* three times, and I DON'T have the time. I admire your pictures.' And I said, 'I was about to say the same thing to you.' Nice guy."

One luminary Payne did not get a chance to speak with is David Lynch, who presided over the festival's feature film jury. Although Payne briefly met Lynch once before, he would like to know him better because he admires his work and what his work represents.

"He's the anti-Spielberg in terms of he doesn't think about the effect of his films on audiences. All he's responding to is how he sees the world and how he catches ideas. It's genuinely approaching cinema as dream. He's creating a certain uneasy, weird, free-associative, Homeric world.

There may be no point to it or there may be, depending on how you see things, but it seems like he wouldn't care how you see it, because he's an artist, unlike Spielberg, who cares where you cry and laugh and, if you don't feel it, he'll make sure you do by making the music tell you to feel that. I'm offended by that kind of very painful attitude toward filmmaking."

Looking ahead

That's not to say Payne isn't above taking commercial assignments. He and writing partner Jim Taylor have become two of the industry's hottest screen doctors since doing rewrite jobs on successive hit pictures: *Jurassic Park III* and *Meet the Parents*. They just completed a rewrite on 20th Century Fox's *Tucker Ames as Himself*. It's a screwball comedy about a Bill Gates–like billionaire, Tucker Ames, who tries escaping media scrutiny over a mega-lawsuit by posing as an actor in an obscure theater that, as fate has it, mounts a socially-conscious play skewering the man everyone says he looks like and secretly is.

Now, the studio is courting Payne to direct the project (which Ben Stiller is attached to) and he's "toying with the idea" of helming it. He will only take the job if Fox meets two demands: they must wait a year while he makes his next film, *Sideways*, which he expects to start shooting in February; and they must "accept a certain independence" from him. He added, "If they don't want to do that, then I've told them, 'Let's part friends.'"

With *Sideways*, which Payne–Taylor are adapting from a never-published Rex Pickett novel by the same name, the filmmaker will be making his first feature outside Nebraska. He will shoot in California, whose wine country is the setting for this story of two male buddies binging on a weekend fling before one is married. Along the way, they hook up with two women and trouble.

Right now, Payne is sure of only one casting decision and that is that Sandra Oh will play one of the women. "It's not just because I'm involved with her," he said, "but she'd actually be great. She's a really good actress." Although *Sideways* marks a departure for Payne in that it will be shot out of state, he said, "I don't see it as a break. It's very much in a continuum. The sensibility will be the same. The approach will be the same. I will be working with the same creative team." He added, however, he does intend doing "a little formal experimentation" with his camera style on the new flick.

With everything on the rise, Payne could be excused for playing the big-shot. The amazing thing is, he doesn't. If ever tempted, he can always think back to how his ego got checked at Cannes. "So, one night I'm walking up the red carpet with Jack Nicholson and there's hundreds of people taking my picture, er, taking Jack's picture. I just happen to be the guy standing next to Jack. The next night, Sandra and I are back. Nobody's taking my picture. I'm in my tux again—it's got a long black satin tie instead of a bow tie, which is passable everywhere except Cannes. They won't let me through. They tell me I have to buy a bow tie for fifteen euros. They keep a supply, like the 21 Club does with suit coats. My girlfriend goes, 'Don't you know who he is? He had a film in competition here last night.' And they're like, 'Yeah, yeah ... whatever, where's your fifteen euros?' "You see? Nobody knows who I am."

Schmidt, Payne and an intersection

Published in a 2002 issue of the *Omaha Weekly*

Playing the field

In a gathering of the cool and cognoscenti, the Blue Barn Theatre presented its October 5 On the Set with Alexander Payne program at the Omaha Community Playhouse. The fund raiser, patterned after the Bravo cable network's *Inside the Actors Studio* series, gave a few hundred cinephiles the chance to see and hear first-hand the homegrown film icon ruminate about everything from his art to his career to his Greek heritage.

Payne, whose presence looms ever larger on the world cinema stage, was his usual charming, witty, erudite self while fielding questions from moderator Hughston Walkinshaw and audience members. Payne and the Blue Barn are a perfect match as each is an irreverent provocateur. So it's only fitting Payne would be what Blue Barn co-founder and executive director Walkinshaw called "our moneymaker for the year." The occasion featured excerpts from the artist's films, including *About Schmidt*, and offered a timely retrospective of the work of this insightful commentator on the American scene.

As excitement builds around *Schmidt*, opening nationally December 13, Payne finds himself at an intersection in his professional life. The Omaha native has carved out a niche as an original, independent filmmaker. His first three features, all critically praised, were made on his home turf, where he's explored a Midwest cultural landscape that is stolid and steadfast on the surface yet riddled with angst beneath. *Citizen Ruth*, *Election*, and *Schmidt*, all written with Jim Taylor, examine the fallout of private moral issues gone public and the politics of relationships gone awry. The conflicts in his movies revolve around the bad choices people make under stress and the folly of trying to cover their tracks. His misbegotten characters are, as he puts it, "working out their personal psychodramas for the first time . . . and there's no map. It's just funnier when they're doomed to failure."

Now, having completed what might be considered his Omaha trilogy, he's preparing to leave his familiar filmic territory behind for new horizons. Or is he? He's committed to filming outside Nebraska with his next project, *Sideways*, a comedy set in the Santa Barbara wine-tasting region. He and Taylor are nearly done with the script for *Sideways*, to be shot next year.

Payne talks about his desire to stretch beyond borders and make movies around the world, including Greece and Spain, two nations he has strong ties to. His grandparents hailed from Greece and the former Spanish lit scholar studied in Spain: "I feel Spain in my heart."

He also talks about one day returning to make his long-awaited Western in out-state Nebraska. Given his acerbic nature, one imagines his vision of the West as closer to Robert Altman's *McCabe & Mrs. Miller* than, say, Clint Eastwood's *Unforgiven*. As stylistically different as those two films are from each other and from such standards as *The Searchers*, virtually all great Westerns deal with the very theme of alienation that permeates Payne's urbane comedies. It may just be that Payne, regardless of genre, will be what Martin Scorsese calls "a smuggler" who infiltrates his ideas, concerns, and obsessions into the guise of the Western.

The Schmidt effect

Everything is pointing to *Schmidt* being a crossover hit and awards contender. Jack Nicholson seems assured a Best Actor Oscar nod for his star turn as Warren Schmidt, a dour Everyman vainly searching for contentment in the throes of a mid-life crisis. Payne and Taylor should be in line for another Best Adapted Screenplay nomination for their finely observed American Gothic story.

After its smashing debut at Cannes, *Schmidt* opened the 40th New York Film Festival at Lincoln Center on September 27 to uniformly enthusiastic reviews. Payne was particularly heartened by Stephen Holden's unqualified rave in the *New York Times* that lauded the film's honest take on a certain way of life that inhibits or distorts real human connections. "Even though I kind of really didn't care what he said and I may not agree with him, what made me happiest about Stephen Holden's review was that it was on the level of ideas ... about ideas being expressed or explored in the film," Payne said. "Most film criticism is just about looking at the mechanics of it, but I liked that he talked about ideas and world view."

Much of the film focuses on the conventions and rituals of middle-class America. After, in short order, retiring from his actuarial job and losing his wife, Schmidt discovers he's dissatisfied with his life and sets off on an existential road trip to try and make amends with his estranged daughter. In one scene of profound awkwardness between Schmidt, his daughter, and her dimwitted fiancé, the threesome cannot bring themselves to talk about anything other than traffic even though they brim with seething emotions.

"For me," Payne said, "it's all about what's not being said. I've just seen that so many times. You talk about the most trivial things and you never get to the juicy stuff. That seems very true to me." Then there is Schmidt trying to play father to his daughter, on the eve of her wedding, after years of sequestering his feelings from her. "It's totally rooted in his own needs and his own selfishness," Payne said. "He's reaching out to her because he's so desperate in his life, but it's too late, man, it's too late. And so many people have told me, 'I saw my father in that film.'"

Most of what Schmidt utters is heard in voice-over, including a funny, absurd one-way correspondence he has with Ndugu, an African orphan he's ostensibly supporting but whom he uses as a sounding board for his own tortured soul. Schmidt, of course, could not be more removed from this poor African child's reality. According to Payne, "One of the biggest laughs in the film is early on when he's finishing up his first letter to Ndugu and he says, 'Well, here I am rambling on and on and you probably want to hurry on down and cash that check and get yourself something to eat.'" The Dear Ndugu device is a carryover from a 1991 original Payne script, *The Coward*, which served more as the basis for the movie than did the Louis Begley novel *About Schmidt*. Payne uses the device to expose that strange phenomenon whereby "some people can only tell the real truth to persons who are otherwise completely uninvolved in their lives."

The New York reception to *About Schmidt* was, Payne said, "Really warm and inviting. They were prepared to like the film because of the reviews. There had been kind of a donor's dinner beforehand and everyone was a little loosened up on booze, and Nicholson was there, which made people feel good."

In good company

For Payne, the highlight of that gala night, which he described as "a New York society event more than a film event," was "a compilation of moments from movies that have opened the festival." As he watched the highlight reel unfold on a monitor backstage, waiting to go on to introduce his film, something happened that overwhelmed the usually implacable artist.

"At the end there was a countdown" of all the legendary directors whose films have opened the prestigious festival, from Fellini to Bergman to Buñuel to Godard to Kurosawa to Almodovar, "and finally ending in 2002 with Alexander Payne, *About Schmidt*. And that I was not prepared for ... to be in that company," he said. "I couldn't believe it. I'm still not sure how to process it. It just reminds me I'm first and foremost a film buff. I just love good movies. I like to watch movies, and that's what I've spent most of my life doing. I like making 'em too and I'm getting better at it. But to suddenly be included with such figures ... at this time in American cinema, which is so bad . . . made me all the more grateful to go out there to say my obligatory but also heartfelt thanks to festival organizers."

Hitting the zeitgeist

He feels that, more than his previous pictures, his new film taps into a shared national consciousness. "I had the sensation that night in New York and again in Omaha that somehow *About Schmidt*, and you hope to do this as a filmmaker, is hitting some part of the zeitgeist. And that's a new thing for me. You can either hit the zeitgeist fully dead center, like *The Piano*, or one of these films the whole world sees, or you graze it and just skim off the top. Only time will tell where it will fall in that sliding scale . . . but it's like people somehow are ready to see this movie and to get something out of it, and a lot of them. I never expected this to be a huge commercial success, and it may not be, but I have the feeling it's going to be somewhere in the zeitgeist."

He's just not sure exactly what people are connecting with. "We'll be able to figure that out better after it comes out," he said. When it's suggested they are responding to the separation so many of us feel from society he said, "Alienation and loneliness ... yeah, maybe. I know I respond to American movies from the '60s and '70s, which is the cinema of alienation. You can feel sort of personal alienation in life just as a way of being but also in a larger sense. I mean, I don't know who I am in society anymore. I don't relate at all to our President. I don't relate at all with the five corporations that pretty much control everything. It's like, Who am I? Who are we anymore as individuals? How is it making us feel and how can we fight back?"

Talking shop

The many sides of Payne were on display during his recent Omaha stay. He enjoys discussing the filmmaking art, his working process, his celluloid passions (It turns out he's a huge fan of Westerns and samurai films.) and even his life outside cinema. At once a scholar and a celebrity, he is at his core a filmaholic grateful to be working in the field he loves. Payne even gave some advice to aspiring filmmakers attending On the Set: "Filmmaking is a struggle. It's just kind of sticking with it and not having a backup plan—I've never had a backup plan—and looking at every obstacle as an opportunity to be more creative."

On the role filmmakers play in culture and society, especially in tense times like these, he said, "One of the things I like about art and about film is when it questions, in a healthy way, the status quo and asks, Do we live in the best of all possible worlds? And the answer is usually no. In fact, it's always no. Your responsibility as an artist is toward yourself and what you think is good and honest and creative. I think even films which seem cynical or critical or satirical actually have a positive message, which is, How can we improve this?"

On the craft of filmmaking, he said, "Anyone can really learn how to make a film in about a week," and in response to laughter from the On the Set crowd, he added, "No, it's true. The principles of film are very simple, but it's a matter of what you're going to film, what story you want to tell, and what eye you want to cast on the world that's important."

As far as choosing the subjects he builds scripts around, he said, "It's really more true that those stories choose you. It kind of takes you over. I just try to stay open to life. I read a lot, I listen a lot, I look at a lot of stuff for story ideas." He recounted how a *New York Times* article filed out of Fargo, North Dakota, served as the inspiration for *Citizen Ruth*, right down to the inhalant-addict pregnant protagonist becoming a pawn of the pro-life–pro-choice camps. He began writing his own scripts "just to get stuff to direct," he said, again eliciting laughter while being dead serious. "No, it's true," he said, adding that he views writing as a basic element of his craft.

"I regard the term filmmaking as a three-part process: writing, directing, and editing. And I've tried to become as proficient as possible with all three." Always on the lookout for a script to direct that neither he nor Taylor has written, he has yet to find one. "I open up every script with a prayer." Writing is an evolutionary process in which the story is revealed through the act of creation. "You discover it while you're writing it," he said. "Writing takes a long time, and it's full of depression and agony." As half of one of Hollywood's most respected and successful writing teams, Payne discussed the collaborative relationship he has with Taylor and how it helps each check the other.

Two heads are better than one

"The nice thing about writing with a collaborator is it makes the process less hideous. You're always fighting against discipline problems.

It's hard sticking to a routine and sitting your butt down every day. But if you know you have an appointment with someone (to write), it's harder to blow it off. You have someone around you to help you identify the one good idea you may have all day."

Unlike collaborators who write separately and then fashion a screenplay via email or fax or phone, the pair "actually have to be together to write," which requires that either Payne, who lives in L.A., and Taylor, who lives in New York, travel to the other. "We have one monitor with two keyboards," Payne said of their writing setup. "I take the lead sometimes in the grunt work, putting it into some basic form on the page. We don't outline. We don't plan all that much what we're doing. We really try to get as firm an idea as we can . . . but it's always the process of writing that brings the ideas. Often times, when we have an idea, I'll write half a page or a page and then Jim will jump in. But weeks can go by and we don't write anything other than notes. We talk. What's it going to be? How are we going to do it? Who are the characters? It's a slow process."

In the end, the two feel "lucky for having found a collaborator in each other. It's like finding a mate in a way. There's no formula and you can't predict it." Payne, who said he and Taylor "try to make each other laugh a lot," is big on creating a light tone on the set of his movies. "I like to have fun. I like to work with people who kind of have a similar, perhaps joyful, attitude about the work we do. It's play. It's hard play. And that's an attitude, I think, that's helpful."

He said, "There's always a bit of nerves between actors and directors the first couple weeks as you're learning to trust one another." That was true at the start of *Schmidt*, as Nicholson felt Payne out, but in short time "he made it very easy to direct him. He put a lot of appreciated effort into breaking the ice with those around him. He was very professional and very cool and very kind."

Balance

During his Omaha stopover Payne revealed a measure of grace in the way he balances his two identities as a cosmopolitan cinema figure and as an ordinary guy with deep ethnic and community ties. At a press conference, he addressed how the fame that's come his way makes him a little uneasy. "I like just making the movies. It's nice that people like 'em, but I get uncomfortable when too much attention is on me personally. Knowing I was going to have to introduce my film in front of three thousand people at Lincoln Center, I was nervous for two straight weeks. That's pretty much all I thought about. And even five minutes before going on I still hadn't figured out what I was going to say. And I don't know why people would want to be famous because everywhere they go people know who they are. I mean, they can't do anything fun—they can't even buy porn."

Even with his growing celebrity, Payne has remained amazingly accessible. He accepted the Blue Barn's request to lend his name and presence to their fund raiser because, he said simply, "They asked me." He's one of the theater's biggest fans. "The first thing I ever saw there was *Go Go Boys from Planet X*, which was fantastic and ribald and subversive against the city fathers of Omaha, and I said, 'Who are these guys?' I haven't liked everything they've done, but I support what they're doing . . . and they should be more known, funded, and respected."

The night of On the Set, Payne was gracious with reporters, patrons, and sycophants alike. When the throng of admirers got to be a little much, though, he slipped out, alone, to take in a midnight screening of *Midnight Cowboy* at the Dundee Theater. The next day, at Caffeine Dreams, where he arrived in a wood-paneled station wagon, he rhapsodized about *Cowboy's* gentle, tender love story between two men. Later, at the coffeehouse, he was patient and generous with a high school journalist who collared him for an impromptu interview. Later, during yet another interview, he took a call from his fiancé, screen actress Sandra Oh, who's in Italy making *Under the Tuscan Sun* with Diane Lane. After telling her, "Yes, darling," and "Of course, darling," he pledged to call back "my future wife." Then, he politely excused himself from any more questions, explaining, "I'm so behind in my life right now," and escaped to the Omaha apartment he keeps as his private sanctuary.

Getting personal

Payne, who guards his personal life, is close to his family. His parents and bride-to-be were with him in New York. His folks were with him again at the Playhouse. The youngest of three brothers, he grew up in a household steeped in Greek heritage. Until his immigrant grandfather changed it, the family name was Papadopaulos. The family patriarch, Nick, was a founder of Omaha's St. John's Greek Orthodox Church. Nick was perhaps best known as the entrepreneur of the Virginia Cafe, a 24-hour eatery that Payne said "was an institution" downtown. The cafe, which Payne's dapper father, George, helped manage, burned down in 1969.

Payne, who said, "I'm proud of being Greek-American," has visited Greece many times and knows the large Papadopoulos clan there. For Payne, who intends to shoot a movie in Greece within the decade, the success of *My Big Fat Greek Wedding* "shows very wonderfully how audiences want to see sincere and human stories amid all this dreck the studios burp up. It's so wonderful. All ethnicities are seeing themselves in it. It's recognizing what an ethnic country we are."

Even with his success, he sometimes wonders whether films really matter anymore in this age of boundless media, but he feels reaffirmed again when he sees something like Martin Scorsese's documentary *My Voyage to Italy*, which lovingly traces the Italian cinema. "It's one of the most inspiring things I've ever seen," he said. "It's fantastic. It reminds me of ways in which cinema can be urgent and important and meaningful and comforting. It's helped given me strength not to sell out and to stay the course." It's why, despite the headaches that crop up when making films, he knows he's exactly where he wants to be. "If I'm having the worst day directing, it's still one of the best days of my life because I'm so happy doing it. I feel lucky to have found so early in life what I love to do."

On December 10, *About Schmidt* opened the new Mary Riepma Ross Media Arts Center in downtown Lincoln. The screening and post-film party (at the Rococo) were fund-raising events for the Center, formerly known as the Mary Riepma Ross Film Theater. Following a cast and crew sneak preview of *Schmidt* at the Joslyn Art Museum on December 11, the film opens in Omaha, New York, and Los Angeles on December 13 and in other markets on December 20.

Alexander Payne on his new film: Nicholson and the comedy of deep focus

Published in a 2002 issue of *The Reader*

Jack Nicholson as Warren Schmidt

Schmidt's big score

Bolstered by rousing receptions at prestigious film festivals, critical kudos from leading reviewers, widespread predictions of Oscar nods, and loads of studio marketing behind it, the momentum attending *About Schmidt* surpasses anything Alexander Payne saw for his previous features' openings.

Where *Citizen Ruth* and *Election* were accorded the kind of lukewarm studio backing (from Miramax and Paramount/MTV Films, respectively) that idiosyncratic movies get when "the suits" don't fully endorse or understand them, *Schmidt* is getting the type of red carpet treatment from New Line Cinema execs that signals they see a potential winner, read—moneymaker, here. And why not?

The film, making its Nebraska premiere December 10 at the new Mary Riepma Ross Media Arts Center (formerly the Mary Riepma Ross Film Theater) in downtown Lincoln, appears to have everything going for it heading into Hollywood's big ticket winter season, when prestige pictures are positioned at the cineplex for box-office leverage and Academy consideration.

The timing of *Schmidt*'s release seems right. There's the snob appeal that comes from boffo Cannes and New York Film Festival screenings of the film this past spring and summer. There's the raves it received from Stephen Holden in the *New York Times*, Kenneth Turan in the *Los Angeles Times* and a slew of other name critics for major media outlets. There's also serious Oscar talk for Jack Nicholson's celebrated turn as dour Omaha Everyman Warren Schmidt and for Payne and writing partner Jim Taylor's sardonic take on middle-class American mores. Then there's the priceless mojo Nicholson's mystique brings to the Nebraska-made project.

Of course, none of this guarantees *Schmidt* will do any business, especially in light of the fact Payne's films have so far fared better in home-market release, where they have time to be discovered and appreciated, than in theaters. That his films appeal to a discriminating audience is logical given his wry, sagacious work, which is really in the realm of social commentary. Film critic David Denby called Payne and Taylor "perhaps the only true social satirists now working in American movies." But satire can be a hard pill for filmgoers to swallow. They may feel the sting hits too close to home or they may prefer something lighter to go with their concessions.

According to Dan Ladely, director of the Ross Media Arts Center, *Schmidt* is "a little bit of a departure from Alexander's two previous films, which were known for their kind of biting satire. This film is a little bit more nostalgic." While perhaps gentler, it is, like the others, a painfully honest and ironic examination of how good people lose their way and court despair even amidst the so-called Good Life.

Disconnection

In today's spoon-fed movie culture, bleak is a hard sell unless accompanied by big action set pieces, and the only thing passing for action in *Schmidt* is Nicholson's comic struggle atop a water bed. That scene closes a sequence in which the tight-assed, buttoned-down Schmidt is disgusted by the outrageous new family he inherits via his daughter's impending wedding. The son-in-law's mother, Roberta, is, as deliciously played by Kathy Bates, a brazen woman whom, Payne said, "Is the type of person that will say anything to anyone." At one point she tries seducing Schmidt in a hot tub by "telling him about how sexual she is and how she had her first orgasm in ballet class at age six," said Payne, delighted with offending every propriety Schmidt holds dear. "Oh, it's so fun to torture your characters."

In this scene, as in much of the film, Nicholson's performance rests more on his facial-physical reactions than words. Indeed, instead of explosions, verbal or otherwise, moviegoers get the implosion that Nicholson's Warren Schmidt, a retired and widowed Woodmen of the World Life Insurance actuary, undergoes.

Severed from the twin tethers of job and wife that defined him and held his orderly life together, he begins questioning everything about his existence, including the choices he made. He lets himself go. The state of his disillusion is captured in the film's ad campaign in which Schmidt appears as a shell-shocked, disheveled man shadowed by a dark cloud overhead in an otherwise clear blue sky. In the throes of this mid-life crisis, he sets off, in a huge, unwieldy motor home that is an apt expression of his desperate inadequacy, on an existential road trip across Nebraska. His destination is Denver, where he heads ostensibly to heal his wounded relationship with his daughter and to save her, as he sees it, from the mistake she is about to make in marrying a frivolous man. Along the way, he conveys his troubles to an odd assortment of people he turns to or rails against in a kind of unfolding nervous breakdown. Unable to express his real feelings to those closest to him, he instead pours out his soul, in writing (and in voice-over), to an African orphan he sponsors, Ndugu, who can't possibly understand his dilemma.

Jack digs deep

Regarding Nicholson's portrayal of a man in crisis, Dan Ladely calls it "probably one of the most subdued performances he's ever given and maybe one of his best. I'd be really surprised if he doesn't get nominated for an Oscar. It's a role where he really stretched himself, and I think probably a lot of the credit for that could be given to Alexander, because Alexander is a director who works well with actors. He gets a lot out of them."

Directing Nicholson allowed Payne to work with an actor he greatly admires and solidified his own status as a sought-after filmmaker. He found Nicholson to be a consummate professional and supreme artist. "Nicholson does a lot of work on his character before shooting. Now, a lot of actors do that, but he REALLY does it. To the point where, as he describes it, he's so in character and so relaxed that if he's in the middle of a take and one of the movie lights falls or a train goes through or anything, he'll react to it in character. He won't break." Payne said Nicholson doesn't like a lot of rehearsal "because he believes in cinema as the meeting of the spontaneous and the moment. His attitude is,

'What if something good happens and the camera wasn't on?'"

As for the film, Ladely said it holds up well with the best of "the really interesting work" being done in American cinema today. "It has an incredibly good supporting cast, including Kathy Bates, who's just wonderful and almost steals the show from Jack, but not quite. Actually, *About Schmidt* is almost a Nebraska travelogue. Jack sets out on a little trip from Omaha to Denver and in the process kind of wanders all over the state, so you get to see a lot of scenery from Nebraska along the way, and it looks very good. It's of course what Alexander knows. It's where he's from. He knows the territory. But at a time when almost every independent film you go to is made in New York or Los Angeles, it's nice to see a film that was made somewhere else. I think the fact he has been able to do that makes him unique."

Coincidentally, *Schmidt* is one of three made-in-Nebraska films being released this winter to critical acclaim. The others are *Tully*, a Nebraska farm story, and *Skins*, a modern Native American Indian tale. "All of a sudden Nebraska is at the forefront of the film industry," said Ladely, whose Center showed *Tully* and will screen *Skins*.

Getting at certain truths

With *Schmidt*, Payne is once again exploring facets of America that reveal our insecurities and incongruities. For example, the way Schmidt opens up to total strangers while concealing his true feelings from loved ones reflects a phenomenon, Payne said, whereby "some people can only tell the real truth to psychiatrists or therapists otherwise completely uninvolved in their lives. That's why the confessor is traditionally faceless in the church. It's really interesting."

Payne said the scenes where Schmidt and his family "talk about the most trivial things" rather than "the juicy stuff" is "all about what's not being said." As anecdotal evidence of this, he added, "A friend of my mom's is Jewish and married into a prominent Omaha WASP family and one time she asked someone in the family, 'Why do you only talk about the weather and golf?' And the reply was, 'What are we supposed to talk about, how much we hate each other?' That seems very true to me. One of the most Midwestern things about *Schmidt* is its looking at what happens when you're not encouraged to talk about your emotions."

All this subtext makes for the kind of iconoclastic, acutely observed cinema that is the signature M.O. of Payne, whose storytelling aesthetic and sensibility is more aligned with the social satirists of the 1950s, '60s and '70s than today's cynically hip filmmakers who choose posturing over incisive narrative. Although Payne isn't banking on the film being a breakout hit, his instincts tell him its discerning look at the sad, absurd quagmire that is Warren Schmidt's middle-class American life is somehow intersecting with the deep current of alienation, anxiety, and anger running through the culture these days.

"It's like people somehow are ready to see this movie and to get something out of it, and a lot of them. I never expected this to be a huge commercial success, and it may not be, but I have the feeling it's going to be somewhere in the zeitgeist," he said. "When people tell me the film is really sad, I take it as a compliment. I mean, I'm happy to make people laugh. I think that's fantastic. But my comedy is based on a very melancholy sense of life, and in this film if people come away with that then that's nice."

Then again, it may not be for everyone. "My mom finds *About Schmidt* very depressing," Payne noted. "She said it made her want to blow her brains out," a sentiment which could be bad for business. Preview cards on the film, Payne said, consistently come back with comments like "real," "true-to-life," "genuine," and naturalistic." A *New York Times* reporter who shadowed Payne in Omaha for a profile told him it has the look and feel "of a well-shot documentary," which Payne thought "a very nice articulation of something that maybe I've been trying to achieve. I mean, that's great when there's little difference between what exists around a spectator and what's on the screen. It's nice when movies ring really true. Not related to something true, but kind of actually true."

Also apparently resonating with viewers is the repressed character of Schmidt and his struggle connecting with people, especially his estranged daughter. "So many people have told me, 'I saw my father in that film,'" Payne said.

Factors that make the film what it ss

Unlike *Election*, which has a kinetic pacing befitting its hyper antagonists' screwball antics in trying to win at all costs, *Schmidt* has, by comparison, a deliberate rhythm keyed to its single plodding protagonist and his befuddled attempts to make things right. Payne said while both films share a similar satiric spirit, the brooding landscape of *Schmidt* demanded a camera and editing style different than the earlier film's more manic tone.

"It has I think the same sensibility as *Election*, but it's slower and it lets the drama and emotion play more often than going for the laughs. I think it just called for that. In *Election* the camera has a very fluid style, it's almost constantly in motion, and the editing is snappy. You'll find that the camera in *About Schmidt* is relatively static, and then when the camera does move it has meaning. And the editing is less jarring." He said he keyed the new film's visual style "not only to the somber nature of the story and to the stolid character of Schmidt, but also to the conditions under which" he made the film.

"On *Schmidt*, I was told I had to make all my days, that I couldn't fall behind schedule and that I couldn't have any extra time to shoot. Because I was under the gun I was forced not to come up with the cleverest way to shoot a scene, but the simplest. What it did is force me to think, which I think about anyway, of absolutely the best place to put the camera to tell the story. I obviously try to pick framing which is funny and also tells the story efficiently. So I had to work quickly, which is not a bad exercise to have. Since I come from low-budget filmmaking, I've always had to work fast and to do as many setups as I can."

In discussing the way he blocks out a scene, Payne revealed his approach to comedy vis-à-vis the camera or, specifically, the lenses he uses, which determines the way he sets off characters visually and thematically. "In all three of my films I like deep focus. I shoot with wide lenses . . . not by design but I just start fishing around with lenses and asking, What would look good? And I rarely come up with long lenses. Typically, Hollywood movies shoot close-ups with a 75 millimeter lens; whereas, I typically shoot close-ups with about a 35, so the camera is closer to the actors, which is not always so good for the actors, but it's just . . . I don't know . . . a little bit funnier. They look realer. Those longer lenses make 'em look more pretty, and I'm usually not interested in making the actors look more pretty."

Deep focus, wide-angle shots are also preferable because they help fix characters in the context of a scene. "The circumstances characters find themselves in are always very important. The longer the lens, the more the surroundings tend to blur away, and I so very much like to get a sense of the set and surroundings and to fill the frame with jokes or meaningful things. It's like in *Mad* magazine when they have the tiny, tiny cartoons in the sides of the pages, whether it's a movie parody or "The Lighter Side" or "Spy Versus Spy," and you look in the corner and there's little things going on. It's fun to have that kind of stuff going on."

Early into Schmidt's road trip he visits the Great Platte River Road Archway Monument near Kearney. Ascending an escalator, the gray, forlorn figure of Schmidt, attired in his ever-present trench coat, is framed against the loud, colorful, gargantuan museum displays, summing up in one shot how small, disjointed, and insignificant he feels in life. This classic image of a lone man dwarfed and dumbfounded by his surroundings is remindful of those great Chaplin and Keaton silent screen scenarios that juxtapose their Everyman alter-egos against giant forces and environments they can't possibly comprehend.

In devising the visual style for his films Payne said that while he works closely with his cinematographer, James Glennon, who has lensed all his features, he personally "figures out every shot. I mean, there's never a time where I just sort of stage the action and turn to the cameraman and say, 'You shoot it.'"

To Payne's way of thinking, "There's no such thing as a second unit, even when I have two cameras going at once." In film parlance, a second unit is comprised of an assistant director, camera operator, and sound man who pick up background, establishing shots, or added coverage. Often, what's captured is considered throwaway material. For Payne, there's no such thing. "Usually, if there are second-unit shots at which I'm not present," he said, "they never get used in the film because in every shot there's the opportunity for something extra."

On the set, Payne is his own master, but he likes having writing partner Jim Taylor, with whom he has a symbiotic relationship, on hand for counsel. "He's another side of me and I of him," he said. "If I ask his advice or he asks mine, we always know we'll get the purest answer about what's creatively best for the film with no commercial considerations. He also knows to keep a little distance . . . he completely understands the process. He knows this is the time the director has."

In a good place

Although still a young filmmaker, Payne has a veteran's grasp of the medium, not surprising given how deeply steeped this inveterate film buff is in cinema history. To date, he has wisely chosen projects that best suit his talents. Each film has been progressively larger than the last, but he has thus far avoided taking things just for the money or prestige. As proof, he recently turned down two lucrative directing jobs: a Coen Brothers–scripted remake of *Gambit* and *Tucker Ames as Himself*, which he and Taylor rewrote.

As long as Payne continues writing his own scripts, either alone or in tandem with Taylor, he should remain true to his stated desire of making "increasingly more personal films" and "human films about people." His litmus test for projects is deceptively simple. "You have to feel inspired about what you write about and what you want to commit to film. The reason I choose a book to make into a movie is because it's sparking something in me." He said the collaboration he and Taylor enjoy invigorates them. "It's like somehow in writing together we help bring out each other's voices. I help him achieve his best and he helps me achieve my best. The nice thing about writing with a collaborator is it makes the process less hideous." Viewed as one of Hollywood's top writing teams for hire, Payne and Taylor have done rewrites on *Meet the Parents*, *Jurassic Park III*, and *Tucker Ames*.

It is clear in talking with Payne he approaches his work with growing confidence. "I'm just more comfortable doing it. I don't panic as much if take one is a disaster. In terms of my own craft, I just know I feel more comfortable not planning things. I'm trying to get away from rules. Increasingly, as a director, it's much more interesting for me to approach every day of shooting in as open a manner as I would approach a day of writing. It depends on how I feel that day and what's in the ether and what I did yesterday and if I want to do something different today." By the same token, he said with the start of any new project, "It's a learning process each time. I still think of it as a struggle . . . just less hard."

One can view his three features as a Nebraska trilogy. In dissecting a certain Midwest ethos and way of life, each examines what happens to good people when their beliefs are fundamentally unhinged or subverted. Through his satirist's eye he shows we're all subject to human frailties and, along the way, skewers some sacred cows: with *Citizen Ruth* it's religion; with *Election*, politics; and with *About Schmidt*, the family.

Having explored some segments of Nebraska society and having firmly fixed himself as one of cinema's brightest artists, he is now itching to expand his vision outside the state. His next film, *Sideways,* will be shot in California. In what is another collaboration with Taylor, *Sideways* follows the misadventures of two buddies on a wine-tasting binge in Santa Barbara. As research, he and Rex Pickett, the author of the unpublished novel Payne and Taylor are adapting, went on a wine-tasting spree. Payne is also co-scripting with Taylor a script about Civil War reenactors that Taylor will shoot as his directorial debut.

Payne said he may not make another film in Nebraska for a while and when he does it will likely be his long-awaited Western. Wherever his work takes him, it will be sure to generate interest. If *Schmidt* is any indication, he should remain a vital presence on the world cinema stage. "It opened the New York Film Festival and was one of only three American films to make it into the competition at the Cannes Film Festival, which really attests to how good Alexander is," Ross Media Arts Center director Dan Ladely said. "I think his films will only get better and better. So far, they've gotten better and better. It's going to be really interesting to watch his career, and I think we're going to see a lot more from him in the future. He certainly hasn't reached his peak. His career is really just beginning."

Loyalty

An endearing thing about Payne is that even as his star rises he remains loyal to his roots. In October he graced the Omaha Community Playhouse stage for a Blue Barn Theatre fund raiser. Now, he's returning for the grand opening of the Ross Center, whose December 10 screening of *Schmidt* will christen the new theater. The screening and post-film party (at the Rococo) are fund-raising events for the Center. Payne has a history with the Center, having received the Mary Riepma Ross Award and been a judge for the Great Plains Film Festival. "We're very grateful to him," Ladely said. "He was gracious enough to help make this happen."

Payne is also slated to appear in Scottsbluff next October for a film festival at the restored Midwest Theater, which he happened upon during a stopover in the western Nebraska town. Tentatively joining Payne for the Scottsbluff event will be Oscar-winning film editor Mike Hill and novelist-screenwriter Richard Dooling, whose *White Man's Grave* was a National Book Award finalist.

Following a December 11 cast-crew sneak preview at the Joslyn Art Museum, *Schmidt* opens in Omaha, New York, and Los Angeles December 13 and other markets December 20.

3

The *Sideways* Diaries

∽৵৵৲

Introduction

The next two stories grew directly out of my being on the set of *Sideways* for a week in the fall of 2003. In some ways the experience forever spoiled me. I was the only journalist on set the entire time. My access to Payne and his process was as complete as one could possibly expect.

Literally, I stood beside him or directly in back of him as shots proceeded. I listened in on otherwise private asides and conversations he engaged in with cast and crew. I was free to interview anyone in the company. I was assigned a driver who picked me up at the crack of dawn each morning from my motel to escort me to the set and deposited me back at the motel at the end of the day's shoot. I was present for virtually every setup and take during the week. I got to eat with the company at the big craft services buffet held at or near the end of each shooting day. I got to visit a winery location used for the film, and I shared a dinner-interview with Payne one evening after a day's shoot.

As I was still getting my bearings the first forty-eight hours or so, there was a distinct learning curve as I attempted to understand the routines and rhythms of a working Hollywood film set. I felt like a third wheel at times. It took me a while to find the right balance of being in the most advantageous position to see and hear everything pertinent happening while not being a distraction or nuisance or obstacle. The last thing I wanted to do was to get in the way; therefore, I was acutely conscious of where I stood and what was happening around me.

My fondest desire was to become one with the production, and I knew when I achieved that state of integration or acclimation because there came a time when I felt so embedded in the workings of it all that I finally blended in as an invisible cog in the apparatus. That was not the case at the start, when I recall tripping over my own feet as I scrambled to keep up, stride for stride, with Payne as he followed the camera mount on a tracking shot. I did not stumble and fall or ruin a shot, but I easily could have, which I suppose might have jeopardized my assignment or at least curtailed my access. I suspect though that if somehow I had fouled things up Payne would have gracefully handled the situation, chastising me firmly but gently, and making me feel better by reminding me it's only a movie.

Payne proverbially rolled out the red carpet for me. He ensured before I ever arrived that cast and crew knew I was there at his express invitation, which of course made all the difference in the world in terms of cooperation and transparency. Therefore, when I got there, I felt I was indeed a welcome guest rather than some interloper they felt constrained to tolerate. The fact that Payne and I had a history is why I was invited there in the first place, and it is why I felt I belonged on his turf even though it was foreign territory to be sure. Speaking of turf or territory, his film sets are sanctuaries that he understandably protects with guarded precaution. It is his world, and one I am not ordinarily privy to.

Until *Sideways* all my encounters with Payne had been off set, in cafes or coffeehouses, at event venues, or at my house or his apartment, and so it was invaluable for me as the outsider and visitor to see him in his natural habitat, so to speak, in order to place him in that environment. It was remarkable to note how unchanged he was from the settings I knew him in to the worksite, where he is completely at home. His ability to relate to anyone and everyone with equanimity and authority and to create a set at once highly professional and tightly run, yet warm, friendly, and loose does not happen by accident. It happens because he is intentional about it. But it is also just a reflection of who he is and how he likes to work, and not surprisingly he draws people around him who follow suit.

I remember how impressed I was by how intense and concentrated he was, on the one hand, and by how relaxed and even playful he was, on the other hand. It was also uncanny how he seemed to be aware of everything happening around him in spite of the focused scrutiny he had to give to each setup and shot. Perhaps the act of directing heightens his acuity to give him a kind of hyper sensitivity to his surroundings.

My intention was to use the material gathered from observations and interviews to feed a truly behind-the-scenes look at the filmmaking process and to give the reader a kind of running insider's view of the way Payne works. Through comments from some of his collaborators I also tried providing additional insights into how *Sideways* came about and how he approached the project from both a macro and micro perspective.

Hollywood dispatch: on the set with Alexander Payne—a rare, intimate, inside look at Payne, his process and the making of his new film, *Sideways*

Published in a 2003 issue of *The Reader*

On assignment

I find myself taking Alexander Payne up on his invitation to view the making of *Sideways*, his first movie made outside Nebraska. My America West early-bird-special from Omaha to Phoenix, Arizona, on this Oct. 27 morning gives me plenty of time to think. From Phoenix I'm to catch a commuter flight to Santa Barbara, California, the nearest city to the *Sideways* shoot and the start of wine country.

In this $17-million project lensed for Fox Searchlight Pictures that began filming September 29 and wrapped December 6, Payne is once again exploring the animus of dislocated characters running away from their problems and seeking cures for their pain.

Coming off *About Schmidt*, the 2002 hit that played more sad than funny for many viewers, but that garnered critical plaudits, a juried Cannes screening, a handful of Oscar nods, and the biggest box-office take yet for any of his films—an estimated $106 million worldwide—one might expect Payne to lighten up a bit.

After all, his films have thus far fixed a withering satiric-ironic eye on human frailties. *Citizen Ruth*, *Election*, and *About Schmidt* heralded him as an original auteur, a considered observer, and a strong voice in the emerging post-modern cinema. One only has to recall: paint-sniffing Ruth Stoops, the unlikely poster girl for the embattled-exploitative abortion camps, in *Citizen Ruth*; student election-rigging teacher Jim McAllister acting out his frustrations against the blind ambition of student Tracy Flick in *Election*; or the existential crisis of Warren Schmidt, an older man undone and yet strangely liberated by his own feelings of failure in *Schmidt*, a funny film that still felt more like a requiem than a comedy.

While *Sideways* will never be confused with a Farrelly Brothers film, it's a departure for Payne in its familiar male-bonding structure, its few but priceless slapstick gags, and its romantic, albeit dysfunctional, couplings. Its surface contours are that of a classic buddy movie, combined with the conventions of a road pic, yet *Sideways* still fits neatly within the Payne oeuvre as another story of misfit searchers.

In *Sideways*, the search revolves around two longtime California friends, the shallow Jack and the intellectual Miles, who ostensibly set off on a fun, weeklong wine-tasting tour in the verdant rolling coastal hills northwest of Santa Barbara. Their trip soon turns into something else, a walkabout, pilgrimage, forced march and purging all in one, as they confront some ugly truths about themselves en route. The buddy pairing is built on a classic opposites-attract formula.

If, as they say, casting is most of a film's success, then Payne's home free. After seriously considering filling the rich parts with mega-stars George Clooney (Jack) and Edward Norton (Miles), he went with "the best actors for the roles" and found perfect fits. Jack, played by Thomas Haden Church (best known for the '90s TV series *Wings*), is the dashing, skirt-chasing extrovert, a former soaps actor reduced to voice-over work. Now in his forties, he's about to be married for the first time, and this inveterate womanizer goes on the wine tour not to enjoy the grape but so he can go on one last fling. As he tells his well-moneyed bride-to-be, "I need my space." Code words for philandering.

Miles, essayed by Paul Giamatti (*American Splendor*), is the smart, neurotic introvert—a failed writer unhappily stuck as a junior high English teacher and still obsessing over the ex-wife he cheated on. Miles concocts the tasting tour as much to indulge his own seemingly perfect passion for wine, which he still manages to corrupt with his excessive drinking, as to treat Jack to some final bachelor debauchery.

When Jack announces his intention to get himself and Miles laid, it's clear that as much as the repressed Miles expresses dismay and outrage at Jack's libidinous behavior, he lives vicariously through his friend. And as much as Jack is irritated by Miles's depression, often on the verge of, as Jack says, "Going to the dark side," and by Miles's warnings that he curb his unbridled sexual appetite, Jack understands his friend's dilemma and appreciates his concern.

Eventually the two hook up with a pair of eager women whose presence upsets the balance in the buddies' relationship and redirects the tour. Jack loses his mind over Stephanie, a hottie party girl of a wine pourer played by Sandra Oh, a darling of indie cinema. Longtime companions, Payne and Oh were married in January. Miles tentatively feels things out with Maya, a nurturing waitress and fellow wine buff portrayed by Virginia Madsen, a veteran of features and television.

In classic road picture fashion, the foursome traverse a string of wineries, diners, motels, and sundry other stops on the highways and byways in and around Santa Barbara, Los Olivos, Solvang, and Buellton. Along the way, relations heat up with the gals before a reckoning—or is it bad karma?—causes things to come crashing down on the guys. Each has his own cathartic rude awakening. A pathetic, repentant Jack goes through with the wedding. A wizened Miles, perhaps finally outgrowing Jack and exorcising his own demons, takes a hopeful detour at the end.

I'm about to take my own detour.

During a brief layover in the Phoenix airport, where faux Southwestern themes dominate inside and tantalizing glimpses of real-life mesas tease me outside, my fellow travelers and I are reminded of the raging California wildfires when flights to Monterey are postponed due to poor visibility. On the hop from Sun City to Santa Barbara, sheets of smoke roll below us and billowing plumes rise from ridges on the far horizon beyond us.

I've arranged for the Super Ride shuttle to take me to Solvang, the historic Danish community I'll be staying in the next six nights. At the wheel of the Lincoln Town Car is James, a former merchant mariner who describes the Marine Layer that drifts in from the Pacific, which, along with moderate temps and transverse valleys, makes the area prime ground for its many vineyards.

We cut over onto U.S. 154 and then into Buellton, home of Anderson's Split Pea Soup, passing an apple orchard and ostrich farm en route to the kitschy, friendly tourist trap of Solvang and its gingerbread architecture. Everything is Danish, except the Latino help. Michael Jackson's Neverland Ranch is not far from here and I'm told the veiled pop star is a familiar sight in town.

After settling into a low-rent motel where most of the crew stays, I unwind with a walk through the commercial district, ending on the outskirts of town, where a mini-park overlooks the Alisal River Course below and oak-tree-studded hillsides beyond. The brushed, velvety blue-green hills resemble a Bouguereau painting of French wine country. All that's missing are the peasant grape-pickers. Wildfire smoke filters a screen of sunlight across the hills, obscuring outlying ridge lines in a ragged gray silhouette.

After a Danish repast in the afternoon and a burger-malt combo at night, I make last-minute preps in my room for tomorrow, my first day on the set.

On the set

It breaks a sun-baked Monday. As I soon learn, mornings start chilly, afternoons heat up, and nights cool down again out here. On what becomes my daily ritual, I take a morning constitutional walk to the overlook.

At 8:30, the publicist assigned to escort me, Erik Bright, arrives. He sports the cool, casual, hip vibe and ambitious aura of a Hollywood PR functionary, a sort of modern equivalent of the hungry press agent Tony Curtis played in *Sweet Smell of Success*. He's eager to please.

We drive directly to the set, the location of which these first two days is the nearby River Course. Once parked, Bright commandeers a golf cart to transport us on set, where a semi-circle of crew and cast is arrayed on a fairway, not unlike painters considering subjects in a park. As we approached at a whisper, a take unfolds. After intoning "Cut" in a businesslike tone, Payne's band of grips, gaffers, assistant directors, and production assistants busily attend to setting up the next take of this scene.

Seeing me out of the corner of his eye, Payne halts what he's doing to come over and greet me. "Welcome," he says, shaking my hand, before excusing himself to resume work. It's the official seal of approval for me, the outsider. He seems totally in his element, directing with calm acuity. The closest he comes to raising his voice is when he politely asks the set to be quieted, explaining, "I've got to focus here."

Nearing middle-age, he certainly looks the part of the legendary artist with his intense gaze, his piercing intelligence, his shock of black hair, now peppered with gray, his lithe body, his grace under fire, and his immersion in every aspect of the process, from fiddling with props to getting on camera. Then there is the relaxed Mediterranean way he has about him, indulging his huge appetites for life and film. He burns with boundless curiosity and energy and embodies a generous *La Dolce Vita* spirit that makes work seem like play. Clearly the journey for him is the joy.

The producers

By the time I meet the film's producer Michael London and co-producer/first AD George Parra, a few takes are in the can. The elegant London, often seen on his cell phone, takes a laissez-faire approach to this project. The strapping Parra, often in radio contact with crew, acts as Payne's right-hand man and gentle enforcer.

"OK, AP, we're ready, sir. Let's go. Rolling." That's Parra talking, overseeing the production's moment-by-moment organization, efficiency, and schedule. Because time is big money in film, his job boils down to "keeping Alexander on track."

"What stands out for me is how much he loves the actual day-to-day process of filmmaking," said *Sideways* producer Michael London (*Forty Days and Forty Nights*), "and how much he loves the camaraderie with people on the set. Filmmaking has become this kind of process to be endured. And it's the opposite with Alexander. He actually loves the details. It's wonderful—his enthusiasm and appreciation and work ethic. He's so happy when he's in his element, and the pleasure he takes out of it is so palpable to everybody. This is kind of what he was born to do."

Amid the disaffected posturings, digital imaginings, and nonlinear narratives employed by so many hip young filmmakers, Payne is something of a throwback. Steeped in film history and classical technique, he eschews neo-genre stylistics for storytelling. Rather than bury a scene in sharp camera moves or extreme angles, special effects, and draw-attention-to-itself editing, he's confident enough in his screenplay and in his direction to often let a scene play out, interrupted by few cutaways or inserts. It's an apt style for someone attuned to capturing the real rhythms and ritualistic minutiae of everyday life.

It's all part of the aesthetic he's developed. "Alexander has an evolving philosophy he's begun to articulate a lot more clearly in the wake of *About Schmidt*, which is that contemporary movies have begun to focus more and more on extraordinary characters and situations," London said, "and that filmmakers have lost touch with their ability to tell stories about real daily life, real people, real issues, real feelings, real moments.

"Where most filmmakers would run screaming from anything that reminds people of everyday life, he loves the fact you can film everyday life and have people take a look at themselves in a different context than what they're accustomed to. And I think it's really important and admirable. It's also a very humble skill.

"Instead of trying to imagine and exaggerate, it's really just observing. It's a more writerly craft and a more European sensibility. I think it's an underrated gift. I don't think people realize how difficult it is to create that kind of verisimilitude on screen. That's why he's always at war with all the conventions of the movie world aimed at glamorizing people."

Lights, camera . . . harvesting

Upon casually saying "Action," Payne watches takes with quiet intensity, afterwards huddling with actors to add a "Let's try it faster" comment here or a "Why don't we try it this way?" suggestion there and listening to any insights they may impart. Reacting with bemused delight to a performance, he says, "That's funny" or flashes a smile at no one in particular. After announcing "Cut," he typically says "Good" or "Excellent" if pleased or "Let's try one more" if not. Takes, which can be spoiled by anything from planes flying overhead and car engines firing in the background to missed cues and flubbed lines to the film running out or a camera motor breaking down, are also opportunities to refine a scene. As the takes mount, Payne remains calm. As he likes saying, "Filming is just all about harvesting shots for editing."

Payne speaks with the actors about a moment when they confront other golfers, going over various physical actions. "Let's see how real that feels," he tells Haden Church, who carries the brunt of the action. "Now, knowing all these options, just follow your instinct. You're a medieval knight. Be big." "Be bold," Haden Church replies, before screaming profanities and brandishing his club as the bellicose Jack.

Several times during the two-day golf shoot, stretching from early morning through late afternoon and encompassing several setups, the PanaVision-Panaflex cameras are reloaded after their film magazines run out, often spoiling takes. A film magazine has one thousand feet or ten to eleven minutes of film. At one point Payne asks for "Camera reports?" and when none are forthcoming calls for "a little tighter" shot. The camera dollies are moved closer. Payne later tells me the shoot was "slightly more unbridled" than normal for him, meaning he shot more coverage than usual.

By afternoon, the sun and heat grow fierce. With little or no natural shade, people seek protection in golf carts or under various flags and screens used to bounce light off actors. Sunscreen is liberally applied, and bottled water greedily consumed. Heat-related or not, a camera's motor gives out, rendering it inoperable. A replacement is ordered.

Payne, who enjoys a sardonic give-and-take with director of photography Phedon Papamichael, says, "I brought you this far, now make it brilliant." The DP responds, "I want my second camera back."

When the situation calls for it, Payne maintains a professional, disciplined demeanor. Setting up a shot, he gives precise directions while inviting input from collaborators, especially Papamichael (*Identity*), a native of Greece with whom he enjoys a lively working relationship. Papamichael says they take turns getting on camera to view setups, each prodding the other with ideas and inevitably admitting, "We pretty much end up where we started."

Before the cast arrives on set, Payne often acts out the physical action himself for the benefit of Papamichael and crew. He checks cheat sheets, including his "sides," a printed copy of the script pages being shot each day, and his "shot list," a personal breakdown of what he's after in terms of camera, lighting, movement, motivation, and mood.

Before filming, he often has actors run through scenes in rehearsals. Sometimes, surreptitiously, he has ADs and PAs shush the throng of crew and extras while signaling the cameras to roll, hoping to pick up more natural, unaffected performances that way.

Payne acknowledges Papamichael's influence on his visual sense: "I'm working with a DP who calls for that [lush] stuff more easily than my previous crew did. Sometimes, early on, I would say to him, 'It's too pretty,' and he'd go, 'No, it's just another side of yourself you're afraid of.' So, what the hell, it's another side of myself and I'm just going with it."

Papamichael also pushed Payne, albeit less successfully, to steer away from his favored high camera angles to more eye-level shots. "He was accusing me the first couple weeks of always wanting to go high, as though I'm God or something, to look down on characters," Payne said. "I don't know, sometimes I get bored looking at people straight-on, so I go higher or lower. It just makes the angle more interesting to me, unless I'm missing something unconscious in myself about some hideous superiority complex."

Papamichael, a favorite cinematographer of Wim Wenders, is working with Payne for the first time though they've known each other for years. The cinematographer said it takes a while for a director and DP to mesh but that "every picture finds its own language pretty quickly. You can sort of talk about it in theory, but then very often it happens. The picture will sort of tell you what needs to be done. This show has not had the extent of coverage and camera movement we usually have on shows because we're playing a lot of things in close and letting the actors operate within that frame. It sort of seems to be playing better with simpler shots."

During a lull, I learn from London and Payne that the owner of a location slated for use in the film is refusing to honor a signed agreement, thereby trying to hold up the production for more money. London slips off to deal with the problem.

Lunch break finds cast and crew descending on base camp a few blocks away. Here, the caravan of *Sideways* trailers and trucks is parked, along with a mobile catering service doling out huge varieties of freshly prepared food. An American Legion Post hall serves as the cafeteria, with people sitting and eating at rows of long tables.

After eating very little, Payne said, "Now, if you'll excuse me, I'm going to take my nap," a daily ritual he's followed since *Election*.

Tuesday is a reprise of Monday's heat, schedule, and location.

Payneful reality

That night, I interview Payne over dinner at the Los Olivos Cafe, an intimate spot reeking of laid-back California chic and, de rigueur for this region, an extensive wine list. It's where the film shoots the next three days. As usual, his careful attention to my questions and to his answers is surprising given all that's on his mind. Like any good director he has the gift for focusing on whomever he's with and whatever he's doing at any given time.

Nothing's too simple or small to escape Payne's attention, "Well, all I can say is details are everything. I don't really conceive of broad strokes. If you're kind of operating from a type of filmmaking that sees art as a mirror of life and film as the most capable and verisimilar mirror, than you've got to pay a lot of attention to details, and I kick myself when I miss them." For him, it's a philosophy that informs, at the most basic level, the very nature of his work.

"You want things to ring true to the audience, and you want to inspire in the audience what literature does and what poetry sometimes does, which is the shock of recognition—having something pointed out to you which you've lived or intuited or thought on an unconscious level and suddenly the writer brings it to your consciousness. I just love that: the recognition of until this moment, of an articulated truth. I'm not saying my films are doing that on a very profound level, but at least in the minutiae I want those things right. Again, it's all about the details, and a lot of times story operates within those details. I don't know if it's just story, because I'm acting instinctively, but it's probably all these things—story, character, and then the texture of the reality you're recreating, presenting."

In pursuit of the real, Payne vigorously resists, or as London puts it, "crusades" against the glam apparatus of the Hollywood Dream Factory.

"You have to fight a couple things. One, is the almost ideology—it's that deeply entrenched—in American filmmaking that things have to be made beautiful ... more beautiful than they appear in real life in order to be worthy to be photographed, and I just oppose that," Payne said. "And you have to really oppose it intensively because there are people around you, hired with the best of intentions ... who are trained to brush lint off clothes, straighten hair, erase face blemishes, and I just think, Why? And then you have to fight against Kodak film stock—we're mostly shooting Fuji on this one—and against lenses that make things look too pretty.

"Now, having said that, this film is going to be a lot more beautiful than my previous films have been because of the locales. It's pretty. And it's a bit more of a romantic film, at least it's kind of turning out that way."

Dailies from the first few weeks of shooting confirm a warm golden hue in interior and exterior colors, which may come as a relief to critics who've decried the heretofore dull, flat, washed-out look of his work.

Not to be confused with dramedies, a hybrid form languishing in limbo between lame comedy and pale drama, Payne films resemble more the sublime bittersweet elegies of, say, James L. Brooks and the late Billy Wilder. Like these artists, he does not so much distinguish between comedy and drama as embrace these ingredients as part of the same flavorful stew, the savory blending with sweet and the spicy mixing with the pungent, each accenting the other. With the possible exception of *Schmidt*, which as London said—in paraphrasing Payne—"defaulted to drama," Payne films use comedy and drama as intrinsic, complementary lenses on human nature.

"I don't separate them. It's all just what it is," Payne said. "I tend to make comedies based in painful human situations that are filled with ferocious emotions. I find ferocious emotions exciting. The actor and director have to trust the writer that the absurdity or the comedy is there in the writing. You all know it's there, but you don't play it.

"Sometimes, I think, in my films I've so not wanted to play the comedy of it that it gets too subtle, where then people don't get that it's funny. I mean, some do, like my friends. Like I think people took *About Schmidt* much too seriously sometimes, and I don't know if it's because they're Americans and Americans are literal and non-ironic, or what. I'm also afraid of being too broad . . . of having caricatures. Not so much on this film, but on previous films."

It should come as no surprise then that Payne and writing partner

Jim Taylor, with whom he adapted the *Sideways* screenplay from the unpublished Rex Pickett novel of the same name, draw on characters' angst as the wellspring for their humor since tragedy is just the other side of comedy, and vice versa.

Payne's finally leaving Nebraska to film was inevitable. Tempted as he is to go elsewhere, including his ancestral homeland of Greece, he said, "I don't think I would have been prepared to shoot in California or anywhere had I not first shot in Nebraska." Despite proclamations he would not film here again for a while, he may return as soon as next fall to direct a screenplay set in north-central Nebraska. It, too, is about a journey. It chronicles an old man under the delusion he is a winner in an Ed McMahon-like sweepstakes. Enlisting his reluctant son as his driver, the man sets off on a quest from his home in Billings, Montana, to claim his "winnings" at the home office in Lincoln, Nebraska.

Along the way, the two get sidetracked—first, in Rapid City, South Dakota, and then in rural Nebraska, where the codger revisits the haunts and retraces the paths of his youth, meeting up with a Jarmusch-esque [in the style of director Jim Jarmusch] band of eccentric Midwesterners. Payne plans shooting in black-and-white Cinemascope.

"I'm happy to come back to Nebraska," he said, adding, "You know, I feel like Michael Corleone—every time you try to get out, they just pull you right back in." Payne's clearly here to stay, just as his connection to Nebraska, where he may direct an opera, remains indelible.

After dinner he gives me a ride back to my motel in his new white convertible sports car, handling the curves with aplomb.

The macro and the micro

There's an ebb and flow to a working movie crew. Everybody has a job to do, from the Teamsters grips and gaffers to the ADs and PAs to the personal assistants to the heads of wardrobe, makeup, et cetera. As a setup is prepared, a flurry of activity unfolds on top of each other, each department's crew attending to its duties at the same time, including dressing the set, rigging lights, changing lenses, loading film, laying track, moving the dolly.

Amid all this movement and noise, Payne goes about conferring with actors or discussing the shot with his DP or else squirrels himself away to focus on his shot list. A palpable energy builds until the time shooting commences, when nonessential personnel pull back to the sidelines and calls for "Quiet" enforce a collective hush and rigid stillness over the proceedings. As the take plays out, an anticipatory buzz charges the air and when "Cut" is heard, the taut cast and crew are released in a paroxysm of relaxation.

Chalk it up to his Greek heritage or to some innate humanism, but Payne creates a warm, communal atmosphere around him that, combined with his magnetic, magnanimous *je ne sais quoi* quotient, engenders fierce devotion from staff. Evan Endicott, a personal assistant and aspiring director, said, "I really don't want to work for anyone else." Tracy Boyd, a factotum with feature aspirations, noted, "Alexander always pays attention to the process of the whole family of collaborators that go into making the film. His sets reflect a whole lifestyle."

My challenge proves staying out of the way while still watching everything going on. The first couple of days, I sense the crew views me as a curiosity to be tolerated. I feel like an interloper. By the end of my stay I feel I blend in as another crewmate, albeit a green one. I become one with the set. Payne periodically comes up to me, asking, "What do you find interesting?" or "Are you getting what you need?"

I tell him it's all instructive—the waiting, the setups, the camera moves, the takes—fun, fascinating, exhausting, exhilarating all in one.Wednesday morning Erik drives us, via the Santa Rosa Road, to the Sanford Winery, a rustic spot nestled among melon fields and wildflower meadows on one side and gentle hills on the other. The landscape has a muted beauty. The small tasting room, with its Old Westy outpost look, and its charismatic pourer, Chris Burroughs, with his shoulder-length hair, Stetson hat, and American Indian jewelry, appear in a scene where Miles tries educating Jack about wine etiquette, only to have his buddy commit the unpardonable sin of "tasting" wines while chewing gum.

Sanford is famous for its Pinot Noir, the variety Miles is most passionate about. It was here and at other wineries Payne visited in prepping the film that he, like Pickett before him, discovered California's wine culture. On our visit, it isn't long before spirited discussions ensue between Chris and customers on the mystique of wine characteristics, vintages, blends, trends, and tastes.

Rejoining the production, I'm deposited in the town of Los Olivos for three days and nights of shooting in and around the Los Olivos Cafe. Space is tight inside the eatery, with crew, cameras, lighting, and sound mixer Jose Antonio Garcia's audio cart crammed around the fixtures. For this sequence, which finds "the boys" meeting two women for a let's-get-to-know-you dinner and drinks icebreaker, Payne breaks up the shooting into segments—from Jack forcing Miles to screw up his courage to their entrance to joining the girls at the table to the foursome exchanging small talk. Payne later pulls the camera in tight to pick up a series of reaction shots and inserts for his "mosaic" of a montage that will chart the progression of the evening and of Miles's panic.

As this is played without sound, Payne directs the actors as they improvise before the camera, tweaking things along the way. Much attention is paid to the moments when the drunk Miles shambles off to the restroom and, slipping over "to the dark side," detours to a pay phone to make an ill-advised call to his ex-wife, before arriving back shit-faced.

Like any experience bringing people together in a close, intense way, a film set is replete with affairs and alliances emerging from the shared toil and passion. Cliques form. Asides whispered. Inside jokes exchanged. Payne and his new bride, Oh, one of *Sideways*'s two female leads, manage being discreetly frisky. While he shows remarkable equanimity in interacting with everybody, he keeps around him a small stable of trusted aides in whom he confides.

Parra is one. For the soft-spoken Parra, who's worked with Payne on all his feature projects, *Sideways* is a golden opportunity toward his ultimate ambition of producing. The two have an easy rapport. Parra said of Payne, "He's kind of calm, no-nonsense. He really knows what he's doing. He's real clear. He thinks things through and figures it out, and I love that, and that's the way I am, so it works really well. It's great to facilitate his needs as a director."

Script supervisor Rebecca Robertson-Szwaja, a Payne regular since *Election*, said, "I think on the one hand there's a lot of fun on his shows, yet people are very focused. So there's that dual edge of relaxed and playful but absolutely serious. You definitely want to make sure you do your work well because you respect him."

Set dresser Cynthia Rebman, working with him for the first time, added, "In feature films the director really does set the tone. . . . All the way from Alexander and Michael London to line producer and first AD George Parra, this is an exceptionally well-adjusted, highly professional crew. Several of the people have worked with Alexander on several projects, which doesn't surprise me because he instills a certain sense of loyalty just in the way he conducts himself and in the way he treats people.

"He's paying attention to every detail in every department and quite often directors don't bother . . . even all the way down to introducing himself to the background extras and discussing with them what the scene is about. It's a genuine pleasure, because then you feel like you're contributing and your contribution is appreciated."

Sardonic Tracy Boyd, called "factotum" for his wide-ranging roles, admires how Payne's process is inclusive of the entire "family of collaborators." Earnest young personal assistant Evan Endicott is, like Boyd, an aspiring feature director. He tells me one night at dinner why he doesn't want to work with anyone else besides Payne: "He takes risks. He's willing to show humanity in a way that few comedy directors do, especially these days. There isn't a lot of artifice in his work. It's very hard to be that honest about human beings. Then there's the control he takes and the attention to detail he gives, whether it's what sneakers a character is wearing to the location he's gone and scouted himself to the lines coming out of the actors' mouths to each camera shot. That takes a lot of commitment and it's not that common anymore. I came out here to be a writer and he has inspired me now to be a director," Endicott said with a gleam in his bright eyes.

Building shots and observing takes, Payne's focus is seemingly everywhere at once. One day, he adjusts bits of business the actors do in a golf sequence and, later, he runs flat-out down a fairway to tweak the placement of a golf cart or the action of an extra. Another day, he obsesses over stemware and wine in a cafe dining scene, making sure the right number of glasses are placed in frame, the correct red or white is poured, and the right amount is consumed. Often times, he rearranges extras in the background, even feeding them back stories on the spot, or quickens the pace of line readings. Always he envisions how each moment will meld and cut together with those already filmed and others yet to be shot. Casting his eye wide and narrow at the same time defines directing.

"Yes, always the macro and the micro," he said between setups at the Los Olivos Cafe in the prosaic town of Los Olivos, whose actual names, along with every place appearing in *Sideways*, are used in the film. "You're always holding two things in mind and on a few different planes. It's like in painting. You're here looking at the stroke and it's not just later but simultaneously that you're looking at its placement in the entire canvas. Even on the technical side, knowing what the sound is doing, what the film stock is doing, but also emotionally . . . storywise, what's going on at once in the many vivisected ways that a director has to think about, and also being surrounded by tons of people yet also remaining alone and watching the movie. Because my only job is to

SEE the movie. I'm the only one who this entire time is sitting in the theater watching the movie or possible versions of it."

Unusual for him, he also encourages the *Sideways* cast to improvise, particularly in a long cafe sequence shot in "little pieces" for "a mosaic" he and editor Kevin Tent will fashion a montage from in post-production this winter. "I like very controlled shots and really micromanaging performance and camera movement, but it's also nice to be free and let go and have kind of a documentary approach, too," he explained.

The conductor

My last hours with *Sideways* are spent watching a Halloween night shoot outside the cafe. A few trick-or-treaters sneak on set. Earlier I said my goodbyes, informing Payne I'll miss the costume bash he's throwing Saturday. Like the first two nights here, they won't wrap until well past midnight.

This is magic time, when everything glows under the glare of movie lights arrayed on rooftops, in a crane's nest, and in the street. The track's laid. The street barricaded. A phalanx of jacketed crew and extras await cues. Once "Action" sounds, the scene is set in motion. Papamichael, poised over camera, his eye on the viewfinder, is gracefully pushed on the dolly by Tony, the muscular dolly grip, while Don, the focus puller, operates a knob on the side of the camera to keep the image in focus. As the actors make their way from the Saab to the cafe, the whole works moves with them, with Payne, the ever-present Parra, Boyd, boom man and script supervisor, scrutinizing the action.

"I always think that when it's the middle of the night and everyone's exhausted, that's when filmmaking is distilled down to its essence," Boyd said. "All the periphery is removed away, and you're really just going for it. It's really quite elegant in a way, even though it's miserable to get there."

If there's a lasting image I take away, it's Payne, the conductor, orchestrating things with a discipline that invites serendipity.

"Sometimes, I think perfect is the enemy of good," he tells me, invoking a famous saying that encapsulates the story and his approach to it: In going straight ahead, he's still prepared to go sideways.

A road trip sideways: Alexander Payne's circuitous journey to a new film

Published in a 2004 issue of *The Reader*

Sandra Oh, Thomas Haden Church, Virginia Madsen, Paul Giamatti

The project

Charting the circuitous development of Alexander Payne's new movie *Sideways*, opening in a limited national release October 20, offers an inside look at how feature film projects come together. During an afternoon golf shoot on location at the Alisal River Course in Solvang, California, near Santa Barbara, the film's shrewd, glib producer, Michael London, detailed how this romantic comedy of a buddy/road picture went from high concept to stalled project to hot property in the span of its four-year evolutionary process.

The inspiration for the film came from that most prosaic of sources, a book, only this time it was a 1998 unpublished novel by Rex Pickett, who drew closely from his own life in telling the sad and comic story of two loser buddies on a wine tour. Adapted into script form by Payne and writing partner Jim Taylor, the pic follows best buds Jack and Miles on a road trip that finds their addictions, obsessions, and neuroses with wine and women catching up with them, turning an idyll into a comedy of errors. It's a classic men-behaving-badly tale. In Jack, the lame-brained serial seducer who never grows up, and in Miles, the anxious intellectual alcoholic who can't take a stand, the two sides of the modern American male are on display.

With a director in as complete command of his craft as Payne (*Citizen Ruth*, *Election*, *About Schmidt*), who also has final cut, producer London (*Thirteen* and *House of Sand and Fog*) is left with little else to do but sign-off on expenditures, smooth-over ruffled feathers, cast a keen eye on dailies, and keep the train that is a film production on track, meaning, on-schedule and on-budget. Payne found London a good fit. "In terms of working with me and the actors and then working in an effective way with the studio, he just speaks everyone's language."

Very unique to Alexander

While *Sideways* marked the first time London and Payne worked together, when London optioned the Rex Pickett novel of the same name in about 1999, Payne was near the top of his list to adapt the book for the big screen.

"I was really just a fan of Alexander's before this. I really didn't have any particular history or connection with him other than meeting him very briefly at the Sundance Film Festival the year Citizen Ruth played there," London said. "I'd read an early draft of my friend Rex Pickett's novel and we'd started talking about it as a movie. At one point, Rex was thinking of adapting it himself and at one point we were going to adapt it together ... I had really liked the book and had started talking to a couple of filmmakers about it. Alexander recently asked me, 'Who passed on it for me to get this?' I don't think anyone passed. I think it's a very particular type of material, and I think the instinct he was right for it was probably a good instinct.

"It's not like there's fifty directors in the world who could have done this story, and I think that's probably true of most of the things Alexander does. They're very unique to Alexander. At the time I started pursuing him I don't think I'd seen *Election*. I was quite obsessed that he would relate to these characters (Jack and Miles) and to the whole idea of this kind of wasted wine trip and of men in mid-life crisis. It just felt like he would do something really special with that. I chased him through his agent and all the ordinary avenues, but without much luck."

In that variegated, Byzantine way in which Hollywood deals get made, London said during the period he was trying to contact Payne in order to court him, the book somehow ended up in the filmmaker's hands via another source. "But it wound up sitting in his hands for about nine months because he was finishing *Election*, and then he was touring and doing press." Payne was in Scotland of all places when he finally called London to put his dibs on the project.

"He wound up going to Scotland for a film festival," London said. "I walked in my door one Friday night and there was a phone message saying, 'This is Alexander Payne. . . . . I just got off a plane in Scotland and I want to do this movie *Sideways* next.'" London said Payne felt so strongly about the material that he became boldly proprietary about it, making his directing it a *fait accompli*. "From our first conversation he was like, 'I have to direct this. No one else can direct this.'"

A long, tortured path

Securing the writer-director he wanted for *Sideways* was one thing, but getting the project off the ground was quite another.

"That began a kind of very long, tortured path," London said, "because as it turned out it was not going to be his (Payne's) next movie. He did *Election* and then Jack Nicholson committed, sort of unexpectedly, to *About Schmidt*, and that movie came together much more urgently than he imagined, and then he went off and made *About Schmidt*."

Three years passed from the time London and Payne first agreed on making *Sideways* together to the film finally being launched. The wait was made longer by delays postponing the start of *Schmidt*. "Every time the schedule got pushed back he would call me in sort of an embarrassed voice, because Alexander really doesn't like disappointing people, and he would very courteously ask if he could have a little more time to finish what he was doing. And, obviously, there was no real conversation about taking it (*Sideways*) to anyone else at that point because his passion for it was so great and his connection with it was so complete."

Then there was the initial campaign to sell the project, an experience which provided a lesson in how quickly things change in the industry. Soon after committing to making *Sideways*, London said, "We went out and took it to a whole bunch of companies. It was right after *Election* opened and everybody wanted it. It was kind of like an auction thing. We set up a deal with a fantastic amount of money for everybody at a company called Artisan, which had then released a movie called *The Blair Witch Project* (the indie project that became a phenomenon). They were the most sought-after independent company in the business."

Slow fade to black. Fade in on a low-slung Hollywood bungalow. Cut to interior view of an office, where huddled men speak anxiously in conference.

"Now, by the time Alexander had gone off to do *Schmidt* and come back," London said, "Artisan was on the verge of going bankrupt and the company we had sold the rights to, which made so much sense before, no longer had the marketing clout to take care of the movie properly." What could have been a sticky situation was resolved when London reminded Artisan, which still wanted in on the deal, that neither party was legally obligated to make the movie with the other.

"We had been quite careful not to sign contracts with them," London said, "because when it looked like Alexander might go away and make another movie first, just in the back of our minds we thought, Well, we don't really know what Artisan is going to be like in a couple years. We were cautious, and properly so, and that gave us freedom so that when Alexander resurfaced and Artisan didn't feel like the right home anymore, we were able to work out a departure from them."

The frustration of putting off *Sideways*, London said, was offset by the relationship he forged with the filmmaker over that time. "During those three years I came to know him very well," the producer said. "Our friendship kind of grew up during those years, which was actually very nice because it meant that instead of being out here (on location) shooting with someone I've just gotten to know recently, we feel like we've been through a couple wars together."

In the interim, London "went off and did a couple other movies," and Payne made perhaps his most mature film up to that time in *Schmidt*, a jury selection at the Cannes Film Festival, one of the best reviewed films of 2002, and the filmmaker's biggest money maker (more than $100 million worldwide). "It all worked out very well because by the time he was ready to do it, it was a good time for him and a good time for me."

Despite the delays, there was never a question *Sideways* would get made. "Michael and Rex were hoping *About Schmidt* would not have come first. But I just kept promising that I'm going to do this (*Sideways*) next, and I kept putting my hand in my pocket every year to renew the option on the book and then I kept to my word," said Payne. "As soon as *Schmidt* was finished, I began work on this one. I think it all worked out great. Because of my experience on *Schmidt* I think *Sideways* is a better film than it would have been otherwise. Rex says jokingly, but he means it too, that I needed to make a film about maturity before I could go back and make a film about immaturity. It all seems right."

Packaging Sideways

With Artisan out of the picture, London and Payne hit on a new strategy for packaging *Sideways*—using Payne's hot status as leverage to sell a ready-made project that retained full creative autonomy for its makers. "Really, at that point, instead of selling it we decided the smarter way to make the movie was to have Alexander and Jim (Payne's screenwriting partner, Jim Taylor) write it on spec and for us to figure out what we thought the right budget and cast for the movie was, instead of allowing the studio to own it and dictate those things," London said.

"Alexander was in a unique position of creative power because he's riding high right now. The material's commercial. Financiers knew if they invested in a movie about two guys on a comic journey through the wine country they were probably going to be able to sell it. It's not like it's a little, precious arty movie. It's a buddy picture. It's a classic buddy picture."

The producer and director put the pieces of the package together and formed a group to get financing in place. They used a bold, ballsy, take-it-or-leave-it, we're-calling-the-shots approach, and it worked. "We rolled the dice. Alexander and Jim wrote it on spec. We found the cast we wanted. We did our own budget. And then when we were about eight weeks before we needed to start shooting—we waited absolutely until the last possible minute—we said, OK, who wants to make this movie?

"We took it to the half dozen or so studios and said, 'Here's the movie . . . this is the script, this is the cast, this is the budget . . . We hope you love it. If you don't love it, you shouldn't make it. Alexander has final cut. We're not really looking for your input. We'll listen to your input. Don't tell us the script is too long, because we know it's too long. Don't tell us you think this casting is not starry enough, because Alexander's met with a bunch of movie stars and he's decided these are the best actors for the roles.' And we did that and very quickly weeded out who was really serious from who wasn't," London said.

For its casting, which by all accounts is as crucial to a film's success as the script, Payne applied his acute eye to the task, especially for the juicy parts of Miles and Jack, which he filled, as is his custom, with character actors. For Miles, he chose Paul Giamatti (*American Splendor,*

Confidence) and for Jack, he chose Thomas Haden Church (*George of the Jungle II, 3,000 Miles to Graceland,* TV's *Wings*). For the main two women roles he went with Virginia Madsen (*The Haunting, The Rainmaker*) as Maya and Sandra Oh (*Under the Tuscan Sun,* HBO's *Arli$$*) as Stephanie. Longtime companions, Payne and Oh married in January 2003.

Usually not inclined to go with stars, Payne considered several, including a pair of male leads that would have raised the ante and the buzz. "I was open to it," Payne said. "The star version of this film would have been George Clooney as Jack (the hedonistic actor) and Edward Norton as Miles (the neurotic writer). And I like them both very much. I think they're both terrific and they both expressed interest in these parts. And I was tempted. Actually, not with Clooney, and I told him to his face. I said, 'I think you're great but to ask the audience that the world's handsomest, most famous movie star is the biggest loser actor is too much. If you were a loser in some other profession, maybe OK, like in the Coen Brothers movies, but as a loser actor? That becomes a joke of the film, and I don't think that's right. He was fine with that. Norton, I thought more long and hard about."

That he went with lower profile actors again doesn't mean he was going through the motions to placate producers or executives. "Look, my life would have been easier and certainly the marketing guys would have an easier time if I had picked stars," Payne said. "I met everyone. I met famous, not famous. Bring 'em on. No prejudice. But, ultimately, I just wanted to really be able to cast the actors that best fit the parts." He said producer London signed off on his choices with some trepidation. "He would have, at one time, preferred I selected more famous actors. But now he understands why everything happened the way it did. He just couldn't be happier. He's only about the quality of the film and not about making it more commercial, although I know he likes me to make commercial choices."

Payne respects London. "If we look to directors to influence our cinema and make less false and fraudulent films and more affective ones about people, you need other people doing that, too—studio heads, producers, financiers. I think he'll ultimately be known as a producer who helped change our cinema."

Even sans stars, *Sideways* grew as a project from the time London–Payne partnered on it to when they finally inked a deal for it with Fox Searchlight Pictures. "The movie had gotten bigger. When we were talking to Artisan we were going to make it for seven to ten million dollars. On a shoestring. *After Schmidt*, Alexander now had the power that we could actually get a healthy budget and do it on a larger scale," London said, "without compromising. It was budgeted at 16--17 million dollars for a fifty-day shoot, which by the standards of contemporary studio movies is a tiny, tiny movie, but by the standards of a movie about a couple guys running around in wine country, is plenty of money to do it well and plenty of time to do it well."

More money means more of "everything" on a movie, London said. "It's having more time, more crew, more resources." And having things like big trailers for the stars, producers, and director. Regardless of the trappings, it's still a small, personal film driven more by the passion of its makers than by the perks, extras, paychecks, points and back-end deals negotiated into their contracts.

Stand the test of time

When all is said and done, the *Sideways* creative-producing team envision this as a potential modest hit in the near term and as a stand-the-test-of-time project in the long term. One of those movies that has legs well after its initial release. "We would like the financiers to make back their money, and we would like it to be a beloved movie that lasts a really long time," London said. "We would trade an awful lot of short-term success for this to be a movie that thirty years from now people say about, God, do you remember that movie about those two guys...?"

Already netting strong reviews from its Toronto International Film Festival premiere last month, *Sideways* is more a love story than Payne or London ever imagined. The romance was evident on the shoot and in dailies and became even more obvious during post-production. Editing is the insular phase of the filmmaking process when Payne and his longtime editor, Kevin Tent, collaborate to find the nuances, rhythms, grammar, and subtext they hope make the film warmly referenced and regarded for years to come.

As much as Payne enjoys the process of shooting a movie, there are the inevitable hassles and unavoidable grind that come with working on location over many weeks. Invention proceeds in workmanlike fashion as Payne goes about the business of capturing and bringing to life on film the narrative described on the script pages. Take after take is recorded. Before what we call a movie is ready for screening, the whole post-production phase unfolds. The shooting phase is all about getting to that point. As he's fond of saying, "Shooting is just harvesting shots to edit."

As good as he is at handling the social-political-communal aspects of filmmaking that come with setting up the deal and shooting the project, Payne enjoys losing himself in the editing suite. There, alone with his precious images and away from the distractions of the set, he can finally see, all at once, what he's got before him and then proceed to shape the movie into the form it tells him to take.

It's where the filmmaking process comes full-circle and is ultimately completed and where the road for *Sideways*'s commercial run finally headed down the home stretch. It should be quite a ride.

4

Taking Stock

❧

Introduction

It is useful for me to think of Alexander Payne's career in terms of before *Sideways* and after *Sideways*. I do not mean to make too much of that project as a demarcation point, but it did represent a new chapter in his filmmaking in a number of ways.

Sideways was the first feature he made outside of Nebraska. As the previous stories noted it saw him indulge a side of himself that the film's cinematographer, Phedon Papamichael, felt Payne had been reluctant to express before, namely an appreciation for beautiful landscapes in his work. The DP, who went on to shoot *The Descendants* and *Nebraska*, also prevailed on the filmmaker to frame shots at eye level rather than from above.

Tonally and thematically, *Sideways* was the first time in features that Payne dealt with love in any substantive way. He was, after all, in the throes of a serious romantic relationship when he wrote it and shot it. And he freely admitted that the finished film became as much a love story as a buddy story, or more so than what he initially imagined or what the Rex Pickett novel he adapted portrayed. He just kind of went with it. The theme of love is one he returned to again with his next feature, *The Descendants*.

Yes, dysfunction, conflict, and betrayal attend his cinematic forays into love, but that is the métier in which he grounds all his reality-based films and storylines. His is the cinema of truth and humanism, and just as the truth often hurts, so is the human condition fixed in pain alongside joy.

More than anything, though, the runaway success of *Sideways* made things blow up for Payne in a career sense. Then, just as he was poised to strike again with another feature while the iron was still hot, life intervened and he turned his attention to a series of new writing and producing projects, plus directing two short subjects. Before he and the rest of us knew it, seven years passed before his next feature hit the screen. To casual film fans and critics it appeared as if he had disappeared or taken some kind of ill-advised sabbatical, when in fact he was working the entire time. It is just that none of his work resulted in an Alexander Payne feature film.

The following four pieces were completed during this somewhat awkward period that found Payne having arrived at a new, not altogether comfortable place in his life and career. As these stories recount he was left reeling a bit by everything that came at him in the wake of *Sideways*, and the usually deliberate artist became even more deliberate before taking any new leap. He spoke candidly to me about various aspects of his working life. Though he kept very busy and did some satisfying work in this somewhat limbo or transitional time, he made it abundantly clear that what he most wanted to do was to direct —and by direct, he meant a feature film.

Even though his not directing a feature for several years was in no way a calculation on his part to increase anticipation about his next project, that is in fact exactly the effect it had. When *The Descendants* was formally announced in early 2010, with George Clooney in the lead no less, the buzz surrounding the project made it one of the most anticipated films of 2011. Its excellent box-office performance (about $178 million worldwide as of this printing) justified the mojo attending it, including mostly glowing reviews and oodles of award nominations and wins.

Viewed in another light, however, this kind of small, personal film is precisely the type that increasingly gets lost in the flood of big-budget, heavily marketed franchise films that are more and more dominating the commercial feature world. Only once in a while does an art film break through all the noise to find a large audience, and when it does there is no predictable formula for why it happens for one picture and not another. Ultimately, Payne is more interested in creating stand-the-test-of-time pictures that continue finding audiences over the generations than making movies that cause a splash but that do not endure.

He will also take his own sweet time to get a script exactly as he wants it before shooting. If that means an extra six months or a year, then the project will just have to wait. Every word is there for a reason. It's why when the cameras roll the actors almost always say the dialogue verbatim, as written, because he's gotten it to the point where it can't be improved. Everything is vetted for accuracy too. He has a journalist's instincts (he once seriously considered studying journalism and making it his career) for getting things right. The same attention to detail applies to his casting and location scouting and, frankly, to every aspect of his films.

With his last four pictures, *About Schmidt*, *Sideways*, *The Descendants*, and *Nebraska*, he has achieved unqualified success with both critics and audiences. In an industry that is one part art and one part business, this balance is what every serious filmmaker with a desire to continue working strives for but few realize. Even fewer realize it from film to film to film as Payne has.

Therefore, he has entered that most rarefied company of directors to have had an unbroken string of art house and box-office successes. The string is bound to end or to be broken sometime. Then again, who is to say it will not continue? If anything, this uninterrupted streak of excellence is a testament to just how carefully he selects his material, goes about casting it, and then meticulously executes it on set and in the editing room.

Alexander Payne's post-*Sideways* blues

Published in a 2004 issue of *The Reader*

What sets Sideways apart

Even before Alexander Payne's *Sideways* premiered September 13 to ecstatic reviews at the Toronto International Film Festival, where he soaked up the accolades, it was hailed as a refreshing change from an artist whose previous harsh satires (*Citizen Ruth*, *Election*, *About Schmidt*) made you squirm as much as laugh.

Sideways, whose national release launched on October 27, marks a departure for Payne in two ways. For the first time in his feature career, he's left behind Nebraska's familiar confines to cast his sardonic gaze elsewhere. Using as a starting point Rex Pickett's unpublished novel of the same name, Payne and writing partner Jim Taylor found the book's central California wine country the perfect setting and context for a story about love. Yes, love. Love of wine. Love of self. Platonic love. Brotherly love. Romantic love. Ah, love. It's something in short supply in Payne's earlier films, where emotions are savaged and relationships discarded.

After Toronto came the New York Film Festival, where *Sideways* was the official closing night selection on October 17. Payne said he was "very happy" with the prestigious NYFF closing night slot. A darling of the NYFF, where *About Schmidt* was accorded opening night honors in 2002, Payne is being feted like the star he is in the international film community. In a statement announcing the program, festival chairman and Film Society of Lincoln Center program director Richard Pena said: "Even with now just four films to his credit, Alexander Payne has established himself as a major voice in contemporary American cinema. I can't think of another filmmaker working today who is able to create characters as complex, as contradictory and as richly human."

The early warm reception for *Sideways* bodes well for its commercial potential. The Hollywood buzz says Oscar nods are in store for Payne and star Paul Giamatti. Payne feels what audiences and critics are responding to is a product of an evolving process he's taking with his work. Having returned from the highs of Toronto and New York, he is now preparing to write a new project that promises to be "current and political."

Humanism and character-driven

Leading film industry trade reviewers Todd McCarthy of *Variety* and Kirk Honeycutt of the *Hollywood Reporter* see in *Sideways*, a Fox Searchlight release, something Payne's long been striving for—a return to the character-driven movies he cut his teeth on.

McCarthy wrote, "Moving away from his native Nebraska for the first time onto what proves to be even more fertile soil ... Alexander Payne has single-handedly restored humanism as a force in American films." According to Honeycutt, Payne captures in his "hysterically funny yet melancholy comedy ... subtle undertones of the great character movies of the 1970s and a delicate though strong finish that fills one with hope for its most forlorn characters."

"If it's true, that's a nice thing for someone to say," said Payne, whose intimate cinema explores the wreckage of ordinary people doing desperate things to reclaim their lost lives. His films are never just funny or dramatic. They are, like life, a mix.

"I aspire to a certain humanism in my films in that they're films just about people," he said. "I don't need to see a gun. I don't need to have a chase. I don't need highly contrived situations. I just want to have situations which will bare open, in a humorous way but also in a dramatic way, what's going on in the hearts and souls of people. And they're comedies. This one gets huge laughs. I think, too, people like the emotion in it and the hopeful note at the end. Yet, there's nothing sentimentalized. It feels earned and felt.

"Also, what I hear is that the film is intelligent. Like hopefully my other films, too, it doesn't talk down to the viewer. It respects the viewer. I mean, I always think an audience is smarter than I am, not dumber. So often, at least in recent American filmmaking, there's a pressure—however spoken or unspoken—to dilute the intelligence or the sophisticated references or the quality of the jokes or something for a more general audience, and I just don't like to do that."

Payne's comedic sensibilities and instincts have never been sharper. Three scenes in particular stand out, and all involve Paul Giamatti as the lovably neurotic wine junkie Miles. In one, some bad news sends Miles careening for the nearest bottle, which he grabs like a suicide weapon and proceeds to drain while stumbling down a hillside. In another, the idiocy of winery etiquette sets him off and he loses it in a fit sure to join Jack Nicholson's famous diner rant in *Five Easy Pieces*. Finally, to help his buddy Jack out of a jam, Miles retrieves some valuables left behind in a house, and nearly gets killed for his trouble.

A lighter touch, loosening up and love

Unlike the acclaimed *Schmidt*, which played cold and dour for some viewers, *Sideways* displays, even in its despair and dysfunction, what he calls "a lighter touch." He adds, "*Schmidt* didn't turn out to all viewers as entertaining as I thought it would have. It's a little slow and I guess people took those depressing scenes a little more seriously than I ever imagined. I just thought I was making a comedy. With *Sideways*, I wanted it to be a really entertaining movie. It has some similar themes as *Schmidt*, like loneliness and depression, but it's a better film. It has more laughs and it has a quicker pace. It also contains something new for me, which is a love story.

"That's what it ends on. It ends on the possibility of this guy being able finally to reopen himself to love ... to loving. I wasn't even actually anticipating how much of a love story this film would be, but it turned out that's really equal to if not slightly greater an element in the movie as the buddy story."

In keeping with the romantic vibe, Payne encouraged composer Rolfe Kent "to concoct a jazz-infused score. I thought jazz would go well with wine." Payne's inspiration were the jazz-tinged Italian comedies of the late 1950s, particularly *Big Deal on Madonna Street*. "Its jazz music kind of washes over whole scenes. It doesn't really score or hit emotionally what's going on. It's just kind of there, and I thought that would be nice. And I think it (Kent's score) turned out really well."

That the film's more of a love story than he ever envisioned comes from his growing assurance in letting a film find its own mood rather than grafting one onto it.

"I just think I'm a little bit more confident and looser with how I make a movie," he said. "I think a lot of my evolving craft is that I have something in mind about how a film should be or could be and when I encounter problems in getting it there, I'm less likely to be freaked out by those problems. I move more quickly in identifying those obstructions and knowing how to dissolve them. I find that in writing too. I just know *Sideways* would be a different film if I chose other actors or if I chose a different cinematographer."

Men behaving badly

Paul Giamatti as Miles and Thomas Haden Church as Jack play middle-aged men acting out their inner child. These lovable buffoons careen out of control in encounters that veer from high drama to sweet romance to slapstick to farce.

"Those two actors—they're just so funny," said Payne, who chose them over mega-stars he had read for the part. "I auditioned all sorts of actors . . . and I just picked the ones that were best for the movie and that I thought were the funniest." They also project a profound vulnerability and fragility, particularly Giamatti, that make their behavior both pathetic and heartbreaking.

In what is a combination buddy picture, road movie, and romantic comedy, *Sideways* gives us two losers whose pairing is remindful of Ratso Rizzo and Joe Buck in *Midnight Cowboy*. Like those bottom-feeding hustlers, Miles and Jack are on the make. The repressed Miles, an unhappy teacher and wannabe writer with a fetish for wine that numbs the pain of a failed marriage, just wants to feel again. The shallow Jack is a former soap opera actor reduced to playing on his old fame to get laid. He wants to relive his youth again and again, without heeding any of the consequences. Alone, they're sorry. Together, they're a co-dependent disaster. Yet, there's also a genuine love they embrace but never quite verbalize. They are *The Odd Couple* for a new age.

On the eve of Jack's marriage, the boys go off on a wine tour. Each has his own agenda. For Miles, it's an escape into fermented melancholia. For Jack, open season on every piece of ass he can get. Things change when they meet a couple of women. Miles falls for Maya, a beguiling waitress and soulmate played by Virginia Madsen. Jack flings it with Stephanie, a frisky hottie of a wine pourer played by Sandra Oh. While Jack's caddish ways set off repercussions that scare him back into facing the music, Miles rediscovers the possibility of love. It's with this romantic turn Payne shows a side of his oft-stated humanism unseen before.

Working with director of photography Phedon Papamichael for the first time, Payne complained on the shoot his DP was making things look "too beautiful," prompting Papamichael to observe, "No, that's just a side of you you haven't embraced." Giving in to the lush golden hue of the Santa Ynez wine country and the romantic arc of the story, Payne said, "I just went with it." He's happy with the results. "I think it's my best film." Others are noticing too. "Some of the critics are saying it's the film that least seems to satirize its protagonist (Miles). It seems to accept him more and to be a little more tender toward him. And that might be true."

As Miles fumbles toward fledgling romance, there are mishaps Payne comically exploits at his protagonist's expense, just as he did with Ruth Stoops, Jim McAllister–Tracy Flick, and Warren Schmidt. But in

Sideways there's a more merciful, sympathetic look at the plight of its poor wretch. This more forgiving treatment, suggests Payne, who's now a married man, is an expression of his own maturity.

"Because of my experience on *Schmidt*, I think *Sideways* is a better film than it would have been otherwise. Rex (Pickett) says jokingly, but he means it too, that I needed to make a film about maturity before I could go back and make a film about immaturity. It all seems right. I hope I'm learning not just more about craft from year to year, but more about life and more about myself and more about subtleties of human experience. I want my work to deepen."

Perhaps it took getting away from Omaha, his hometown, before he could explore more colors. "It doesn't matter Omaha–not Omaha," he said. "They're all just films." But he's clearly annoyed by questions like, "Wow, what was it like not to shoot in Omaha?" and yet he insists that "doesn't have anything to do with my decision not to shoot there anymore, or at least for a while."

New projects and new directions

Until this summer Payne was coming back to shoot a Robert Nelson script titled *Nebraska*. Then, Payne fell in love with another story that he and Jim Taylor are now making their next project. "I don't want to say too much, because it's just in its early stages, but I will say we want to delve into our times," he said. "There's a lot wrong going on right now, and I think film has to be bold in addressing both the human and political arena."

He's eying a sprawling, nonlinear narrative. "I want to work on a little bigger scale and canvas. I don't mean effects-wise. But I want a longer film. I'm thinking at least two and a half hours long. And, structurally, not a straight-ahead three-act structure, but more like five or six sequences. I've been thinking a lot of Fellini's *La Dolce Vita* and Robert Altman's *Nashville* as a kind of inspiration."

The genesis for this unnamed project, which will not shoot here, arose when Tyler Bensinger, a friend from Payne's UCLA film school days, suggested a concept that got Payne "thinking about a whole lot of different things." Payne expects he, Taylor, and Bensinger, a writer and producer on *Cold Case*, will "hash out the ideas."

As for *Nebraska*, the film Payne was to helm, he said, "I'm putting that on hold. That's a wonderful screenplay I would like to make one day, but there are things more pressing right now in our world that we all kind of have to respond to."

Another film on Payne's mind these days is *The Assassination of Richard Nixon*, a Sean Penn–starring vehicle Payne helped get made. Directed by another UCLA film school bud, Niels Mueller, who co-wrote it with Omaha native Kevin Kennedy, *Assassination* shot two days in Omaha last year. It's played the Cannes and Toronto fests. "I'm always interested in helping my buddies get their films made," Payne said. "I used a few of my show biz connections to help get it to Cary Woods, who produced *Citizen Ruth*, and then we got Sean Penn involved. I also did some advocating for the film's inclusion at Cannes this year. The filmmakers were nice enough to give me an executive producer credit on it. I'm happy for its success."

Sideways's success is no sure thing, but Payne seems confident he's made his most accomplished—read: accessible—film to date. Getting it done on time for festivals and a fall release pushed him and editor Kevin Tent to the max. "Post got really tough. The hours were long. We worked basically from nine to eight every day," he said. "I got really sucked into this one and I'm just now starting to look up from it." A big reason the edit took eight and a half months was the personal record in footage he shot.

He got an early reading on *Sideways* at informal screenings he held in the cutting room and at official test screenings Fox ran in theaters. "I make comedies, so I need to screen my films a lot," Payne said. "The first group to see my films is always my old UCLA film school friends, the collaborators from the film, and some other friends. So, maybe a group of about thirty. Then, I take them all out to dinner and we talk about it. The studio may offer input from their test screenings, but it's always about 'make it shorter.' I listen, but I don't necessarily make any changes based on what they say. I learn from it all. But the changes I do make are never about making it more commercial or palatable for the audience, other than what I want."

With a new picture out that many are calling his best, Payne's sitting pretty. Still basking in the glow of the triumphant 2004 Summer Olympic Games held in his ancestral homeland of Greece, whose success "made us all proud," he said, he's set to serve on the jury of the Thessaloniki Film Festival (November 19–28) in Greece. Grecian officials have long courted him to come make a film there, a move that would fit nicely in his expanding vision as a filmmaker.

In his early middle-age he's reached a level of respect few other filmmakers enjoy. All of which reminds the ironical Payne of a line from *Chinatown*. "Of course I'm respectable—I'm old. Politicians, ugly buildings, and whores all get respectable if they stick around long enough." Add filmmakers to the list.

This privileged moment of the filmmaker at a lake near Livonia, Michigan, on location for the HBO pilot *Hung* reminded me of the existential place he found himself after *Sideways* and before *The Descendants*. During that between and betwixt period he still walked with great purpose, but with no definitive feature project on the horizon it seemed as though he was adrift at times. (photo by Anna Musso)

Scuba diving with Alexander Payne: in the wake of his Oscar win and divorce, the filmmaker draws inward and reflects on the new status he owns and what it may mean to his work

Published in a 2005 issue of *The Reader*

Surrender

Alexander Payne's Oscar win for *Sideways* officially anointed him a member of American film royalty. His ascendancy to Hollywood's ruling class, no matter how short-lived it proves, increased the already intense courting of him that began when the picture morphed from nice little adult comedy to big fat hit. With his coronation complete, everybody wants a piece of him, all of which makes the reflective Payne deliberate ever more carefully about his next move.

On a recent Omaha visit, the filmmaker looked tired describing the deluge of requests, deals, offers, and scripts he gets these days. This followed an exhausting awards and festival season that saw him do extensive media. He presided over the *Un Certain Regard* jury at Cannes. As the breakup of his marriage to actress Sandra Oh goes through the courts, he's in the process of moving. With so much in the offing and at stake, grabbing at just anything would be a mistake.

After all, when the world is offered up on a silver platter, you don't bite off more than you can chew. As Payne recently put it, "You eat too much birthday cake and you get sick." With "a whole new level of having to deal with stuff coming at me," he said, he's taking a step back to "catch my breath" and to go into "life maintenance" mode before "getting back to work."

"I'm just surrendering for about four more months. I'm really not doing anything for a feature film, other than thinking and reading some scripts that come in," he said. "I'm getting a knee operation. I'm moving from one house to another. Dealing with the divorce. I've a little more travel to do. After I do this life stuff then I'll start to think about what my next film is, because once you start a feature film you're scuba diving under water for two years. The rest of your life goes away, which I prefer. I prefer to be scuba diving."

He almost forgot to mention an international project he's part of called *Paris, I Love You*. This anthology or omnibus film will interweave some twenty commissioned shorts, each a rumination on Parisian culture, by some of world cinema's leading artists, including Payne, into a feature-length tribute to the City of Light.

He'll shoot his five-minute segment there, specifically in the 14e arrondissement, in September.

"From where I am in my life right now, the idea of making a short film in a distant city sounded appealing," he said. "And part of the reason is precisely that I don't know Paris well at all."

Reassessment and rejuvenation

Paris sojourn aside, he's retreating for the moment to let things die down and sink in before taking the plunge again.

The eminence attending Oscar has vaulted Payne into rarefied company. It began as soon as he accepted his statuette. "People wanted to hold it. It was a little like handing over the ring in *Lord of the Rings*. Then, other people didn't want to touch it thinking it would jinx their own chances of winning one day," he said. "It's too early to tell whether it has changed my own perception of my worth." He expressed mixed feelings about what it all confers.

"On the one hand, I think, Oh, I guess I'm a 'made guy' now. On the other hand, I think, Oh, I've won an Oscar, mainstream seal of approval. What did I do wrong?"

The real question is where does he go from here and how does he remain true to himself amid all the swirl?

This is not entirely new territory for the writer-director. Even with only four features to his credit, he's enjoyed an exalted position for some time now. He was a previous Academy Award nominee for *Election*. His *About Schmidt* was selected for the main competition at Cannes, closed the 2002 New York Film Festival, and received several Oscar nominations in addition to grossing more than $100 million. Moreover, *Schmidt* proved to Hollywood insiders that Payne could shepherd a successful vehicle with a major star, Jack Nicholson, thereby making the filmmaker more packagable. As Payne said, "Anymore, I view success as a commodity to help get the next film made."

Often overlooked in his rise up the industry ladder is the "sell-out" work he and writing collaborator Jim Taylor, the co-Oscar-winning scenarist of *Sideways*, do as script doctors. They did rewrites for mega-hits *Meet the Parents* and *Jurassic Park III*. They just finished their latest job-for-hire on Universal's *I Now Pronounce You Chuck & Larry*, a comedy about a pair of Phillie firefighters who feign being a gay couple, all the way to the altar, to qualify for job health benefits unavailable to single straight men. "We want to rename it *Flamers*," Payne said, smiling.

Then there's what he calls the *Sideways* "tsunami." Even though he went through the gauntlet on *Schmidt*, he was taken aback when *Sideways* hit. Its success, and all the attention it brought, he said, has been "the most disorienting" experience of his career. Before its general release, he perceived the project as "a nice little movie." He politely turned down a request from the Cannes Film Festival to submit the pic for competition, explaining to officials, "I don't think it's big enough.'" His view was reinforced when it was "turned down for competition" in Venice. So when the buzz ignited, he was naturally surprised.

"I was caught off guard for the amount of stuff coming at me. I don't want to look a gift horse in the mouth, but it's put me in a highly reactive rather than active mode. Like, much more of my time is spent answering inquiries about using me than doing my work. It's meant a lot of travel. My number of emails has increased vastly. Also the number of requests I get to read scripts and to do things for charity. Don't get me wrong, it's been great. I'm grateful. I have interesting access to people nowadays. But nothing in life is clean cut. It's all a mixed bag. Like all these people asking, 'Will you read my script?' I don't even have time to go to the gym. If I say no to being on a charity's board of directors, does it mean I'm an asshole? When Jim and I started we never hit anybody up for anything. It's like, not cool."

An example of the heat surrounding him, even pre-Oscar, came at a University of Nebraska at Omaha symposium he gave in December, when an overflow crowd of students, aspirants, and acolytes energized the Eppley Auditorium, charging the air with adulation and fascination. Sure, that was on his home turf, but cut to a scene six months later at the prestigious Walker Art Center in Minneapolis for a June 3 program kicking off a weeklong retrospective of his work. *Los Angeles Times* and National Public Radio film critic Kenneth Turan interviewed Payne on stage of the Walker cinema before a full crowd every bit as juiced as the one in Omaha. Yes, Payne's a hot ticket wherever he goes these days.

As his fame grows Payne finds some see him differently. "They see me in a new context. Not everybody. Not close friends. That doesn't change. But sometimes I experience the perception of others change more than I change. I'm like, 'Are you sure it's me? I mean, I didn't return your phone calls before.'"

Even before opening nationwide, *Sideways* caused a stir at the Toronto Film Festival that carried over to its closing night slot at the NY Film Festival, where Payne's a favorite son. By the time *Sideways* cleaned up at the Independent Spirit Awards and earned five Oscar nods, including for Best Picture and Best Director, it was a bona fide commercial/critical success. To date, the film has grossed some $115 million worldwide after topping out at $75 million domestic.

While the film won but a single Oscar, for Best Adapted Screenplay, an award Payne and Taylor shared, the fact that it was in the running at all in the major categories and that it did this without the benefit of a name actor, has given Payne a cachet only the regal and the hot are accorded.

Committing Omaha and other environs to the screen

Then there's the breakout aspect of *Sideways* that, as Payne's first feature made outside Nebraska, perhaps once and for all removed the Omaha tag from his filmmaker's profile, a label some sought to define him and his work by.

As he told Kenneth Turan that night at the Walker, "I get so sick of the question, 'Why Omaha?' because I always think you never ask Spike Lee, Martin Scorsese, and Woody Allen that question about New York. It's just that they happen to be from there. Quentin Tarantino and Paul Thomas Anderson happen to be from L.A., and you don't ask that question, Why L.A.? And, you know, I like to point out that Fellini shot early on in Rimini (the Italian filmmaker's hometown) and he returned later on in *Amarcord*. And I just think in many arts you feel a necessity somehow to connect to that home base. I was and I am sick of seeing films really only set in L.A., which I feel is an anomalous place within this country and yet it's shown to the world as being typical. It's only because the film business is located there and they're too lazy to get out of town.

"Excuse my tirade, but we're all so anxious to see a version of ourselves mirrored in art and in cinema. I didn't grow up seeing myself—a Midwesterner—in film. Instead of asking me how did where I come from shape me as a filmmaker, the real question is, how does where I come from have to do with me as a person? It's a great place to grow up. You know, good values and a good rhythm of life. A certain honesty and a certain sense of humor. Omaha is of the Midwest that way, but also specific to itself. I like to get reality in film and to somehow take a documentary approach in fiction filmmaking, and yet I felt I needed to get it right first in Omaha— in the place I knew best—before I could move on.

"I think if *Sideways* is successful at all in terms of getting a sense of Santa Barbara, it's because I was armed with tools I had learned in finally starting to get it right in *About Schmidt*, which was made in Omaha." By proving he could apply the same precisely-honed satire and well-observed scrutiny to character and place in Santa Barbara as he did in Omaha, he's opened a universe of possibilities once denied him by the suits.

Opportunity

"Generally, when you finish a film and it has some notoriety, there's a short window of opportunity where stuff comes at you and people are interested in you before they move on to the next big thing. From observation, successful directors generally have about ten years where you are in touch with the zeitgeist. You can go from film to film, like a monkey swinging from branch to branch. Before that and after that it's a little harder. You might still be doing good, honest work, but it's not hitting. You don't generate excitement. Your films are not met with a sense of event. You're still respected, but it's not quite the same thing. Knowing how to capitalize on that window is something I continue to witness and is something I haven't known how to do until recently," he said.

He intends using his new-found leverage by not going after riches but staying close to his heart. That's why he's taking his time before inking his next project. "I always do really think out what my next film is going to be. I mean, that's a big commitment, so you always want it to be right, and yet not overthink it. But I'm thinking how could I use this opportunity to get something made which otherwise would be difficult to get made. And I don't know exactly what that is ... Ideally, I want to use whatever 'power' I'm getting to make increasingly more personal films, not impersonal films. That's where you can really use your power—to make more personal films more successfully."

A critical overview of cinema

Payne's insistence on adhering to his vision fits squarely within his overarching concern for the state of American cinema today, which he feels is disconnected from the potent issues of our time. He awaits a film movement, akin to what evolved in the '70s, that closely reflects what's happening in society.

"In what's a horrible time for the world in general and particularly for America, I'm hoping that will translate into a wonderfully vital time for cinema. Now, I think it's a time when in many aspects of life we need to change the form and change the language a little bit. Drive around Omaha and you see a homogenization of architecture and commerce that didn't used to be here. Where there used to be something individual, there's now a Walgreens or Walmart. Like what corporations have done to the look of this country and the feel of the country, in my little corner of activity there's a homogenization going on in the movies of this country. So individual practitioners have to avoid homogenization, which means coming up with new and personal things and getting them out there."

Always the film buff, Payne applies an informed analysis to cinema trends and influences. He's intimately familiar with such models of ground-breaking cinema as the Italian Neo-realist movement and the French New Wave. But, as with any cineaste, he has his own favorite patterns to draw on.

"For me, I look at Italian films of the '60s and American films of the '70s. Certainly with the great Italian films of the '60s, each new film was positing a new idea of what a film could be. *8 1/2. La Dolce Vita. The Leopard. L'avventura. La Notte. The Good, the Bad and the Ugly. Once Upon a Time in the West*. Bertolucci's *1900*. They're all really different. All narrative. All entertaining. All meaningful and humanist. But all different forms with different and new uses of film language. In American films of the '70s, there is, among others, *Little Big Man, Nashville, McCabe & Mrs. Miller*. Film was very political then. At least you had consistent themes of an individual alienated within the society he lives. We need movies like that now. That's the kind of American cinema I want. Maybe it's going to take a little while, because from idea to getting it out there is at least two years."

Weighing what's next

Prior to the *Sideways* crush, he was thinking in terms of his next film being political and referring to some of America's disturbing actions and policies that make the nation a corporate-run caste system at home and a reactionary military-industrial pariah overseas. That still seems to be the general direction he's leaning, although there's no single core idea for a film that's coalesced yet with him and Taylor.

He's aware of the expectation to make large-scale, star-heavy pics now that he's in demand and in line to get them made, but that's the farthest thing from his mind.

"Often, in superficial interviews, people ask, 'So, are you going to make your big movie now?' Well, what does that mean? That's such an American question. As if these little films don't really exist other than as a stepping-stone toward ultimately making big-budget, very commercial films," he said. "And, I guess, I could make one of those films in the way they mean, but the final consideration for me is always—what's the story? I mean, if I had gotten into this for the money, I wouldn't have gotten into this. I would have gone to law school or gone into another field because certainly success in film is most unassured. It's nice to know it's out there if you come up with a story that needs a lot of money behind it. Who wouldn't like to say, Action, and see a bunch of people on horses come over a hill? That might be fun. What is it Orson Welles said? A movie set is the greatest electric train set a kid ever had. On the other hand, it gets back to—what's the story?"

Clearly, whatever he decides to make, his next film will evolve organically, not as some take-the-money-and-run career move.

"I remain very inner-directed. There's the films you choose and the ideas that choose you," he said, "and, anymore, I believe ideas really choose me. I'll be thinking about one thing and suddenly this other idea comes and I'm like, 'Oh . . . go away . . . ugh,'" he said, clasped hands mimicking an idea grabbing him by the throat.

Meeting up with the right idea is a state of mind. "You have to be open, and that's really what I've set out as my task these months—being open," he said, adding that discovery is at the core of cinema. "Making a film is not the execution of an idea, it's a process of discovering what that film is. And, so, you just discover day by day. In screenwriting, Jim and I don't outline. Every day, it's, What is this film going to be? When making a film you have two questions boomeranging in your mind. One is, What is a film? And the other is, What is this film? You remain open to what ideas come to you in your sleep or that a PA brings you on the set."

One for all, all for one

In that discovery, his collaboration with creative department heads is key. Payne's working relationships with Taylor, art director Jane Ann Stewart, editor Kevin Tent, composer Rolfe Kent, and producer George Parra go back to the early '90s.

"We elicit the film from one another, and it's all due to the quality of questions we ask each other. Often, we don't have to say anything. We have a shorthand. We're a team. We feel like family. When there's love on the set and not just professional associations, it makes a difference," he said. "We look forward to each new film so we can spend more time together."

Payne said the way he and Taylor apprehend the world is why their films are the way they are. "The films are very much an expression of how we occur together and hang out. The critics talked a lot about how *Sideways* successfully mixes comedy and pathos or makes some hairpin turns in tone, which we're not necessarily aware of when writing it. It's just all what we like, without prejudice. We're like, Oh, that's funny ... that's meaningful, whether looking at other people or at the pathetic aspects of our own lives. That's the type of stuff we talk about."

More and more, his process resonates with something author Gabriel Garcia Marquez said: creation is memory. Whether drawn from memory, a book, a play or an article, Payne feels whatever film story he writes is an original; whereas, Taylor feels every story is an adaptation. In any event, Payne said, "We write a script based on our memory" of the source material, thereby making it their own.

Until further notice, Payne's being a receptacle for ideas, one or two of which he hopes triggers that instinctual response, "Oh, that's a comedy." He wouldn't mind a great script "dropping in his lap" either. However it happens, he'll soon enough don his scuba gear for another dive into the filmmaking depths.

Meanwhile, he's got the shards of a life to pick up and reassemble. Truth be told, it's all a distraction until his muse fixes him up with his next exploration of flawed, unscripted lives going off track. Then it's magic time again, when he and his movie family reunite to find the discoveries that go into making cinema art.

"I've got to get back to work ... and have a vacation."

'

'Every day I'm not directing, I feel like I die a little.' Catching up with Alexander Payne—after a year of largely producing-writing other people's projects, he sets his sights on his next film

Published in a 2006 issue of *The Reader*

Busy work

Appearing calmer than he did in 2005, when still in the exhausting grip of *Sideways* mania and the fallout of his divorce from Sandra Oh, a relaxed Alexander Payne was back in Omaha the past couple weeks, eager to resume work. For those curious about what's he been up to since *Sideways*, he answers, "I got busy." It's why he's been out of touch so long. "It's not just a line, I've been busy," he reiterates. True enough, but aside from a short film project he did in Paris he's largely been embroiled in work not his own. And that drives him crazy.

He's helped produce two feature films due out next year. *The Savages* stars Philip Seymour Hoffman and Laura Linney. *King of California* stars Michael Douglas and Evan Rachel Wood. Payne's a close friend of the filmmakers. He's an executive producer on *Savages*, written-directed by Tamara Jenkins (*The Slums of Beverly Hills*), the wife of Payne's writing partner Jim Taylor. He's a full producer on *King*, whose writer-director Michael Cahill was a film school buddy of Payne's at UCLA.

Payne's been collaborating on the script of Taylor's first directing job, *The Lost Cause*. The pair also did a rewrite on *I Now Pronounce You Chuck & Larry* before Adam Sandler signed on opposite Kevin James and "brought in his own people" to, as Payne put it, "Sandlerize it and, quite frankly, dumb it up. We read a draft of what they're shooting and it's more than a little different from what we wrote."

A new feature project

The real news is the Omaha native has finally fixed on what his next film will be and it turns out it'll bring him back home, perhaps by late 2007. He won't say much else other than it's the long, episodic, "Altmanesque" film he's referenced in the past. He and Taylor are well along on the script, a first draft of which they hope to complete by next spring. The idea for it is one he's kicked around a while but it was only in January he "began to think of it in a new way" that made it click. In the past he's referred to the concept as a vehicle for expressing his dismay and disgust with American attitudes and policies. He won't go as far as calling it politically charged, but he gives the impression it will be a pointed satire.

"All I know is I hope it will be funny," he said in what's become his stock answer to queries about his works in progress. "The only thing I'll tell you is what's new about it for Jim and me is it has a little bit of a science-fiction premise, which functions more as a metaphor than a ... anyway, that's all," he said, catching himself in mid-teaser lest he reveal too much of the still fragile script.

Also new is that "Omaha figures a lot in this one," he said. "As we have it currently configured about a third of the film would shoot here, but it's a much longer film than any I've made before, so even a third of the film is a good hunk." He would never consider covering Omaha somewhere else. "I believe in place," he said.

Ad Hominem Enterprises

Payne's growing place in the industry, which avidly awaits his next film, was made tangible last fall when he, Taylor, and producer Jim Burke formed the production-development company Ad Hominem Enterprises. In the process they struck a first-look deal with Fox Searchlight Pictures that gives the studio first dibs on any projects the filmmakers develop. A producer on *Election*, Burke was brought in to manage the Santa Monica–officed Hominem's small staff. Taylor also has a support person in New York, where he lives. Fox Searchlight did such a good job handling *Sideways* that Payne inked the studio pact, a move he'd avoided doing until now.

"We'd been talking about it for a while," he said, "but it wasn't until after *Sideways* we decided to take the possibility more seriously. Actually, Jim (Taylor) is the one who kind of spearheaded it. I've never wanted to have one of these deals before because you never know whom you're dealing with exactly, and I've never had as harmonious a filmmaking experience as I had with *Sideways* and Fox Searchlight. We'd be happy to make another movie with them. They were great. Jim really thought it (the deal) would be a good idea and he was right.

"A first-look deal is where a studio just kind of pays for some overhead and you have people working for you in an office and in exchange they (Fox) get first right of negotiation . . . first crack at anything we do. It doesn't necessarily mean they're going to make it, but they get a short window of time in which to decide if they want to do it and, if not, it's in effect a free ball. And it just kind of formalizes good will and relationship between filmmakers and studio. Besides . . . the company allows Jim and me to have extra eyes and ears out there reading books or accepting scripts, taking phone calls. Otherwise, we're doing it all ourselves and not getting our work done. It's just sort of there to facilitate us."

Hominem serves another purpose, one taking more and more of Payne's time, namely to help nudge friends' projects from limbo to realization. He said the company gives him and Taylor a framework to "on a very selective basis help, enable or foster ... those films getting made. And we've done one so far—Tamara Jenkins's *The Savages*, which is turning out quite well. She was having a very hard time getting that film off the ground, even with the wonderful cast of Laura Linney and Philip Seymour Hoffman. So, finally our agreeing to come on as executive producers helped it reach the tipping point to getting it made."

He said the resulting film, shot mainly in New York and a bit in Sun City, Arizona, is "ultimately funny and sad and real. Great performances. They're very human."

Wanderings

Sporting a Hydra-head of overflowing locks, Payne broke his long silence to sit down for an exclusive interview with *The Reader* one October afternoon at M's Pub in the Old Market. It felt like catching up with someone returned from an odyssey. That's how removed he's been from the media these past several months. It's not that he disappeared in the wake of *Sideways,* the little picture that blew up bigger than anyone expected and deservedly won Payne and Taylor Oscars for Best Adapted Screenplay. But after the barrage of press junkets, film festivals, awards shows, and requests came at him faster and heavier than for any of his earlier films, he did retreat inward, largely avoiding any public life.

Last summer he spoke of "trying to get away from letting myself be trapped by the demands of others on my time. I mean, leave me alone, I'm trying to get back to work." This time, he said, "I'm trying to be a private citizen." He's managed to avoid the tabloids, but he's had mixed success with the bit about getting back to work.

There was *Paris, je'taime* (*Paris, I Love You*), a made-in-Paris anthology film that commissioned twenty-one filmmakers from around the world, Payne among them, to ruminate about love as manifested in Old Paree.

Payne wrote-directed one of the twenty-one segments, *14e arrondissement*, and portrayed Oscar Wilde wandering in a cemetery in another—director Wes Craven's *Père-Lachaise*. The film opens in the U.S. in March. He enjoyed the experience if for no other reason than, as he told a Canadian reporter at the recent Toronto Film Festival, where he hosted a screening of the film, "The timing was right, and I never really spent time in Paris, only as a tourist once."

This time he spent two months there, late August through late October 2005, prepping three or four weeks, filming two days and editing over three or four weeks more. He got to enjoy some of the Parisian milieu, including a celebration marking the restoration of the Le Grand Palais, complete with a light show and the music of Debussy and Ravel. "It was delightful to be in Paris," he said, adding the best part was being back at work again. "It was really great to make a film. And it turned out pretty well." His segment is seen last in the anthology.

He wrote *14e arrondissement* for actress Margo Martindale (the white trash mom of Hilary Swank in *Million Dollar Baby*). She plays a dour Denver letter carrier living out a dream to visit Paris only to be depressed once in the City of Lights. He first noticed her a decade ago in *Lorenzo's Oil*. "She's a wonderful actress," he said.

The way the French production was set up recalled his old UCLA days. "Making *Paris, je'taime* was a little like film school, which is at any given time there were two or three directors working and it was literally on one floor of a building in Paris," he said. With filmmakers, cast, and crew around in a communal setting, a director might ask anyone passing by—"What are you doing tomorrow?"—and stick them in front of the camera. That's how he ended up getting cast for his onscreen gig.

"As I was finishing my segment, Wes Craven was about to shoot his and they needed someone to play Oscar Wilde," he said, "and I got the part the way most actors get parts, which is that three other actors passed.

"They just saw me in the hall walking from the editing room to the bathroom and they saw my long hair ... I didn't want to do it. I told them I'm a terrible actor, but they didn't care. So Wes Craven put me in it. It was fun. I acted opposite Rufus Sewell and Emily Mortimer, a couple of English thesps. It was fine. But I'm really glad I don't want to be an actor."

Upon his return to the States he spent late 2005 and early 2006 working on *The Lost Cause* and *I Now Pronounce You* and searching for a project to direct. At one point last year he came back to research a pic focusing on the lives and journeys of Latino immigrants who migrate here to work in south-central Nebraska meat packing plants. He audaciously envisioned it as a Spanish-language film.

"I went to Lexington and Schuyler, Nebraska and started to talk to people at UNO [University of Nebraska at Omaha] and UNL [University of Nebraska–Lincoln] who are studying this phenomenon," he said. "I like immigrant stories. I don't think we've had one for a while and since I speak Spanish it just makes sense. You know, who are these people? How do they live? And if he likes the part, I would offer the lead to Javier Bardem (*The Sea Inside*) . . . the greatest European actor of our generation and I would bring him to Nebraska."

Payne's put the project aside for the time being, just as he's done with a road trip comedy he adores called *Nebraska* that he pledges, "I'm still going to do some day."

Much of his 2006 though was taken up by producing, something he gladly did to help friends out but that he's also had his fill of for now. The title "producer" has many variations and meanings. Someone in a full producing capacity pulls projects together, brokers deals, keeps productions on track, troubleshoots, et cetera. An executive producer pulls strings. Some producers are glorified consultants or go-betweens. Payne's received producing credits before on projects outside his own, most notably his friend Kevin Kennedy's *The Assassination of Richard Nixon*, which filmed a scene or two in Omaha.

For *Savages*, which tells the story of two adult siblings (Hoffman and Linney) obliged to care for the ailing elderly father (Philip Bosco) who never cared for them, the executive producer title Payne assumed fell in the advisory realm. Taylor's also an executive producer on it and Jim Burke is one of its sundry other producers.

Playing producer

Savages writer/director Tamara Jenkins said Payne "has really great instincts" when it comes to suggestions for improving the script or refining the edit. She said rather than making conceptual or esoteric comments, his are "utterly practical and very helpful. I like that about Alexander," she said.

Payne said his "own personal role" on the project has been more "as creative advisor. I read the screenplay very thoroughly and gave notes. I watch all the cuts and give notes. I show up at all the meetings. I'm just sort of there." He visited the set two or three times. Otherwise, he said, Jim Burke spent the most time on set, dealing with "some difficulties in production that needed the extra care our involvement was able to provide.

"You know, it probably kind of formalizes something I probably would have been to a great extent doing anyway as a friend of the project. Jim Taylor, because he's married to the director, would have got sucked-in regardless. But it makes the director feel as though there's one more official element of protection and makes the studio feel there's one more official element of expertise involved."

Jenkins said Payne encouraged Fox Searchlight, which earlier passed on *Savages*, to reconsider the project. When Jenkins went to pitch Fox again, Payne, Taylor, and Burke accompanied her. "Nobody said anything but I did have all these men sitting behind me that were pretty formidable," Jenkins said. "It certainly made me feel good and it sort of created a sense that somebody should pay a little bit more attention than they were. And I think that's what happened. It was kind of like walking into a room with back up."

"Precisely," *King of California* director Michael Cahill said of the support and influence Payne's provided him. "Alexander has helped me to get things creatively I might not have been able to get just by the force of his imprimatur. At the same time I've been able to run things by him, this being my first feature film, to sort of understand how the machine works. He's helped me with that quite a bit."

Novelist (*A Nixon Man*) turned filmmaker Cahill's *King* is a story of a mentally ill man (Douglas) who goes on a quest with his daughter (Wood) to find a treasure of gold doubloons he's convinced lies beneath their suburban neighborhood. "The film is very much a whimsical comment on how real estate development is killing our planet," Payne said. "The father and daughter are a little bit like Don Quixote and Sancho with this impossible dream, but using their astrolathe and compass and old charts they end up by Chuck E. Cheese Pizza or the 24-Hour Fitness. It shows how man's defecated" on Mother Earth. The King "finds the heart of gold he's looking for beneath the floor of a Costco."

As Jenkins found, Cahill couldn't get his project launched despite a strong script. When Payne read it and loved it, he passed it on to *Sideways* producer Michael London with the recommendation, "You should produce this." London agreed but on the condition they make it together. Payne balked before giving in. Landing Douglas, Payne said, was a real "coup." As a full producer, Payne made it on set most days and continues to have a post-production presence.

"I watch cuts and give constant comments and monitor where they are. Go in the cutting room a little bit," Payne said. "Because I'm an old colleague of the director's, I can give him comments. I've had some liaisons with the financiers. When they see the film and express concerns I'm kind of the catcher . . . the interpreter, so I hear what they say and help deliver it to the director in a way that is most helpful for him. At least that's what I aspire to do."

When you need a friend

Payne's serving as "a filter" or shield, Cahill said, is "a fantastic advantage . . . that cannot be overestimated. Everyone should be lucky to have that. That's huge." "You try to be the type of producer you yourself would want," Payne said. "The best producer though does nothing because the film has been set up so well you just let it go . . . you just let it run. The thing about producing is, it's like parenting—it's not even important what you do, it's just that you're there."

When friends become collaborators it risks straining their relationship. "That can happen," Payne said, "but if you're good enough friends with someone then that can weather storms. It doesn't work with everybody. You've got to be careful. But when it works, it works very nicely." He and Taylor's partnership is a model for it.

As much as he enjoys helping friends, it's still a distraction from his own work. "I mean, all of this is fine, but I don't want to produce anymore. I didn't get into film to be a producer. That's the last thing I want to be. I'm happy to help my friends when I can. I've done it and I'll do it again, but I can't for a while. Not the way I did it this year, because I need to do my own scuba diving"—his metaphor for immersing himself in his writing-directing—"and be utterly free to do my own thing. Every day I'm not directing I feel like I die a little."

To be or not to be

During the first part of his recent Omaha stay Payne was called away to California to attend a memorial service for the late Jim Glennon, his director of photography on *Citizen Ruth*, *Election*, and *About Schmidt*. Despite advanced prostate cancer, Glennon worked up till the end, lensing the acclaimed HBO shows *Deadwood* and *Big Love*. "He died too young at 64," he said. "A fantastic guy. It's just very sad."

As he expects to be back here for his new film, Payne's rented a mid-town Omaha home. He satirically described his relationship with the Big O. "After *About Schmidt* I was anxious to leave and now I'm anxious to come back and shoot," he said. "I think one's relationship with Omaha is like the tide. It comes in, it goes out. It never leaves shore. But after it's been in for a while it wants to go out. After it's been out, it wants to come back in."

He expresses enthusiasm for the "new Omaha in the making. Omaha is changing so much right now. It's kind of exciting," he said. He's most enthralled by the maturation of the cultural scene, with the Qwest Center, the Holland Performing Arts Center, the Great Plains Theatre Conference, the Omaha Film Festival, Lit Fest, the coming Kaneko Center and the emerging riverfront-condo landscape.

A project he's more than an idle observer of is the Saddle Creek Records build-out in NoDo (North Downtown). To show his support for the Film Streams art cinema that's a part of it, he sits on the theater's board of directors. He's a fan of Film Streams director Rachel Jacobson. "She's got it all going on," he said. When open next summer the venue will give film buffs what they've never had here: a state-of-the-art theater dedicated to art film exhibition and education.

"That's so fantastic that very soon in downtown Omaha you can go see *The Seven Samurai* projected. A huge contribution to the cultural life of the city as far as I'm concerned," he said. At her request he's submitted a list of ten of his favorite films for screening at the theater. He'll write program notes and be on hand to introduce as many of his picks as possible. Anyone who knows his tastes can expect some Kurosawa, Fellini, Antonioni, Visconti, maybe Ashby or Forman.

When all is said and done, Alexander Payne is a film geek.

"I've welcomed this because it's giving me a chance to ask myself why are these ten of my favorite films. What really do they have? And really to articulate what it is," he said. He feels we should all immerse ourselves in the films we love. "You have to memorize your favorite films ... just watch them over and over and over again. Scorsese says a film is part of your life, like a favorite record or painting on the wall. It's not just something you look at once or twice."

If we're lucky, Payne will keep blessing us with films we can watch again and again.

Size matters: the return of Alexander Payne, not that he was ever gone

Published in a 2009 issue of *The Reader*

A long time coming

Has it really been five years since *Sideways*? The 2004 film's success gave its director and Oscar-winning co-writer Alexander Payne the kind of career momentum few filmmakers ever enjoy. What did he do with it? From a crass POV, he squandered the opportunity when instead of leveraging that critical-commercial hit to make some dream project, he chose not to make anything.

Well, not exactly. He did write and direct the short *14e arrondissement* for the 2006 omnibus film *Paris, je t'aime* (*Paris, I Love You*). He and writing partner Jim Taylor took passes at the scripts for *I Now Pronounce You Chuck & Larry* and *Baby Mama*. In 2007 the pair also began work on a script that turned into an unusually arduous process. Payne hopes to direct that script, *Downsizing*, next year.

Also, Payne helped produce two films, the disappointing *King of California* and the sublime *The Savages*. All those commitments kept him busy, which is how he likes it, but they also made it more difficult to launch a new feature of his own.

Besides the Paris short, he'd actually exposed no film for six years from the time *Sideways* wrapped in 2003 until last summer, when he shot the pilot episode for the new HBO comedy series *Hung*. Thomas Jane stars as a typical middle-class American man driven by economic distress to offer his gift to women as a high-class escort. The opening episode Payne helmed premiered last Sunday.

Paris notwithstanding, the gap between *Sideways* and *Hung* was interminable for this celluloid junkie who once said, "Every day I'm not directing I feel like I die a little." OK, maybe he was being overdramatic, but the point is he went a long time not making cinema. He presumably could have had he really wanted. But Payne is nothing if not a considered, deliberate study. Anyone who knows him understands how particular he is when it comes to his work. Everything must be done on his terms. He'll only shoot after a script's gone through endless permutations, revisions, drafts. It must be solid as gold. No question marks, no loose ends.

Given the choice of rushing to follow up *Sideways* or stepping back to survey his options, he chose the latter course. Thus, the last five years was about regaining his personal/artistic bearings. Things came at him so hard, so fast after *Sideways* blew up that he lost his equilibrium there for a while. A breather was in order.

It didn't help that in the wake of the film taking off he was reeling from his and Sandra Oh's divorce. Amidst all that, he moved, he had knee surgery, he did a ton of press, and he fielded multiple directing offers. He discovered what it's like to be a hot commodity. It all got to be a bit much, and in typical Payne fashion he didn't want to compromise his principles by just jumping into anything that came along or feeling pressured into a project he really wasn't passionate about. So, he entered a self-imposed hiatus from shooting. He would only break this pact with himself in the event the right assignment came along at the right time. *Paris* was such an assignment. He filmed his segment in 2005.

Hung

Until last year he hadn't found anything conducive enough with his sensibilities and schedule to compel him to shoot again. That all changed with *Hung*. The new HBO series equates America's desperate new straits to the plight of ex-golden boy Ray Drecker, a one-time athletic hero turned high school basketball coach whose life has soured after a run of bad luck that leaves him feeling worthless.

As Payne noted in a recent interview at mid-town's Caffeine Dreams, this is the first television pilot he said yes to after years of courting by producers. So what made the ever cautious one bite? "Every May I get a couple offers to direct a pilot and I've never done so until now because the scripts weren't good or at least I didn't like them, or I was busy. But this time Jim Taylor and I had just finished a draft of *Downsizing*, and I was just so eager to shoot something and maybe let *Downsizing* simmer before coming back to it to do yet another draft, because the script has been so difficult. I thought, just go make something short, go shoot some film, go beat up some actors, assemble my team."

Itching to shoot aside, he clearly responded to the series developed by *Hung* writers-producers Colette Burson and Dmitry Lipkin (*The Riches*). "What interested me," said Payne, "is that it's about a guy who loses everything. His house burns down when he's uninsured, he's been hit hard in a divorce, and he ends up turning to the only asset he thinks he has left, one that he was born with. And I thought that maybe somehow that was a symbol for America in a way, where so much has been taken away from it that it only has its large member, and however it uses that. So it's kind of a whacky metaphor but it's something I could hang my hat on," he said, smiling wryly, pun fully intended.

The premise may not be Payne's but given his track record it's not hard to imagine him envisioning *Hung*'s scenario. In line with his taste for discerning, critical, original material, *Hung* explores the nation's economic, moral downturn through the prism of an All-American male's experience gone awry. In this downward spiral Ray does what the sorry, wounded protagonists in Payne's conception of the world do, he acts out. In this case, the beleaguered Ray turns the one endowment he feels he can market into a second career turning tricks.

Familiar territory

Is what Ray does really so different than Ruth Stoops playing her pregnancy off the pro-life–pro-abortion camps for cold hard cash (*Citizen Ruth*)? Or Jim McAllister giving Tracy her comeuppance by rigging the student body's vote (*Election*)? Or Warren Schmidt asserting his emancipation by rashly making an RV road trip and assuaging his guilt by supporting an African orphan (*About Schmidt*)? Or Miles going off on a self-loathing jag and Jack having his last fling (*Sideways*)?

Payne's less sure how consistent *Hung* is with his oeuvre. "I don't know if it fits into the body of my work or not, but it was fun to do, and I was certainly able to bring something to it. I'm proud of the work I did on it. I can't speak for the rest of the show because they just finished shooting it, but I know the pilot. It speaks well for the pilot that the network did select *Hung* to be a series because part of that decision is the pilot. And it was really great to work with HBO. They're awesome." As he didn't write the script, he said, "It's nothing from my soul," but that he would respond to *Hung* makes sense as its creators had his tone in mind when conceptualizing the series.

"It's funny because we recently found our very first notes from our very first session and we had said months before we had Alexander on board that it should be a comedy with 'a Paynesian sensibility,'" said Burson. "Alexander finds both the humanity and the comedy in everyday life. His movies feel very true and yet they're very funny. It's comedy that emerges from truth. Comedy without a wink."

Further, Burson said, when it came time to pitch a director to HBO Payne's name was at the top of her and Lipkin's list. "When we met with HBO and they said to us, 'Who is your dream director?' we said our number one choice would be Alexander Payne." To HBO's credit, she said, the network didn't blink. "Two days later he had the material and he called us up."

Making it his own

Once attached to the project Payne gathered his core crew and went to work. "I then was able to use my line producer, my editor, my costume designer, my second-unit director, my assistant. I kind of got my team on board. It was like, let's just stretch our legs a little before getting back to a feature. And so it was fun." He only had a small window of time to mount the pilot. "I said yes in May and we were casting and working on the script and scouting locations over the summer and then shooting in September. I finished editing picture at Thanksgiving. And then I did the final sound and music work last month. So I was on the show for a long time."

He meticulously cast the show and selected its locations. "The way we're cast has everything to do with Alexander," said Burson. "Alexander is very old school about it. He insisted on auditioning everyone. He has such an eye for it and such a clear notion for what we should be looking for. The other thing he was very demanding about was locations. He really wanted just the right house (for Ray). A lot of people assume it's a set, it's not, it's the house Alexander found next to the huge mansion Alexander found. He searched for it for weeks." The ill-fated house and McMansion next door sit on a Michigan lakefront beach.

Payne has a theory why feature directors like himself are sought after for pilots: "They figure a feature director might be a little bit more adept at creating the world of the show, helping cast it, helping determine the look, helping pick some of the creative and then beginning to shape something out of nothing that can then be used as a template for the show henceforth." Not only is it a chance to shape a world but to work on a more intimate scale. "It's fun to work in miniature and one puts no less attention," he said. TV production is faster and cheaper, but he said the budget and schedule allotted *Hung*'s pilot was generous.

"The nice thing about a pilot with respect to the rest of the episodes is that typically a network lavishes more time and money into the making of the pilot. I was able to direct it in a way as a very small feature as opposed to a TV show." His pilot does indeed read richer and deeper than episode two. Where his work has the fullness of a lush feature, the other is flat, plastic, unrefined. Double entendres only take you so far.

Like Ray calling himself "a happiness consultant."

As Payne was regarded a kindred spirit, he came in not just as a hired hand but a full-fledged creative collaborator. "We're very aligned creatively with him. We tend to be very particular. With almost every scene he shot we felt he would almost be reading our minds," said Lipkin. Added Burson, "He kept telling us, 'I'm your faithful gardener and I just want to nurture your vision and help it to grow.'"

One way he did that was to emphasize place. Set in Detroit, the pilot parallels the city's and car industry's dissolution with Ray's. Just as longtime titans Ford and GM have devolved into corporate derelicts seeking bailouts and Detroit a wasteland awaiting rescue, Ray's a former Mr. Big turned nobody who prostitutes himself. The series means to be a running commentary on the middle class being marginalized. Payne liked the rich subtext Burson and Lipkin gave him to work with.

"It's rare for me to direct something I haven't written, although Jim Taylor and I did do a little bit of polishing to the script, but it's still basically the vision of the writers/producers," he said. "But actually they were collaborative enough with me. In bringing me on, they allowed me to kind of take their work and interpret it my way and bring concerns I would find interesting into relief, like the fact that it was set in Detroit. Now it was set in suburban Detroit because they wanted to have somehow the idea of lake houses as symbols to explore class. You know, where there are these huge nouveau monstrosities being built next door to old mom-and-pop cabins on lake shores. The creators wanted that dynamic.

"The car companies faltering and the recession beginning were elements I wanted to bring out more strongly in this pilot. I wanted to make Detroit much more of a character and to really bring the foundering economy and car business into focus because it's about a guy who's down on his luck."

He's particularly successful at that in the opening montage. He portrays iconic American symbols in assorted states of desolation, from heaps of discarded cars in junkyards to abandoned auto manufacturer headquarters and factories to the razing of Tiger Stadium, all punctuated by Ray's bitter, ironic narration: "Everything's falling apart and it all starts right here in Detroit, the head waters of a river of failure. Thank God my parents aren't around to watch the country they loved go to shit. They were proud Americans. They had normal jobs and made a normal living. They fit in. They weren't kicked up the ass every day of their lives by property taxes and home owners associations

... What would I tell them if they saw me? That I'm not to blame, that it's not my fault? They didn't raise me that way. They taught me to take responsibility and get the job done. No excuses. You do your best with whatever gifts God gave you. . . ."

As the American empire declines, the nation resorts to defining itself by its big stick. Now that America doesn't make anything anymore, it's all about posturing. Ray Drecker's an emblem for that warped psyche. Show creators Burson and Lipkin describe "the burden of being hung" that Ray carries with him as an "existential state." In a Shakespearean sense, Ray's dilemma is what he and his dick are meant to be or not to be. Or, if you prefer a classical Greek analogy, Burson and Lipkin suggest that Ray accepts his burden as "his calling." Prostitution as quest.

Everything is up for sale in America

It is the oldest profession. Ray discovers selling yourself as a sex toy in this social media age is as easy as posting online ads of your attributes and services. A good hook helps. Transactions are fast, easy, anonymous. Safe? You be the judge. A victimless crime? It depends. After all, who's using whom here? Then again, there's little overhead and you're your own boss. Did anyone mention it's illegal?

Ray soon finds prostitution a cold, hard business that leaves him feeling rather, well, empty when he's through. As with everything, illicit sex comes with a price. Leading a double life means lying in order to skip out of classes, practices, games, and family doings to attend to business. That means complications. The guilt, the hypocrisy, the fear of being found out come with the job. Boundaries get blurred. Maintaining his alter ego, not to mention living up to his appendage, is hard work. There's real pressure to perform. A lot of these clients are demanding.

There's also Ray's journey in the land of estrogen. In school he got any girl he wanted and he stayed married twenty years to his wife, Jessica (Anne Heche), so he's not had to work very hard at understanding women. Now that Jessica's left him and he's in the trade of servicing females, he gets a rude awakening into what women want. "The gender dynamics," as Burson calls them, are more than Ray bargained for. In episode two he asks, "Why can't they just fuck me for me?"

Thomas Jane plays Ray with the crumbling sardonic veneer of William Holden in *Sunset Boulevard*. Holden's character, Joe Gills, is a once promising screenwriter now on the skids who deals with the degradation of being a gigolo to an aged ex-screen goddess. Jane's character, Ray, is a once Saturday hero who must come to terms with being reduced to a human dildo. As Ray's new at this he needs a "business manager."

Enter Tanya Skagle, a minor poet who is his occasional lay and full-time pimp. Jane Adams plays Tanya with the nihilistic cynicism of Jane Fonda in *Klute*. Ray and Tanya make a matched set. He's the sad picture of what happens to many sports stars after the parade's gone by and they wind up whores in the broadcast booth, in commercials, in movies, in books, playing off their old glory. Ray's not in that league and so his prostitution is of the down-and-dirty variety. Tanya's the classic starving artist with no real prospect of being discovered and, so, she sells out. In lieu of a grant or residency she rides the next best thing that comes around and prostitutes her own creative bent to exploit it.

Circumstances bring these seeming opposites—the macho jock and ditzy Beat—together. Deep down, they're not so different. Each leads a life of quiet desperation. Each feels at the end of the rope. Each hungers for a way out: Ray from under the mess he's in; Tanya from the treadmill she's on. They also fit the classic addict mold of using sex to fill the void they feel inside. Even though Payne didn't conceive these characters, he could have. They resonate with his universe of flawed, disaffected souls in search of, if not love, then attention, affirmation.

It is a Paynesian world all right and he could have easily made *Hung* a comfortable, ongoing gig. "They wanted me very much to direct as many episodes as I wanted," he said. But, he added, "Doing the pilot was enough for me."

Development hell

The last thing he wanted was getting stuck on a show that delayed his return to features anymore. Not when he's close to finally sealing the deal on *Downsizing*, the epic comedy with sci-fi trappings whose script he and Taylor have labored over for three years.

Several factors contributed to *Downsizing*'s protracted development. There were the script-for-hire projects Payne and Taylor did and the films Payne produced. The fact the filmmakers live on separate coasts means they can't always get together and write when they'd like. Then there's the mind-numbing process of inking a deal. "I am in that hideous process of trying to find financing for it. It has to do with casting, it has to do with a lot of stuff. These things always take a little longer than you think. I'm working on it every day," he said eight weeks ago." Little had changed by mid-June except that the final draft was complete and he was anxious for a green light.

But the main problem with *Downsizing* has been accommodating its ambitious themes. "Without giving the concept away, the concept is so big that it's been difficult to tame the idea into a manageable size," said Payne. "Feature filmmaking is frustrating a little bit in that you have to keep a two-hour limit in mind. You can't add on to the world of the story you're telling like you can in a novel or in a mini-series. Filmmaking is a search for economy, so you're always finding ways to tell more story in less time. That's why the script is as concentrated as possible.

"It's just been a challenge because there are two stories at work in the script: one is the story of the world and the other is the story of our lead character (reportedly Paul Giamatti's part but Payne won't confirm). To tell both of those stories responsibly, in a way I as an audience member would be satisfied, and then have it all wrap up in a manageable, directable length, within a certain budget . . . "

Ironically, in a film about scale, Payne's agonized over cutting it down to size. He refuses to be constrained by "the burden of making it like this or that. Like any film, I want it to be what it wants to be," he said. That means "taking artistic risks."

The high concept behind it will require visual effects, and the sprawling story it tells will necessitate a four-month shoot, making the film a big-budget undertaking, at least by his standards. That's why securing financing has been a struggle. Well, that and the rather odd hook the story hangs on. "It's about the idea of people miniaturizing as a panacea to the world's ills. It's a comedy with that premise but that takes that idea very seriously, like that it actually happens and what might be a consequence of that," he said.

He discussed the social-political issues that are its context. "Overpopulation is our single greatest problem," he said. "So many things stem from that—famine, disease, war, climate change, over-fishing the seas, cutting down the rain forests. They say this planet is sustainable for about one hundred million people, and we've long passed that. So, long term, what are we going to do? Start slaughtering? Or let war, famine, natural disasters do that for us? Or colonize other planets? Or what if we just reduce our mass and volume?" he said, laughing. "So I've said too much."

If things go to plan he'll do pre-production in the summer-fall and start shooting after the first of the year. About a third of the film would be Nebraska-based. If there's a hang-up, he has a backup project ready:

Nebraska, a father-son road pic he "can jump into." *Downsizing* "is by far my priority," he said. "But *Nebraska* would be a very attractive film to make at any time. I'm just ready to shoot."

Looking ahead

Until cameras roll his next public gig here will be the September 13 Film Streams fundraiser, A Conversation with Debra Winger. He'll interview the actress on stage at the Holland per the Laura Dern program he did last year. Payne's a Film Streams board member.

He admires the mercurial Winger. "I think Debra Winger is so interesting. Meryl Streep–like early on. Like, wow, is there nothing she cannot play and bring such emotional depth to? And then the fact she's disappeared from movies, so there's a mystique about her. She rarely does this kind of stuff, like never, and so when I called her up the first thing I said was, 'You will not get an award and you are not being honored. It's a retrospective of your films at a very serious film place.'"

To sweeten the pot, she will select films from her career along with two that have inspired her. The idea of Payne having her back on stage helped. He assured her their conversation will not be personal "but just about film nerd stuff." "We're really excited to have her," he said.

Film nerds are excited Payne's back too.

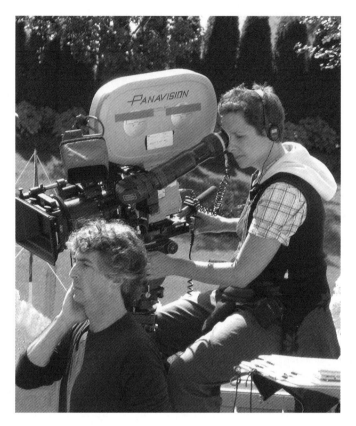

Payne and cinematographer Uta Briesewitz in a Michigan suburb on the set of *Hung*. The filmmaker is at once methodically deliberate and wide open to serendipity when approaching a shot, and thus he's equally prepared to stick to his preconceived ideas or to be struck by inspiration in the moment.

5

Payne as Auteur and Collaborator

Introduction

The much discussed auteur theory is helpful in some respects and not so helpful in others. I believe there are filmmakers whose body of work clearly establishes them as the primary authorial voice of their films, complete with revisiting personal themes, motifs, and stylistic flourishes that only they as the director or writer-director could insert from project to project.

But taking the auteur notion too far can unfairly negate or diminish the undeniably vital roles of many collaborators whose contributions are essential pieces in the whole. Film is perhaps the most collaborative of mediums. Making the case for a director, or even a writer-director like Alexander Payne, as an auteur is a valid exercise but caution is advised so as not to distort the facts.

Yes, any reasoned, careful examination of Payne's work would lead one to conclude he is most definitely an auteur. Count me among that camp. As many of the stories included in this compilation note, he is a filmmaker with a distinctive satiric tone as evidenced in words, visuals, protagonist types, dramatic situations, and, when you come right down to it, every facet of his work.

However, and this is where the auteur theory tends to fall short, he has also collaborated with screenwriter Jim Taylor on four of his five features. That means, if a shared writing credit means anything, Payne and Taylor are demonstrably and unarguably the co-authors of those four films. No one, including the screenwriters themselves, would be able to extract what one or the other wrote—so enmeshed are they and their work.

Furthermore, all but one of those films was also adapted from a book. More recently, Payne wrote *The Descendants* "alone." But it should be noted he worked from the Kaui Hart Hemmings novel of the same name and rewrote an earlier screenplay by Jim Rash and Nat Faxon, with whom he shared screen credit and the Oscar.

But when all is said and done, Payne and only Payne directed *Citizen Ruth, Election, About Schmidt, Sideways, The Descendants* and *Nebraska*. As I quote him in one of my articles, though I am paraphrasing here, the director is the only person on a movie who at any given time has the whole story in his head and therefore knows precisely what is needed in a scene in order to best realize it in context with the scenes that precede and follow it.

What's more, Payne is a fully hands-on presence with editor Kevin Tent during the edit phase. That has been true on all of his features. Additionally, he has kept final cut on each. And while it is true that Payne or anyone else for that matter cannot make a multi-million-dollar film without the assistance of many others, his authorial voice and eye are enhanced by the company of collaborators he gathers about him over and over again.

The very fact he works repeatedly with assistant director George Parra, art director Jane Stewart, cinematographer Phedon Papamichael (the late Jim Glennon lensed Payne's first three pics), Tent, and composer Rolfe Kent helps him realize his vision because they are of one mind. It is no different than how John Ford, Alfred Hitchcock, Francis Ford Coppola, Steven Spielberg, and Martin Scorsese worked time and again with their own company of collaborators.

Even though Payne did not partner with Taylor on two of his last films, *The Descendants* and *Nebraska*, there is no doubting their collaboration is, other than the one he enjoys with Kevin Tent and Phedon Papamichael, the most significant in his career. Taylor and Payne co-authored the newest film directed by Payne, *Downsizing*. For anyone interested in how these two screenwriters approach working together, this next story is a must-read. They also talk some about the art of adaptation.

In a later story Payne and actress Laura Dern talk about their working together on *Citizen Ruth*. Other stories shed light on some of the filmmaker's cinema passions, including his admiration for film artists Debra Winger and Steven Soderbergh, two figures he brought to Omaha as part of his hands-on involvement with the Film Streams art cinema. You will also read about his efforts to sway Nebraska legislators to pass a film tax credits bill. His interest in growing the cinema culture in Nebraska is sincere. He grew up at a time when there was no equivalent model to himself today, which is to say there was no home-grown filmmaker shooting studio pictures in the state.

Omaha native Joan Micklin Silver was busy making her own sublime satires (*Hester Street, Between the Lines, Chilly Scenes of Winter, Crossing Delancey*), only back East, not anywhere near where a young film fanatic like Payne could see up close for himself that it was indeed possible for a Nebraskan to realize that dream.

Hollywood films have only sporadically shot there. Until Payne began making movies here the two biggest film ripples in these parts came when *Terms of Endearment* and *The Day After* shot in Nebraska. Payne was already off at college when they happened. Later, Sean Penn shot *The Indian Runner* in Nebraska and *To Wong Foo* principally filmed there, but by then Payne was actively engaged in developing his own feature projects.

He has single-handedly increased the state's features profile with his own projects, but even as much as he wants to film in Nebraska again, the lack of incentives (tax credits) offered to the film industry makes it increasingly difficult for him to justify shooting here. Should push ever come to shove and force a film he wants to make in Nebraska elsewhere, it would be an incalculable loss for Nebraskans. Locals could be employed on his productions, thus gaining valuable experience and exposure to the workings of feature films, not to mention the inspiration that aspiring or emerging filmmakers could be drawing on.

When Payne made his first three features in Omaha, he served as the very model he did not have years before. Talk to any young filmmaker in the state and he or she will credit Payne's success and his work in state as inspirational. Omaha native Nik Fackler, whose *Lovely, Still* (2008) starring Martin Landau and Ellen Burstyn was entirely filmed in the city, is among those filmmakers from Omaha who readily acknowledge Payne's impact.

Payne grew up at a time when there was no dedicated art cinema in Omaha. The presence of Film Streams, which opened in 2008, has been embraced by the filmmaker. He serves on its board in a quite active capacity. He uses his clout and connections to bring in film artists who otherwise would not come there. Now that he is in the position he occupies, he is reaching out to notable Nebraskans in Film to celebrate their ties to this place. He was responsible for bringing Jane Fonda to Omaha. He's working hard to convince Joan Micklin Silver to come for a tribute program.

Silver left Omaha at age eighteen but she still has family in town, and this is where her cinema stirrings were first fired. She has graciously given this reporter several interviews over the years. A Film Streams program with her and Payne would reconnect me with my two most enduring cinema subjects.

Though Jane Fonda is not a Nebraska native, she and her brother Peter spent considerable time in Omaha while growing up, often staying summers with their Aunt Harriett. Their late father, the great American actor Henry Fonda, most certainly was a born and bred Nebraskan. What's more, Henry Fonda retained deep bonds to the state. He got his start in theater at the Omaha Community Playhouse, and he, along with another famous Playhouse alum, Dorothy McGuire, repeatedly lent their names and talents to aiding the theater.

Notably, in 1955 the two superstars played the leads in an Omaha benefit production of *The Country Girl* whose proceeds helped fund the construction of a new Playhouse facility. Henry's then-teenaged daughter, Jane, played a suitable ingénue role in what was perhaps her first professional-level acting appearance.

Nearly three decades later Jane appeared in Omaha at the gala Midwest premiere of *On Golden Pond*, the film that she acted in so memorably alongside her ailing father and the great Katharine Hepburn. Fonda's screen actor brother, Peter, went to college in Omaha, where he performed in both student theater and Playhouse productions, and he has been known to make impromptu visits to commune with the Playhouse spirit of his father.

Payne's 2012 *Inside the Actors Studio*–like interview of Jane Fonda at the Holland Performing Arts Center in Omaha attracted a sell-out crowd. The programs raised funds for Film Streams.

He appreciates the reverberations he feels with these peer artists and he is generous enough to share their artistry with his fellow Nebraskans. As noted earlier, this state has produced a rich cinema legacy in terms of the talents who have come out of this place, but in my estimation it has done a very poor job of celebrating these figures and their contributions.

Other than occasional nods to these folks by the Playhouse, the Mary Riepma Ross Media Arts Center, and the Omaha Film Festival, precious little has been done to recognize them. I appreciate Payne taking the lead in this regard. He is doing everything he can to put Nebraska on the cinema map as a relevant film location and as a film friendly environment. He is also extending the welcome mat to fellow Nebraskans in Film and helping give them the home-cooked esteem they deserve.

My secret wish is that Payne bring Omaha native Nick Nolte back home for a program. It may be the only way I get to interview the actor.

Jim Taylor, the other half of Hollywood's top screenwriting team, talks about his work with Alexander Payne

Published in a 2005 issue of *The Reader*

Alchemy

There's an alchemy to the virtuoso writing partnership of Alexander Payne and Jim Taylor, Oscar winners for *Sideways* (2004) and previous nominees for *Election* (1999), that resists pat analysis. The artists themselves are unsure what makes their union work beyond compatibility, mutual regard, and an abiding reverence for cinema art.

Together fifteen years now, their professional marriage has been a steady ascent amid the starts and stops endemic to filmmaking. As their careers have evolved, they've emerged as perhaps the industry's most respected screenwriting tandem, often drawing comparisons to great pairings of the past. As the director of their scripts, Payne grabs the lion's share of attention, although their greatest triumph, *Sideways*, proved "a rite of passage" for each, Taylor said, by virtue of their Oscars.

Taylor doesn't mind that Payne, the auteur, has more fame. "He pays a price for that. I'm not envious of all the interviews he has to do and the fact his face is recognized more. Everywhere he goes people want something from him. That level of celebrity I'm not really interested in," he said by phone from the New York home he shares with filmmaker wife Tamara Jenkins (*The Slums of Beverly Hills*).

With the craziness of *Sideways* now subsided and Payne due to return soon from a month-long sojourn in Paris, where he shot a vignette for the *Paris, I Love You* omnibus film, he and Taylor will once again engage their joint muse. So far, they're being coy about what they've fixed as their next project. It may be the political, Altmanesque story they've hinted at. Or something entirely else. What is certain is that a much-anticipated new Payne-Taylor creation will be in genesis.

Taylor's an enigma in the public eye, but he is irreducibly, inescapably one half of a premier writing team that shows no signs of running dry or splitting up. His insights into how they approach the work offer a vital glimpse into their process, which is a kind of literary jam session, game of charades, and excuse for hanging out all in one. They say by the time a script's finished, they're not even sure who's done what. That makes sense when you consider how they fashion a screenplay—throwing out ideas over days and weeks at a time in hours-long give-and-take riffs that sometimes have them sharing the same computer monitor hooked up to two keyboards.

Process and ritual

Their usual M.O. finds them talking, on and on, about actions, conflicts, motivations, and situations, acting out or channeling bits of dialogue, and taking turns giving these elements form and life on paper.

"After we've talked about something, one of us will say, 'Let me take a crack at this,' and then he'll write a few pages. Looking at it, the other might say, 'Let me try this.' Sometimes, the person on the keyboard is not doing the creative work. They're almost inputting what the other person is saying. It's probably a lot like the way Alexander works with his editor (Kevin Tent), except we're switching back and forth being the editor."

For each writer, the litmus test of any scene is its authenticity. They abhor anything that rings false. Their constant rewrites are all about getting to the truth of what a given character would do next. Avoiding cliches and formulas and feel-good plot points, they serve up multi-shaded figures as unpredictable as real people, which means they're not always likable.

"I think it's true of all the characters we write that there's this mixture of things in people. Straight-ahead heroes are just really boring to us because they don't really exist," said Taylor, whose major influences include the humanist Czech films of the 1960s. "I think once we fall in love with the characters, then it's really just about the characters for us. We have the best time writing when the characters are leading us somewhere and we're not so much trying to write about some theme."

Sideways's über scene, when Miles and Maya express their longing for each other via their passion for the grape, arose organically. "We didn't labor any longer over that scene than others," he said. "What happened was, in our early drafts we had expanded on a speech Miles has in the book (Rex Pickett's novel) and in later drafts we realized Maya should have her own speech. At the time we wrote those speeches we had no idea how important they would turn out to be. It was instinctive choice to include them, not something calculated to fill a gap in a schematic design."

He said their scripts are in such "good shape" by the time cameras roll that little or no rewriting is done on set. "Usually we'll make some minor changes after the table reading that happens right before shooting." Taylor said Payne asks his advice on casting, locations, various cuts, music, et cetera.

Their process assumes new colors when hired for a script-doctor job (*Meet the Parents, Jurassic Park III*), the latest being *I Now Pronounce You Chuck & Larry*.

"With those projects we're trying to accommodate the needs of a different director and we generally don't have much time, so we don't allow problems to linger as long as we would, which is good practice," said Taylor. "It's good for us to have to work fast. We'll power through stuff, where we might let it sit longer and just let ourselves be stuck."

Serving the script

Ego suppression explains in part how they avoid any big blow-ups. "I think it's because both of us are interested in making a good movie more than having our own ideas validated," Taylor said. "So we are able to, hopefully, set our egos aside when we're working and say, 'Oh, that's a good idea,' or 'That's a better idea.' I think a lot of writing teams split up because they're too concerned about protecting what they did as opposed to remembering what's good for the script. We can work out disagreements without having any fallout from it. It's funny. I mean, sometimes we do act like a married couple. There's negotiations to be made. But mostly we just get along and enjoy working together."

As conjurers in the idiom of comedy, he said, "I think our shared sensibilities are similar enough that if I can make him laugh or he can make me laugh, then we feel like we're on the right track."

Collaboration is nothing new for Taylor, a Pomona College and New York University Tisch School of the Arts grad, who's directed a short as well as second-unit work on Payne shoots (most of the 16 millimeter footage in *Election*) and is developing feature scripts for himself to direct.

"For me, I didn't set out to be a screenwriter, I set out to be a filmmaker," said Taylor, a former Cannon Films grunt and assistant to director Ivan Passer (*Cutter's Way*). So did Alexander. And we kind of think of it all as one process, along with editing . . . . People say everything is writing. Editing is writing and in a strange way acting is writing, and all that. Filmmaking itself is a collaborative medium. People drawn to filmmaking are drawn to working with other people. Sure, a lot of screenwriters do hole up somewhere so they're not disturbed, but I'm not like that and Alexander's not like that. I don't like working on my own. I like to bounce ideas off people. Filmmaking demands it, as opposed to being a novelist or a painter, who work in forms that aren't necessarily collaborative."

One is a lonely number

Simpatico as they are, there's also a pragmatic reason for pairing up. "We just don't like doing it alone and it's less productive, too. And we sort of have similar ideas, so why not do it together? Even beyond that, it's like a quantum leap in creativity. You're just sort of inspired more to come up with something than if you're just sitting there and hating what you're doing. At least there's somebody there going, 'Oh, that's good,' or 'How do we do this?' And you sort of stick with the problem as opposed to going off and cleaning out a drawer or something."

Payne said scripting with someone else makes the writing process "less hideous." For Taylor, flying solo is something to be avoided at all costs.

"I hate it. I really hate it. I mean, I do it, but it's very slow and I don't think it's as good," he said. "I'm getting Alexander's input on something I've been working on for a long, long time on my own, a screenplay called *The Lost Cause* about a Civil War reenactor, and I expect it to became fifty percent better just because of working with him. We'll essentially do with it what we do on a production rewrite."

Lost Cause was part of a "blind deal" Taylor had with Paramount's Scott Rudin, now at Disney. The fate of Taylor's deal is unclear.

Writing with his other half, Taylor said, opens a script to new possibilities. "I'll see it through different eyes when I'm sitting next to Alexander and maybe have ideas I wouldn't otherwise."

The pair's operated like this since their first gig, co-writing short films for cable's *Playboy: Inside Out* series. The friends and one-time roommates have been linked ever since. "It's pretty hard to extract the friendship from the partnership or vice versa. It's all kind of parts of the same thing. We don't end up seeing each other that much because we live in separate cities, unless we're working together," Taylor said. "So our friendship is a little bit dependent on our work life at this point, which is too bad." However, he added there's an upside to not being together all the time in the intense way collaborators interact, "It's important to not get too overdosed on who you're working with."

He can't imagine them going their separate ways unless there's a serious falling out. "That would only happen if we had personal problems with each other. Sometimes, people naturally drift apart, and we're both working against that. We're trying to make sure that it doesn't just drift away, because that would be sad."

Keeping the alliance alive is complicated by living on opposite coasts and the demands of individual lives/careers. But when Taylor talks about going off one day to make his own movies, he means temporarily. He knows Payne has his back. "He's supportive of my wanting to direct. But I'm so happy working with him that if that were all my career was, I'd be a very lucky person."

Jim Taylor, Jim Burke, Alexander Payne accepting
Best Motion Picture of the Year Award for *The
Descendants* at the Golden Globes Awards in 2012

Film currents

The next two entries are not about Alexander Payne per se; rather, they are glimpses of his film passions and predilections. Among the ways he takes an active hand in things as a Film Streams board member is by programming an occasional repertory series there. In fact, he was the guest programmer for that cinema's inaugural repertory series in 2007 and what follows is a compilation of musings by Payne, myself, and others on the international slate he picked.

Another series he had much input into was one celebrating the New Hollywood that emerged in the late 1960s and early 1970s, the very period of filmmaking that most influenced him. In interview after interview he has mentioned how he aspires to make films that capture the humanist spirit of that era's films. Included here is a story I did about a Film Streams series centering on American cinema from that decade, and some of his insights into what made those works so resonant for him and others.

A further indication that his involvement in Film Streams is far more than cosmetic is the role he plays in its annual film event fund raiser. He has personally invited and arranged for Laura Dern, Debra Winger, Steven Soderbergh, and Jane Fonda to be special guests at these *Inside the Actors Studio* programs. He interviewed Dern, Winger, and Fonda on stage. Author and journalist Kurt Andersen, another Omaha native and Film Streams advisory board member, interviewed Soderbergh. My stories about these programs are included here.

Of Nebraska's many film luminaries Payne is among the few to have retained a strong connection to this place. Robert Taylor, Henry Fonda, and Dorothy McGuire did. Lew Hunter, Marg Helgenberger, Gabrielle Union and Yolonda Ross do. Now retired Oscar-winning editor Mike Hill never left. Oscar-winning cinematographer Mauro Fiore has remained even after the phenomenon known as *Avatar*. Payne has taken it to a new level by principally filming the majority of his films in Nebraska, including, as you will read later, his masterpiece *Nebraska*. Payne has taken it to a new level by filming three of his five features here. *Nebraska* makes it four out of six. His newest, *Downsizing*, was only partially filmed in Omaha. His Film Streams support is unwavering.

He has also played the role of advocate and activist by testifying before Nebraska state senators on the need for film tax credits to be adopted by the state. He has told legislators in no uncertain terms that the only way to grow production in the state is to sweeten the pot, so to speak. At various points he applied what leverage he has to the incentives debate by suggesting what a pity it would be if he had to film his project *Nebraska* in, say, Kansas or Oklahoma should push come to shove and investors insist it be made where incentives are offered. Enough lawmakers finally listened that the Legislature advanced and passed an incentives bill during the 2012 legislative session.

Then there is his visible support for community anchors. Besides Film Streams, he has thrown his weight behind the Holland Performing Arts Center, the Blue Barn Theatre, the Omaha Community Playhouse, the Mary Riepma Ross Media Arts Center in Lincoln, the Midwest Theater in Scottsbluff, and the World Theatre in Kearney. Though his portrayals of Omaha and greater Nebraska have often not been flattering, his devotion to his roots makes him a popular, even beloved figure. It is a love affair sure to continue.

Film Streams Founder and Director Rachel Jacobson, Laura Dern, Jane Fonda, Alexander Payne, Jane Fonda's son Troy Garrity. (photo credit: www.JaneFonda.com)

Film Streams Ruth Sokolof Theater, Omaha

Alexander Payne's 2007 curated World Cinema Series

The Seven Samurai
1954, Japan (dir. Akira Kurosawa, 207 mins. Japanese, English subtitles)

PAYNE: "Japanese director Akira Kurosawa's grandly entertaining historical epic is an achievement like climbing Mt. Everest. My vote for the best movie ever made."

Sweeping action and intimate emotion are captured in a dynamic story that thrusts viewers right into the volatile mix on screen. In this prime example of kinetic cinema the actors and camera seem in constant motion—the action driving the story inexorably forward.

If you've never seen a Kurosawa film, Samurai's a good start. His ability to layer the screen with detail is evident in every frame. Note the 16th-century Japanese village. Its residents hire a band of seven itinerant samurai to protect them from marauding bandits. Note too the intricate fortifications the samurai build. With the battle lines drawn, two opposing forces clash. Kurosawa finds the most telling ways to depict the action. It's take-your-breath-away stuff.

What's sometimes lost amid the visual mastery is what a great storyteller he is. He dramatizes the classic stand off with not only great physical direction but well delineated characters that inform and enrich the conflict. So influential was the film that its reverberations are seen in *Rio Bravo, The Dirty Dozen, The Wild Bunch, The Thing* (1982), et cetera. John Sturges based all of *The Magnificent Seven* on it.

Kurosawa's frequent collaborator, Toshiro Mifune, heads the cast.

Viridiana
1961, Spain (dir. Luis Buñuel, 91 mins. Spanish, English subtitles)

PAYNE: "A deeply subversive, clear-eyed, brutal, compassionate, thrilling, obscene masterpiece from the great Spanish director Luis Buñuel."

Provocateur Buñuel delighted in offending the official, sanctimonious piety of his native Spain, filling his films with religious, sexual, violent themes certain to outrage the largely Catholic conservative majority. *Viridiana* is no exception. Any façade of decency is stripped away to reveal his dark vision of humanity. Anything smacking of moral authority is exposed as hypocrisy or fantasy or madness.

When we meet the title character played by Silvia Pinal, she's a demure, novice nun so devout she wears a crown of thorns and sleeps in the shadow of a life-sized crucifix. That makes her a perfect foil for Buñuel who, characteristically, has her transvestite uncle Don Jaime (Fernando Rey) defile her.

She tries to repent by saving the souls of beggars, but they have sex not salvation on their minds. As things get out of hand, *Viridiana* gives in to her own base desires. Long a target of censors who branded his work indecent and blasphemous, Buñuel seems to say repression begets its own punishment.

Room at the Top
1959, U.K. (dir. Jack Clayton, 115 mins.)

PAYNE: "Worth seeing just for French actress Simone Signoret's Oscar-winning performance, it's a powerhouse British tragedy about class, money and power, and how sex, which is used to get them, traps the user."

This is an example from Great Britain's cinematic New Wave of the late '50s and early '60s. The movement parted company with the studio-bound, genre-based artifice of the first half of the 20th century for more naturalistic dramas inspired by the era's angry-young-man/kitchen-sink plays and novels. Adapted by Neil Paterson and Mordecai Richler from John Braine's novel, *Room* stars Laurence Harvey as Joe, a young opportunist and misogynist whose boorish behavior crosses class lines.

Always looking for a new conquest and perhaps an entree to high society, Joe pursues Susan (Heather Sears), the young daughter of a local industrialist. The disapproving father sends Susan abroad, whereupon Joe takes up with the older, unhappily married Alice (Simone Signoret), who falls hard for him. When Susan returns, Joe seduces her. The father tries buying Joe off, but can't. Marriage is broached. Joe's then forced to choose between his mistress and his fiancé and to deal with the consequences that result. It all plays out in a realistic manner aided by Freddie Francis's black-and-white photography.

Clayton went on to direct the 1961 masterpiece *The Innocents*.

La Notte

1961, Italy (dir. Michelangelo Antonioni, 122 mins. Italian, English subtitles)

PAYNE: "Marcello Mastroianni stars in Michelangelo Antonioni's look at the breakup of a marriage over a single night during which the couple attend a party. A challenging, rewarding, mysterious film."

The cinema of dissolution-dissipation is the province of Antonioni, whose existential characters drift in a perpetual state of alienation and melancholia. The difficulty of finding meaningful human connections in the modern industrialized world is one of many themes in his work that surface in *La Notte (The Night)*.

Giovanni (Mastroianni) is a noted author. Lydia (Jeanne Moreau) is his wife. When we meet the couple they are diffident to each other, looking to others to assuage whatever hurt they carry. Their strained relationship is not explained, only offered as a symptom of the barren times. These two metaphorically lost individuals wander from place to place, their sense of detachment and isolation expressed in the empty streets and situations they find themselves in.

La Notte is part of a trilogy of films, with *L'Avventura* and *L'Eclisse*, in which Antonioni examines the despair of failed human relations. It's also part of an Italian New Wave in the '60s that marked a departure from the neo-realism of that nation's cinema in the immediate post-war years to a more impressionistic style.

Modern Times

1936, USA (dir. Charlie Chaplin, 87 mins.)

PAYNE: "The miracle of cinema is the miracle of Chaplin, and for personal reasons this consistently hilarious satire of the machine age is my favorite."

The dehumanizing effects of mechanization run amok are fodder for serious exposé and humorous send up in *Modern Times*. It's Charlie Chaplin's most visually striking and imaginative film. No doubt influenced by the Sinclair Lewis muckraking classic book, *The Jungle*, and Fritz Lang's cautionary futurist film, *Metropolis*, Chaplin's vision suggests the Everyman embodied in his Tramp character is in danger of becoming an assembly-line cog or slave in the machinery of corporate society. The only way to assert one's individuality is not to conform to the state-mandated mold.

As in most of his narratives (*The Gold Rush, City Lights*), a sentimental love story is interwoven with the action, which pits the

Tramp against The System. His struggle is expressed in pantomime and slapstick executed with grace and ingenuity. Physical comedy as sublime art. Part of the joy of *Modern Times* is discovering an appreciation for "silent" film language. Released nearly a decade after the advent of sound pics, this film proved the swan song for silents. Chaplin was Hollywood's last superstar holdout. Following the film he relented to changing tastes and made his last four films talkies. None approached his early work.

His *Modern Times* co-star, Paulette Goddard, was his lover and future wife.

McCabe & Mrs. Miller

1971, USA (dir. Robert Altman, 120 mins.)

PAYNE: "Warren Beatty and Julie Christie in Robert Altman's great, mysterious Western about the opening of a brothel in a Northwest boom town. A landmark film in its use of cinematography and sound for mood and texture."

Altman loved reinterpreting genres. Just as he took a fresh approach to the war film in *M*A*S*H*, the private-eye flick in *The Long Goodbye*, the buddy pic in *California Split*, the historical bio in *Vincent and Theo*, and film noir in *The Player*, he imploded the Western here. The story focuses on the mislaid fortunes of professional gambler, cum entrepreneur John McCabe (Beatty) and madam/opium addict Mrs. Miller (Christie) in the Northwest frontier mining town of Presbyterian Church. He's a dreamer, she's a cynic.

Within this familiar template Altman examines old themes in new ways: from the individual squashed by the corporate syndicate to the exploitation implicit in male-female relations. Trouble looms when the stubborn McCabe decides to fight the-powers-that-be. In the end his only ally sees their relationship not as a romance but as a business proposition. He is expendable.

Never before *McCabe* and not again until *Deadwood* did the Old West look as gritty, grimy and in progress as it does here. Much of that is due to Vilmos Zsigmond's cinematography, Leon Ericksen's production design, and Philip Thomas's art direction. Everything seems up for grabs. In reality, big money interests control what the future holds. The stakeholders in this Manifest Destiny brook no opposition. Altman, Beatty, and Brian McCay adapted the story from Edmund Naughton's novel.

The Wild Bunch

1969, USA (dir. Sam Peckinpah, 145 mins.)

PAYNE: "Film Critic Pauline Kael said it best—'Pouring new wine into the bottle of the Western, (director) Sam Peckinpah exploded the bottle.' Staggeringly well-crafted movie about aging outlaws in 1913 Mexico."

Crazy cinema poet Peckinpah made two Western epics. *Major Dundee* is a sprawling work of post–Civil War tensions and Indian War exploits that doesn't quite jell as a cohesive drama. His fights with the studio on the project didn't help. He lost final cut. *The Wild Bunch* is a bleak, violent, fully realized fever dream about a band of merciless outlaws on their last legs in an Old West fast giving way to civilization.

Pursued by mercenaries every bit as cutthroat as they, the gang seek refuge in Mexico, where they make a last stand. Everything in the film is finely nuanced—from the brutal carnage to the native rituals to the stark landscape to the archetypal characters and their world-weary speeches to the filtered lighting, ironic musical score, and dynamic photography/editing.

Consistent with Peckinpah's other great films (*Ride the High Country, The Ballad of Cable Hogue, Pat Garrett and Billy the Kid*), *Bunch* is a lyrical ballad that for all its violence and mendacity renders a tender human portrait of loss. The work is an odd blend of romanticism and realism, as it at once celebrates the misfit-rebel and rues the passing of a communal way of life. In the end, Peckinpah sides with the wild bunch, even as he acknowledges that resisting change exacts a heavy cost.

The Last Detail

1973, USA (dir. Hal Ashby, 103 mins.)

PAYNE: "Hal Ashby's uproarious, bittersweet, beautiful story about two Navy lifers ordered to take a childlike, oafish sailer to the brig. A film I watch about twice a year, and my favorite Jack Nicholson performance."

Profanity gets raised to high art in this road pic adapted by Robert Towne from the Darryl Ponicsan book. Lifers "Badass" Buddusky (Nicholson) and "Mule" Mulhall (Otis Young) inherit the shit detail of escorting the naïve Meadows (Randy Quaid) to prison. En route, the escorts snub their nose at authority by showing the kid a good time.

As the rite of passage plays out, a bond forms.

With the sodden weekend drawing to a close, the reality awaiting Meadows sinks in and he tests his guards' loyalty. The end is a cynical comment on brotherhood.

Nicholson manages to be naturalistic and over the top at the same time. *Detail* has an as-if-it-were-happening-for-the-first-time spontaneity that distinguishes '70s pics. Funny, vulgar, real, Detail seems as fresh and raw today as it did thirty years ago.

Detail was among four strong films by Ashby, a former film editor, that helped define the '70s vital cinema—*Harold and Maude, Bound for Glory, Coming Home.*

8 1/2

1963, Italy (dir. Federico Fellini, 138 mins. Italian, English subtitles)

PAYNE: "Italian director Federico Fellini's self-portrait never fails to astonish with its technical virtuosity, imagination, and honesty. My other vote for best movie ever made. With Marcello Mastroianni."

The self-reflexive impulse of the artist is embodied in the character of a film director, played by Mastroianni, who's really a stand-in for Fellini. *8 1/2* came in the throes of Fellini's own struggle to follow up the hit *La Dolce Vita*. The striking imagery, enhanced by high-contrast black and white, is full of symbology, flights of fancy, archetypal faces, and self-referential bits.

8 1/2 is much-admired by directors, who see in it an auteur's personal expression of and meditation on the art and business of moviemaking. Fellini is their hero, as he insisted on following an idiosyncratic vision uncompromised by studios, critics, or audiences. *8 1/2* is his manifesto and therefore a kind of creed for all filmmakers.

Any examination of the internal and external landscape of art after 1963 must acknowledge *8 1/2*. Bob Fosse's *All that Jazz*, Woody Allen's *Stardust Memories*, and Richard Rush's *The Stunt Man* are just some of the films that pay homage to it.

To Be or Not to Be

1942, USA (dir. Ernst Lubitsch, 99 mins.)

PAYNE: "One of the first American movies to deal with the Holocaust—and of course, like *The Great Dictator*, a comedy. From director Ernst Lubitsch, and starring never-better Jack Benny and Carole Lombard."

Farce turns poetry in this classic that works as light romance, screwball comedy, and biting social satire. In Nazi-occupied Warsaw a Polish troupe of Shakespearean players is pressed into espionage when its hammy lead actor Joseph Tura (Benny) is moved to action out of patriotism and jealousy.

A handsome young Polish flier, Sobinski (Robert Stack), needs help to complete a secret mission. Joseph, who suspects his wife Maria (Lombard) is having an affair with Sobinski, agrees. The company impersonate German officers and soldiers in an effort to thwart enemy plans. As the intrigue plays out in ever more complex ruses, Joseph keeps a wary eye on Maria.

The film was the last the luminous Lombard made before her death. Her ethereal yet earthy persona captivates. Benny strikes the right balance of insecure egomaniac and indignant nationalist with his signature slow burns and double takes. Like any great film, *To Be* has a never-to-be-recaptured magic, a maxim proven by the lame Mel Brooks remake. Lubitsch made a handful of masterpieces (*Trouble in Paradise, The Shop Around the Corner*) but this is arguably his best.

In this next story Payne shares some thoughts on the seminal decade of American film that more than any other shaped his aesthetic, but most of the analysis is my own.

A decade under the influence

Published in a 2009 issue of *The Reader*

A new Hollywood

By the dawn of the 1960s, the stagnant American cinema scene was due for a rude awakening and it got one. Only the real fallout wasn't felt until the 1970s, a decade regarded as the last Golden Age of U.S. filmmaking.

Celebrate the New Hollywood that emerged then by indulging in an eighteen-film, ten-week repertory series at Film Streams opening this week and running through December 24.

This country didn't invent the movies but the Hollywood Dream Machine's factory-like assembly approach raised the medium to the height of its commercial potential during the first half of the 20th century. Within the cold efficiency of that apparatus, great art was made alongside schlock. By the late '50s the studio contract system was dying. In response to television's inroads, studios turned to spectacle with sand-and-sandal epics, wide-screen photographic processes, and 3D gimmicks.

Genre pictures constituted Hollywood's staple fare, but in the counter-culture '60s the old reliable programmers—Westerns, musicals, film noirs, war stories—were increasingly out of favor with moviegoers and out-of-step with the times. As censorship boards and production codes produced a chilling effect on content, world cinema enjoyed greater freedom.

Hollywood filmmakers traditionally came up through the studio ranks or from the theater. A new breed began entering the picture. Sidney Lumet and Arthur Penn were among directors who earned their chops in live TV. They instilled a vibrant new energy in features. They were joined by directors from episodic TV—Sam Peckinpah, Robert Altman, William Friedkin—in forming a new creative corps.

Other artists, such as Peter Bogdanovich and Woody Allen, came from the worlds of film programming/criticism and comedy, respectively. Others, like Roman Polanski and Milos Forman, came from the New Wave in Europe.

The biggest sea change though came via film schools, which began popping up in the late '50s–early '60s. Film studies grads like Richard Rush, Francis Ford Coppola, George Lucas, Brian De Palma, and Martin Scorsese inched their way into the fringes of the studio system with low-budget indie projects. By the '70s, Steven Spielberg could gain entry to the game on the strength of his student work.

With studios struggling to maintain huge backlots, soundstages, and talent rosters, everyone became a freelancer for hire. The new model saw producers, directors, agents, and actors assemble projects for studio financing-distribution.

By the late '60s, studios reeled from big-budget pics that no longer resonated with audiences. Young studio-production heads replaced the old pioneering moguls. The suits began giving the reins to the new barbarians at the gate. A handful of films nobody expected much from changed the rules by making cinema relevant again and opening the door to new voices-visions.

Setting the stage for the "New Hollywood American '70s" revolution were seminal '60s films from America and abroad that touched a nerve with bold treatment of subject matter, reinvention of old genres, and use of racking focus and jump cuts.

Payne's perspective

"It was just a very, very special time coming on the heels of the breakthroughs of the late '60s," said filmmaker Alexander Payne, a Film Streams board member who often cites the films of the '70s as a major influence on his cinema sensibilities.

Dennis Hopper and Peter Fonda's little road picture about personal expression, *Easy Rider,* tapped the zeitgeist. Its success gave the keys to the palace to a brash new generation whose work spoke to audiences in more direct, mature ways. The best '70s films were marked by invention and liberation. Themes of alienation, paranoia, rebellion, and iconoclasm ran rampant. One original work followed another. A new realism tinged by humanism was born.

"Like many people it's one of my favorite decades of film, and it has special meaning to me personally and to people my age because I was a teenager in the '70s, and that's the decade that defined what I thought an American movie was," said Payne. "I graduated from high school in 1979 and all these movies now considered the great classics of '70s cinema, my buddies and I saw in theaters. I was very lucky to have seen them when I did."

The decade established a cadre of artists as the new vanguard, led by Coppola, Scorsese, Altman, Lumet, Penn, Malick, Polanski, Forman, Hal Ashby, Bob Rafelson, Alan Pakula, Richard Rush, Bob Fosse, John Cassavetes, John Schlesinger, Peter Yates, and John Boorman.

Old Hollywood veterans made great films then, too, notably John Huston. The age of the auteur took full force and directors gained unprecedented freedom, sometimes to the regret of studios (*Heaven's Gate*).

Payne said the '70s "has come to have this special meaning . . . where auteurism hit the modern vernacular, where you could say bad words and have nudity. And you had a lot of heavy stuff coming down in the country. And the costs weren't as exorbitant as they are now," he said wistfully.

The Film Streams series represents a key chapter in American movies. Seventies personal filmmaking bridged the fall of the old studio system and the rise of the special effects-laden, super-sized, franchised blockbuster era. Many cineastes wish for a return to that decade's intimate, idiosyncratic storytelling, which we glimpse today with films like *Little Miss Sunshine*, *Juno*, and *In the Valley of Elah*.

Payne said the series' "extremely impressive lineup includes one of my favorite neglected films, *The Landlord*, Hal Ashby's first film as a director." He said the series is sure to offer fellow film buffs some "new gems to be discovered."

The series (each title has a one-week run):

Easy Rider (Dir. Dennis Hopper, 1969)
Raging Bull (Dir. Martin Scorsese, 1980)
Chinatown (Dir. Roman Polanski, 1974)
The Landlord (Dir. Hal Ashby, 1970)
The Exorcist (Dir. William Friedkin, 1973)
Gimme Shelter (Dir. Albert Maysles, David Maysles, Charlotte Zwerin, 1970)
The Long Goodbye (Dir. Robert Altman, 1973)
Nashville (Dir. Robert Altman, 1975)
Apocalypse Now (Dir. Francis Ford Coppola, 1979)
Taxi Driver (Dir. Martin Scorsese, 1976)
Five Easy Pieces (Dir. Bob Rafelson, 1970)
The Last Picture Show (Dir. Peter Bogdanovich, 1971)
Dog Day Afternoon (Dir. Sidney Lumet, 1975)
Days of Heaven (Dir. Terrence Malick, 1978)
Sleeper (Dir. Woody Allen, 1973)
A New Leaf (Dir. Elaine May, 1971)
Shampoo (Dir. Hal Ashby, 1975)
The Parallax View (Dir. Alan J. Pakula, 1974)

Two film events Payne did his best James Lipton imitation for are the subjects of the following stories. For the first, he played interviewer with Laura Dern and for the second he did the same with Debra Winger.

Alexander Payne and the women in his films

It is ironic Payne has become so strongly identified as the satiric observer of middle-age male crisis when the protagonist of his first feature, *Citizen Ruth*, was a young woman undergoing an existential melt-down of her own. In the figure of Ruth Stoops, however, he portrays a perpetual loser and user whose crucible experience is thrust upon her by outside forces, though she ends up manipulating events and people just as surely as they manipulated her. She may be less shrewd than Payne's later protagonists, but, like them, when she senses her position threatened, no matter how unhinged or damaged her life is, she takes actions, right or wrong, to protect herself. It's human instinct.

A woman character of a very different sort was portrayed in Payne's second feature, *Election*. Reese Witherspoon stunningly captures Tracy Flick's obsessive-compulsive perfectionism and win-at-any-cost drive. Her character is the antithesis of Ruth Stoops. Both behave equally badly but Ruth is branded a social pariah and defect because she lacks the looks and charm and guile that Tracy possesses and uses to her advantage. When Tracy finally confronts an adult who sees through her and is therefore her nemesis, in the person of Jim McAllister (Matthew Broderick), she defends her territory and status with a zealousness that is frightening and hilarious to behold.

There have been no female lead characters in Payne's subsequent works about middle-aged men stumbling through mid-life angst. But upon review the women in *About Schmidt*, *Sideways*, and *The Descendants* all figure prominently if secondarily in the throes of the meltdowns the male protagonists undergo. In *Downsizing*, one female character betrays Matt Damon's Everyman Paul and another both challenges and inspires him

Jack Nicholson's buttoned-down Warren Schmidt is in a state of dispirited conformity under the thumb of his bossy wife (June Squibb).

When she suddenly dies, he is both set adrift and free. Though he may never fully reconcile the distance he feels from his distracted daughter (Hope Davis) and may never feel comfortable around her earthy mother-in-law (Kathy Bates) and may never connect with a woman again, he at last has the opportunity to be the man he felt he was meant to be. At the close of *About Schmidt* we sense Warren will never be at peace with himself or with another human being, but that he has grown some through his painful encounters with women.

In *Sideways* women are either anchors or sirens in The Odyssean sense. As Jack and Miles go off on their bacchanal in wine country, the former is running away to cheat on his unsuspecting bride-to-be, and the latter is stealing from his addled, overbearing mother and is paralyzed by anger and insecurity in the wake of his ex-wife dumping him for another man.

It is no surprise then that when these two emotional midgets in the bodies of men meet up with women and wine they behave badly. Sandra Oh's Stephanie is a free-spirited single working mom who has the misfortune or bad judgment to get sucked in by Jack. Virginia Madsen's Maya is perhaps the most mature female in all of Payne's films. She is smart, intuitive, and caring and though she is hurt by Miles, or more precisely by how Miles enabled Jack to betray her friend Stephanie, she is also wise and kind enough to give him a second chance.

By the end, Jack has left a trail of destruction en route to marrying his fiancé, with little hope he will remain faithful to her. Miles, meanwhile, has overcome his resentment and fear to connect with a woman again and perhaps to reopen a facet of life he no longer thought possible.

The central woman in *The Descendants* is for all practical purposes dead. Liz King (Patricia Hastie) lies in a coma and her husband Matt (George Clooney) and their kids try coping as best they can. Complicating matters are revelations of Liz having acted badly, and the fresh wounds caused by these revelations propel Matt and his kids on a search for answers and remedies. Matt's oldest daughter, Alexandra (Shailene Woodley) behaves true to how a very together yet still fragile teenager would in her position, which is to say impetuously one moment and adult the next.

In some ways the most intriguing woman in a Payne film thus far is Judy Speer, the wife of the man who had an affair with Liz King. As written by Payne and essayed by Judy Greer, she is that most unenviable figure of a woman who has been cheated on. Greer plays the part with a compelling mixture of broken heart, rage, bewilderment, and love.

When her philandering husband is too ashamed to visit Liz, Judy Speer steps up to do the right thing to pay her respects. But even in that moment, Payne and Greer veer from any pat happy resolution because they know that life does not offer such tidy clean-ups amid the mess of human failings and emotions.

Naturally, Speer feels a mix of sorrow and anger at Liz, and wants more than anything to vent at this woman who stole her man's affections. Matt won't allow it, though he does give himself permission to rage at Liz, alone, in private. At the end, with Liz gone and her ashes having been scattered in the ocean she loved, Matt and his two girls are getting on with their lives as a family, wrapped in the embrace of love and the quilt that covered Liz in the hospital. It is the most affectionate portrait of a nuclear family, albeit minus one, Payne has put on film.

There is no doubt though that his most concerted focus on a female character came in *Citizen Ruth*.Laura Dern gives one of her finest performances as the incorrigible Ruth Stoops, making her simultaneously unsympathetic and sympathetic by always playing the truth and never edging toward sentimentality or camp. No matter how absurd or weird things get, and they get plenty strange in the trajectory of the story, she remains grounded in Ruth's reality, even as warped as it may be. And that is precisely the point: Dern plays Ruth's reality without hesitation or hedge, therefore giving this derelict of a character and the crazy events that unfold around her an authenticity that another actor might have been tempted to dilute.

It's all in the writing, of course, and Dern and Payne made a great team in remaining faithful to the script when they might have felt entitled to soften things working with someone else. Neither artist offers an excuse or an apology for Ruth. She is who she is. They also do not glorify or negate her very bad decisions and behavior. We clearly see the consequences of her addictive, rootless life and can only look on as she brazenly defies being saved or made a symbol. At the end we are left feeling just as ambiguous about her as we were at the start. We admire her defiance but despair her destructive choices.

As you will read here, the actress and the filmmaker enjoyed a fruitful collaboration that will remain a highlight of each of their careers.

When it comes to Debra Winger, Payne has never worked with her, but it is not hard to imagine he might have and still could. He is an unabashed admirer of the feisty actress, whose brave choices and full-out commitment are very remindful of Laura Dern. Payne has expressed fascination for her leaving the business at the peak of her career and then only returning to it on her terms.

There is also a local connection involving Winger that gives Nebraskans, including Payne, a proprietary interest in her: when portions of the film *Terms of Endearment* were filmed in Nebraska, she and then-governor Bob Kerrey struck up a romance that lasted for more than a sound bite. The pair were never officially the First Couple of Nebraska, but for a brief time they gave this rather dull, ultra-conservative state a taste of our own Camelot.

When Laura met Alex: Laura Dern & Alexander Payne get deep about making *Citizen Ruth* and their shared cinema sensibilities

Published in a 2008 issue of *The Reader*

Alexander Payne and Laura Dern at the Holland Center

Citizen stirrings

When Alexander Payne and Laura Dern chat on the Holland Performing Arts Center main stage July 13 for Films Streams' first annual fundraiser, they'll naturally get around to *Citizen Ruth*. The 1996 abortion comedy he co-wrote with Jim Taylor marked Payne's directorial debut, and Dern's portrayal of title character Ruth Stoops earned her critical acclaim.

What the pair may or may not discuss is how pivotal their collaboration proved. Sixteen years ago Payne was still an aspiring feature filmmaker. His UCLA graduate thesis project from a few years before, *The Passion of Martin*, turned heads. The newcomer showed enough promise to land a studio development deal, analogous to a college baseball star getting drafted by a major league franchise, inking a fat contract, and getting assigned to the high minors.

But he hadn't broken through yet. He and Taylor did finish their abortion comedy script, then-known as *The Devil Inside*, that fall. They were trying to get it set up for Payne to direct. The script made the rounds, generating heat, but nobody wanted to finance it. Too risky.

Too political. Too controversial. It didn't help that Payne was untested in features.

Cut to Dern, by then established as an edgy screen actress for bare-her-soul performances in Joyce Chopra's *Smooth Talk*, Peter Bogdanovich's *Mask*, David Lynch's *Blue Velvet* and *Wild at Heart,* and Steven Spielberg's *Jurassic Park*. She was already Oscar-nominated as the free spirit title character in Martha Coolidge's *Rambling Rose*, for which her mother, Diane Ladd, was also nominated. Her acting genes extend to her father and fellow Oscar nominee, Bruce Dern.

Reminiscent of a young Barbara Stanwyck in her ability to play innocence and guile, sweetness and toughness, Dern was a catch for any director. Payne was a big fan of her work but never thought of her for messed-up Ruth Stoops. He probably didn't think he could get her. That changed when, unbeknownst to him, Dern's then-beau, actor Jeff Goldblum, got ahold of the *Devil* script and gave it to Laura. "And I just was obsessed the moment I read it," she said by phone from the L.A. set of a short film she's appearing in. "I just forced their hands."

Shared cinephile leanings

What did she respond to so strongly? "Well, in terms of the material," she said, "it's a very unique and hilarious and extremely honest voice about this country and about what happens when you get two opposing sides in America, on any subject frankly. And the idea of putting this not just flawed but impossible protagonist at the middle of it is just completely genius. I felt I had something to bring to it that was unique.

"My love for finding empathy and voice in untenable human territory made me determined to force myself on them. I could love nothing more as an actor than one specific challenge, which is finding an empathetic place for a character we would ordinarily have disdain for, and Alexander happens to love that too. Alexander, Jim (Taylor), and I have the same sensibility and that's a very rare thing to find."

Studio execs often express dismay at Payne's unsympathetic protagonists. "My response is always, 'It hasn't been cast yet.' I think it's the actor who brings the humanity and the sympathy to that part," he said. "Yeah, of course, how the film is directed and the tone contribute also, but that's the actor's job—to bring us a really full human person, and I'd like to think that truth is always sympathetic." "And the goal probably isn't finding the sympathy, the goal is finding a multi-dimensional authentic person," Dern said. "Everyone is filled with their own dark and light places."

Laura Dern and Mary Kay Place in *Citizen Ruth*

She said the sensibility she and Payne share derives from their cinema weaning. "Alexander and I both grew up on the humanist films from the '70s. In the '70s there was a blossoming of the auteurist view and in the very specific way directors worked with their actors to find a singular voice. I think probably because humanity was the goal. The bottom line is it's up to your actor to find the humanity in a way that can only happen through behavior. That was the focus those directors had, and it seems to be such a focus of Alexander's work as well."

Putting herself on the line

The only other time Dern's gone after a role so aggressively, she said, is *Rambling Rose*. Her commitment to Ruth changed everything. "Laura's presence helped finance the film," Payne said by phone from his Topanga Canyon, California home. Her involvement also lured other cast members. "I know Laura's presence helped woo Burt Reynolds. These things catch their momentum however they catch their momentum. The script opened doors and then Laura liked the script and then the snowball started growing."

Finally, Payne secured the financing, which, he added, "Was still hard to get even with Laura attached. This film almost wasn't made." He said it was only by the slimmest of margins the money came through.

Few besides Payne and Dern know how close it all came to not happening and how long it took to be realized. "We finished our first draft in the fall of '92 and I wasn't shooting until fall of '95," he said. "I was so frustrated I left L.A. in a kind of self-imposed exile, wondering, What does it take to get a film made?"

Without Dern the project might have died or at least been delayed and Payne's dream to direct deferred. When she signed on, he recognized his good fortune. "Yeah, and the exciting thing was that she kind of came after me," he said. "I had lunch with her and she evinced such enthusiasm for the part and understanding of the role that she was the one."

To help make the small-budgeted indie pic feasible, Dern agreed to work for SAG or Screen Actors Guild scale along with everyone else. "Here she was, a big movie star coming to Omaha, Nebraska, to play a pregnant drug addict," he said. "She was getting, I don't know, $4,000 a week or something, so that proved she was there because she wanted to be there. It wasn't for any other reason than for the pleasure, for the joy of it."

Said Dern, "We were all there for our passion and it made for an incredibly creative and professional experience for all of us." On the set he soon discovered her reputation for putting herself out there, on the line, totally exposed, for her art is well deserved. "Yeah, that's where she's most comfortable," he said. "She gives one hundred percent to the role."

A safe place

Ruth Stoops is among many roles in which she's gone to emotional extremes and done provocative scenes. There's no holding back. No hedging or softening. She lays it all out to see. She clearly enjoys pushing boundaries.

"I mean, for whatever reason it is my favorite thing to do," said Dern, who won her legal emancipation from her parents at age sixteen in order to pursue her craft full-time. "And I have a feeling that being raised by Bruce Dern and Diane Ladd had something to do with it, both in my film life and in my life. I definitely seek it out."

Before she can put herself out there she has to feel she's in good hands. Despite Payne's inexperience, she felt protected.

"I must say I had implicit trust in him. I never questioned him. I don't think I ever will. I believed in him and I think like we felt we knew each other, and that's a bond where you can't go wrong. That's some kind of innate knowing. If there was a feeling-out process, it was really just—What do you like? How do you like to work? On that level. Just on the day-to-day things."

Payne said it's inevitable a director and a lead actor size each other up. "Oh yeah, you know I was so happy she was going to be in my movie but still the director thinks, I hope this person doesn't screw up my movie," he said. "And the actor might think, Who's this director who's going to screw up my performance?"

In their case, he said, it helped that she'd checked his work out. "She liked *The Passion of Martin*, my student film, so she did her homework in watching that." Still, he was a newbie. He soon found out about her astute grasp of cinema. "Of course she was justifiably concerned as to who my other partners were going to be—who my cinematographer was, my editor . . . because that's the thing, she really understands the filmmaking process and how it's not just about the actor or the director," he said, "it's about everyone involved. It's such a huge effort. And she really gets all of that."

"So, yeah, she wanted to know she was going to be placing her hard work in safe hands and I think once she felt that, then she was able to give her all. And once I felt she was going to give me what I wanted and even more, then I felt safe, and then we just skyrocketed."

Dern had a hand in a key crew member coming on board. "One thing that worked out really well on the film—it both made her feel safe and it began a friendship and a professional collaboration that lasted through three films—is that she introduced me to Jim Glennon, the cinematographer," he said.

"Jim had shot her in *Smooth Talk*, her kind of star-making film, back in '85, and she recommended him. I went to meet him, if nothing else just as a courtesy to Laura, thinking, Well, I'll be able to tell her I met him but I didn't like him. And I adored him, and so that was a right move in many ways."

The late Glennon went on to shoot Payne's *Election* and *About Schmidt*.

In synch

Payne and Dern meshed in that way only two artists who respect each other can. "Look, we worked together extremely well," he said. "It's one of the richest collaborations I've ever had with an actor, and I was so happy it was happening on my first feature film. We really got in tune with each other pretty early on, and we really felt a partnership.

"I mean, when you make a film, your production designer is your partner and your cinematographer is your partner, and your editor is your partner. And it's nice when the lead actor is your partner in the same way and it's not somebody you have to handle or manipulate or anything."

For her part, Dern said, "I consider one of the best moments of my life was working on *Ruth* with Alexander. I had been acting for sixteen-seventeen years. I'd worked with extraordinary people, for sure. I think that speaks so much to his innate abilities and instincts."

The comfort level she felt with him and Glennon helped her tap into an aspect of Ruth and women like her she feels deeply about. "One of the things I always loved about Ruth, why I felt like I understood her so completely, was that Ruth isn't just a character trying to find her voice, but she's a character who doesn't know she's entitled to one, and I long to play women who are in that struggle," Dern said. "I think Rose in *Rambling Rose* is similar that way.

"And I know they're the two that have probably penetrated my heart the most as characters I really love and find really relatable for women in this country. I really crave playing women who are on that discovery.

Mutual admiration society

Payne said Dern's commitment to craft isn't a self-absorbed ego trip. She's not just concerned with her own performance but with contributing to a fully realized film.

"She gives a hundred percent to the role and she also is a good kind of team captain for the entire cast," he said. "The rest of the cast look to the lead actor—how is he or she feeling about the film . . . and she always had such great enthusiasm and professionalism."

Payne couldn't have asked for anything more. But he got it. When he and Kevin Tent were editing the film he got another glimpse of Dern's cinema savvy. "She has such a knack for film acting. I mean, many months later when I was editing I would talk to her by phone or she would come by the cutting room, and I'd say we're cutting a scene a certain way or she'd see how a scene was cutting and she'd say, 'You know, I think in that shot on take three I did something kind of interesting. You might want to take a look at that.' She had a prodigious memory for what she did in what scenes and what other actors did.

"I've read recently about her performance in *Recount*. That she would do many scenes three ways—underplayed, over the top, and then kind of neutral, so that Jay Roach, the director, would have choices to calibrate her performance in the cutting room. And that's just like textbook Laura. She understands film to the nth degree. She knows it's about editing and she gives you choices in editing."

Payne went on to have the same experience with Jack Nicholson on *Schmidt*. "Oh, yeah, that's the kind of actor you want. Everyone has to understand it's not about what happens on set, it's about what you harvest on set to get to the cutting room."

For Payne, Dern's enduring gift was the example she set "that one can work the way one wants to, which is with a real sense of partnership with the lead actor," he said. "That it really can be the way it should be. And have fun. I mean, we all had a really good time making *Citizen Ruth*. A really good time. She's a blast. I'd like to think it set a tone for what the rest of my films have been."

Both would like the opportunity to work together again. "We've definitely talked about it," Dern said. "I'd love to work with her again but I haven't had a part for her," said Payne, who doesn't know yet whether his upcoming film, *Downsizing*, may include a role for her. An original screenplay written with Jim Taylor, *Downsizing*'s described by Payne as "a large-scale, possibly 'epic' comedy that uses a science-fiction premise as a way to paint a fairly large satiric mural of today's world."

Just as Payne surrounds himself with a family of film artists on project after project, Dern enjoys longstanding collaborations."I'm a big believer in it and I feel like I have found a tribe of people I've worked with over and over again, someone who gets you, and you feel like you can do your best work with someone who gets you."

The two know each other so well, he said, he's not preparing copious James Lipton notes for the Holland event but rather winging it. "I mean, look, all we have to do is start talking and it'll all come out." Maybe he'll wear his lucky *Ruth* pants, white jeans whose pants leg was torn by a dog that bit him on a location scout.

Alexander Payne and Debra Winger hold court for Feature Film Event '09

Published in a 2009 issue of The Reader

Debra Winger (Wikimedia Commons)

A kindred spirit

Debra Winger reviews her career with Alexander Payne for the Film Streams Feature Event this Sunday, September 13 at 6:30 p.m. As prep, he's immersed himself in her work. Long an admirer of the "emotional depth" she brings to her craft, he's "impressed" by how well her seminal performances and films "are holding up."

Though they've not worked together, he sees in her the virtuosic method and recurring personal stamp he found in Laura Dern, Jack Nicholson, and Paul Giamatti.

"These are actors whose body of work as artists acquire something approaching a singular voice. You almost detect themes running through their performances. It's a matter of who they are as people," said Payne. "It's cool when actors can penetrate through the character to reveal their actual concerns as artists."

There's a fearlessness to Winger he's eager to explore during the event at the Holland Performing Arts Center. Excerpts from her films will be screened. A patron reception follows the program, a fund raiser for the art cinema.

Winger curated a repertory series of her work showing this month at Film Streams, 14th and Webster. She also selected two films not her own that have inspired her: John Huston's *The Night of the Iguana* and Patrice Leconte's *The Hairdresser's Husband*. The series unreeled last week with *Cannery Row* (1982) and *A Dangerous Woman* (1993). The remaining lineup is:

Sept. 10: *The Sheltering Sky* (1990, Bertolucci); *Shadowlands* (1993)

Sept. 11–17: *Terms of Endearment* (1983, James L. Brooks); *Big Bad Love* (2001)

Sept. 18–24: *The Night of the Iguana* (1964); *The Hairdresser's Husband* (1990)

Sept. 25–Oct. 1: *Mike's Murder* (1984); *Urban Cowboy* (1980)

The artist owns a special kinship with Nebraska via her 1980s romance with then–Governor Bob Kerrey. Sunday, she'll undoubtedly discuss *Terms of Endearment*, the project that first brought her here and introduced her to Kerrey.

Her local ties include an association with Omaha's Rose Theater. She was to star in a production of Robert Bly's play, *Tatterhood*, but her schedule didn't allow it. Artistic director James Larson did arrange for her to come record the narration for its *Why Mosquitoes Buzz in People's Ears*, in 1998. "She was very precise, very professional, and she put a high level commitment to it. It was wonderful," said Larson. "The whole show was improvised without dialogue. The only spoken words were Debra Winger's recorded voice."

Another local connection comes from her twice starring opposite native Omahan Nick Nolte—in 1982's *Cannery Row* and in 1990's *Everybody Wins*. While Payne's sure to chat up her Nebraska ties, don't expect Kerrey stories. Payne assured Winger the focus will be on her "life in film," not her personal life.

It's easy to overlook her as one of her generation's top actresses. After all, she made few films before walking away in 1995, at age forty for a six-year hiatus. Yet she was already an indelible screen presence by then, updating the tough, street-smart persona of Barbara Stanwyck to create her own saucy, sexy, truculent, wrong-side-of-the-tracks broads. Winger's been back working since 2001—in HBO's *Sometimes In April*, Lifetime's *Dawn Anna*, and in the indie film *Big Bad Love*. Her performance in 2008's *Rachel Getting Married* sparked serious comeback twittering.

After an inauspicious start in schlock pics and on TV's *Wonder Woman*, her memorable breakthrough came as bull-riding ball-buster Sissy in *Urban Cowboy*. She parlayed that by playing the ambitious Paula in *An Officer and a Gentleman*. She raised the long-suffering Emma's woes above maudlin in *Terms*.

Some good work in so-so films followed before she took off again. Her sensuality imbued the searching Kit in *The Sheltering Sky*. Her frankness found full expression as Joy Gresham in *Shadowlands*, a performance that brought a third Best Actress Oscar nomination. Next came the repressed Martha in *A Dangerous Woman*.

Then Winger disappeared. A measure of her impact was Rosanna Arquette's doc, *Searching for Debra Winger*, using the artist's dissatisfaction with Hollywood to examine how women find quality parts scarce once reaching a certain age.

But as Winger's said, she never set out to be "the poster child" for ageism or sexism in film. Her own problems with Hollywood were more intrinsic. She decried the double-standard that labeled her "difficult" in an industry run by ruthless men. She rarely found parts sufficient for her talent. She turned down several roles that proved iconic and lucrative for the women that played them. She didn't seem to care. Fame and its trappings didn't interest her. Good work did.

Her return included projects directed by her actor husband, Arliss Howard. Her latest role, as Anne Hathaway's mother in *Married*, has people talking about her in the present tense, not in the whatever-happened-to-Debra-Winger mode, which is how she wants it. It's not like in her self-imposed exile she sat around stewing, waiting for the phone to ring. She lived life. She and Howard share an upstate New York farm they tend themselves. She raised their son, Babe, she taught a course at Harvard, she acted at Lincoln Center, she wrote an intimate book, *Undiscovered*.

She's a more mature artist since first visiting here. Her career is now in its second half. It's not unlike Payne's own journey. He's matured since *Citizen Ruth*. After his last feature, *Sideways*, he seemed to go underground even though he worked the whole time. With the economy scuttling plans for *Downsizing*, he's now adapting a novel, *The Descendants*. Shooting starts early 2010 in Hawaii. Both artists then are in the midst of a "comeback," although neither really ever went away.

❧

Another story considers the prolific Steven Soderbergh, a filmmaker Payne appreciates for the depth and breadth of his work. In another example of Payne being proactive where his film connections are concerned, he arranged for this fellow world-class filmmaker to come to Omaha.

❧

The Soderbergh experience: Alexander Payne and Kurt Andersen weigh in on America's most prolific and accomplished filmmaker of their generation

Published in a 2011 issue of *The Reader*

Steven Soderbergh, *The Reader*

A career unlike few others

Steven Soderbergh may not generate the snobby, effete buzz of some name directors, yet he's arguably the most prolific and accomplished American filmmaker over the past twenty years. As special guest for the Feb. 20 Film Streams Feature Event III, An Evening with Steven Soderbergh, he headlines Omaha's must-see cinema event of 2011.

Skeptics must concede he has the juice to qualify as an elite director. There are the awards (the Palm d'Or and the Oscar), the glowing reviews, the productive collaborations with mega-stars (George Clooney), and the clout or charisma to get both commercial (*Erin Brockovich*) and fringe (*Che*) works produced.

He did one early game-changing film (*sex, lies, and videotape*) and he's followed with some prestige mature projects (*Traffic*). Yes, naysayers point out, but he can't claim a seminal work like *The Godfather* or *Taxi Driver* as his own.

What he does possess is a supple technique he applies to a broad canvas of genres he crosses and bends with equal amounts of restraint and respect and reinvention. He's not even fifty, and his oeuvre may ultimately contain more stand-the-test-of-time credits than any of his flashier contemporaries or senior counterparts.

Yes, but is he an auteur? That may be among the things novelist and *Studio 360* host Kurt Andersen explores with Soderbergh during their on-stage interview-clip program at the Holland Performing Arts Center.

For now, Andersen ventures while it's hard to instantly identify a Soderbergh film the way one can a Scorsese or Allen or Tarantino or Coen Brothers film, or for that matter a Tony Scott film, "He is an incredibly ambitious artist, and that's an interesting combination."

Count Andersen an admirer.

"He's done television as well as feature films, he produces (*Syriana*, *Michael Clayton* as well as directs), he does documentaries, he does these big kinds of pure entertainment features as well as these very strange little features, and all of that range continues," he said. "It's not as though he did these little movies and then graduated to payday movies. That he continues to be as diverse at age forty eight as when he was twenty five–thirty is really singular.

"When you look at the body of work and career, there's nobody of his generation who comes close I think in having all of that, as well as the half dozen or whatever master works you can argue about and point to."

An appreciation

Before the auteur theory messed with cinephiles' conceptions of where ultimate film authorship lies, name-above-the-title directors were rare. Today, even hacks are accorded that once privileged status. Soderbergh is anything but a hack. Indeed, Andersen calls him "the anti-hack."

Alexander Payne, who approached Soderbergh to headline the Film Streams fundraiser and will introduce the program, summed up his fellow artist with:

"I count Steven as a friend and colleague, and I have tremendous respect for his career and his purity, and certainly for his work ethic. He admires the directors of classical Hollywood who honed craft through continuous work, and he has miraculously enabled himself to equal their prodigious output. Some hit, some miss, but craft sharpens and roves. And he supports other filmmakers without question."

A great filmmaker doesn't have to also be a screenwriter like Payne. John Ford and Alfred Hitchcock produced great art with recurring personal themes and motifs without scripting a word. Soderbergh has writing credits on a third of his features.

Neither is a clearly defined style a prerequisite for a great director. Witness John Huston and Elia Kazan, whose subtle styles changed from film to film in service of story while their own preoccupations shone through. Soderbergh is in their chameleon tradition.

The fertile mid-1960s through 1970s era saw personal filmmaking flower in and out of Hollywood with Cassavetes, Scorsese, Coppola, Ashby, Altman, et al. In the 1980s this trend retreated in the face of mega pics, sequels, and special effects.

A bridge figure

Soderbergh is a bridge figure who helped usher in the independent film movement with his 1989 debut feature *sex, lies, and videotape*. A searching period followed that film's breakout success. Since the mid-'90s he's evolved as a director of high gloss studio projects, including the *Oceans* series, that win critical and industry praise—and also make money—yet also as the maker of art pieces that exercise other creative muscles.

University of Texas at Austin film scholar Tom Schatz said Soderbergh's arrival on the scene marked a turning point.

"1989 was perhaps the most important year for Hollywood in the past half-century," said Schatz. "It was the year of the Time-Warner and Sony-Columbia mergers, which began the trend toward conglomerate control that now defines the movie industry. It was the year of *Batman*, the first modern blockbuster. And it was the year of *sex, lies, and videotape*, which ignited an indie film movement and alongside *Batman* set a dual trajectory that continues to this day.

"Interestingly enough, Soderbergh is among the very few contemporary Hollywood filmmakers who can move effortlessly and successfully from one of these tracks to the other, segueing from modest, innovative, character-driven films to big-budget franchise blockbusters. In the process he has steadily produced a body of work that is unmatched in contemporary American cinema."

Andersen said Soderbergh shook things up around the same time the Coens, Tarantino, Gus Van Sant, and Spike Lee emerged as a brash new guard. Andersen wonders how *sex, lies, and videotape* plays to 2011 eyes inured by YouTube, Web cams and reality TV. When the film came out, voyeurism was not the ubiquitous leisure activity it is now.

"It was the germinal moment of a certain era of American films that were strange and singular and idiosyncratic and that everybody was suddenly talking about in a way they hadn't since the '70s," notes Andersen. "What's so kind of heartening and praiseworthy about Soderbergh's career is he continues really risky formal experiments."

Take the director's choice of revolutionary Che Guevara as the subject of a four-hour-plus, two-part film in Spanish. The sheer length and scope leaves Andersen wondering, "Why do you do that? It's almost a different thing than a conventional feature film. At one point in the process did he decide this needs to be this epic thing?" He plans to ask Soderbergh that very question.

Andersen's also fascinated by Soderbergh's take on the ferment of that time. "I've just written a novel, much of which is set in the '60s, and about politics. I'm eager to talk to him about how we're maybe now just getting far enough away from the '60s, with all their power and electricity and iconic resonance, where we can make interesting art about them and talk about them in ways that are not quite so hot and bothered."

Film Streams director Rachel Jacobson said she appreciates Soderbergh's "transparent awareness of the commercial pressures that compromise the art of film" by his jumping back and forth between the two extremes of feature filmmaking. She adds, "He's also interested in challenging traditional distribution channels. Both *Bubble* and *The Girlfriend Experience* were released On-Demand and on Blu-Ray the same day and date they were released theatrically. His visit is such a terrific match for us as an art house theater dealing with these issues from the other end."

Film Streams Feature Events I and II guests, Laura Dern and Debra Winger, respectively, discussed acting and offered anecdotes about projects and collaborators. Alexander Payne, who directed Dern in his first feature *Citizen Ruth* and admired the commitment Winger made to her roles, conducted soft interviews with the stars. This time, with a director in the spotlight and a veteran journalist asking penetrating questions, a different dynamic is in the offing. Both Payne and Andersen work with the art cinema (Payne's a board member, Andersen's an advisory board member).

"Having had two terrific actors at past Features, I feel like the acclaimed director's visit is a terrific way to mix things up," said

Jacobson. "Everyone has seen a Soderbergh film but not everyone pays attention to the director. It's really important to our mission of promoting film as art that people think about the artist with the vision behind the work, the decisions that go into every shot, and the talent it takes to create a good movie.

"We're thrilled that Kurt is coming to do the interview this year."

Balancing act

The balancing act of Soderbergh, who's publicly bemoaned the unwieldy, antiquated system for getting films made and released, intrigues Andersen. He said he's eager to ask "how he convinced-persuaded the money guys to let him do what he wanted to do" in that limbo period following *sex,* when the perceived failures of *Kafka, King of the Hill, Underneath,* and the TV series *Fallen Angels* seemed to signal a fall to irrelevance.

Then came five films that made Soderbergh not only relevant again but gave him cachet: *Out of Sight, The Limey, Erin Brockovich, Traffic, Ocean's Eleven.* From then till now Soderbergh's moved from obscure projects like *Solaris* and *The Good German* to star-vehicles like *The Informant* and the forthcoming *Haywire.*

As Andersen noted, "There's talent and luck and then there's the personality-temperament things that allow you to make that Hollywood ATM machine cough up the money." Andersen's curious to know how artists like Soderbergh "actually manage to have other people pay for the courage" of their "private, quirky convictions."

Even when Soderbergh has played it "safe" with forays into genre themes and variations, whether the caper buddy pic (*Oceans*) or the romantic suspense flick (*Out of Sight*) or the revenge story (*The Limey*) or the underdog-against-all-odds chestnut (*Brockovich*), he's made the conventions his own.

"He's broad enough in his vision of interesting material that he can take something that's been seen a thousand times and make it a memorable thing," said Andersen.

The Good German finds Soderbergh taking the duplicity and intrigue and look of *Casablanca* or *The Third Man* and at once remaining true to it and tweaking it. His black-and-white milieu and mis en scene boast mystique with a modern edge.

"You see him setting up a particular kind of obstacle course for himself. He's doing not just a modern version of a film noir," said Andersen, "but he's actually trying to do it in a virtual simulation way—to try and figure out how movies were made then in ways that we don't now, and yet trying to make it work as a film that comes out in 2006.

"It's interesting to me to talk to an artist about the kinds of puzzles he sets for himself." Andersen admits to being a sucker for spy stories anyway, and he said Soderbergh's riffs with the well-worn form made it a must-see for him. "That's interesting in a personal way for me," said Andersen. "I'm fascinated by the intelligence agencies. In this new novel of mine the serious research I had to do was about how the intelligence business works, so I actually was thinking about *The Good German*. I rewatched that film in anticipation of talking to Soderbergh."

Kurt Andersen (www.kurtandersen.com)

Traffic is another example of an overused, often cliched subject—illegal drug trafficking—that in the hands of an imaginative filmmaker becomes a kind of elegiac opus about human greed and frailty told in overlapping storylines.

"A really interesting film," said Andersen. "It's the kind of movie that in description could be such a hack work thing. If in a blind taste test that film was simply described to you, you'd think, Yeah, maybe, but you'd expect it to be mediocre. But again with this kind of genre material he brings both this interesting, complicated structure, TV-like in a way because of course it's an adaptation of a television series—and turns this pulp material into something so much better. Into a work of art."

Andersen said *The Informant* portrays business management's "moral ambiguity" and "murkiness" in a way "that fiction and film seldom do. It's so unpigeonholable. Is it a comedy? Is it a drama? What is it?" He likes too the improvisational and enigmatic qualities of *The Girlfriend Experience*.

In the end, Andersen said, Soderbergh distinguishes his work above the fray. "There's so many like big tent-pole movies that get made just because the deal was made," he said. "He's one who clearly takes seriously the fact that somebody's going to pay ten bucks and spend two hours of their life, and so I better try to entertain them. He kind of gives more than necessary. When any artist over-delivers in what they're strictly required to do, it makes for a great artist and for a career that really lasts.

"You never get the sense he's phoning it in in any sense, which isn't to say it always works. I mean, he has lesser movies and greater movies, but he's always trying. His work never goes off the rails. There's always a sense of rigor about it."

6

The Descendants

❧

Introduction

When Alexander Payne returned to feature filmmaking in 2010–2011 with *The Descendants* he very much picked up where he left off on *Sideways* to make a work with deep currents running through it. Here, those currents are not only personal for the protagonists, as they are in *Sideways*, but cultural, ancestral, and historical as well, thereby making this the most complex tapestry he has woven yet.

While there is no doubting Payne had a small army of devoted fans and critical champions prior to *The Descendants*, I still intuited there was a sizable body of film viewers who hedged when it came to his work. Why? Because to their tastes he never quite went all in with the comedy or the drama, preferring instead to not so much straddle both sides of tragedy but insisting on having it both ways and thus going back and forth between the two, even within the same scene. I think that left some viewers feeling dissatisfied or cheated.

It is clear by now though that that is who he is as a filmmaker and he is not about to change. Why should he? His films are increasingly nuanced, mature works that take you through an emotional journey full of revelation. They also leave you hanging to an extent ruminating about what next lies in store for their characters. That is more than most films do.

In addition to that segment of viewers who wanted more clarity or resolution I think there were those who wanted him to take on more challenging stories, as he did with his first two features, and there is a point to be made there. One could argue that from *About Schmidt* on, Payne has revisited stories that share much in common and that can be considered variations on a theme: *Schmidt*, *Sideways*, and *The Descendants* all focus on middle-aged or older male protagonists at some crisis point or crucible in their lives that propels them on a physical and emotional journey.

All are, in one way or another, road pictures. There is a quest or search involved as well. As a Greek-American writer-director steeped in the classics, he may be at some level, whether consciously or unconsciously, retelling elements of *The Odyssey* from film to film. After all, his protagonist(s) only sets off on his journey after some sort of fall or loss, and in the course of the adventure he encounters all manner of characters who variously help or hinder his progress.

Not surprisingly then his next film, *Nebraska*, is almost quite literally a road picture from start to finish. Its primary character is a miscreant older male who's managed to alienate himself from everyone in his life, including his son. Faced with a willful, foul-mouthed, somewhat addled father who believes he's won a sweepstakes, the son indulges the old man on a journey to claim a prize that isn't there. En route, the son decides to grant his father the gift of redemption. And in a grace note ending that beats all, the son lets the old man get the last laugh for once.

Cinematographer Phedon Papamichael, who did the photography on *Sideways* and *The Descendants*, once again helped Payne realize a visually stunning landscape, only this time the desolate and sublime stretches of Nebraska prairie and Sandhills. Together, they found the poetry of its wide open spaces. Capturing these settings in black and white added dramatic effect.

Downsizing turns out to be the ultimate journey story told by Payne with its epic tale traversing time and space, philosophy and culture. Of course, as Payne points out, the road picture template or device is both a convenient and effective one for propelling a story. The notion of a journey framing a story is as old as *The Odyssey* itself. When applied to film, it offers a perfectly legitimate dramatic means for opening up a picture and having protagonists meet up with interesting characters and adventures. Besides, who doesn't want to spend two hours in the company of Paul Giamatti and Thomas Haden Church, or Jack Nicholson, or George Clooney on a virtual road trip filled with laughs and heartache?

As the following stories delineate, *The Descendants* project came into focus for Payne after he was unable to pull the financing together on *Downsizing*. It had already been some years since *Sideways* and the questions were mounting as to why he had not yet followed up that success with a new feature. Then when *Downsizing* proved too big a gamble for investors in the depths of the recession, he was left somewhat in the lurch. Or so it seemed.

In truth, he had a number of feature options to pursue, including the long announced project, *Nebraska*. But it was *The Descendants* he committed to making. It meant working with a superstar for the second time in his career and certainly his experience with Jack Nicholson on *About Schmidt* informed his handling of Clooney on *Descendants*. Like *Sideways*, the project took Payne far from the Omaha-based locales of his first three features and planted him in a landscape full of picaresque beauty and cultural-historical import.

Much as he did on *Sideways,* Payne fully embraced the emotional and dramatic palette of his characters and their situations, only here he avoided even more the comic deflections, distancing devices, and set pieces he has sometimes over relied on to the detriment of the films. Oh, he still infused *The Descendants* with humor, only more subtly, grounding it in greater reality. Perhaps it is the melancholia at the heart of the story, perhaps it is a more wizened and assured Payne extracting what the material offered, but there is a difference to be sure, and I think it helps account for why the film did so well around the world. *The Descendants*'s worldwide box office take makes it by far the most popular and biggest money-making work of his career.

The material may not have been any more challenging on its face, but I think it was for Payne because the story required him to articulate in words, visuals, and sounds the complexity of a cross-cultural setting and a panoply of personal dramas unfolding within it that were largely outside his own experience. There was a lot he had to get right in order for us to care enough about these characters and situations to want to take this journey with them.

Therefore there were a lot of things that could go wrong. Because he would be operating in unfamiliar territory, he probably did more preparation for this project than he did on all of his other pictures combined. As the following stories elaborate, he literally schooled himself on the intricacies of Hawaiian culture so that the characters and the actions would be naturally immersed in those attitudes and rituals and signposts, rather then feeling forced or imposed or artificial. He not only achieved that but he also managed to convincingly tell this moving, funny, sad story of a family on the brink of collapse coming together in the midst of tragedy, and did so without making it cloyingly sentimental. The laughs and tears are honestly earned.

His growing finesse as a visual artist is perhaps best expressed in the boat scene near the end, when Matt King and his daughters scatter Liz's ashes in the ocean and Payne uses the water and light to cast an abstract hue of hope and the hereafter over the somber proceedings. Earlier, Alexandra's imploding rage is released under water in the family's backyard pool.

Then there are the Paynesian touches that make it his own. Matt King's flip-flop run to confirm his wife's cheating and his peering over a hedge to spy on the target of his revenge are homages to the silent film comedies Payne loves. His knack for summing up characters and situations with a single image reaches a zenith at the very end, when the final shot holds on Matt, Alexandra, and Scottie for a remarkably long time as what remains of their battered family regroups around the sofa watching TV. They share an unspoken, easy affection, accentuated by their physical contact, that tells us they are going to be okay. They have made it to the other side of their ordeal and are back to the simple yet profound rituals and routines of everyday family life.

The fact that Payne does not cut away from this portrait signals to me he is more comfortable letting the subtext of a moment speak for itself through characters' nonverbal cues than perhaps he was before. Similarly, he seems more comfortable letting emotional or dramatic scenes play out longer without visual interruption or cinematic comment, though as he has rightly pointed out to me he's always favored long takes, certainly more than many of his contemporaries.

For these and other reasons this Payne film reads as his most accomplished achievement. It is the closest thing he has done to a traditional or mainstream film from Old Hollywood. It is also completely in synch with the sensibilities of that 1970s humanist strain of films he was weaned on and that he so admires. The picture is wholly accessible to general audiences while retaining the quirkiness and acerbity that has in part defined his work.

In my view his work is likely to veer ever more in this direction, and I think that is a good thing.

Alexander Payne, George Clooney and Co. find love, pain and the whole damn thing shooting *The Descendants* in Hawaii

Published in a 2010 issue of *The Reader*

Paradise Lost

Alexander Payne's version of *Paradise Lost*, by way of *Terms of Endearment*, describes the emotional arc of his new $24-million George Clooney vehicle, *The Descendants*, which wrapped shooting in Hawaii at the end of May.

Arriving to interview Payne at his swank new downtown digs, he gave this reporter the nickel tour of his pad—more properly termed a penthouse loft that overlooks the Gene Leahy Mall. The place has the spare, chic, movie-movie look straight out of a Hollywood art director's sketchbook. Workmen finished making fixes around the condo while we sat at a heavily lacquered round wooden table. As the tape started rolling, a thunderstorm unleashed wind and rain, enveloping the downtown canyon in sheets of gray. The curious director noted the commotion, but quickly carried on.

A premise of the Kaui Hart Hemmings novel, which Payne adapted for the film, is that life's messiness proceeds the same in a supposed paradise as it does in, say, drab Omaha. Eden doesn't exempt one from loss or burden. Payne revealed as much in *Sideways,* where errant pals turned nirvana into a pitiful wasteland.

It's clear the writer-director prefers protagonists undertake an ironical journey. Whether Ruth Stoops (*Citizen Ruth*) Jim McAllister (*Election*), Warren Schmidt (*About Schmidt*), Miles and Jack (*Sideways*), or Clooney's Matt King, Payne plunges anti-heroes down a rabbit hole of self-discovery.

A seriocomic odyssey writ small unfolds, ending with the beleaguered character completing and/or embarking on a trek, wizened or not along the way.

Matt King is the most emotionally mature adult male seen in the Paynesian world, but he's not without issues. The middle-aged A-hole is a well-off attorney troubled by his identity as a landed descendant of a white missionary who married into Hawaiian royalty. What's worse, he's pining and worrying over his wife, who's in a coma after a boating accident. This was not how their golden union was to end. They were the couple others envied. But we learn that things between them had been less than idyllic for a while. Matt settled for things; Liz did not. Beautiful, free-spirited, attention-grabbing Liz always got her way. Even in her vegetative state, Matt feels betrayed by her restless, reckless vibe. Two thankless deadlines hang over Matt: to pull or not pull life support, and sell or not sell the valuable land entrusted him and his large extended family.

Bring on the drama

Much of the story revolves around Liz in the ICU. Payne does not shrink from depicting her fragile, wasted-away existence. "It's meant to be startling," he said, adding that actress Patricia Hastie went to extremes—losing weight, growing her body hair and nails, skimping on sleep—to achieve stark realism. Even when not on camera, her presence is felt, lending a more serious tone than usual to the satiric Payne universe.

"It's more of a drama than I've done before, and I'm curious to see how that turns out," he said. "I think it'll be OK, but I haven't seen a lot of the footage. I thought in the past I would be afraid of drama, because I'd always made comedies. Often comedy directors have the best touch with pathos. The jury's still out with this one."

Then there are the two strange creatures in the form of Matt's daughters. He tries making up for lost time with them contemplating how they should deal with their mom's condition. It turns out the older one, Alexandra, and her father have reasons to hate Liz. Not that Liz didn't have her reasons for her actions. Payne predicts big things for Shailene Woodley, who plays Alexandra. He said the chemistry she and Clooney developed "totally shows up on screen."

Matt's also put upon by cousin Hugh (Beau Bridges) eying a windfall land sell, and by his feisty father-in-law (Robert Forster), who blames him for Liz's accident. It would seem an imploding family could send Matt off the deep end, but it doesn't—except for getting back at Liz by making a brave, albeit misguided trip with the girls and a slacker hanger-on. It's a risky venture, full of pain and humor.

Clooney as Matt King, said Payne, "is asked to run a full spectrum of emotions and ways of presenting them. I already admired him as an actor in movies but I didn't know how good he was until I got to watch him live and see what he could do with certain scenes, how nimble he is as an actor, how nimbly he can do emotions and turn emotions on a dime. He's a really good actor."

The ruddy good looks and exasperated charm of Clooney made him everyone's choice as Matt, who's wounded but not the damaged goods of other Payne protagonists. He comes out of his crucible fairly whole and ready to meet an ambivalent new reality.

Wending his way to the film

Payne went on a literal and figurative journey of his own to make *Descendants*. After his Oscar-winning buddy road picture, *Sideways,* hit big in 2004, he spent the next few years, if not in self-imposed exile from features, distracted from making another. He got divorced (from Sandra Oh), he formed his own production company (Ad Hominem Enterprises), he produced films (*King of California, The Savages*), he and longtime writing partner Jim Taylor did script doctoring work (*I Now Pronounce You Chuck & Larry*). Payne also directed a short (*14th arrondissement*) and an HBO pilot (*Hung*).

The project he and Taylor labored on three years, *Downsizing,* became a casualty of the recession when its $65-million special effects–laden budget scared off investors. Then Payne's producing partner Jim Burke asked him "for the umpteenth time" to helm *Descendants*. Payne liked the material but wouldn't commit with *Downsizing* still in play.

The Hemmings book was among the first properties Ad Hominem optioned. Nat Faxon and Jim Rash wrote a script, which director Stephen Frears was slated to make. When Frears bailed, Payne gave the novel another read. This time he said yes to adapting it himself.

"I basically threw out the draft other writers had done and then started anew," Payne said. He wrote it, alone, without Taylor. "All writing is scary, with someone or without someone, and in this case it was fine," said Payne. "Jim and I had spent so much time writing on *Downsizing* together that I think we just needed a break. It's not my story. Hawaii exists in a different dimension. It's a different country. So I sort of wanted to find my own personal way into that story by adapting it myself.

"About the only thing I have in common with the story ostensibly is the protagonist and I are the same gender and age. So it's a little bit like acting—if I had been born or somehow brought into that set of circumstances, who would I be, how would I react? I wanted to do that a little bit just to find my own way into the story emotionally."

Working with Jack Nicholson on *Schmidt* schooled Payne on the superstar factor. Though he hung out more with Jack, he and Clooney, both nearing fifty, have more in common.

"We both got to L.A. more or less at the same time, I in the film school circle, he in the acting circle ... so we have many of the same cultural reference points. It was nice having something more of an alter ego in the lead part."

The project reunited Payne with veteran collaborators, including director of photography Phedon Papamichael from *Sideways*.

Steeped in Hawaii

Beginning last summer, Payne did Hawaii— "getting to know that world so I can represent it accurately," he said. "I took three or four one to two-week trips between August and December. That's time I was dividing between sniffing around Hawaii, finishing the screenplay in Los Angeles, and casting in Los Angeles and in New York (with casting director John Jackson of Omaha). Then on Jan. 10, I moved to Hawaii full-time," remaining there for the duration of the March 15–May 26 shoot.

Throughout, he relied heavily on Hemmings, a Hawaii resident, to "vet things in the dialogue." Hemmings said, "It was as much about getting the lingo right as anything." "I often asked for her input, even on casting," said Payne. "Sometimes I'd be stuck between two people and I'd ask, 'Who rings more true to you?' Again, it's not my world, I needed help from her, from a lot of people. And I'm sure I still have a million mistakes in the film, but I'm sure I would have had more had I not gone out there. It's all about trying to aspire to catch a sense of place in a film."

Hawaii, he said, "is very specific and there's great consciousness about who's from Hawaii, who's not, who's just out here from the mainland." Ultimately, it comes down to interpretation. "What does getting it right mean?" Payne said. "It's so subjective. It's still going to be this white guy from the mainland going out to tell this Hawaii story, although the emotional story could be set anywhere. But, of course, the land is everything. Land and power, the whole setting of it, the landed upper class of Honolulu, which I then had to do a kind of thesis paper on in a way."

Researching his subject, he became friends with noted Hawaii historian Gavin Dawes, who impressed upon him the complexity of the place. "At lunch he told me, 'After living here for more than fifty years it's more mysterious to me than ever,'" Payne said. Oddly enough, Payne said capturing Hawaii "all comes back to Omaha," adding, "It's an exciting, logical extension of my process begun here in Nebraska, of how do you tell a story in the foreground and have a place in the background? Starting with *About Schmidt* I began to get the hang of that. I took those skills and learned some new ones on *Sideways*. So I pretty much see *The Descendants* as an extension of that same work, in a place where I haven't been before. It's telling a personal story in the foreground and maintaining a sense of the landscape in the background. There's one director in particular whose work I've studied, Anthony Mann, who was very good at that. But he went one step further by having the changing physical landscape often mirror, like a projection, the protagonist's inner landscape."

Payne said he didn't even try muting Hawaii's stunning beauty, just as he didn't suppress the splendor of *Sideways's* Santa Barbara wine country. "I went with it. It's just so pretty. We were shooting in Hanalei Bay on the island of Hawaii, and I didn't realize how beautiful it was until I saw it on film watching dailies."

Improvs and do-overs

Owing to the newness of it all, he was more open to script revisions on set than ever before. "It's the first time I've ever done a little bit of rewriting of scenes, because I would learn new things along the way." He also re-shot a scene, again something he's rarely done. It's a "money" scene with Matt and the two girls on a boat.

"It turns out shooting on boats is very difficult," he said. "I've done road movies, which has taught me how much I hate shooting in cars. It's just a drag. George Clooney, who had done *A Perfect Storm*, said boat work is car work on steroids, and he was right. You know, most of filmmaking is hauling equipment around, so just getting the equipment out there, securing the actors, one of them a little girl, on a small boat, then dealing with the swells, and how to shoot it. The light continuity was very different shooting one side of the boat to the other. It'd be in clouds and then in sunlight. It'd be a calm ocean and then rough. The little girl got tired easily. It was laborious.

"We shot that first, toward the beginning of the schedule, and then it just didn't look so good in dailies, so I said we should just re-shoot it and get it right. In doing so it turned out to be a gift. When I came back to re-shoot it at the very end of the schedule, I had learned more about the emotional journey of the characters and so I was able to have that inform more specifically their attitudes."

Happy accidents. More than once, he said, he or the actors or the DP or all three were inspired during a take to do something unscripted that made magic. "In filmmaking you're supposed to have a day of shooting be executing a preconceived plan, and that's fine, it makes everybody feel secure you're getting done what you're scheduled to do. But it's nice also where within that structure you're able to have moments that are as spontaneous an act of creation as painting or writing, and I had some of those, and that felt good."

Descendants proved a welcome break from *Downsizing* and the green screen work it would require. "It was a breath of fresh air to get away from it for a bit. It was nice to just have a camera and shoot people. That's where it's at," he said. He fully expects to still make *Downsizing* one day, he said, "because it's a good one."

After spending early June in Omaha, Payne joined his longtime editor Kevin Tent in L.A. to edit. Payne wants an all-Hawaiian soundtrack. The film's due for a 2011 release.

As for his next project, he intends coming home to make, what else?—a road pic named *Nebraska*.

The interview complete, Payne ushered me past some freshly arrived white cane chairs he bought in Hawaii and bid me adieu with a hearty, "Aloha."

Composer Rolfe Kent, left, and sound mixer Jose Antonio Garcia, right, flank Payne on the set of *The Descendants*. Payne is clearly always in charge but he engenders great loyalty among his crew, many of whom he's worked with time and again, because he treats people right and part of that is letting them do their jobs. There's a mutual regard and a warm, easy rapport on his sets that can't be faked and that many film artists envy. (p. 189)

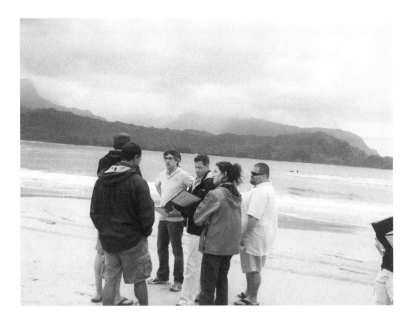

Payne and select crew at Kauai on Hanalei Beach for *The Descendants*. Left to right: Line producer George Parra in windbreaker, cinematographer Phedon Papamichael wearing cap, Payne, first assistant director Richard Fox holding script, second assistant director Amy Wilkins-Bronson, and second unit director Tracy Boyd. (photos courtesy of Anna Musso)

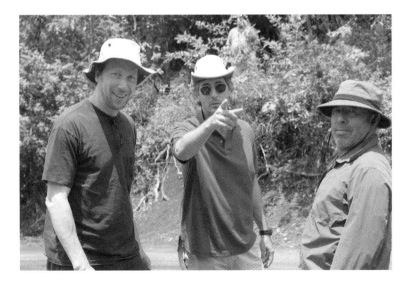

Hail, hail *The Descendants*: Alexander Payne's first feature Since *Sideways* a hit with critics, George Clooney-starring comedy-drama sure to be an awards contender

Published in a 2011 issue of *The Reader*

Back in the saddle

However you feel about Alexander Payne's work, you must concede the cinema landscape is richer now that he's back with his first feature since *Sideways*. That's certainly the consensus among reviewers who've seen his *The Descendants*.

The September 10 world premiere of the much-anticipated comedy-drama at the Toronto International Film Festival officially launched the George Clooney–starring vehicle as a must-see this fall movie season. The film's screenings in Toronto, where Payne, Clooney, and co-star Shailene Woodley appeared, came just a week after a press sneak preview at the Telluride Film Festival.

The next big splash comes in October when *The Descendants* is the closing night selection at the New York Film Festival, and Payne will be on hand. It's reminiscent of how his highly lauded *Sideways* and *About Schmidt* scored major points at prestige festivals. He will also accompany his film at festivals in London, Honolulu, Greece, Turin, and Dubai. The Fox Searchlight release opens theatrically Nov. 18. Payne will be at special November screenings of *The Descendants* at Film Streams. Details coming.

Shot in Hawaii in 2010, the film is Payne's faithful adaptation of the Kaui Hart Hemmings novel. Clooney's Matt King is a father-husband forced by circumstance and legacy to face some hard truths, such as his dying wife having cheated on him. This rude awakening propels a journey of revenge and reconciliation.

Payne re-teamed with *Sideways* cinematographer Phedon Papamichael and worked for the first time with Clooney, Woodley, Beau Bridges, and Robert Forster. Given Payne's track record and the talent surrounding him, it's no surprise the project's getting big love or that his return is being warmly embraced.

Though an old hand at the dog-and-pony hype of festival, and soon enough again, awards show hype, it's been a while since he's been through the media grinder. So what does it feel like to unveil your precious creation to the expectant film world? He answered that and other questions by phone from Toronto the day after his picture was accorded a standing ovation there.

"I guess you feel a combination of panic and calm," he said. "Panic in that people are going to see it for the first time and you really hope it works. And calm in that, well, there's nothing I can do. I've already done the work and it is what it is, and it's ready to have its own relationship with the public. Now it belongs to the ages.

"So it's panic, morbid curiosity and relief. And the fact that it's been well-received both at Telluride and here . . . the big feeling is relief. When a film is well-received it doesn't bring me profound happiness necessarily, but it calms my nerves."

In an out-of-sight-out-of-mind industry, Payne's relative absence since 2004 amounts to an eternity, though he insists, "I personally never think about that, only when all the reporters ask, 'Why's it been so long?' and I say, 'Well, because I've been busy—I had a bunch of other stuff going on.' It's not going to be that long for the next few. I'm going to go quickly now from film to film." He may begin shooting *Nebraska*, his black-and-white, father-son road picture, as soon as spring 2012.

Meanwhile, Payne is paying attention to reviews. But in an era when, as he puts it, "every Tom, Dick and Harry is an online film critic," he's selective about whose criticism he reads. He prefers "the old standby critics," by whom he means figures like Todd McCarthy of *The Hollywood Reporter.* "I respect him, he's a real film guy. He's a cinephile. And I do care what he thinks," Payne said of McCarthy. "I'd like for him to like it. And I like Leonard Maltin. I like good critics. I want anyone to tell me what I'm doing wrong and what I'm doing right so that I can keep learning."

For the record, McCarthy called *Descendants* "one of those satisfying, emotionally rich films that works on multiple levels." Maltin termed it "an exceptionally fine film." Payne's familiar enough with what's been written that he said, "Some film journalists suggest, 'It's like your other work, it has a certain combination of comedy, pathos and following the journey of a flawed protagonist, but somehow this one has more acceptance and less condescension,' which I personally have never aspired to. But anyway they think it's more open-hearted and nuanced."

His own production company, Ad Hominem Enterprises, acquired the novel before it was published but not for Payne to direct. He eventually came around to the material as a project for himself, then rewrote the script by Nat Faxon and Jim Rash. Did Payne's life catch up with the emotional arc of the story? "It could be," he said. "I think if you're trying to do sincere and honest work, then the work you do corresponds somehow to where you are in your life. It has to. I do know that an emotional anchor that kind of made me want to do it are two acts of love or forgiveness in the novel. When Clooney's character decides to track down his wife's lover, he wants to kill the guy, but tells him she is going to die imminently. He just reckons this guy would want to know. That's an act of love.

"And then later at the end when the lover doesn't show up but his wife does, and she says, 'My husband was too cowardly to come and that didn't seem right—I thought someone from my family should come.' It's also an act of difficult love. And I thought those would be nice to represent."

Descendants resonates with Paynesian themes and motifs. "I'm just always drawn to material that remains human and devoid of contrivance, that stays on the credible human plane. I try to somehow explore, express and mock the human heart." He said a friend who saw the film "enjoyed having a constantly shifting relationship" to the coma-stricken Mrs. King, who is variously an object of love, hate, pity, and indifference—both for the other characters and the audience. Similarly, the story often shifts from comedy to drama and back again.

"One thing I witness with audiences is what someone described as hairpin turns in tone. That within a scene you can be laughing one moment, crying the next, and then laughing again. A couple journalists asked me about that and how it's accomplished and of course I have to say, I don't really know, but I do think life is like that. Life has laughter and drama all going on at the same time. So I don't really see hairpin shift in tone but rather a thicker tone or fabric of life."

Letting the picture go

During the premiere Toronto screening at the Elgin Theatre Payne said he was a picture of nervous energy. He began the night seated in the middle of the house, then went to the back to request the sound be raised. He watched from the rear, then moved to the balcony. He asked for another sound spike, before finally returning to his seat. All the while, acutely aware of how the film played.

"I just make the films, I don't really know what they are until I watch them with an audience. It's just interesting to see how this one functions and what I think I can do better next time and what I think works pretty well this time around."

As for the marketing, he called the trailer "OK," but acknowledged this film, like his others, is "hard to sum up," adding, "You just have to see the film." How Fox positions it is beyond his control. "The studio, I trust, is going to do a great job. I completely trust in their greed."

Payne and cinematographer Phedon Papamichael on the set of *The Descendants*. The two artists have formed a fruitful working relationship that began with *Sideways*, continued with *The Descendants*, and extended to the writer-director's next film *Nebraska*, which saw the collaborators and friends working in Payne's home state and in black-and-white for the first time. They have since worked together a fourth time, on *Downsizing*.

Cinematographer Phedon Papamichael, producer Jim Burke, and actress Shailene Woodley discuss working with Alexander Payne on *The Descendants* and Kaui Hart Hemmings comments on the adaptation of her novel

Published in a 2011 issue of *The Reader*

Hawaiian Eye

In his well-reviewed new film *The Descendants* Alexander Payne reframes the Hawaiian idyll as gritty American terrain where history and culture intersect with human aspirations and failings.

The festival favorite follows a Hawaiian clan set askew by trauma, infidelity, greed, and legacy. Feeling the weight of it all is reluctant land baron Matt King (George Clooney), who tries salvaging what's left of his family and life by practicing forgiveness and finally growing up. Clooney's called the film a coming-of-age tale for his fifty-year-old character and his estranged seventeen-year-old daughter, Alexandra, played by Shailene Woodley.

The Fox Searchlight release has two preview screenings Nov. 20 at Film Streams, where the pic plays exclusively beginning Nov. 23.

For this project that's put Payne back in the game after a seven-year feature hiatus, he reunited with producer Jim Burke, who goes back with him to *Election*, and cinematographer Phedon Papamichael, who lensed *Sideways*. Payne and Papamichael use Hawaii's natural beauty to inform its prevailing island insouciance and to counterpoint its hard realities. Burke is a partner with Payne and his frequent screenwriting collaborator Jim Taylor in Ad Hominem Enterprises, which produced the project. Woodley worked with Payne for the first time on the new film.

Descendants also marks the first time since *Election* Payne's worked with two young actors in crucial roles in Woodley and Amara Miller as her younger sister, Scottie."It's all about casting," Payne says of getting kids' parts right. "Shailene is a total pro. She's on a TV show (*The Secret Life of the American Teenager*). She's going places. She's excellent. Amara, who turned ten while we were shooting, had never been in anything. She's just a complete natural."

Payne collaborated once again with his longtime casting director, John Jackson (an Omahan). Kaui Hart Hemmings, a Hawaii native and resident, who authored the novel the film's based on, closely vetted the script at Payne's request to ensure authenticity and was on set for the duration. She praised his "attention to the minutiae of Hawaiian life, his humor and restraint, his casting decisions," adding that the adaptation "brings Hawaii to the big screen—something that's never been done before in an authentic way."

Whether bucolic wine country gone sodden or stolid Omaha's underside revealed or paradise undone, Payne indelibly places broken characters in their milieu. Rather than *Hawaii Five-O* gloss or native exotic allure, here he focuses on the mundanity of familial disputes, personal tragedies, and inconvenient truths. In the Paynesian scheme, life happens messily everywhere and comedy springs from desperate people making mistakes.

Nuance

Burke said Payne's deft sardonic touch has, if anything, ripened. "My feeling is Alexander has made his finest film. It's sort of a maturation of filmmaker that is actually beautiful to see. Tonally, it still has many of the hallmarks of Alexander's previous work, but it is a bit more emotionally penetrating. I think the stakes are sort of serious in this picture."

The stakes are high for Payne, too, after being away so long and failing to get his *Downsizing* project made. He needed this. "Well, I mean from a straight kind of careerist point of view it's important," said Burke, "but that's not really what he is, he's more of an auteur. He's going to make movies when he's ready to do that and when he's ready to work on something he feels a connection to, and sometimes that takes a while."

Payne as collaborator

Woodley experienced the warm, laid-back set Payne's famous for. "He really gives you the freedom to express in whatever way you want to," she said, "and you don't feel weird being vulnerable around him because he creates such an accepting and open environment." She said Clooney was equally comfortable to work with and she now regards the two men as her industry "mentors."

Papamichael said Payne betrayed extra "nervousness" at the start but soon fell into a rhythm. Despite having worked only once before they quickly hit their stride.

"It was pretty instant. We were able to dive right into it. On *Sideways* it took about ten days for me to figure out the way he sees things and understands coverage. Sometimes the camera is not as intimate as I'd like to place it. He's very much an observer—he likes to stay a little wider, a little distant, and I pushed it a little bit and we got in tighter.

"We're still exploring our aesthetic as our collaboration continues. It's all very subjective, all very personal. Everybody sees things a little differently."

Each has a propensity for stripped-down, naturalistic, location-driven shoots that are a function of their low-budget roots. "I didn't come through the system of operators and gaffers, it was always do-it-yourself, use natural light, move quickly, keep it as simple as possible, be as unobtrusive as possible, so it was a good fit," said Papamichael. "On *Sideways* we tried not letting the camera, the craft, get in the way of the story, and that was the approach to *The Descendants* as well. Both are picturesque settings you put these conflicted, troubled lives into," he said.

Place as character

"What was important to us was to show a range of Hawaiian society. It's not just what's presented to people through the tourist boards," said Papamichael. "I mean, it has traffic jams, it has poverty. There's a great discrepancy between wealth and locals living in slums along the beach, where these tent towns go on for miles. It was important for us to show people who live in Hawaii are Americans like everywhere else. They have all the same problems."

Deep reverberations of place and heritage assail Matt King, he said.

"It was important to show the psychology of the land and the strength of nature as Matt goes through the conflict he's dealing with and feels the healing power and purity of nature. It helps him sort of resolve certain things he's torn about, and he gains respect for recognizing those values. There's so many layers in it."

The reportage-like approach subtly reveals layers.

"It was important for the photography not to be flashy, but to feel real," Papamichael said. "Alexander has this saying: 'Keep the banality of things.' So we don't touch anything on locations."

The joint where one of King's cousins, played by Beau Bridges, holds court is a genuine bar and the extras glimpsed there its actual denizens. "Even when we shoot somebody driving somewhere, we shoot on the road the character would have to take. It's not like, 'Oh, let's do some drive-bys on the north shore because it's really pretty.' It extends to casting. Alexander instinctively finds people that feel real.

"All that authenticity audiences do feel somehow. It's not manipulative, it's not some artificial world we're creating. I think that's why his stories, other than the brilliant writing, are so effective. They are real."

How Papamichael and Payne work

He says the two of them work intuitively, starting in pre-production. "We don't really shot list or storyboard. What we do is we watch movies we feel are more or less relevant to what we're doing. We're drinking wine and eating pasta and showing each other films."

For *Descendants*, he said, "I showed him *Walkabout* because it deals with nature and how society and humanity are in conflict with that. We always end up watching some Hal Ashby or Italian movie (at Payne's insistence)." This show-and-tell sparks a running conversation. "It's nothing specific, nothing designed. We don't analyze it. We just get a sense for the tone or the framing. We do go scout and pick locations together. We do talk a little bit about color palette when we're dealing with (production designer) Jane Stewart, but it's very nontechnical—the whole thing.

"He's open, he listens to people. Sometimes he's looking more for help, sometimes less. He has a very particular, very unique way of seeing things in the way he directs, the way he cuts. He takes a long time to cut his movies. He really fine tunes and finds the little moments with (editor) Kevin Tent. It's very precise in a way."

That precision extends to Payne's scripts. "I remember Thomas Haden Church once asked if he could change one word in a sentence (on *Sideways*) and Alexander thought about it for a really long time and he was like, 'No, I think we'll just do it the way it's scripted.' He surely thought about that line a really long time when writing and that's why it's in the script that way." He said even dialogue that sounds improvised is scripted. "It's exactly the way it's written, word for word, there's no veering off into any ad-libbing."

Papamichael and Payne are slated to work together again soon. They've done scouts and made tests for *Nebraska*, a black-and-white, father-son road pic for Paramount to be shot in state next spring. Word has it Payne's trying to seduce Oscar-winner Gene Hackman out of retirement to play the derelict father who enlists his estranged son in driving him to claim a supposed winning lottery ticket.

Alexander Payne and Kaui Hart Hemmings on the symbiosis behind his film and her novel *The Descendants* and her role in helping get Hawaii right

Published in a 2012 issue of *The Reader*

Kaui Hart Hemmings

Giving credit where credit is due

When Alexander Payne's turn came to speak in the glow of *The Descendants* winning Best Motion Picture Drama at the Golden Globes, he made sure to thank the people of Hawaii and author Kaui Hart Hemmings.

He did something few directors do by involving Hemmings, a Hawaii native and resident, in the adaptation, pre-production, and production of the George Clooney–starring film. He's widely credited her vital role in helping him get a fix on the island state's particular culture, or as much as a mainlander like himself can attain. For all the time he spent researching, writing, prepping, and shooting there, he never lost sight of being a visitor in need of expert advice.

Of course, the 2007 Hemmings novel is the reason there's a movie at all. He knows golden material when he sees it and he remained true to the book beyond her expectations.

"I've had the privilege of seeing Alexander making this film, from location scouting and casting to directing and filming. His attention to the minutiae of Hawaiian life, his humor and restraint, his casting decisions—I felt like I'd be surprised if it wasn't a good film. Still, I couldn't prepare myself for how good," said Hemmings. "It's a film that sticks with you, teaches you something without being at all didactical.

It brings Hawaii to the big screen, something that's never been done before, in an authentic way. I never insisted on him being faithful to my novel, but he did, and I'm pretty happy about that since it led to results like these."

His respect for her work and inclusion in his process is why he told a worldwide Globes audience, with some prompting from Ad Hominem Enterprises producing partner and former co-writer, Jim Taylor, ". . . thanks to Kaui Hart Hemmings—she gave us a beautiful gift."

"I don't need the public thank you but . . . it sure does please the locals. I spent a lot of time with Alexander, the crew and George, so it was just fun times," said Hemmings. "I'm a big fan of this movie. I have the privilege of feeling like I contributed to it in some way and so it's nice to be acknowledged."

In good company

Sticking closely to her tale of a man desperately negotiating personal upheavals, Payne's film has struck a responsive chord. It's made $52 million-plus in domestic box-office revenue while playing in fewer than one thousand theaters. The success is not surprising given Payne's track record, then again this was something of a risk as his first solo feature script after collaborating with Taylor on his first four features and numerous for-hire gigs. It also took Payne far afield from the worlds he'd portrayed.

He did surround himself with a company of longtime collaborators in producer Jim Burke, co-producer–production manager George Parra, production designer Jane Ann Stewart, cinematographer Phedon Papamichael, and editor Kevin Tent.

On the strength of a robust showing, the film's pegged a strong Academy Awards contender. Tuesday, it nabbed five nominations—for Best Picture; Payne for Best Director; Payne, Nat Faxon, and Jim Rash for Best Adapted Screenplay; Clooney for Best Actor; and Tent for Best Editing. Even if it should fizzle Feb. 26, it won't change the fact Payne's made arguably his most accessible work without comprising artistic integrity.

Nailing Hawaii

Among the reasons to admire the film is the authentic glimpse it offers of a little-seen Hawaii stripped bare of any gloss. As Payne's quick to point out, he didn't arrive at this informed, insider's look alone. Hemmings became his primary guide in seeing past the surface, touristy Hawaii into the deeper machinations of its internal society.

"It's not my world. I needed help from her, from a lot of people," he said. "It's all about trying to aspire to catch a sense of place. It is very specific and there's great consciousness about who's from Hawaii, who's not, who's just out there from the mainland."

The beautiful gift of Hemmings's debut novel is a multi-layered story anchored in family, heritage, betrayal, and forgiveness. Land baron Matt King and his comatose wife Liz are the pivot points around which the drama revolves, yet the pull of Hawaii and the weight of legacy are equally indelible characters. The plot plays to Payne's strength of peeling away a protagonist's façade in crisis. In an *Odyssey*-like journey King tries rectifying the damage of his failed marriage, salvaging what's left of his family, saving face, and exacting revenge. Through missteps and all, he becomes a better man and father. In doing right by his ancestors, he becomes an honorable descendant.

As a mixed heritage islander herself, Hemmings is well attuned to the delicate balance of Hawaii's haves and have-nots. As landed gentry by virtue of ancestry King is an object of envy and resentment. He feels guilty about his privileged status and burdened by the riches he controls. When he discovers Liz and her lover Brian Speer were conspiring to manipulate the impending sale of the family's land, he's dismayed.

Telling the story through King's acerbic POV, the author deftly moves from pathos to humor in her book. She's satisfied Payne's filmic voice stays true to the material. "I think my biggest concern was tone. You know, forget all the cultural things, I felt like tone came first and I think I really lucked out with getting a director like him. It could have been either really glib and slick or it could have just been so melodramatic and so focused on culture and setting, and ignoring the fact this is a universal story that's heartbreaking and funny and true. He gets that obviously.

"So much of the humor depends on these really small observations, a piece of dialogue or what someone's wearing, their choice in magazines. Alexander makes fun and yet he lets you know he likes the people. It comes across as kind and not condescending at all, which is so great. That makes me appreciative he is the person dealing with my book because there are judgments to be made, yet in the end I love this place and I love the people and I think he does too."

Faithful translation

Anyone who both reads her book and sees Payne's film will recognize her characters have been fully realized in the translation. "I'm so pleased with the script and I definitely think he got them. In fact. I think he improved on a lot of them," she says. "I think he improved on the older daughter character (Alexandra) or just added some more layers to the relationship with her father. I think the character of the younger daughter, Scottie, was hard to translate to screen ... I thought she came off as a kid who is precocious but you can also see it's sourced in this anger and pain."

Surrendering her book to the adaptation wasn't traumatic for Hemmings. "I never saw it as a book that's so sacred it can't be touched ... so if anything I freely gave it up, put it on the altar and said, Do what you will, because the book is done and no matter what a movie does to it it's still there, it's not going anywhere, it can't be ruined. It's been enjoyable to see how others interpreted it. I just sort of sat back enjoying the ride and helping where I could."

She confirmed an earlier script by Nat Faxon and Jim Rash "was a lot different" than Payne's. "I enjoyed both, but enjoyed his a lot more." Payne's other Ad Hominem producing partner, Jim Burke, optioned the novel for Payne to produce. Faxon and Rash wrote a script Stephen Frears was once attached to. When Payne couldn't find financing for his pet project *Downsizing*, he revisited *Descendants* at the urging of Burke. Once committed to it, he delved into Hawaii and wrote an entirely new script.

Notably, he wrote the script alone, not with Taylor. "I needed to find my own personal way into Matt King, just to feel him a little bit more," he says. "The other thing was I needed this one to be a little bit more personal to me because I thought the story was so outside of me. I'm not from Hawaii, I'm not from one of those families, I'm not married with kids. So somehow to find personal connections to Matt King I wanted to write it alone and by that I mean without speaking. When you write with someone you have always to speak: 'Oh, why don't we try this ... what if the scene was this?' But often the best writing is without speaking because you're just working, at least the more personal writing.

"To give an example of it, I think I would have felt more rage than how Matt King felt at the betrayal and finding out about Brian Speer so I wrote that scene not in the book where he yells at her (Liz). He tells the girls, 'Let me alone for just a minute,' and he lays into her. That came from a kind of personal place. I'm not saying I would have the courage to do that, or I might ..."

The grace note the film ends on of King and his girls joined at the hip is a Payne invention that packs a punch without going overboard.

"I'm getting lots of compliments on the final shot where they're all together on the sofa, of course covered with the mother's blanket (quilt). I'm happy that worked out. That's a movie ending. It's a landing strip." The accumulated weight of all the storylines becomes distilled in this living family portrait of redemption, reconciliation, mourning, togetherness, and moving on.

"The other thing I added that's not in the book, because this is a movie I thought we should see the land, is that scene in Kauai where they go, 'Let's go see the land.'" A largely wordless scene plays out between King, Alexandra, her friend Sid, and Scottie as they take in the beauty and enormity of the coastal land entrusted to Matt and his fellow heirs. It's a perfectly nuanced blend of profundity and emotion.

Just as director of photography Phedon Papamichael helped Payne capture the wine country of *Sideways*, he subtly brings out Hawaii's splendor. He'll presumably do the same for the Sandhills and Panhandle when the two film *Nebraska* this spring.

"It's a nice feeling too to be working with someone I like working with so much," Payne says of Papamichael. "You need to feel great complicity with your DP. You have to have a great unspoken, wordless communication, where something an actor's doing with just a quick look at each other we indicate we have to find a way to trick him into another take, that the acting wasn't very good. Or just the shared excitement at executing a great shot. You both have to be really excited about filmmaking, and of course the DP has to give the actors the impression he's making them look fantastic.

"And we have the Greek thing in common."

Checks and balances

Before filming commenced Hemmings acted as Payne's editorial eye. "I feel like I set him up on little play dates where I set him up with different people. I sent some people his way who I thought would fit the role of some minor characters. We went over the script on two different occasions, where we'd just go through it line by line and I would add my two cents. Again, it's just all about these small details that you think are mundane, but for me that's what makes a story.

"And as we'd go through the script he'd have specific questions: 'Who do you see as Shelley?' I'd go through a bunch of actors I was thinking of as I was writing it. When I first met Jim Burke in 2007, before the book was even published, he asked, 'Who do you see in this role?' (of Matt King) and I was sort of shy to say George Clooney. It felt sort of presumptuous. But that's the only person I imagined. I had no idea they would actually consider that and he would actually be cast in it."

Hemmings, who plays King's secretary, is in two scenes with Clooney. In one, she utters a line about his cousins arriving. Later, she's among friends of the family he admonishes to visit Liz in the hospital. Members of her family also appear as extras.

But her main role was off-camera. She said, "A lot of things were just the lingo. Nobody really says, 'Are you from the island?' It's just these stupid little things, and yet for someone from Hawaii it's jarring when you say it the wrong way. You want to be authentic. Alexander was really concerned about getting things right as far as place."

She said Payne "had a bunch of questions about land." He explains, "The emotional story could be set anywhere but of course the land is everything. Land and power, the whole setting of it, the landed upper class of Hawaii." Hawaii historian Gavin Dawes impressed upon him "the complexity of the place."

In the end, he said capturing Hawaii "all comes back to Omaha. It's an exciting, logical extension of my process begun here in Nebraska of—how do you tell a story in the foreground and have a place in the background? Starting with *About Schmidt* I began to get the hang of that. I took those skills and learned some new ones on *Sideways*. So I pretty much see *The Descendants* as an extension of that same work ..."

If *Descendants* should score at the Oscars, Payne is sure to express appreciation again to Hemmings and Hawaii. Her novel was a gift, and now his film is one in return. The film's success certainly can't hurt its sales. "I don't know exactly," Hemmings said, "but I know this is the best thing that ever happened to my little book."

The following is a capsule take on Alexander Payne and *The Descendants* I did for *Omaha Magazine* just before the Oscars. In this piece I tried to give readers a brief rundown on the filmmaker and his seriocomic forays into the existential angst, folly, fragility, and yearning of the human condition.

Two-time Oscar-winner Payne delivers another screen gem with *The Descendants* and further enhances his cinema standing

Published in a 2012 issue of *Omaha Magazine*

Until *The Descendants* opened to golden reviews last fall, seven years elapsed between feature films for its celebrated writer-director Alexander Payne.

The Omaha native and Creighton Prep grad came of age as a film buff here. He made his first three features (*Citizen Ruth*, *Election*, *About Schmidt*) in his hometown, each moving him up the ranks of elite moviemakers. His surprise 2004 hit, *Sideways*, took him to Southern California's wine country. The combination road-buddy picture and unconventional love story confirmed Payne as a film industry leading light, earning him a Best Adapted Screenplay Oscar.

He then busied himself writing-producing films for other directors. When he couldn't find financing for his own pet project, *Downsizing*, he made *The Descendants*. Before shooting it in late 2010 the only directing he did in this period was a segment of *Paris, I Love You* and the pilot for HBO's *Hung*.

The Golden Globes won by *Descendants* star George Clooney for Best Dramatic Actor and by Payne and producing partners Jim Burke and Jim Taylor for Best Drama harbors well heading into the Oscars, where the film will be well-represented with five nominations (for Best Picture, Best Director, Best Adapted Screenplay, Best Editing, and Best Actor). The three friends share their own production company, Ad Hominem Enterprises, which produced the picture for Fox Searchlight, with whom Ad Hominem has a first-look deal. The pic's strong showing with critics and award shows is reminiscent of *Sideways*. Like that film, this one took Payne far from the Midwest—to Hawaii. A decade after working with iconic Jack Nicholson on *About Schmidt*, Payne teamed with another icon, Clooney.

As land baron attorney Matt King, Clooney is a man in crisis. His wife Liz lies in a coma after a boating accident. After years of indifferent parenting he's suddenly in charge of his two girls. He's burdened, too, by the valuable land entrusted to his care by ancestors. When his older daughter Alexandra (Shailene Woodley) reveals her mother's infidelity, Matt sets off on a journey that begins in retribution but ends in forgiveness. Payne said "two acts of love" are what drew him to adapt the Kaui Hart Hemmings novel.

The story shares in common with *Schmidt* and *Sideways* and Payne's forthcoming *Nebraska* a beleaguered protagonist trying to mend an unraveling life. "It's just the comic archetype Jim Taylor (his producing partner and former co-writer) and I came up with and I'm continuing of the middle-aged guy who's really unconscious and has a bunch of anguish and frustration in life," said Payne. "It's a guy with good intentions but who's bought the wrong package. I think it's funny."

Extracting equal amounts pathos and humor from human folly is what Payne does. "I'm just always drawn to material that remains human. You don't need guns and spaceships and great contrivance to have a movie and a meaningful one. I don't think those elements are necessarily bad—I like movies of every genre, but what I'm drawn to is trying to somehow explore and express and mock the human heart."

Descendants is being called Payne's most fully realized work. "I hope so," he said, adding that any new maturity reflects his more accrued life experience at age fifty and his evolving film craft. Some observers note he seems more comfortable letting tender emotions play out on screen. "Well, that's what this story called for," he said. "I mean, it could be a new vein of filmmaking in me or could just be I was serving this particular story as a professional, workmanlike director. I have no idea."

Staying true to his Omaha roots, he attended the movie's local premiere at Film Streams, where *Descendants* smashed box office records. Payne enjoys sharing his work at the art cinema whose board he serves on. Before an appreciative crowd of friends and supporters he announced the film was among the highest grossers nationally its first week. By early February its domestic take stands at $66 million-plus, making it the top indie flick released in 2011.

Exuding grace and humility, Payne personally greeted audience members before and after the opening night screenings here. In accepting his Golden Globe, Payne deflected praise to cast and crew, to the people of Hawaii and to Hemmings, whose "beautiful gift" of a novel he made his own.

"He made this movie that's hugely successful and he made sure that success was also Film Streams' success, and hopefully Omaha's success," said Film Streams founder-director Rachel Jacobson. "We had so much fun at the premiere. It was just a blast. I wondered if we should do it at a bigger venue, and he said, 'We've got to do it at our home.' Getting the exclusive from Fox Searchlight was all him. That was huge for us."

He's conquered Cannes, Toronto, New York, Hollywood, but he proves he can come home again. Payne, who keeps a condo here, plans shooting the father-son road pic *Nebraska* in various in-state locales come spring. Home is where the heart is and he's always happy to return where his cinema dreams were first fired.

While *The Descendants* did not clean up at the Oscars as it might have some other years owing to multiple wins by *The Artist* and *Hugo*, Alexander Payne added to his growing legendary status by picking up his second Oscar for Best Adapted Screenplay. He, Nat Faxon, and Jim Rash shared the Academy Award for their work on what was perhaps the best reviewed film of the year. Payne shared the same award with Jim Taylor for their *Sideways* script. It seems only a matter of time before Payne is recognized with a Best Director Oscar.

Payne's love affair with the movies began when he was a child in his hometown of Omaha. The nascent cinephile's frequent filmgoing companion then was his mother, Peggy Payne, who recognized her prodigy of a son expressed far more interest in grown-up films than children's fare, and she indulged his serious passion by taking him to screenings of art movies.

Decades later the world-class filmmaker told the planet how much he appreciates what she did for him when he dedicated his Oscar to her. In doing so he said, "I love you," in Greek, thus acknowledging his family's heritage, which he's extremely proud of. He also singled out one of his producing partners, Jim Burke, star George Clooney, and author Kaui Hart Hemmings, whose novel he, Faxon, and Rash adapted.

Alexander Payne delivers graceful Oscar tributes— the winner for Best Adapted Screenplay recognizes Clooney, Hemmings, and his mom

Published in a 2012 issue of *The Reader*

The obvious and not so obvious came into focus when native son Alexander Payne accepted his second Oscar in front of a live audience of his peers and a television viewing audience estimated at one billion-plus viewers during Sunday's Academy Awards.

He shared Best Adapted Screenplay for *The Descendants* with Nat Faxon and Jim Rash, whose mimicking of presenter Angelina Jolie's power pose seemingly distracted and peeved Payne as he tried beating the clock with his thank-yous. Always the pro though, he quickly collected himself and offered one of the evening's best grace notes with this tribute:

"We share this with George Clooney and the rest of the cast for interpreting our screenplay so generously and we also share it in particular with Kaui Hart Hemmings, our beautiful Hawaiian flower, for her novel."

A radiant Hemmings sat next to the debonair Payne and his date for the evening, his well-coiffed mother Peggy, and it was to her and their shared Greek heritage he made the most moving gesture.

"And on a brief personal note if I may, my mother is here with me from Omaha, hold the applause, and after watching the show a few years ago she made me promise that if I ever won another Oscar I had to dedicate it to her just like Javier Bardem did with his mother (eliciting laughter). So, Mom, this one's for you. Se agapao poly. (Greek for "I love you very much.") And thanks for letting me skip nursery school so we could go to the movies. Thanks a lot."

Payne has sometimes mentioned his mother and father both indulged his early childhood fascination with film, but it was she who took him to see the cutting-edge grown-up movies he preferred over children's fare.

He could have quipped about her insisting that only her Countryside Village hair stylist attend to her tresses, which meant he had to fly the hairdresser out to L.A. He could have used the stage to poke Nebraska legislators, as he did six weeks ago in Lincoln, for leverage in trying to get film industry tax credits passed here, lest he have to take his planned Nebraska project to, say, Kansas. He could have tweaked the noses of Paramount suits who gave him a hard time about his insistence in wanting to shoot *Nebraska* in black and white.

That he didn't show anyone up speaks to his respect for the industry and his desire to not burn bridges. Besides, as he recently told a reporter, "I like the Oscars." It's obvious the Oscars like him. The only question is when he will take home Best Picture and Best Director awards.

7

Nebraska

❦

Introduction

Even though Alexander Payne demonstrates time and again that commercial considerations mean very little to him, following the breakaway success of *The Descendants* (2011) there was every reasonable expectation he might lean a bit more again in the direction of mainstream with his next film. I say again because I count *The Descendants* as a conventional, even mainstream work even though its protagonist rails against his comatose wife and sets out to wreck the life of the man she was cheating with, all the while trying not to lose it with his two grieving daughters in tow.

Payne soon quashed any notion of playing it safe when he announced the small, insular back roads comedy-drama *Nebraska* (2013) as his new feature project. It did not help its bottom line chances that the film is set in rural Nebraska, which for most filmgoers may as well be the dark side of the moon for its unfamiliarity, remoteness, and perceived barrenness. Indeed, if Nebraska conjures any image at all it is of endless cornfields, cows, and monotonously flat, uninspired scenery. When the story laid over such a setting features a confused, depressed old cuss alienated from family and friends and wandering around in a bleak wasteland made even bleaker by black and white photography and desolate late fall, post-harvest locations, it does not exactly engender excitement. The prospect of a dour, feel-bad experience devoid of life and color does not get tongues a-wagging to generate the all important buzz that sells tickets.

Of course, anyone who has seen *Nebraska* knows the film is not the downer it may appear to be from glimpsing a thirty second trailer or hearing a thirty second sound bite, but that it is ultimately a sweet, deeply affecting film filled with familiar truths amid its very Nebraskaesque yet also quite universal archetypes.

Payne's insistence on shooting in black and white was a completely legitimate aesthetic choice given the storyline and tone of this stark, autumnal mood piece about an old man having his last hurrah. But it also meant a definite disadvantage in appealing to average or general movie fans, many of whom automatically pass on any non-color film. Compounding the aversion that many moviegoers have with black and white is the fact that most studio executives, distributors, and theater bookers share this aversion, not on aesthetic grounds, but based on the long-held, much repeated argument that black and white films fare poorly at the box office. Of course, there is a self-fulfilling prophecy at work here that starts with studio resistance and reluctance to greenlight black and white features and even when a studio does approve the rare black and white entry executives seem to half-heartedly market and release these pics. It is almost as if the bean counters are out to perversely prove a point, even at the risk of injuring the chances of one of their own pictures at finding a sizable audience. Then when the picture lags, it gives the powerbrokers the platform to say, I told you so. No wonder then – and this is assuming the argument is true – most black and white flicks don't perform well compared with their color counterparts. Except, how does one arrive at anything like a fair comparison of films based on color versus black and white? Even if the films under review are of the same genre and released in the same period, each is individually, intrinsically its own experience and any comparison inevitably ends up being a futile apples and oranges debate. Besides, there are exceptions to the supposed rule that all black and white films struggle. From the 1970s on *The Last Picture Show*, *Paper Moon*, *Young Frankenstein*, *Manhattan*, *Raging Bull*, *Schindler's List*, *Ed Wood*, and *The Artist* are among the black and white films to have found wide success. It is admittedly a short list but it does prove black and white need not be a death sentence.

To no one's surprise Paramount did what practically any studio would have done in the same situation, which was to fight Payne on the black and white decision. In no uncertain terms Payne wanted to make *Nebraska* in black and white and just as adamantly the studio wanted no part of it. He pushed and they pushed back. He would not compromise his vision because from the moment he first read Bob Nelson's screenplay he clearly saw in his mind's eye the world of this story play out in in shades of black and white. It just fit. It fit the characters and the settings and the emotions and as far as he was concerned that was that. No questions asked. No concessions made.

I do not claim to know all the details of this protracted dispute or should I say discussion but I do know from what Payne and cinematographer Phedon Papamichael have told me that the issue became a point of some contention. I do not know if it ever reached an impasse where Payne more or less indicated by word or action he was prepared to walk and take the project with him (his own Ad Hominem production company brought the property to Paramount). It certainly wouldn't surprise me that he let it be known, subtly or not, that he was willing to make the project with another studio if it came to that. It is a moot point now since Paramount eventually acceded to his wishes, though not insignificantly the studio did cut some of the picture's already small budget as a kind of hedge I suppose against the small business they expected the film to do. The smaller the budget, and in this case it was $12 million, the smaller the risk of not recouping its cost.

Given Payne's even temperament and gentility, I doubt if things reached the level of shouting or angry exchanges, though he undoubtedly expressed displeasure with their interference and pettiness. I have to think he wore the execs down with his patience and persistence to win the black and white battle but at the end of the day he was willing to give up a couple million dollars in exchange for realizing his vision. I know he said that losing a million dollars is a huge loss when it comes to small-budgeted films like this one and I understand that in order to get the film made within those constraints he and others worked for scale in return for some points on the back end. But I have to believe those "sacrifices" were completely worth it in the long run. I would even argue that having to work on a bare bones budget and a tight schedule worked in favor of getting this simple story right. It required cast and crew to live frugally like the characters and the frugal shoot placed a premium on efficiency, ingenuity, and everyone pulling together to make the most of what they had to work with. In truth this esprit de corps is evident on all of Payne's projects anyway because of the tight, loyal stock company he works with from film to film to film. They are a family and a team dedicated to one purpose: getting the film made to his specifications.

I asked Payne if it ever seems like a studio plays this game in order to gauge just how strongly the filmmaker is invested in a choice or preference as well as to what extent the filmmaker can be manipulated.

He seems to believe there is some truth in that. Perhaps it really is the studio's way of testing how firm the filmmaker's convictions are and how much the filmmaker is willing to give up or to stand fast in terms of creative control. As Paramount surely knew going in and if they somehow didn't know they surely soon discovered in the process of setting up the film, Payne is no push over and he brooks no fools. That is true at every juncture in the process, from making the deal to pre-production to the shoot and on through post-production. It is his film and he will not be budged from any creative choices he feels are necessary, which is to say he will not be pressured into doing something for the sake of added commercial appeal. Because Payne is not about burning bridges, except for his public displeasure over the way his first two films (*Citizen Ruth* and *Election*) were handled by the studios and releasing companies behind them, he is not saying on the record what he thinks about the way Paramount handled *Nebraska*. I have to think he is not pleased with the extremely limited release they gave it. At no time during its release did the film ever play more than nine hundred sixty eight theaters according to the website Boxoffice Mojo. That is anywhere from two-thirds to a half to a third the number of theaters its main awards competitors played at during their runs. It is hard to understand why the film was not given more opportunities to find a wider audience given the outstanding reception it received from critics (making most Top Ten lists), the foreign press (five Golden Globe nominations) and the Academy (six nominations).

Hampered as it was by the limited release, *Nebraska* still pulled in nearly $18 million domestically and I am sure when all the figures are added up from North America and overseas, where I predict the film will fare well, especially in Europe, its total gross will be in excess of $25 million. By the time all the home viewing rentals and purchases are taken into account a year from now, I wager the film will have done some $30 million in business, which would more than double its production costs. That is quite a return on a small film that did not get much studio support beyond the bare basics.

Payne could have made things easier for himself and the studio by filming in color and securing a superstar. *Nebraska* marked quite a departure from the lush, color-filled canvas of Hawaii he captured in *The Descendants* and the equally verdant California wine country he committed to celluloid in *Sideways*. Never mind the fact the stories of those earlier films, despite the radical differences of their physical locations, actually share much in common tonally and thematically with *Nebraska*. The dark comic tone and theme of Payne's films can threaten to be overshadowed when a star the magnitude of Jack Nicholson (*About Schmidt*) or George Clooney (*The Descendants*) attaches himself to one of his projects. But as anyone who is familiar with the subdued star turns of those two actors in those particular films will tell you, Nicholson departed far from his trademark insouciance and braggadocio to totally inhabit his repressed, depressive title character in *Schmidt* just as Clooney left behind much of his breezy, cocksure charm to essay his neurotic somewhat desperate character in *Descendants*. Each star was eager to shed his well-practiced, bigger-than-life persona in service of scripts and parts that called for them to play against type. Instead of their usual live-out-loud, testosterone-high roles, they play quiet, wounded, vulnerable men in trouble. For that matter, the men-children Paul Giamatti and Thomas Haden Church play in *Sideways* are seemingly complete opposites but in actuality are emotionally-stunted, damaged souls using oblivion, alcohol, and sex to medicate their pain and avoid reality. The beauty of the California and Hawaii locales work as contrast and counterpoint to the chaotic lives of these lost figures careening toward catharsis. In *Schmidt* Omaha is the perfect washed-out backdrop for a man undergoing a full-scale identity and spiritual crisis once he retires and his domineering wife dies.

That brings us to Woody Grant, the crotchety so-and-so at the center of *Nebraska*. When we meet this reprobate he is near the end of a largely misspent life. Facing his inevitable and nearing mortality he doesn't much like what he sees when he reviews his life and where he has landed. He is dealing with many deficits in his old age. His body is falling apart. He walks stiffly, haltingly. His alcoholism has been unaddressed and it contributes to his foggy mind, mood swings, propensity to fall and hurt himself, and to utter hurtful things. He seems to derive no joy or satisfaction from his wife of many years and his two adult sons. He almost regards them as inconvenient reminders of his own failings as a husband and father. On top of all this, he is poor and in no position to leave his family anything like a tangible legacy.

This miserable wretch has seized upon what he believes to be his last chance at assuaging a deep well of shame, guilt, bitterness, and resentment. His mistaken belief there is a sweepstakes prize for him to redeem becomes a search for his own personal redemption or salvation. He desperately wants something, namely a truck, to leave his boys. The true meaning of the road trip he embarks on with his son David is only revealed to us and to his boy along the way and that gradual discovery adds layers of poignancy to the story.

When Woody arrives back in his hometown of Hawthorne, Nebraska word spreads he is on his way to collect a million dollars sweepstakes prize. For a few moments he becomes a person of substance in the eyes of his extended family and the town's other residents. Some family members and one old friend turn vultures and demand they get a share of his windfall as compensation for favors they did or loans they made that were never returned. But there is another side to that story. We find out Woody has a kind heart beneath his gruff exterior, so much so that he's been known to do favors and to give money away without ever expecting repayment. That has led him to be taken advantage of over the years. Then when the truth gets out Woody has not won anything but has misinterpreted a marketing piece for a confirmation letter of his supposed million in winnings, he is publicly humiliated and made out to be a fool.

For *Nebraska* Payne went one step further in distancing himself from commercial considerations by casting as his two leads Bruce Dern and Will Forte, who at first glance form an unlikely combination but in fact play wonderfully off each other. Dern's acclaimed performance as Woody Grant earned him a Best Actor prize at Cannes and nominations from the Golden Globes and the Academy of Motion Picture Arts and Sciences. *Saturday Night Live* alumnus Forte is triumphant in his first dramatic role as the sympathetic son David. The next largest part belongs to June Squibb, who until this film was a somewhat familiar face if not a household name (she played Nicholson's wife in *Schmidt*). Her stellar work in a colorful role as Woody's piss-and-vinegar wife Kate has brought her the most attention she's received in a very long and productive career. Arguably, the biggest name in the picture belongs to Stacy Keach, a veteran of film, television, and stage who has little screen time in the picture but makes the most of it in a powerfully indelible turn as the story's heavy, Ed Pegram. As strong as these performances are Payne did not do his film any box office favors by choosing actors so far off the radar of moviegoers. That is not a criticism, it is simply a fact. At least a dozen more speaking parts are filled by no-name actors, nonprofessional actors, and nonactors, all of whom add great authenticity to the film but whose obscurity hurts rather than helps the marketing cause.

The choice to populate the film with zero star power ultimately is not the reason the film failed to pull in more of an audience because there are plenty of films that do well with little known, non A-list names, and nonactor finds. No, the real problem with how *Nebraska* fared had more to do with the perception the marketing campaign for the film imposed on it. The film's trailers did not communicate the heart and soul of the picture. None of the warmth or depth or populist appeal at its core registered in those clips. Instead, the film was represented as a cold, mean, depressive, rather flimsy sketch concept blown up to fill two hours. Anyone who has seen and appreciated *Nebraska* will tell you it is far more than that. It is a work replete with deep currents of regret, disappointment, melancholia, rage, nostalgia. and love. Alongside that run streams of humor, sweetness, irony, and slapstick. Then there is the sheer poetic evocation of hauntingly beautiful visuals that turn the wide open flyover terrain, roadside stops, and played-out small towns of Montana, Wyoming, South Dakota, and Nebraska into haunting fields of dreams and symbols of neglect. Not to mention centers of quirky, silly, sometimes surreal goings-on.

Plenty of small indie films about similarly unglamorous subject matter have struck a responsive chord with the masses. So what kept *Nebraska* from resonating the way, say, *Juno* did or *Little Miss Sunshine*? No one really knows. If the creatives who make the films and the suits who finance and sell them did, if there was some sure-fire magic formula at their disposal, then every film would be packaged into a box office winner. The truth is some films catch the wave and most don't and there doesn't seem to be any reliable rhyme or reason for why some hit and others miss that elusive, always moving wave everyone is after.

It may take a while, but I am quite confident *Nebraska* will eventually find the large audience it deserves. In my opinion it will be a much viewed and discussed stand-the-test-of-time film for its many cinema art merits. As good as Payne's earlier films have been I believe this to be his finest work to date because it is in my view the fullest expression of his filmmaking talents. Visually, it is a tone poem of the first order and on that basis alone it is a film to be reckoned with. Payne and cinematographer Phedon Papamichael have achieved an expressive black and white palette whose hues perfectly articulate the heavy heart of the story. But Payne also found unobtrusive ways to position the camera and, with editor Kevin Tent, to cut scenes so as to amplify its many moments of humor without ever detracting from its elegiac, soulful mood. Mark Orton's original music, plus the incidental music used here and there, add more nuances of mood. Payne artfully composed images for the wide screen format he shot in to glean added depth and meaning from the action. Within the same frame he intentionally juxtaposed characters with the stark landscapes, townscapes, and homes they inhabit. Many of these scenes emphasize sadness, stillness and desolation. Irony infuses it all. The result is an ongoing dialogue between people and their environments. Each informs the other and by consequence us.

The filmmaker's economy of style has never been more evident. He has reached the point of communicating so much with simple brush strokes. Take for instance the way Woody's harsh childhood experience is encapsulated when the old man and his family visit the abandoned farm house he grew up in. Payne has the camera fluidly glide over the detritus of this once proud home turned wreck and to peak into rooms that carry so much psychic-emotional pain for Woody, who was beaten as a boy. Payne clearly indicates this is a private, anguished, cathartic return for Woody, who has avoided this place and its memories for years.

Or consider that gathering of taciturn men in Woody's family at his brother's home in town. Payne arranges the uncles, brothers, sons, nephews, cousins in an American Gothic pose around the TV set, where the men engage in the almost wordless ritualistic viewing of a football game. It is at once a funny and powerful expression of their tribal, tight-lipped bond. A bond more about association by blood than affinity.

Then there are the almost incidental shots of boarded up buildings in town that symbolize and speak to the economic hard times to have befallen so many small towns like the fictional Hawthorne. In a short scene Payne conveys an important way in which the times have changed there and in towns like it when he has Woody visit the auto service station he used to own and he finds the new owners are Spanish-speaking Hispanics. Woody thus personally encounters a demographic shift that has altered the face of his hometown and much of rural Nebraska. No more is made of it then that simple reality and the brief exchange between Woody and the "newcomers," but it is enough to say that times have moved on and the Hawthorne he knew has evolved in some ways and remained unchanged in others.

Perhaps the best example of Payne distilling things down to their simplest, purest, most elemental form is the end sequence when David and Woody are in the truck David has purchased and registered in his father's name. David, who is at the wheel with Woody beside him, stops the truck on the edge of town and invites Woody to take the wheel and drive down main street in his new rig. What follows is one of the most moving denouements in contemporary American cinema. Woody is granted a rare gift when he accepts the invitation to take a celebratory ride down main street. As the truck slowly passes through town he wins more than any prize money could provide when four people from his past catch sight of him and look at him with a combination of awe, admiration, and surprise. It is a perfect moment in the sun vindication for a beleaguered, bedraggled man who suddenly brims with confidence and purpose. Woody leaves town on his own terms, his dignity and pride intact.

What makes that valedictory ride so special is that his sympathetic son David is there to grant him it and to bask in it with him. These two who began the road trip not really knowing each other and often at odds with each other have traveled a journey together that has brought them a measure of acceptance, healing, and peace. David has finally come to understand why his father is the way he is. His fondest desire is realized when he gives Woody that movie-movie opportunity to prove he is not the loser or fool this day. As Woody sits high in the cab of the truck, with David lovingly looking on from the floor, and drives past the artifacts of his past and the denizens of that town, he may as well be a cowboy sitting tall in the saddle of his horse riding into the sunset. He graciously accepts the congratulations of town chatterbox Bernie Bowen. He stares down his former friend Ed Pegram, who now looks the shamed fool. Woody's heart stirs again for old flame Peg Nagy, whose wistful expression wonders what might have been. As he heads out of town Woody said a fond goodbye to Albert, the Grant brother whose favorite pastime is siting beside the road waving at the occupants of passing cars.

Outside of town the truck stops at the bottom of a hill and Woody and David once again exchange places. Doing this out of the view of onlookers preserves Woody's glorious farewell and signals Woody now accepts his limitations and David's love for him. With David back behind the wheel and Woody beside him father and son drive off to meet the future together. The fact that almost all of this sequence plays out wordlessly and still conveys so much meaning is a testament to the work of Payne and his collaborators in extracting the essence of these scenes through beautifully executed shots that give full weight to glances gestures, postures, and backdrops.

I had been anticipating the ending for a long while because it was some years ago Payne first shared the Nelson screenplay with me. The script had come to him way back around the time he was making *Sideways* (2004). He kept it in reserve all those years that passed between *Sideways's* production and release and his starting production on *The Descendants*. By the time he shared the *Nebraska* script with me Payne had already changed the ending (he always rewrites scripts he inherits) and I remember him being particularly proud of what he had achieved with the close of that story. I was completely taken by the entire script and especially that ending. In my book he really nailed it and came as close as one could to realizing what was on the page.

It is hard to find antecedents for the film. The closest I came up with are Frank Capra's *Meet John Doe*, Preston Sturges's *Sullivan's Travels*, Federico Felllini's *La Strada*, Jerry Schatzberg's *Scarecrow*, Peter Bogdanovich's *Paper Moon*, Paul Mazursky's *Harry and Tonto*, and David Lynch's *The Straight Story*. That is quite a range of work and it gives you an idea of the breadth of potential influences that can be found in it, though I am not suggesting Payne had any of those specific films or others in mind when he made *Nebraska*. There is at least a similar sense of alienation and a crazy intrepid spirit running through their restless storylines. They share a similar visual sensibility as well. Of course the most obvious thing they share in common is the road story template. While the protagonists are very different from each other, they are all running to or from something.

In terms of my coverage of *Nebraska*, I interviewed him twice before he began production, I visited the northeast Nebraska set for a couple days and witnessed a few scenes being shot, including one major exterior scene (outside the abandoned family farmhouse) and one major interior scene (at the home of Woody's brother in Hawthorne). I did followup interviews with Payne during and immediately after the shoot. Then I traveled to Los Angeles to sit in on five days of the final mixing process just before the film had its world premiere at Cannes. During my L.A. stay I got to see many fixes made to the film and watched a private run through of the entire film at a screening room on the Paramount Studios lot.

I got a second opportunity to watch the film ahead of its general release at a special Paramount screening put on by the Nebraska Coast Connection, an affiliation of Nebraskans working in the film and television industry. The organization hosts a monthly Hollywood Salon that features guest speakers and I attended the fall salon featuring Payne, who was interviewed by NCC founder and president Todd Nelson before a live audience at the Culver Hotel in Culver City. Much of that event focused on the making of *Nebraska*. I also attended the fall Film Streams Feature Event in Omaha that saw novelist and *Studio 360* host Kurt Andersen interview Payne, co-stars Dern, Forte, and Squibb live on stage at the Holland Performing Arts Center. In addition to the earlier interviews I did with Payne, I had interviewed all of those actors, with the exception of Squibb. I also interviewed Keach, screenwriter Bob Nelson, producer Albert Berger, and cinematographer Phedon Papamichael.

All in all, I accumulated as much or more material about *Nebraska* than I did for any of Payne's previous films and more than enough to warrant this new edition.

Much of what is communicated in *Nebraska* has to do with dislocation and disconnection. The characters harbor potent, not always pleasant memories of their shared past. Woody is a man broken off from the people and places of his past and when he revisits them in pursuit of his phantom winnings he is flooded with mixed feelings he doesn't quite know what to do with. Woody's woundedness is bound up in the incidents of his childhood and young adulthood. Distancing himself from that past has only separated himself from himself. Thus, he is a broken man who has left pieces of himself scattered in his wake. The story is not so much about him picking up the pieces of his life and putting them back together, although some of that occurs to make him more whole again, as it is about his son David using those fragments as puzzle pieces to more fully appreciate who his father is and the path he's walked. Because the story is about people who don't have much to say to each other, at least emotionally speaking, the emotional life of the story is rooted as much in the subtext as it is in the context of scenes. Therefore, the film's power resides as much in what is left unsaid or in what is referred to as it is in what is actually said and shown. This nonliteral approach is unusual for American films. Indeed, the film's oblique style and deliberate rhythms are very much those of a European or a Latin American film.

A final note about *Nebraska* and its reception from Nebraskans is in order. As respected and admired a figure as Payne is among the home state set, his films made in Nebraska elicit strange reactions from a certain segment who bemoan the unflattering light they feel he presents the state and its residents in. This is a classic case of it-is-what-it-is. There is no doubt *Citizen Ruth*, *Election*, *About Schmidt*, and *Nebraska*, his quartet of films made almost entirely on his native turf, focus on mundane and malicious aspects of life that, though found everywhere, no one wants associated with their state. It can be a particularly sensitive subject in Nebraska. because this small population state already battles an image problem. That is to say greater Nebraska and its one true metropolitan center, Omaha, do not have a strong, readily identifiable or sexy profile and presence on the national-international stages. Nebraska simply blends in with that vast homogenized Midwest and Great Plains. Outsiders dismiss it as a place of no consequence with bland surroundings, unsophisticated inhabitants, and insignificant happenings and therefore the very antithesis of the coasts. Some of those same perceptions explain why Nebraska struggles to retain its best and brightest and rarely draws a major new employer.

Nebraskans upset by Payne's portrayals of their state refer to the dull, dingy, dysfunctional portraits he paints, forgetting that he is in service to the stories he tells. Some wonder why he doesn't make Nebraska look better, more colorful, more pleasant, more positive, like the way he portrayed California or Hawaii, once again forgetting that aside from the countryside and oceanside idylls briefly glimpsed in those pictures he mainly showed the seamy, messy undersides of people's personal travails.

What Payne-bashers largely don't get is that his "negative" depictions stand out because outside of the films he makes in Nebraska, virtually no other films made there get seen by anything approaching a mass audience. If there were five or ten other filmmakers giving their take on Nebraska then it would be a very different conversation because there would be multiple storylines, interpretations, inclinations, perspectives, not just his. New Yorkers don't complain that Woody Allen only concerns himself with the foibles of upper middle class and upper crust Manhattan. Los Angelenos don't take Quentin Tarantino to task for his focus on violent denizens of the L.A. underworld. Each of those filmmakers is one of many putting a lens on those cities and so the vision and voice of Allen and Tarantino become part of a much greater and diverse whole that contains many different visions and voices. It only follows then that there are many varied looks at New York and L.A. for the taking, some of which may conform to residents' own views and some of which may not. The point is, there is more than enough to go around for you to find something that speaks to you. Unless and until more features get made in Nebraska by more filmmakers, Payne's personal, idiosyncratic representations of the state will remain the predominant ones, if not the only ones. Don't expect him to change. He is only being true to his material and to himself. Hard to fault someone for that, especially when his films are heralded, and rightly so, for the fidelity of their vision. He doesn't pretend his Nebraska films are true to life portraits of all Nebraskans or of all Nebraska He is only being true to the characters and settings of his stories. That is the singular world he plays God over.

It would be good too for folks to consider that in *Nebraska* Payne and screenwriter Bob Nelson have delivered archetypal characters and settings that are true to Nebraska, yes, but to a whole universe of other places as well. The equivalents of Woody and his orbit of quirky family and friends can be found everywhere.

Nebraskans bent out of shape by the bad light they think Payne casts them, in should remember he is an artist unbound by marketing motivations. He has no desire, nor should he, to skew his work to reflect some fanciful postcard image of this or any other place to placate critics or to make insecure folks feel better about themselves. Besides, Payne gives far more back to the state than any potential "damage" his films do because were it not for him bringing his films there Nebraska would have no Hollywood production of any sustained size, much less any kind of frequency. Outside of his *About Schmidt* and *Nebraska* and apart from some micro-budgeted indies (under a million dollars) one would be hard pressed to name another Hollywood project that shot in state for more than a couple days in the last dozen years. His commitment to growing the film industry there is well-documented.

Oh, and by the way, using the state's name as the title for his acclaimed film is a gift that will keep on giving as long as the film endures and in my estimation the film will long outlast any silly quibbles or dissatisfaction from the nitwits who want him to make Nebraska look like everywhere else. Payne actually cares enough to show facets of Nebraska exactly as they are, without artificial adornments that become distortions of his overriding concern – the truth. He also cares enough to faithfully show his home land as it has never been seen before on the big screen. I dare say with *Nebraska* he has given most natives and residents a glimpse at their own state they have never beheld. That is more than most art and entertainment delivers. Indeed, by repeatedly bringing the industry to his home state through the films he makes and the cinema figures he hosts he does far more than what most of the people who purportedly have Nebraska's best interests at heart, i.e. state business leaders and elected officials, do. Outside of Warren Buffett he is the state's leading ambassador to the nation and to the world and the impact he and his work have in enhancing the state's name is incalculable.

Should he never make another film in Nebraska again (in fact he immediately did, by shooting part of *Downsizing* there.) he will have endowed the state with four significant works that bear its imprint and inspiration and in the case of his latest work, its name. Although *Sideways* and *The Descendants* were made elsewhere they cannot be considered apart from his Nebraska quartet. The way Payne observes the human condition and the way he navigates the world in his personal and professional life is inextricably linked to his native experience. He carries it with him wherever he goes. His Nebraskan sensibility informs everything he does. That is why you can only separate his two features made outside Nebraska from his features made in Nebraska on the most superficial levels. Apart from the specific physical locations he must be true to and is, all his films, no matter where they are set and filmed, are cut from the same cloth emotionally and dramatically speaking. Thus, all his work bears a stamp of Nebraska on it. Besides, Nebraskans rightfully claim all his triumphs, regardless of where they were executed, as a part of their own. As a fellow Nebraskan myself, I certainly do.

Payne's affinity for his home state is already one of the great documented love affairs an artist has had with his place of origin and with any luck at all he will only keep adding to this singular narrative.

Payne's *Nebraska* a blend of old and new as he brings Indiewood back to the state and reconnects with tried and true crew on his first black and white film

Published in a 2012 issue of *The Reader*

Coming home in black and white

Alexander Payne's decision to make *Nebraska* in his home state brought into sharp relief some realities with large implications for his own work and prospects for more studio films getting made here.

The state's favorite son had not shot a single frame here since *About Schmidt* in 2001. With *Nebraska*, whose principal photography went from October 15 through November, he continued a tradition of shooting here and surrounding himself with crew with whom he has a long history. Some key locals are part of his creative team, too, including one metro resident he calls "my secret weapon."

Aesthetically and technically speaking, Payne also stretched himself by lensing for the first time in black and white, wide screen and digital. He said abandoning celluloid marks a concession to the new digital norm and to the fact today's black and white film stock options are limited.

Cinematographer Phedon Papamichael said digital "allows us to work more with natural light and not have to carry a larger equipment package. We did specific black and white tests to choose the texture and quality in terms of contrast and film grain level we want for the picture. So we went into it knowing exactly where we want to be at."

Natural light and locations

Papamichael added, "Digital means needing less light, so we can do tighter interiors, which is important on this show because we're entirely a location picture. We don't have anything built. A lot of these interior spaces are very small and whatever space we can save in terms of lighting and camera equipment is helpful. Rather than having traditional bigger car rigs and following cars with camera cars we're able to just get in the car hand-held. Also, these newer cameras allow us to do good car work without lighting. It just helps the whole natural feel we're going for."

At the end of the day, said Payne, digital "doesn't matter to me because my process stays exactly the same." His process is all about arriving at the truth. Capturing the windswept plains and fall after-harvest season figured prominently in that this time. Papamichael and Payne sought ways to juxtapose characters with the prairie, the open road and small town life milieu. In a story of taciturn people rooted to the land and whose conversations consist of terse exchanges, context and subtext are everything. Therefore, the filmmakers extracted all the metaphor and atmosphere possible from actual locations, geography and weather.

Film as business

Payne doesn't belabor the point but he received pressure from various quarters to shoot the picture elsewhere. The suits pressed going to states with serious film tax credits. Many locales could approximate Nebraska while saving producers money. He finds himself in the awkward position of having lobbied long and hard to try and convince the governor and state legislators to support film incentives only to see his entreaties largely ignored. As much as he and his projects are embraced, his moviemaking forays in the state seem taken for granted. But the fact is he only ended up shooting here because he had the motivation and clout to do so.

If not for *Nebraska* there would have been no feature film activity of any significance here during 2012. Minus his *Citizen Ruth, Election,* and *Schmidt*, the state has precious little feature film activity of any size to show for it. Refusing to cheat the script's Nebraska settings, Payne brought Indiewood feature filmmaking of scale back home for the first time in a decade. Basing his production in Norfolk provided a boost to the northeast part of the state.

Norfolk director of economic development Courtney Klein-Faust said the total impact the project had on the local economy has yet to be tabulated but that just in lodging alone the production spent more than a half-million dollars accommodating its one hundred cast and crew members. She said the film bought local goods and services whenever possible. She feels the experience will serve as "a case study" for elected officials to assess the trickle down effect of mid-major features and will be used by supporters of tax credits to push for more film industry friendly measures.

AP's stock company's master of light Phedon Papamichael

Like many filmmakers who develop a track record of success Payne's cultivated around him a stock company of crew he works with from project to project. During a mid-November visit to the Nebraska set it was evident he enjoys the same easy rapport with and loyalty to crew he had before his two Oscar wins. The only time this visitor saw Payne betray even mild upset came after a principal actor was not in place when ready to roll and the filmmaker emphatically tapped his watch as if to say, "Time is money." He expressed mild frustration when cows drifted out of frame and it took awhile for production assistants to wrangle them back in position.

On *Nebraska* he collaborated for the third consecutive time with Papamichael, the director of photography for *The Descendants* and *Sideways*. Their relationship entered a new dimension as they devised a black and white and widescreen visual palette to accentuate Nebraska's stark characters and settings. That meant fixing on the right tools to capture that look.

"We did a bunch of testing and dialed in a look we'd like for our black and white because there are many different ways to go about black and white," said Papamichael. Some of the expressive light and shadow images extracted by Papamichael and Payne recall memorable black and white treatments from cinema past, including *Shadow of a Doubt*, *Night of the Hunter*, *Touch of Evil* and *It's a Wonderful Life*.

Seeking and getting the right look

"It's not really a film noir look, it's definitely a high con(trast) with natural lighting" Papamichael said. "We were very diligent in selecting our lens package, which is Panavision C Series anamorphic. That's from the '70s, so it has a little bit of a less defined, less sharp quality and that helps the look. We're adding quite a bit of actual film grain to it which will feel like you're watching a film projection. We're even talking about possibly adding some projector flicker imposed. So we're really going for a film look. And through a series of tests we've been able to achieve that."

A week into filming, Papamichael was pleased by what he and Payne cultivated. "There's an overall excitement the whole crew has. Everybody feels we're doing something very special and unique and the black and white has a lot to do with it. After you work with it for awhile it becomes the way you see things. In a way we're learning the power of black and white as we go. We're really coming to appreciate and love the poetic power of the black and white in combination with these landscapes and, of course, the landscapes are playing a huge role in this story – just scaling the human drama and comedy. The black and white is becoming a very powerful character in this film just in terms of setting the mood for this."

Grizzled Bruce Dern as the gone-to-seed protagonist Woody is a walking emblem of the forlorn but enduring fields and played out towns that form the story's backdrop. His tangle of white hair resembles shocks of frosted wheat. His drab working man clothes hang on him as if he's a scarecrow. His gait is halting and he lists to one side. His Woody is as worn and weathered as the abandoned farmhouse of the character's youth. But just like the artifacts of Woody's past, this physical-emotional derelict holds on from sheer cussedness.

Papamichael said part of the fun became "discovering Bruce Dern's great visual qualities – his face, the textures and everything that are emphasized through the black and white."

Sense of place

The film's full of Nebraskesque places and faces. There's that farmhouse a few minutes outside Plainview. There's the town of Plainview itself standing in for the fictional Hawthorne. There's an American Legion hall, some bars, farm implement dealerships and mottled fields full of lowing cows. There are earnest farmers, shopkeeps, housewives and barmaids, plain as the day is long.

"Alexander is very diligent about finding the exact right spot for everything," said Papamichael. The original screenplay is by Bob Nelson, whose parents grew up in the very northeast environs of the state the film's set in. He's also impressed by how rigorous Payne is in location scouting. Nelson said "I think he's done a great job of finding a combination of things around Norfolk. I've seen the location photos and it's pretty stunning to see it in black and white. You know it has that *The Last Picture Show* quality to it. It is funny to see these things that were in your mind, like the abandoned farmhouse, come to life. I don't know how they found it, it must have been a chore, but they came up with a good one. Almost everything I saw was spot-on perfect."

The locations are pregnant with memories and incidents, thus Payne and Papamichael chose ones most reflecting the characters and situations and they cast actors and nonactors alike who most represent these places and lifestyles. "For him it's not all about trying to capture something truthful and comedically grim about the American landscape but also something archetypal," said producer Albert Berger.

Completing the stock company

Whenever Payne works with Papamichael it means inheriting the camera and lighting crew the celebrated DP brings with him, including chief lighting technician Rafael Sanchez and key grip Ray Garcia.

Boom operator Jonathan Fuh is a regular on Payne sets as well as costume designer Wendy Chuck.

Then there's veteran Payne collaborator Jose Antonio Garcia, the sound mixer on the writer-director's last three films. George Parra goes back as far as *Election* in capacities ranging from assistant director to co-producer to production manager. He executive produced *Nebraska*.

Production designer Jane Ann Stewart had been on every Payne show since *Citizen Ruth* but J. Dennis Washington took over that job on *Nebraska*. Interestingly, a Hollywood art director who lives in Nebraska, Sandy Veneziano, joined the crew to mark her first Payne production. Omaha resident Jamie Vesay, a key assistant location manager, crewed along with other locals, including set medic Kevin O'Leary.

Screenwriter Nelson is a Nebraskan by proxy. His folks hailed from Hartington and growing up in the Pacific Northwest he visited relatives back here, several of whom were models for his characters. Woody is closely patterned after his father. Payne conferred with Nelson as he tweaked the writer's work. "Yeah, every time I'd do a pass on the script I'd send it to him and see what he thought, and he seemed to like it," Payne said. "Sometimes there were certain moments or a certain scene I'd want a little more information about. Like one scene I really like in the script is when the family visits the house where Woody grew up and it's now an abandoned farmhouse. And there Woody delivers a speech about having found the hail adjuster's knife in the field, and it's really the only time Woody speaks in the film, and I just remember asking Bob where that came from."

Nelson said that American Gothic scene when Woody tells his son David (WIll Forte) "a story about how the hell adjustor tried to screw them out of their insurance is actually a true story based on visiting an uncle near Wausa on his farm. That's almost verbatim." Payne said Nelson also helped inform some creative decisions. "He sent me some old photographs of his actual family from Hartington to serve as something of a reference for casting and costuming."

Casting director John Jackson

The colleague Payne refers to as "my secret weapon," casting director John Jackson of Council Bluffs, is undoubtedly the most influential local in the filmmaker's close circle of collaborators. "We just have really similar tastes and in honing our working method since 1995 we just have developed a very similar aesthetic of what we want to see in a film, the type of reality we want," Payne said of Jackson. "And also I think the two of us have developed a pretty good eye for spotting acting talent in nonactors—talent they may not even know they have —and by talent I just mean the ability to be in front of a camera playing some version of themselves and saying dialogue believably and without getting freaked out."

"People can be cinematic just by being themselves and being appropriately placed where they need to be, people can be brilliant by just doing what they do, listening or talking or moving," said Jackson, who along with Payne is excited about several of their nonactor discoveries on *Nebraska*. "Glendora Stitt, the woman that plays Aunt Betty, what a find. Dennis McColg, who plays Uncle Cecil, is like Gary Cooper. Scott Goodman, the barista who served me at the Scooters drive-thru in Norfolk was hilarious without trying and I cast him in a tiny role. John "Jack" Reynolds, who plays Bernie Bowen, an old friend of Woody's, is right out of a Preston Sturges and Frank Capra movie. He's the face of the rolling plains and hilariously funny."

Jackson said he thinks of filling out the people who inhabit any movie, such as Woody's clan, "in terms of I've got to build the family, and then, 'Who are the next door neighbors? who are his friends? what do they do for a living?' I always have a back story for them. It's not like I sit down and make it up, the script tells me what it is by the things they say."

Kindred Spirits

"Obviously it's worked well," said Payne. "Together we cast Chris Klein, Nick D'Agosto going as far back as *Election*. In the traditional American filmmaking model for casting you have one casting director, typically out of New York or L.A. or Chicago with whom you cast the lead parts, maybe the top five or ten or fifteen speaking parts. And then if you're shooting on location you have a second casting person, a local casting person. That's what John Jackson was for me on the first three films. And then you have a third person who's in charge of extras. And I somehow thought that one person should be in charge of all of the flesh. There should be one vision guiding all of it. You can't get anyone in L.A. or New York to do that, so the person I want to do that is John Jackson." Jackson said his guide in casting is looking at "what does the script say," and then conferring with Payne. "We talk a lot about the characters in relationship to the text. I frequently find myself asking him questions like, 'At this point in the movie what do you want the audience to feel? what do you want them to think? what do you want them to say as they walk out of the theater?' One of the things I learned from him is to look at a moment in the story and to ask questions like, 'Who's funnier doing this? who's more believable doing that? who breaks my heart more?'

"I remember when we were doing *Schmidt* and it was between this woman in New York, June Squibb, and a woman in L.A. the studio was pushing and I said to him, 'Well, it has to be her,' meaning June Squibb, and he said, 'Why?' and I said, 'Because in that moment when she surprises him with the motor home and she's seated at the table and said, Isn't it going to be great? you know he's hating every minute of it. Somebody needs to break my heart, and June Squibb breaks my heart. At that moment I feel for her. I feel pain for him, but I really feel for her, so when she dies I'm going to hurt, whereas this other woman I don't feel anything.'" Squibb plays Woody's wife Kate in *Nebraska*.

Give and take

"Those are the kinds of conversations we have," Jackson said of he and Payne. "We never talk about, as other producers do, 'Well, you know, this person's presence in the film would be great because they're so huge in terms of DVD sales.' I never have those conversations with him. I've tried in the past and he'll just look at me like, 'What the fuck are you talking about? I don't want to hear it, I don't want to know.' So it's cleansed me."

Jackson said he's learned not to try and anticipate what Payne wants. "He constantly surprises me, he constantly challenges me. I wouldn't want it any other way. What he's looking for, I don't know, I don't know that he even knows, but I know one thing – when it's there he recognizes it. That's alchemy."

No two projects are alike, Jackson said. "Every single one of these films is a completely different organic living thing and the challenge is to honor that and to help that grow and evolve and become whatever it's going to become and Alexander is the guide to all of that."

Payne and longtime editor Kevin Tent will be cutting *Nebraska* through the spring and the film will likely start playing festivals in late summer-early fall in advance of a end of 2013 general release.

Cinemaphotographer Phedon Papamichael, Actors
Bruce Dern and Will Forte, Director Alexander Payne.

Director Alexander Paynr on the set of *Nebraska*.

Bruce Dern

Bruce Dern, June Squibb, Will Forte

Will Forte, Bruce Dern, Stacy Keach

(photos by Merie Wallace, © 2013 Paramount Pictures)

Alexander Payne's *Nebraska* comes home to roost

Published in a 2012 issue of *The Reader*

In 1968 Francis Ford Coppola led a small cinema caravan to Ogallala, Nebraska for the final weeks shooting on his independent road picture *The Rain People* starring Shirley Knight. Joining them were future fellow film legends George Lucas, Bill Butler, Robert Duvall and James Caan.

Now a road pic of another kind, *Nebraska*, is underway here by native prodigal son Alexander Payne. For his first filming on his home turf since 2001 Payne's lit out into northeast Nebraska to make a fourth consecutive road movie after the wandering souls of his *About Schmidt*, *Sideways* and *The Descendants*. *Nebraska* began shooting October 15 around Norfolk, where the production's headquartered, and will complete thirty five days of principal photography by the end of November. A week of second unit work will run into early December. The project is by Payne, Jim Taylor and Jim Burke's Ad Hominem Enterprises in collaboration with Albert Berger and Ron Yerxa's Bona Fide Productions and Paramount Pictures.

On the road again

Despite proclamations he doesn't care for road movies, much less shooting in cars, Payne's once again attached himself to a story of lost and broken people careening to some revelation about themselves. Asked why he keeps returning to this theme or structure, he said, "I have no idea, I personally don't really like road movies all that much and it's all I seem to make. No, none of it's intentional, I'm a victim. Yeah, it just happened."

Characters hitting the road is a classic metaphorical device for any life-as-journey exploration and Payne's not so much reinvented this template as made it his own. "I think self-discovery is a big theme in his movies," said Berger. The protagonist of *Schmidt* (Jack Nicholson) goes in search of meaning via his mobile home after his life is knocked asunder. In *Sideways* buddies Miles (Paul Giamatti) and Jack (Thomas Haden Church) indulge in a debauched tour of California wine country that rekindles the love impulse in one and confirms the unreliability of the other. The by-car, boat and foot journey of *The*

Descendants is propelled when Matt King (George Clooney) discovers his dying wife's infidelity and sets off to find her lover. What he really finds is closure for his pain and the father within him he'd forgotten.

The bickering father-son of *Nebraska*, Woody (Bruce Dern) and David (Will Forte), hold different agendas for their trek along the highways and byways of Montana, Wyoming, South Dakota and Nebraska. Woody, a unrepentant, alcoholic old coot estranged from everyone in his life, is hellbent on collecting a sweepstakes prize that doesn't exist. David, the good-hearted but exasperated son, decides to placate his pops by promising to drive him from Billings. Montana to the prize company's home office in Lincoln, Nebraska by way of several detours. He's sure his father will come to his senses long before their destination.

This mismatched pair's road-less-traveled adventure in the son's Suzuki Forenza finds them passing through Woody's old haunts, including his hometown, the fictional Hawthorne, Nebraska, a composite of Hartington, Wausa, Bloomfield, Norfolk and other rural burgs. At nearly every stop they encounter the detritus from Woody's life, which like the broken down Ford pickup in his garage he can't get to run is a shambles of regret and recrimination. Woody's made the fool wherever he goes. A longtime nemesis, Ed Pegram (Stacy Keach), is a menacing presence. By story's end this father-son journey becomes a requiem. To salve his father's broken spirit David performs a simple act of grace that involves a valedictory cruise down main street that gives Woody the last laugh.

Coming to Nebraska-**Nebraska**

Producer partners Berger and Yerxa (*Little Miss Sunshine*), who shepherded Payne's *Election* in conjunction with Paramount and MTV Films (1999), brought Bob Nelson's original script for *Nebraska* to the filmmaker's attention a decade ago. Payne said, "Albert Berger and Ron Yerxa had gotten a hold of it, and asked me to read it, not thinking I would want to direct it myself. They wanted to know if there was some young up and coming Nebraska director I knew about who could make it for a very, very low sum, and I read it and I liked it and I said, 'How about me and for a sum not quite so low?' And so it was, and they've been kind enough to wait for me these eight or nine years since I first read it.

"I read it before making *Sideways* but I didn't want to follow up *Sideways* with another road trip. I was tired of shooting in cars. I didn't think it would take this long, I didn't think *Downsizing* (his comedy about miniaturization) would take so long to write in between. And then *The Descendants* came along and now I've circled back around to this austere Nebraska road trip story."

The story's essential appeal for Payne is its deceptive simplicity. "I liked its austerity, I liked its deadpan humor, I like how the writer clearly was writing about people he knew and representing them faithfully to a certain degree but also sardonically. And I've never seen a deadpan, almost Jim Jarmusch sort of comedy that takes place in rural Nebraska."

A black and white palette

The barren, existential landscape should find ample expressive possibilities in the black-and-white, wide-screen visuals Payne and cinematographer Phedon Papamichael (*Sideways*, *The Descendants*) plan capturing. Papamichael said the palette they've hit upon after much testing emphasizes natural lighting and texture. They're using a high contrast stock from the '70s that's less sharp or defined. Film grain is being added to it. "We're really coming to appreciate and love the poetic power of the black and white in combination with these landscapes," said Papamichael, "and of course the landscapes are playing a huge role in this story. It's scaling the human drama and comedy with this vast landscape. It's a road movie but it's also a very intimate, small personal story."

"Well, I certainly wanted to make one feature film in my career in black and white because black and white when well-done is just so beautiful," said Payne. "And I knew that whatever film I made in black and white couldn't have a huge budget, so this one seemed to lend itself to that that way. Then also in reading it I wanted the austerity of the characters and of their world represented also in a fairly austere way and I thought black and white in the fall could be very nice. By that I mean ideally after the trees have lost their leaves – to just get that look. Sometimes where you're in rural America there is a certain timeless quality in all those small towns which have the old buildings. You know, change comes slowly to these places." In terms of visual models, he said, "we've looked at a number of black and white films and photographs but it's not like I'm consciously saying, 'Oh, Walker Evans or Dorothea Lange' (or *The Last Picture Show*) or something like that. No, not really. I mean, I've seen them. We're just going to follow instinct in how this one should look like."

Albert Berger on Payne and process

Berger supports Payne's aesthetic choice, though it came with a price and a fight as Paramount execs reportedly resisted the decision to forgo color. But Payne and Papamichael held firm. Berger feels the project gives Payne a new creative space to work in. "I always was excited artistically about what he was trying to accomplish," said Berger. "Clearly we would have gotten a lot more money if we didn't film in black and white and life would have been a lot easier for the production. Alexander's films have always had a very authentic look. He's obviously a great appreciator of cinema and he has a wonderful eye and I think in a way this is his first opportunity to showcase a more iconic, archetypal look."

Payne may just do for the north Sandhills what John Ford did for Utah's Monument Valley in capturing a certain beautiful desolation. The play of light on wind, barns, trees and wide open spaces offers evocative chiaroscuro possibilities. "I think it's exciting to see what he and Phedon will come up with here," said Berger. "And it's scope as well and so that will add yet another dimension. And digital for the first time for him and it's going to be interesting how that helps us getting in tight spaces like cars and using low level lighting. There's all sorts of tools at his disposal on this one that he hasn't had before."

Berger's come to know Payne's meticulous eye for finding locations and actors that ring true. "Once the script is right and once the cast and the locations are in place I feel he's completely ready to make the movie. I wouldn't say the rest is easy but I think that is the critical bedrock upon which his movies are made. I think he's a filmmaker who's completely in-tune with what he's trying to say both emotionally and comedically. It's been a real pleasure to be able to watch this evolution in his work."

Casting

Payne said the more specific the character on the page the harder it is to cast, which is why his search for the right Woody and David took so long. "I just know in the time frame in which I was trying to get this film made these guys rose to the top of my research and struck me and John Jackson, my casting director, as being the right fit," he said of Dern and Forte.

The irascible Woody proved most difficult. "In this case Woody's a very, very specifically rendered character and I just couldn't plug any actor in there," Payne said. He interviewed-auditioned many, including big names. For the longest time no one matched his conceptions. "In today's world it was kind of hard to find someone whom I believed in that part and I didn't want it to change the character of Woody." No compromising.

He finally found his Woody in Bruce Dern, whose daughter Laura Dern starred in Payne's *Citizen Ruth* and remains a close friend. What made Papa Dern (*Silent Running, Coming Home, Family Plot*) the perfect Woody? "Well, he's of the right age now and he can be both ingenuous and ornery. And he's a cool actor. And in a contextual level I haven't seen on the big screen a great Bruce Dern performance in a few years and I'm curious to see what he can do. He's a helluva nice guy as well."

Dern and Will Forte (*Saturday Night Live*) didn't meet until they arrived in Norfolk in early October to participate in table readings with other principal cast. Any chemistry they produce will be worked out on set. That's how it worked between Giamatti and Haden Church on *Sideways*. "I cast those two guys in *Sideways* separately. They never met before ten days or two weeks before we started shooting. Or George Clooney and Shailene Woodley, they had never met before. I've just had good luck with that. Actors know it's their job to develop some sort of chemistry, hopefully not force it but develop it, and then of course film has a wonderful capacity to lie."

The casting of Forte surprised many. Not surprisingly, Payne has a considered rationale for the choice. "Will Forte, physically, I believed could be the son of Bruce Dern and June Squibb (who play's Woody's long-suffering wife, Kate). and then I just believe him as a guy I would know around Omaha or meet in Billings. He has a very, very believable quality. And I also think for the character of David he is capable of communicating a certain wide-eyed quality toward life and also damage – like he's been damaged somehow, somewhere."

A singular story by Bob Nelson

Payne's confident he has a stand-alone project. "I don't think you would have seen anyone portray characters like these before. I mean, I've never seen exactly this movie with exactly this dynamic." Payne revised Bob Nelson's script alone, then had Phil Johnston (*Cedar Rapids*) take a pass, before revising it again. He admires how close the material is to Nelson's experience. "His parents were from Hartington, Nebraska and I think Wausa (Nebraska) but he grew up in Snohomish Washington. You know how other people summer in the south of France or the Caribbean? Well, this guy used to summer in Hartington, that's where he would spend time with his many uncles on his father's side."

Nelson confirms the hard-tack individualists and towns of *Nebraska* are composites of relatives and places there and in rural Washington, though Woody is directly based on his late father. He darkened characters and incidents for dramatic effect and invented the sweepstakes storyline. Nelson's best-known writing credit before *Nebraska* was for the award-winning Seattle television show, *It's Almost Live*. He meant to shop his feature script around L.A. but it quickly got into the hands of Payne, who instantly committed to making it and never reneged. Getting Payne behind it, he said, "changed everything." To his surprise and delight, Payne didn't overhaul his script.

"I'm pretty sure I would have been happy no matter what he did with it because I believed in him as a filmmaker. The fact that so much of my dialogue and so many of the scenes remain is really almost unheard of if you have a writer-director taking over," Nelson said. "That's another thing that impressed me. I could tell he didn't go in and try to turn it into his own screenplay. He wasn't driven to put his own stamp on it just to do that. He went through it and thoughtfully changed things he thought could use changing but he left in things he thought could work well. For that I'll always be grateful.

"When he's rewriting it I think he's turning in a way already into a director who's thinking, 'Do I really want to shoot this scene and do I want to shoot it like that? Is there anything that could make this better?' You can almost see that going on in his mind. The one thing you hope when your work is adapted is that it will be made better and he's one of the few guys in Hollywood you're almost certain will make it better. I really trust him."

Rooted in Nebraska

Payne rooted the production in Norfolk after a long search. "I spent a year driving around Nebraska when I had free time—a wonderful education on the state. I considered places like Columbus, Grand Island, Hastings, but I landed on Norfolk because Norfolk has a pretty good number of small towns of about fifteen hundred people orbiting it, and maybe it's also no coincidence that that's the area Robert Nelson was writing about. Hartington is within spitting distance of Norfolk."

Earlier this year Payne and Papamichael followed the route Woody and David make in the film, traveling for three days in a Toyota owned by Payne's mother, Peggy, "just to get a feel for the land," said Papamichael. "He really wanted to convey the feeling of the land to me and that was very helpful. I took a lot of black and white stills." Nelson, who's seen footage and visited the set, found the film's locations spot-on.

Finalizing locations and cast members led Payne to make certain tweaks. "Yeah, as it always does," he said. "I start incorporating locations more into the script and I might steal a line of dialogue or two from an actor in an audition who can't remember his line or adds an improv that I think is quite good. Or as I'm going along I just think of things which could be better." He's continued tinkering.

After seven years between his last two features he's moving quickly from project to project now. He expects to jump from *Nebraska*, whose editing he should finish in the spring, into *Wilson*, his adaptation of the Daniel Clowes' graphic novel slated to shoot on the west coast next fall.

When a film becomes a film: the shaping of *Nebraska*

A shorter version of this story
appeared in a 2013 issue of *The Reader*

After wrapping the *Nebraska* shoot the end of 2012 Alexander Payne holed up with editor Kevin Tent in L.A. to edit the film starting Jan. 7 and finally put the project to bed the beginning of August. When I caught up with Payne and a small post crew in mid-May at The Lot in Old Hollywood they were mere days from completing a mix before the film's world premiere at the Cannes Film Festival in Nice, France.

The edit-mix process is one few outside the inner circle are allowed to witness. It's where a film becomes a film. Over a four-day period at the Audio Head post facility, with its long console of digital controls and theater projection screen, I watch Payne, Tent, mixer Patrick Cyccone, sound designer Frank Gaeta, music editor Richard Ford and others engage in the rather anal exercise of extracting nuance from the minutiae of sound and image, time and space that comprise a film.

I ask Payne how much more can really be massaged this late into the edit. I mean, isn't the soundtrack a relatively simple proposition?

The art and science of sound mixing

"Seemingly simple," he said. "There's always little complicated stuff to modulate and calibrate." It may be a snippet of dialogue or the sound of a character walking across a wood floor or music from a jukebox or the rustle of wind. It may be how long or short an actor's beat or a shot is held. Nothing's too small or incidental to escape scrutiny. Anything even vaguely amiss is ripe for "a fix" often only arrived at after several adjustments that might involve raising a level here, dropping a level there, sweetening the pot with a bank of recorded sounds or snipping a frame.

To the untrained eye and ear, few problems appear obvious or even to be flaws at all. Many are flat out undetectable until brought to your attention. But to the hyper-attuned Payne and his crew, who've watched the footage hundreds, even thousands of times, the slightest element out of synch is a jarring distraction. When something really bothers Payne he's apt to say, "That's hideous."

There's a poignant scene in Robert Nelson's original screenplay when taciturn protagonist Woody Grant (Bruce Dern) looks out on a field spread before his family's old abandoned farmhouse and relates a childhood story to his son David (Will Forte) about his father, a hail adjustor and a knife. I was visiting the northeast Nebraska set in November when the scene was shot. The rather barren, wind-swept location with its forlorn wooden farmhouse and rough-hewn harvested fields made an evocative backdrop for the nostalgic moment. But the part where Woody reveals this incident from the past didn't make it in the final cut because try as he might Payne decided it just didn't work.

"You know, so much of filmmaking is if you can't make a perfect omelette you try to make perfect scrambled eggs," he said. "So we just cut the scene down." As I glimpse the mix process Payne asks me more than once, "Are you finding this interesting or are you bored out of your skull?" I admit the attention to detail is surprising, to which he replies, "It's all important though . . . because there's always discovery. You're discovering it frame by frame. Ways to make it delightful so it never breaks the spell it has over the audience. Kevin (Tent) and I will have knock down-drag out fights over two frames, over tenths of a second." I ask if he ever fears he's micromanaging the life out of a picture. "I never worry about that," Payne answers.

Fractions of frames and seconds

Even to the filmmakers themselves the fixes can be hard to quantify. At the end of July Payne told me in a phone interview, "I was just watching the film with Phedon (Papamichael), the DP. He had seen it in Cannes and then he saw it again here in L.A. and he said, 'It feels so much better,' I mean, it's the same movie but after Cannes Kevin and I came back and spent two weeks doing some more picture cutting. Two frames here, six frames there, twelve frames there, you know, fractions of seconds. And we did another pass of course on the mix. We remixed it. It smoothed out some of the way the music was functioning. It made it less repetitive and more emotional. Film is in detail and squeezing that last one, two, three, four percent out of a film like in any creative work makes a big difference. And there's nothing you can even concretely point to. It just feels better, it just feels more like a real movie."

Tent, who's edited all of Payne's features, said the filmmaker is "more involved than most (directors) with the small details." Payne said what makes he and Tent a good team is, "number one we get along really well and number two we both want to be and are the actor's best friend. We go through the takes over and over again to make sure we're getting the best stuff up on screen in terms of what represents the actor's work and then, of course, what's appropriate for the character. And then beyond that I think we both have a pretty good storytelling sense—telling a story effectively and making it rhythmic."

Located on Santa Monica Boulevard, The Lot owns a storied history as the Fairbanks-Pickford Studio and original home of United Artists. For most of its life though it was the Warner Hollywood Studio that served as the smaller sister studio to the main Warner Brothers Studio in Burbank. Some film-television production still happens in the cavernous sound stages there but today it's mostly a post site for finishing films. It's one of countless L.A. industry venues where films of every imaginable type are supported and tweaked behind closed doors. It's safe to say two-time Oscar-winner Payne was the star resident client at The Lot with his Cannes-bound project.

Payne's sixth feature enjoyed a warm reception at the fabled film bazaar, where star Bruce Dern won the Best Actor prize. Payne, who accepted the award for Dern, said even a stellar performance like Dern's is partly shaped in the editing room. "It's definitely what the actor's doing but its also the work of editing where you're combing through and getting the best of every set up and then creating both from what they gave you and from what you're choosing and culling as absolutely necessary to tell the story. You tease out a great consistency to performance and to the creation of the character and then once we do that the work the actor's done really starts to pop. Bruce did a good job."

During my visit last spring to the Audio Head suite Payne introduced me to the insular post production world where he and his crew were under the gun preparing the film for its Cannes debut. "We've been working twelve-hour days. It's been very much a mad dash to the finish because we're getting ready for Mr. Frenchy," Payne said to me shortly upon my arrival.

Notes and tweaks

Nebraska is a six-reel picture. Each pass through a reel takes put to six hours. It's time consuming because each team member has notes made from previous screenings of what fixes need addressing. With each successive pass, there are new notes to respond to. After a screening of the twenty-minute reel five with a running time count on the screen Payne said to his collaborators, "I have a bunch of little things, so maybe we should fast track." After noting several areas of concern and the corresponding time they appear in the reel, everything from extraneous noises to wanting some bits louder and others quieter, he said, "Sorry, I have a lot of notes here guys."

Then Payne invites Tent and the others to chime in with their own notes. Payne interjects, "I'm looking froward to our whole film playback so we can gauge all of these things." He asks for input from personal assistant and aspiring filmmaker Anna Musso and first assistant editor Mindy Elliott before asking, "Anyone else?" That's how it rolls, day after day.

During my stay I watch an uninterrupted playback of the entire film at a large screening room on the Paramount lot with Payne and the edit-mix team poised with notepads and pens in laps. Several folks are moved to tears despite having seen the film countless times. For the duration of the edit-mix the post crew becomes Payne's family. It's the most time intensive segment of creating a film. "I spend more time with the post production crew than with the other (the shooting crew) and each thinks it's THE filmmaking family. Many of them never meet each other. But I meet all of them, down to the musicians who play on it or to the guy who designs the titles."

Recently, Payne told me that post work on *Nebraska* took twenty eight weeks but even with that it still marked the shortest "period of time I've posted a film. I think *The Descendants* was about thirty eight weeks total. And in these twenty eight weeks I took time out to go to Cannes, I took a week off after Cannes. I went to Bologna, Italy to watch old movies. Even within there it's been a faster process than my previous films."

Austerity

Ever since he began talking about *Nebraska* he's described his vision for it as "austere," referring to the small budget ($12 million), tight shoot schedule (six weeks), short script (ninety five pages) and minimal camera set-ups. The script's lack of a voiceover motif, something most of his films have featured, was the biggest time saver in the edit room. "It was shot in a more austere style so I had fewer camera angles to do deal with. I wanted to be complete in my coverage but very limited in the coverage and to have as much play out as possible in single takes, and cut as little as possible. Plus no voiceover. Ask anybody who does a voiceover picture—voiceover adds a whole level of time to the editing of the film to calibrate, to get the voice over just right. It's a rather musical element really. Dramatic and musical." He said he was never tempted to impose a narrator on the story. "Absolutely not, no way, that's not how it's conceived. Voiceover isn't something you decide to add later. Usually people only do that when the film's in trouble. For me, voiceover's always been an integral part of the conception of a film."

Although a purely aesthetic choice, the film's middle range black and white photography that's neither expressionistic nor impressionistic is congruent with its austerity, Payne said Paramount, the studio that bankrolled the picture and is releasing it this fall, initially resisted his making it in black and white because that's what suits and bean counters do to appease shareholders. Payne held out and when push came to shove he got his way. "They said they were glad I stuck to my guns because they like it so much. They've been great. I've had a great experience with Paramount, honestly. Once we were able to make it at a budget level they were comfortable with given the fact it was black and white with no major stars in a non-rebate state then I couldn't have asked for a more supportive group. I couldn't be more happy about it."

So was their resistance a bluff to see how committed he was to black and white? "Kind of," he said. "I mean, they want you to, they don't want you to, which is fine, that's their job. Color makes more money apparently. But they trusted me and then it's just about the budget at that point." "I guess I traded in my last Oscar for a black and white movie," Payne added jokingly.

Heart and soul getting personal

It's a black and white movie with perhaps more heart and soul than Payne realized. After living with the film for months he recognized it has more emotional depth than he initially appreciated and part of that was him informing the story with things from his own life. "The script had a kind of deadpan hilarity. I think the direction and the acting and the music are bringing out a lot of sweetness in the film thats making it a more heartfelt film than maybe the screenplay might have suggested at first glance.

"The other thing, too, I was able to make it quite personal in certain details related to David taking care of his older folks. I'm at that age and everyone I know of my generation is at that age where our parents are getting on and need a little special attention. We love them to death and they drive us crazy as we figure out how to take care of them and accommodate them and all those things, including how far do we extend ourselves to be dutiful and at what point do we cut it off. All those questions. I was able to insert some of my own experiences with that in the film. Even though I didn't originate it it wound up being because of the time in my life when I was making it quite personal and I think that helps the film. It always helps a film if you can put some of yourself in there." Payne's pleased by a common refrain he hears from those who've seen the film. "A lot of people tell me it makes them think about their parents and I was stopped a number of times in the street in Cannes by people who'd seen the film who said, 'I was very touched by the film.'"

Woody Grant, the geezer Bruce Dern plays so effectively, is a wreck and wretch demanding attention be paid near the end of a misspent life. Payne's appreciation for the character and the way Dern portrays him grew during the project. He said Woody has "a lot more in common" with the title character Jack Nicholson played in Payne's *About Schmidt* than he might have imagined. While Woody's not as articulate as Schmidt is by the end, both share a similar existential angst about the value of their lives. "People sometimes come to the end of their lives and are overwhelmed with the feeling they have nothing to show for it. I think that's certainly whats driving Woody's crazy mission (to redeem a worthless sweepstakes prize mailer) in some part."

While Payne finds "kind of sweet the smallness of Woody's dreams" —he only wants a new pickup truck and a compressor—he said Woody's admission that he wants "to leave something" for his boys is generous but also selfish. "He wants to know he's done something." David, the sweet son who elects to take Woody on the road trip to retrieve the prize, feels many things about his father during the course of that journey but by the end, Payne said, it's "unconditional love." He said David is a classic case of "how you seek the love of those who belittle you. Look at his father, who's a nothing anyway, and how he has to take out his low esteem by belittling others, including his son. So I think the end is complicated. He's still seeking approval but also granting a last wish."

Along the way, noted Payne, David "finds some understanding" for why his father is the way he is. "Like the graveyard scene with the irreverent things the mother is saying about all the deceased but David is taking all this in for the first time and learning. And when they go to the old farmhouse and then in the bar. Why did you have us? David asks his dad. Well, I liked to screw, Woody said. Again it's kind of a weird, disturbing yet comic scene. David drank the elixir and is able to wander into his father's turf and ask him questions he never asked him before."

Payne's appreciation for Will Forte's work also "deepened." As the sweet son desperate for approval Forte plays a guileless Everyman we all know from our own lives.

Little seen America

The film is filled with sweet and savory small town archetypes. After the Cannes screening Payne said many viewers commented, "We haven't seen these Americans in a long time. It's as though they're forgotten. We never see them in the cinema," referring to the average types that populate the pic. "I thought it interesting they really feel they're seeing Americans they've never seen before. Of course I really appreciate that. I've been saying for a long time Americans make films but not American films about Americans. We make cartoons easily digestible for the rest of the world. But we're not showing ourselves to ourselves.

"I like when art is a mirror somehow to represent or reflect or distort or refract just to see ourselves, like our film in the '70s was, to see common people doing every day things to some degree. It makes me think of what Martin Scorsese said in his documentary about Elia Kazan—that when he was a kid and saw the faces from the street used in *On the Waterfront* suddenly it was as though the people he knew mattered. People want to see themselves. In general we Americans need to see Americans we recognize in our films but we kind of don't. Within that to see Midwesterners is an even more uncommon thing."

The film is a singular Nebraskaesque work. There's the title, which has never graced a feature before. Then there's the rarely seen northeast Nebraska locale and by extension the rarely glimpsed denizens of its rural hamlets. And the film's writer and director both have strong Nebraska ties. Of all the Nebraskans who've gone on to Hollywood careers few have been filmmakers. Payne's the only one of note to have returned to make films here about the people and places he knows. "Yeah, it's as though the people I knew mattered and in that way I think I'm lucky I'm from Nebraska in that I have a virgin territory to show in movies," he said. "And maybe the fact I've seen so many movies informs the fact that I can know even unconsciously what would be new. I don't want to make derivative films. I want to do something new.

"Rachel Jacobson asked me to program a series of films in the fall at Film Streams that have influenced this one and I kind of can't think of any. Maybe I can, but in general I can't. It's like the Latin phrase, suis generis – of its own kind or genus."

Nothing particularly emphatic or dramatic happens in the story. The way Payne puts it is: "The movie has a lot of anti-climaxes," What does happen is authentic and delivering the truth is always his overriding goal, which is why he's "proud" of the work of the nonactors he and casting director John Jackson found for the film.

Payne's among the leaders of the Indiewood movement that finds filmmakers like himself making independent movies with studio backing. He's defied all odds by not having a single critical miss in his growing body of work. His last three features (*About Schmidt, Sideways, The Descendants*) have been commercial successes.

How *Nebraska* fares is anyone's guess but it's well positioned to generate buzz between its Cannes reception and expected screenings at the Telluride and New York Film Festivals. After the film opens in late November it should be a prime contender come awards season.

The Nov.ember 24 Film Streams Feature Event welcomes Payne, Dern and Forte in conversation with Kurt Andersen.

Casting director John Jackson helps build Alexander Payne's film worlds

Published in a 2014 issue of *Omaha Magazine*

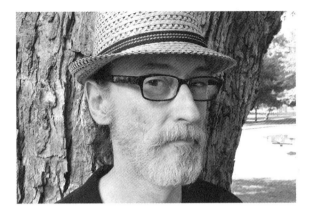

John Jackson (Photo credit: Martin Magnuson, *Omaha Magazine*)

When you watch Alexander Payne's acclaimed new film *Nebraska* keep in mind every acting part was cast both by the two-time Oscar-winning filmmaker and casting director John Jackson. As John Durbin, the Council Bluffs native and resident long ago established himself a character actor in L.A. He returned home in 1988 to run a local casting service while taking acting gigs here and on the coast. For his first feature *Citizen Ruth* (1996) Payne hired Jackson to do Omaha location casting. Jackson filled thirty two speaking roles, plus all the extras. From the start, Jackson said, "We had a great working relationship. The same thing happened when Alexander came back to work on *Election* (1999). And then he began slowly to include me. The New York casting people would send him tapes and he'd say, 'John, why don't you watch this and tell me what you think,' and that built."

On *About Schmidt* (2002) Jackson said Payne entrusted him with ever more responsibility and increasingly sounded out his advice. "Until finally the producer of *Schmidt* said to Alexander, 'Why do you hire these people in New York and L.A., why don't you just get this guy?' Meaning me. And Alexander said to me, 'Do you want to cast my next movie?' and I said, 'Sure, why not.'

Jackson was back home directing and playing a supporting role in a Brigit Saint Brigit show. Payne called to say he was casting *Sideways* (2004) and needed Jackson in Calfornia ASAP. "So that started a process of me being in L.A. Monday, Tuesday, Wednesday, Thursday and then Friday morning I'd get on a plane, fly back home, land, grab something to eat, go to the theater, do the show Friday, Saturday, Sunday. Then Monday fly back. That's the way it went," recalled Jackson.

He said *Sideways* "was a new experience for both of us in many ways." It found Payne shooting his first feature away from Nebraska and it marked the first time Jackson served as the filmmaker's sole casting director. Ever since, Jackson's been Payne's lone CD. He's since teamed with Payne for *The Descendants* (2011) in Hawaii and for *Nebraska* (2013) in the northeast part of the state and bits of Montana, Wyoming and South Dakota,

Cast and catch

Payne said of their relationship: "In honing our working method over the last eighteen years we just have developed a very similar aesthetic of what we want to see in a film, the type of reality we want. Also I think the two of us have developed a pretty good eye for spotting acting talent in nonactors." The pair filled a large number of roles in *Nebraska* with real-life farmers and small town bar denizens. On any project they painstakingly search for the right needle-in-a-haystack fit for characters. Payne's particularly proud of the casting on *Nebraska*, whose leads, Bruce Dern and Will Forte, he asked to "flatten" their performances to be in synch with the low-key nonactors.

Jackson said the cast immersed themselves in the story's "magnificent simplicity." He said his job is to "build the world" Payne envisions for the characters in the script. "We paint with people. We want it to be as authentic as possible." Payne's often praised for his casting and he always deflects credit to Jackson, whom he calls "my secret weapon." Jackson now finds himself in-demand as a CD. He's currently casting two films, *Car Dogs* and *Phantom Halo*.

"Everybody told me when I left L.A. in '88 I was throwing away everything I'd built. But I never believed I was throwing it all away and it was because of moving back here the greatest thing from a creative and professional standpoint happened."

Collaboration

He said Payne engenders loyalty by "building a rapport that ends up showing up in the work." Crew are encouraged to speak their mind. If Alexander and I didn't have that commitment I would cave to the pressure of the producers who say to me, 'You need to convince Alexander these are the people he needs.' Instead, I'm like, 'That's not my job, my job is to to support, encourage and grow his vision."

In their "give and take" the pair always serve the script ahead of commercial considerations. It's all about fleshing out the universe on the page with actors who best inhabit the characters. When June Squibb auditioned to play Jack Nicholson's domineering wife in *Schmidt* and a decade later to play Dern's long-suffering spouse in *Nebraska* she got cast over better known actresses because in each case she was right for the part. Payne and Jackson met with many name actors for the role of Woody in *Nebraska* but only Dern, who was Payne's first choice, was deemed right. Jackson may have favored others but in the end he supported the writer-director's instincts. Since becoming Payne's CD Jackson said he's gladly put his own acting career on hold because "I love what I do—it's very satisfying."

Nebraska opens Nov. 22. Payne, Dern and Forte will be interviewed live on stage by *Studio 360* host Kurt Andersen Nov. 24 at the Holland Center for Feature V to benefit Film Streams.

Alexander Payne's new film *Nebraska* features a senior cast and aging themes in a story sure to resonate with many viewers

Published in a 2013 issue of the *New Horizons*

Oscar-winning native son Alexander Payne famously feels affection for his home state, so much so he's made four of his six feature films here, even titling his new movie starring Bruce Dern and Will Forte, *Nebraska*. Payne, the writer-director of *Citizen Ruth*, *Election*, *About Schmidt*, *Sideways* and *The Descendants*, has with *Nebraska* forever burnished the name of this place in cinema history.

The film stands apart from most flicks today. For starters, it's black and white. Next, it captures elements of this Great Plains state never before seen on the big screen. Largely filmed in northeast Nebraska, the movie shows the rolling landscapes, prosaic farmsteads, played-out small towns and crusty inhabitants of this starkly beautiful rural region.

The Nebraska Gothic picture plays like a funny, tragic and sad still life evocation of people and places rubbed raw by weather and misfortune. But what really makes *Nebraska* a singular work is the preponderance of older folks in the picture and the various aging themes that permeate its storyline. Several senior-aged actors are featured in the nostalgia-laced story starting with Dern as protagonist Woody Grant, June Squibb as his piss-and-vinegar wife, Stacy Keach as his arch nemesis, Angela McEwan as his old flame, Mary Louise Wilson as his chatty sister-in-law Martha and Rance Howard as one of his brothers.

Older cast and aging themes take precedence

Payne's casting director, John Jackson, is impressed by what these actors of a certain age bring to the table. Jackson said, "They are pros. They are inspirational to me. Their desire to create, passion to succeed, pursuit of challenges to themselves as performers—I want that as I age. I can only hope to be as fully functional as Mr. Dern, Mary Louise Wilson, June Squibb and Stacy Keach."

The movie's fanciful tale revolves around Dern's character of Woody, an unrepentant lech and cantankerous cuss who's lost some bearings in old age. He's seemingly unaffected by anything but hides a deep well of hurt, longing and regret. Like many males of his Depression Era generation he's doesn't reveal much in the way of feelings. Much to the exasperation of his wife and two adult sons, he's stuck in his ways and bad habits and refuses to change. He's also facing some challenges that come with advancing years. For example, he's no longer able to drive and he walks with a halting gait. He appears depressed, confused and cut off from others.

When we first meet Woody he's running away from home, intent on walking the nine hundred miles from his home in Billings, Montana to Lincoln, Nebraska to claim a sweepstakes prize he believes he's won. Even when returned home no one can convince Woody he's got it wrong. More than once, he lights out to tramp alongside busy roads, in all kinds of weather, his son David coming to his rescue.

Realizing his old man is still bound and determined to go and afraid his father will be a hazard if he sets out again on his own David reluctantly agrees to take him to Lincoln, convinced Woody will come to his senses before they get too far. But things happen. The father-son road trip turns into a retracing of Woody's old haunts in his native Nebraska. Along the way the son learns some hard truths about his father's past that help explain the way he is and what's behind this crazy Don Quixote quest to redeem a prize.

Art imitating real life issues

Eastern Nebraska Office on Aging experts say they don't know of a senior who's gone so far as to show up at a sweepstakes office expecting to collect their winnings. ENOA Care Management Program coordinator Diane Stanton said some seniors do mistake marketing pieces for actual checks and bring them to their bank thinking they can cash them. "That will happen unfortunately," she said. Legitimate sweepstakes are one thing, but there are scams that prey on the trusting nature and sometimes naivete of seniors.

"We encourage our seniors to never give out personal information on the phone," said Stanton, adding that one should never have to divulge private details or send money as a condition for receiving a prize. "The Better Business Bureau has a Senior Line, 877-637-3334, that we strongly encourage our seniors to keep by their phone and to call anytime they suspect they're being scammed." Stanton said the free service hotline frequently updates the newest scams to avoid.

Whether Woody's gullible or addled or simply wants to believe he's won, it becomes apparent what he's really seeking is redemption. He wants to leave his boys something to salvage his misbegotten life. In an act of unconditional love and forgiveness David poignantly grants him a valedictory moment at the end. Woody's problems are still with him but he and his son have become closer and the lines of communication opened. We're left with the feeling that should something happen to Woody or his wife, David will be there for them.

Experts say adult children need to discuss with aging parents those limitations affecting quality of life and what role they'll play in terms of support and caregiving. ENOS Information and Assistance Program coordinator Gloria Erickson said her office fields a variety of calls each week from adult children inquiring about everything from financial assistance to home care to senior housing to transportation for their aging parents.

If an adult child feels his or her parent is a potential risk driving, a good course of action is to seek professional consultation. "The first thing you need to do is talk to their doctor and get the doctor's perspective and opinion on where they are physically and cognitively in regards to driving," said Stanton. "That's the first step. And then talking about the need for one of the driver assessments." Stanton said Immanuel Hospital and AARP offer assessments or evaluations to help determine if seniors are still able to drive safely. AARP also offers a self-test seniors can take online. Assessments or not, an adult child may still need to have a conversation with an aging parent about surrendering their keys. "Those heart to heart discussions are tough," said Erickson because it means the parent may be giving up some of their independence. "Family dynamics have a lot to do too with how things go."

ENOA Community Services division program coordinator Karen Kelly said whatever aspect of daily living a senior may need assistance with, it's always best to give them options. She said among the changes adult children should look out for in their aging parents are increased memory loss, growing social isolation, worsening sleep issues and increasing difficulty taking stairs and keeping up their home. As adult children notice changes in their parents, she said they need to address what can they "do to help and step in to fill in those gaps" and to determine when to "start looking outside the family for help." Erickson said it's vital family members know "you don't have to do it alone." ENOA offers direct services and refers callers to other resource providers as needed.

Alexander Payne said he was better prepared to tell the story of *Nebraska* in 2012 than in 2003 now than when he first acquired the Bob Nelson script a decade earlier because his own life caught up with the film's themes. His father George was placed in a nursing home and his mother Peggy endured a health scare. Payne's attended to it all. "I was able to make it quite personal in certain details related to David taking care of his older folk," he said. "I'm at that age and everyone I know of my generation at that age have parents that are getting on and need a little special attention. We love them to death and they drive us crazy, and how we take care of them and accommodate them and all those things, and how far do we extend ourselves to be dutiful and at what point do we cut it off, all those questions. It wound up being because of the time in my life when I was making it quite personal and I think that helps the film. It always helps a film if you can put some of yourself in there."

Not every senior needs special assistance. Indeed, most get along just fine on their own and still work, recreate, make love and learn. Take the older actors who populate *Nebraska*. Angela McEwan, who plays Peg Nagy, the editor of the newspaper in Woody's fictional hometown of Hawthorne, Nebraska, said she and her fellow actors of a certain age are busy professionals who haven't lost a beat. In fact, she said, "We're at the top of our game."

Better with age

Casting director John Jackson saw both Mary Louise Wilson and Stacy Keach on stage in New York during the casting process of *Nebraska* and was inspired by their vitality. "Both were terrific. Mary Louise was doing what was essentially a two-person show. That is a tremendous amount of energy to put out each week, each night. Mr. Keach was on Broadway. Big theater. Long run. Lead role. Wow. Good on them. They've set the bar high, both for themselves and others. That's what I want for myself as I age. More. Better."

In the film these actors vividly play characters their own age who still stir with passion and energy. McEwan's character was once in love with Woody. Near the end she gives a wistful look that suggests she still yearns for what might have been. Wilson plays a chattering busybody. Keach portrays an intimidating man set on getting what he feels he's owed. The film overturns aging myths by demonstrating that even well into our Golden Years we can remain not only physically active but cognitively sharp and emotionally full. A positive spin on aging is encouraged by ENOA experts who say it's healthier to think in terms of assets or what can be done versus deficits or what can't be done.

Forte, best known for his long stint on *Saturday Night Live*, was moved by how engaged his veteran co-stars were. "It was just a delight and an honor to get to work with these people," he said. "They're just such amazing actors. I learned a lot from them because I think at times I could be over-thinking stuff and it just reminded me, Oh, don't try to act too much, just be real. Like Bruce (Dern) would always say, 'Just be truthful,' and that always sounded like acting mumbo jumbo to me coming in but for some reason the way he would explain it and describe it it made sense. There's such an honesty that comes from these performances that it really taught me a lot to watch them."

Cast and crew bonding

Forte got close to Dern, who in real life is old enough to be his grandfather, during the two months they worked on the shoot. "It was very similar to our characters in the movie—we really got to spend a lot of time together and by the end of it we were incredibly close. It just feels like we're family now. I learned so much from him. He was good to me. He was such a good teacher and friend. Nurturing, encouraging, patient. I can't say enough about him, and that's just personally. Professionally, to get to watch what that man does in this movie . . . I don't know what I will do in the future but it will be one of the highlights of my life to get to see such a special performance from that close up. It's something I will always remember."

Forte said he was already a fan of Dern's work before the project. "I have watched so many Bruce Dern movies and he is the kind of person who I will rewind scenes to watch because he's so interesting. The performance he gives in this movie is mesmerizing. We've done a lot of screenings of this movie and I've seen it quite a few times now and I'm just always seeing new things I never saw before. He continues to amaze me with different subtleties. It is such a privilege to get to be in this movie with him."

This wasn't the first time Payne's worked with older actors. Jack Nicholson was in his early 60s when he played the title character in the filmmaker's *About Schmidt*. June Squibb, the actress who appears as Dern's wife in *Nebraska*, was in her 70s when she played Nicholson's wife in *Schmidt*. Robert Forster was 70 when he essayed his small but telling part in *The Descendants*. Just like Forte finds it educational working with veterans, Payne does too.

Mutual admiration society

"I've adored working with the 'old pros'—Nicholson, Dern, Keach and Forster. They are the best actors to work with," said Payne. "They know what they're doing and they know how to study the director to see what movie he or she's trying to make. Plus, I have much to learn from them about what it is to have a life in movies. After all, I don't get to work with and learn from older directors, but I do get to have the actors. "

It works the other way, too, as Dern enjoyed working with two talents much younger than him in Forte and Payne. "I grew to respect Will's ability as an actor and I wasn't sure who he was as an actor when we began," said Dern. "He brought his 'A' game every day for forty days (the number of shooting days). One thing I made him know early on is that you have to play every play just as hard as hard as you play the play before and the play after. I told him, 'It's a job and you're supported here. Alexander's got a whole bunch of people on his set every day that have been working every day on every film he's ever made. He's got a family there."

Dern's worked with legendary directors, including Alfred Hitchcock and Francis Coppola, and he said, "They're all wonderful, they all have genius qualities about them," adding, "Obviously, Alexander is maybe at the head of the list now that I've worked with him. He gets it done and gets it done with a style and a grace. I very much liked the experience with Alexander. I mean, the guy has two fabulous qualities that make a great director—he's a great coach and he knows when to up the vibe and down the vibe."

Stacy Keach, who's also worked with many directing legends, said of Payne, "He's like a great painter and a great conductor. He's a great filmmaker. It's a great honor for me to be a part of this movie." Dern was impressed, too, by the work turned in by his fellow octogenarians and near octogenarians. "Just everybody rose to the occasion. June Squibb is in her 80s. Mary Louise Wilson who plays my sister-in-law is in her 80s. Rance Howard is in his 80s. Angela McEwan, I don't know how old she is, but she's got to be up there. I'm 77."

Keach, age 72, calls it "wonderful" that he and his fellow senior actors create such a strong ensemble together. "We still love what we're doing. We're trying to get good, still." He said he and his colleagues not only remain capable but hungry, possessing "a love for our work and a need for our work and for our growth and development," adding, "Hopefully, we've learned something in our many years of experience." He believes his old friend Bruce Dern delivers his finest, most in-depth performance, Dern, who won Best Actor accolades at the Cannes Film Festival and is a favorite for an Oscar nomination, feels his own work in the film is perhaps the best of his long, noteworthy career.

Dern recalled, "The first day of the movie Alexander said to me, 'I'd like you to let Mr. Papamichael (cinematographer) and I do our jobs,' meaning don't show me anything, let me find it with the camera, and that's what he did and that's what you see. That doesn't mean I wasn't acting. It was as hard a role as I've had to take on but I feel I owed it to the material and to my career for just once in my life to try and have as many consecutive moment-to-moment pure moments of behavior. That's what I began when I worked with Mr. (Elia) Kazan and Mr. (Lee) Strasberg in the Actors Studio—how much moment-to-moment real behavior can you have? And I think in *Nebraska* I've done far and away the most I've had in an entire film."

Nearly stealing every scene she's in, June Squibb is the loud, cranky, foul-mouthed wife of Woody. As Kate Grant she makes a formidable partner to Dern's taciturn Woody. Forte said the pair play very different personalities than their own. "If you knew them as people you'd be blown away even more by their performances. June is such a sweet woman and then you see her as Bruce's wife in the movie and she's just ripping him apart. And Bruce, so vibrant and talkative in real life, but then once those cameras turned on he was so believably gruff and a man of few words. It is such a testament to their acting that they can fully inhabit these complex characters."

Payne and casting director John Jackson agree that the older players assembled for *Nebraska* deliver indelible performances. The pair spent much time and took great care finding just the right mix of faces to play the many older roles the story required. This aspect of filmmaking is so critical that Payne asserted, "Casting is the most important thing" and "The best thing I do as a director is cast. You can't mess up casting. You've got to get the right people in every part. The leads and the secondary, tertiary parts have to be exactly right. It's creating a world."

Anthropological casting

He said his movie is as much "anthropological" as anything because he and Jackson found the faces and voices that most authentically represent the specific rural types being portrayed. "Whatever achievements this film *Nebraska* may or may not have," Payne said, "for me its greatest achievement is its most significant marriage of professional and nonprofessional actors and nonactors because to create that world it's dependent equally on production design and casting. That's what suggests that world is that flesh. We spent over a year doing it so that they all seem like they're in the same movie. Finding those vivid nonactors takes time.

Models and regrets

Many characters in *Nebraska*, including the older figures, are based on real life counterparts screenwriter Bob Nelson extrapolated from childhood visits to northeast Nebraska, where his parents were from and where extended family resided. He said the main character, Woody, is closely drawn from his own father.

Will Forte said his actual parents are nothing like his movie parents in *Nebraska*, but his maternal grandfather did share in common with Woody an inability to articulate things. "He was a man of very few words, so I had the experience in dealing with a person like that. I loved him very much and he loved me, so it was never an issue like that. But I had just a taste of that frustration of being with somebody who wouldn't always express themselves so clearly. That frustration mixed with that love. You can be frustrated by somebody and still love them and treat them with respect."

Bruce Dern said one of the reasons *Nebraska* resonates so strongly with him is that it speaks to something in his own life. "One of the things in my life that's bothered me is that when I had an opportunity to say things to people in my own personal life before it was too late, before they were gone, I didn't do it, and that's on me. I thought that was stuff that was inherent in Woody. He was not a guy able to say the things he should have said and nobody in his family was able to say what they really felt to him. That struck a chord immediately. "If there's a message in *Nebraska* it's if you have the opportunity to say the things you want to say, get them said, and if you don't have the opportunity make the opportunity, otherwise you'll carry it around with you the rest of your life."

Local color: Payne and Co. mine the prairie poetry of Nebraska

Published in a 2014 issue of *The Reader*

Local color, of the achingly human variety, is where Alexander Payne's new black and white film *Nebraska* most deeply comes to life. After fall festival premieres abroad and across the U.S., Payne's coming home to show off the film named for his native state and primarily shot and set here. *Nebraska* had an exclusive limited run at Film Streams. On Nov. 24 Payne joins stars Bruce Dern and Will Forte at the Holland Performing Arts Center for the sold-out Film Streams fundraiser, Feature V, that will find the troika interviewed on stage by *Studio 360* host and novelist Kurt Andersen. The following day Payne and Dern travel to Norfolk, Nebraska, the production's base camp last fall while the project filmed in nearby Hartington, Plainview and environs, to premiere the picture there.

Ringing true and finding Woody

Oscar-winner Payne is a stickler for the truth and with the by-turns elegiac and silly *Nebraska* he went to extreme lengths finding the people and places that ring true to his and screenwriter Bob Nelson's vision of Midwest America. "This is the most authentically Nebraska feature film I've released to date," said Payne, who previously made *Citizen Ruth*, *Election* and *About Schmidt* in-state.

Casting director John Jackson and Payne searched long and hard for the right players to animate the oddball yet familiar characters Nelson created on the page. In a rare star turn winning him much acclaim Bruce Dern so fully inhabits his old codger of a character, Woody Grant, that despite the actor's well known face and voice he disappears into the part to become just another of the story's small town residents. Dern plays Woody as written: a taciturn man of stoic roots and repressed pain long alienated from everyone around him. Feeling a failure near the end of his life, he's desperate for some validation and so gets it in his head that he's a sweepstakes winner. His son David, played by Will Forte, takes him on an epic journey to claim the prize. Amid the missteps and detours comes discovery, empathy and closure. As their strained relationship warms the son gives his father a gift born of understanding, forgiveness and love.

One of the reasons Payne said Dern leapt to mind when he originally read the script a decade ago is that like the actor's actress daughter Laura Dern, who starred in Payne's feature debut *Citizen Ruth*, he doesn't worry about what he looks like on screen. To convincingly play the gone-to-seed Woody the actor inhabiting the role had to look a wreck. "Those Derns don't have vanity," Payne said admiringly. "They'll do anything, they want to do anything. When working they're more interested in hitting a certain level of truth, an often ugly truth or pathetic truth, and now you're talking my language."

Payne elaborated on what made Dern the right fit: "Bruce is a handsome guy when he's cleaned up and obviously as you can see in the film when he's not cleaned up he can really look like a coot and a weirdo. If you took many other actors and tried to do the same thing they'd look fake. The guy would have to portray someone cut off from others and lost in his own world. Woody's probably been like that somewhat his whole life but as a young man they just thought he was reticent. Now he's a coot and ornery and pissed off at himself that he hasn't done anything with his life and now he's about to start taking a dirt nap. I think that's certainly what's driving Woody's crazy mission in some part.

"When I thought about who could communicate that I thought of Bruce." Payne felt Dern could express the two sides of Woody as both prick and pushover who can't refuse doing favors, even if it means being taken advantage of. He also detected "a certain childlike nature" in Dern that aligned with Woody's fragility. "I think within Woody's ornery crust there is something of a child – of a very disillusioned and disappointed child." Indeed, we first meet Woody as he's running away from home. "There's also a sweetness about Woody and Bruce is a sweet guy. He hasn't often played that."

Dern acknowledges it's a departure for him. "Throughout my career I've been flamboyant in a lot of roles, especially flamboyantly evil, and there's a certain style that goes with that." *Nebraska* called for him to be a dull, muted, passive presence. "What the role demanded was a character who appeared to not be touched too much or too little," he said, "and probably not touched at all. And if he touches other people it's without planning to do it. He's just who he is and he's always going to be that way. I think he's a fair man, Woody, and that's another thing I based the character on a lot. Because he's fair he believes what people tell him because he doesn't know why anybody would want to lie to him about anything."

The tangibles and intangibles of a character go into any casting decision. "When you cast someone in a lead you're not casting just his or her ability to act," explained Payne. "you're casting the substance or essence of their person. There's two things going on simultaneously seemingly contradictory but not. One is you want them to become that person in the script yet at the same time not act."

Actor and director arriving to the truth

Dern said Payne has an uncanny way of communicating what he wants, variously tapping "your strengths and weaknesses and sometimes invading your privacy" to extract the emotion or tone he's after. Actors Studio veteran Dern believes he achieved a progressive in-the-moment reality in *Nebraska* he'd never accomplished before on a film. "I've always wanted to be a human being and just kind of acting—otherwise leave myself alone and not perform and I don't think there's really a moment in the movie where I perform—in other words take it above the context of what it really is. The first day of the movie Alexander said to me, 'I'd like you to let Mr. Papamichael (cinematographer) and I do our jobs,' meaning don't show me anything, let me find it with the camera, and that's what he did and that's what you see.

"That doesn't mean I wasn't acting. It was as hard a role as I've had to take on but I feel I owed it to the material and to my career for just once in my life to try and have as many consecutive moment-to-moment pure moments of behavior. That's what I began when I worked with Mr. Kazan and Mr. Strasberg in the Actors Studio—how much moment to moment real behavior can you have? And I think in *Nebraska* I've done far and away the most I've had in an entire film."

Forte, a relative newcomer to acting after years writing for television, said he learned a lot from his co-star. "Bruce would always say, 'Just be truthful,' and that always sounded like acting mumbo jumbo to me coming in but for some reason the way he would explain it and describe it it made sense. There's such an honesty that comes from his performance and all the performances that it really taught me a lot to watch everyone work."

Dern said Payne lived up to what his daughter Laura and his old acting chum Jack Nicholson, who starred in the director's *About Schmidt*, told him about the filmmaker: "They both said in separate conversations, 'He'll be the best teammate you've ever had.' They were right. I feel it's the best team, overall, I've ever had."

Payne, whose sets are famously relaxed, said he also casts with an eye to who will "be nice to work with" and contribute to the playfulness he believes essential to good filmmaking. "I want to be there to play. I don't know exactly how it (any scene) should be, I'm there to sort of say, 'Oh, well, let's try this and let's try that, nudging the machine toward a certain direction. It's not all preconceived, you're discovering it day by day, so I think you want actors who are willing to have a sense of, Let's be playful and free. It's all about having fun, and that will create something none of us have thought of exactly."

Dern said he's glad it took nearly a decade to get the film made – the project came to Payne as the filmmaker was setting up *Sideways* – because "I wasn't ready to play this role a few years ago." The passage of time put some more natural wear and tear on Dern, both physically and emotionally. The limp he walks with in the film is real, if exaggerated, and the way Woody leaves things unsaid is something Dern said he's been guilty of himself and regrets.

Life informing art

Similarly, Payne's personal life caught up with the experience of David in *Nebraska* as an adult child dealing with aging parents. Payne's father is in a nursing home and his mother recently survived a serious health scare. "I was able to make it quite personal in certain details related to David taking care of his older folks," Payne revealed. "Everyone I know of my generation at that age has parents that are getting on and need a little special attention. We love them to death and they drive us crazy. How we take care of them and accommodate them and all those things, and how far do we extend ourselves to be dutiful and at what point do we cut it off, all those questions. It wound up being because of the time in my life when I was making it quite personal. The fact that I had that much more life experience for this film with respect to my parents, I think helps the film. It always helps a film if you can put some of yourself in there."

Payne said the bottomed-out economy also enhanced the austere shooting style and stark look of the film, adding, "Those winds blew their way into the film as well and it becomes more of a Depression Era film." Undoubtedly some will take umbrage at the film's portrayals of quirky. salt-of-the-earth types. But if the strong reception the picture's received at the Cannes, Telluride and New York Film Festivals, among others, is any indication, than most audiences realize Payne and his collaborators sought archetype, not caricature in bringing to life small town inhabitants and the dysfunctional Grant family.

"I hope what people take away from this movie is his genuine love for Nebraska because he really does love Nebraska" said Forte. Dern calls the film "a love poem" to Nebraska from Payne.

Payne, Nelson, Jackson, Papamichael, editor Kevin Tent, assorted other crew and the ensemble cast all committed to realizing authentic portraits of this comic-dramatic Midwest Gothic tale. As Payne is both a writer and a director he made his own pass on the Nelson script. He's particularly proud of the simple yet sublime and nearly wordless ending he hit upon that may just go down as one of the most memorable and moving conclusions in the annals of American cinema. A series of telling looks are exchanged that say more than any words can. He's pleased too by his handling of the film's black and white and wide screen that help make *Nebraska* an expressionistic experience for the way he and Papamichael evoke mood from light, shadow, landscape and framing. The juxtaposition of persons and places carries meaning.

Creating a world through casting

But what Payne's most eager to talk about is how *Nebraska* lives and breathes on the strength of its casting and melding of actors and extras. "Whatever achievements this film *Nebraska* may or may not have for me its greatest achievement is its most significant marriage of professional and nonprofessional actors and nonactors because to create that world it's dependent equally on production design and casting. That's what suggests that world is that flesh. We spent over a year doing it so that they all seem like they're in the same movie. Finding those vivid nonactors takes time.

"Official preproduction is going to start maybe fifteen weeks out but I need casting and location scouting to start many, many weeks before that and I do a lot of the scouting way in advance of a greenlight. Whenever I'd have three free days I'd just take off in my car around the state." He's come to know rural Nebraska quite well. It's why he's confident he cast not only the right locales but the right faces and voices. He goes so far as to say, "Casting is the most important thing" and "The best thing I do as a director is cast. You can't f___ up casting. You've got to get the right people in every part and of course the leads and the secondary, tertiary parts have to be exactly right. It's creating a world." He likes saying his movie is as much "anthropological" as anything.

Prepping the movie, he said, "I looked at a number of small town American films. One of them in particular is an excellent film and it has professional actors but also people cast from that small town. But there's a great chasm between the acting styles of the two. It's like the faces of the real people lend what they're supposed to lend which is authenticity, verisimilitude and all that but they're not acting properly, even as versions of themselves.

"So I knew we had to spend time to get local people who could act as vividly as possible as versions as themselves but also to have the professional actors act flatter. They both had to meet in between. I like when professional actors act more flatly like people do in real life. People don't gesticulate, go into histrionics in real life, not Midwesterners anyway."

A cinema seldom seen

Truth is always the litmus test for Payne. "When I'm in a casting session it's no different from how I am on the set, which is the moment they start acting I pretend in my mind that we're not making a movie, that I'm just there invisible watching something. Do I believe it? That's the trick. Do I buy it? Do I think these are real people?"

Payne's likely to return to Nebraska again to make films. It's only natural. "Other directors continue to make films in the cities where they grew up. Paul Thomas Anderson and Quentin Tarantino shoot in L.A. Woody Allen and Martin Scorsese and so many others in New York. Kurosawa would never leave Tokyo. Pedro Almodovar hasn't made a movie outside of Spain. Fellini never made a movie outside of Italy. They were courted and invited a lot. 'No, no, this is where I feel comfortable, where I feel like I know the people and where I can get the details right.'"

It's the same reasoning Payne uses for making movies here. Then there's the fact that by tackling subjects so close to home he can show a segment of America too often missing from today's cinema. "I think in general we Americans need to see Americans in our films but we kind of don't, we see cartoons largely. As Americans we make cartoons easily digestible for the rest of the world but we're not showing ourselves to ourselves. I like when art is a mirror somehow to represent or reflect or distort or refract, just to see ourselves like our film in the '70s, showing common people doing every day things. . . ."

He said a recurring comment he hears about *Nebraska* is that "we haven't seen these Americans in a long time. It's as though they're forgotten, we never see them in the cinema. I thought that was interesting that people really feel they're seeing Americans they've never seen before. Of course, I really appreciate that."

As one of only a handful of Nebraska feature filmmakers who's cultivated the state on screen, he said, "I think I'm lucky I'm from Nebraska and that I have a virgin territory to show in movies. Maybe the fact I've seen so many movies informs the fact that I can know even unconsciously what would be new. I don't want to make derivative films, I want to do something new."

By the same token, Payne, who reveres classic cinema, said, "People have said of *Nebraska*, 'This is a film like they used to make,' and that makes me feel good because I'm trying to make films like how they used to make. I'm trying to make the films I myself would like to see, which is film from the '70s and before."

In truth, Payne's made a timeless film that plays like a loony requiem set to its own internal rhythm and logic. It unfolds slowly but surely and from the mix of somber, sweet and surreal emerges a lyrical comic-drama unlike any other. Because of this cinematic prairie poem the state will surely never be looked at the same again.

Nebraska Coast Connection Salon Q & A with Alexander Payne: the filmmaker speaks candidly about *Nebraska,* casting, screenwriting and craft

Excerpt of Alexander Payne in conversation with Nebraska Coast Connection founder Todd Nelson at September 11, 2013 NCC Hollywood Salon at the Culver Hotel in Culver City

AP: "Hello, good evening, thank you for coming..."

TN: "You have a little movie coming out. A little black and white number you threw together over a weekend or two."

AP: "No, longer than that. But it's a small movie. That doesn't mean it's not dramatically resonant, but it's a small movie."

(Then Payne addressed how the project came to him and the background of how its screenwriter Robert Nelson came to write it.)

AP: "Nine years ago I got a script from Albert Berger and Ron Yerxa, the team that had produced *Election.* They came to me nine or ten years ago with a script called *Nebraska* and it was written by a guy named Bob Nelson out of Snohomish, Washington but his parents were from Hartington (Nebraska). And it was based on his memory of his father's and mother's families. He used to spend his summers out there in Hartington in northeast Nebraska and he wrote this script based on his memories of those summers and it really rang hilariously true. It was a very austere screenplay. Those producers said they suspected it was going to be small for me, too dinky a film."

TN: "They thought you might know someone who..."

AP: "Yeah, 'Do you know a young Nebraska filmmaker who might want to do this?' and I said, 'No, I think I want to do it.' They had wanted to make it for like $2 or $3 million, and I said, 'How about like $10 or $12 million?' I showed it not long afterwards to someone in attendance here tonight, John Jackson, my casting director, because I knew that this film would really live or die on its casting. I mean, all films do but even a couple percentage points more this one would because it's as much anthropological as it is cinematic. And he liked it and thought he wanted to cast it. He said he felt a very personal connection to it through his family, whom he describes as dirt farmers from Iowa. That's a bit of an exaggeration in a way with respect to the script but still it's suggestive. . . .

"A lot of the movie was a road trip and I was just finishing *Sideways*. I didn't want to followup *Sideways* with another road trip film. It's a real drag to shoot in cars and I just couldn't do another car movie again after *Sideways*. Now *The Descendants* ended up having some stuff in cars too but anyway . . . the timing worked out and right after *The Descendants* I made it. They were nice enough to wait—the producers and the writer—and so it happened."

TN: "It has Bruce Dern and Will Forte. Tell us about bringing them on board."

AP: "Bruce Dern had first leapt to mind to play this part. All parts are tricky to cast in general but this one I think for John and me has been the trickiest. You know. I get praised sometimes for getting a certain controlled performance out of Jack Nicholson or that I get stars to create characters, that after ten or fifteen minutes of seeing a big star like George Clooney you can maybe, hopefully, of course it's my aspiration, forget it's a big star and just see the character . . . I never tailor a screenplay to fit the actor. I always demand the actor come to the script—even if it's Nicholson or Clooney, who have certain strengths that most directors and screenwriters would wish to exploit.

"Naw, this is a text and it's a part and yes you're a star but you're also an actor, so come to this and make it your own that way. This though I think has been the most specific lead part we've ever had to cast. Not anyone could play this guy Woody Grant. I looked back in film history and said, 'Well, Henry Fonda could have played it like the way he did *On Golden Pond*,' or Walter Brennan, or for you film buffs out there, Charley Grapewin or possibly John Carradine or possibly Warren Oates had he lived. But all those people are unavailable. After thinking about Bruce Dern, the only other guy who maybe could have done it, Gene Hackman, but I couldn't get a meeting with Gene Hackman because he genuinely has retired. He won't even return a phone call or a query. So it just came down to Bruce Dern.

"We did our due diligence and met fifty other guys and any one of them who could have done it would still be a stretch. Like this one could maybe do it but he has trouble learning lines or this one could maybe do it but you'd have to get him to not do this schtick or this one could maybe have done it but it would have taken more work on my part and every actor requires work anyway. Bruce required work but less work than any of those other guys would have required to get it right, so Bruce Dern's the guy."

TN: "Will Forte?"

AP: "Never would have thought about him in a billion years but he auditioned well. So I know often in these salons we get actors or casting people and I'm always happy to say that John and I rely on auditions, the old fashioned way. Even actors who are well known I still need them to come in and read the text, with all respect. I mean, even if it's ten words, say a few words, help me out, I have a pea brain, I don't want to screw it up, and I don't want to screw up and cast you in the wrong part and then it's not right. We all benefit if we're able to have a meeting. Well, what else are we going to talk about? Read the fucking script.

"And to good pros, the ones who won't audition, but they will deign to have a meeting, the good ones will either consciously or unconsciously find the time in the meeting to say, 'Oh, I loved the moment in your screenplay where he said . . .' and he'll do a little bit of it. That's the courteous thing to do, that's the polite thing to do because those actors who won't even do that don't get the job in my experience.

"Just about auditioning stuff I remember the actress Judy Greer, a super great old fashioned in the best way actor. She's in *The Descendants*. She plays the lover's wife. She calls herself an audition-only actress. She won't take an offer and if there's a meeting she insists on reading the script because she said it's only when I read the text in front of the director do I know if I'm right for the part. So the direct line of communication between actor and director is that text. That's just smart. What the hell else are we doing?

"June Squibb, she played the part of Jack Nicholson's wife in *About Schmidt* (and she plays Bruce Dern's wife in *Nebraska*). . . . I didn't offer her . . . She didn't occur to me, she sent in an audition. Even she had to audition. I had no idea she was going to be right for this part. It's the Geraldine Page part or the Marjorie Main part from *Ma and Pa Kettle*. Basically *Nebraska*'s a glorified *Ma and Pa Kettle* film," he said, deadpanning and eliciting laughs.

(Payne discussed some more actors he's worked with, why's he's particularly proud of the casting he and John Jackson did on Nebraska and how he tried to avoid certain pitfalls that come with mixing professional and nonprofessional actors on screen.)

AP: "Tim Driscoll from Omaha, who had a small part in *Citizen Ruth*, came back for this one. And his sister (Delaney Driscoll) had a significant part in *Election* as Matthew Broderick's lover.

"Whatever achievements this film *Nebraska* may or may not have for me it's greatest achievement is its most significant marriage of professional and nonprofessional actors because to create that world it's dependent equally on production design and casting. That's what suggests that world is that flesh. We spent over a year doing it. The start date is here, the visual preproduction is here, the casting has to start here. You can't fuck up casting, you've got to get the right people in every part and of course the leads and the secondary, tertiary parts have to be exactly right. It's creating a world.

"I looked at a number of small town American films for this one. One of them in particular is an excellent film and it has professional actors but also people cast from that small town. But there's a great chasm between the acting styles of the two. It's like the faces of the real people lend what they're supposed to lend which is authenticity, vermisiltude and all that but they're not acting properly, even as versions of themselves. So I knew we had to spend time to get local people who could act as vividly as possible as versions of themselves but also to have the professional actors act flatter. They both had to meet in between. I like when professional actors act more flatly like people do in real life. People don't gesticulate, go into histrionics in real life, not Midwesterners anyway."

(Nelson and Payne then made a few comments before screening the trailer for Nebraska.)

TN: "It premiered at the Cannes Film Festival in May. A wild success I can witness—I was there. I saw a fifteen minute standing ovation at the end of the film."

AP: "Yeah, I've seen turkeys get a standing ovation at Cannes. It played better at Telluride."

(Then, referring to the trailer, Payne said)

AP: "This is a work in progress print."

(After the screening someone in the audience commented about the

Spanish sounding music, which prompted Payne to describe it as a—)

AP: "More Mexican sounding trumpet piece."

TN: "We have a stack of questions" (on note cards, which he began reading). What was your big break in the business?"

AP: "Uh, probably three. One was getting into UCLA film school. The second was making a hit short film out of UCLA film school, my student thesis film, *The Passion of Martin.* Making a very good film out of UCLA film school, it's like that movie *The Big Picture,* it opened a lot of doors for me. It was still years before I made my first feature. Four big breaks. . . . Another big break I would say was meeting Jim Taylor, my co-screenwriter because, well, a movie can be anything but the types of movies we talk about generally depend on two things, one is screenplay, the other is casting. But screenplay, screenplay, screenplay, and I was very fortunate to find a co-screenwriter early on. And then I have to say *Election.* You know, *Citizen Ruth* was OK, an 'A' for effort and all that, but it tanked at the box office and it was dumped by the distributor, Miramax...

"The same producer who sent me this thing, Albert Berger, (*Nebraska*) sent me *Election,* and that was a big break. In a very good year—for I don't like this name independent, but non-studio, authorial voiced films—1999, it did very well, not at the box office necessarily good but it's still the film I get the most compliments on. It's my mother's favorite of my films. I showed her *Nebraska*—'Yeah, it's OK, but why you cant make more like *Election?*'

(Nelson referred to Payne and Jim Taylor collaborating.)

TN: "I watched you and Jim work together."

(Nelson said Payne and Taylor wrote About Schmidt here, meaning L.A. and Payne corrected him.)

AP: "No, we didn't write *About Schmidt* here. We wrote *Election* here. We wrote *About Schmidt* in Topanga Canyon."

TN: "So tell us about the collaboration. A lot of people in the Coast Connection often ask what it's like to write with a writing partner."

AP: "There seem to be three areas of dramatic narrative writing that lend themselves to collaboration: Musicals, TV writing and screen-writing. A play is never co-written or a novel is never co-written, but movies often are, even by the great directors. Bergman and Fellini and Bertolucci. Billy Wilder always had a collaborator. I think there's something about the process which lends itself to casting a wider net for ideas. Sometimes when people collaborate on screenplays they divide and conquer, where maybe one is better at structure and the other is better at dialogue, or they outline together and one takes scenes one through thirty and the other takes scenes thirty through sixty. Then they reunite and rewrite. We're not like that at all. We're always together in the same room."

TN: "You had two keypads on the same computer."

AP: "Correct. We never outline, we never make out note cards or anything real distinct about what could happen next. Most of the time is spent not writing. Writing alone or writing with someone, in any eight hours you're only writing maybe forty five minutes in that eight hours. The rest of the time you're doing dishes, obsessively checking email, walking around. You need to set aside all that time to extract that hour of writing. One or the other will say, 'I've got an idea, let's do this,' and then you pound out maybe two or three pages, then you sit down and rewrite and we chisel our way through the whole first draft. I wrote *Descendants* alone and I did a rewrite of this one (*Nebraska*)."

(Nelson mentioned that Nat Faxson and Jim Dash wrote a draft of The Descendants and Payne clarified.)

AP: "They didn't do the draft we shot."

TN: "So you polished it up."

AP: "I didn't polish it, I wrote it from scratch. With *Nebraska*, I rewrote it, also uncredited Phil Johnston, who wrote *Cedar Rapids* (which Payne produced), contributed some jokes, too. So I cast a wide net that way. I wrote the ending. I made it personal. I think it's my job as a director to make it as personal as I can to me. It's still Bob Nelson's vision. It would never occur to me to seek screenwriting credit."

(In answer to questions from the audience about how he finds the material that he makes into films, Payne said he turned to writing his own scripts out of necessity.)

AP: I've always written out of desperation. I never imagined in film school, Oh, I need to write and direct all my films. Who wants to write? Writing is awful. I had to do it because I never find anything, other than *Nebraska*. Soon after film school I wanted to direct *Wilder Napalm*, which was written by Vince Gilligan of *Breaking Bad*. That's the only thing I wanted to direct was the Vince Gilligan script and I didn't get the job. And then they made an unwatchable film out of it. They should have hired me. But, yeah, I open every screenplay with a prayer, 'Please Lord let me want to direct it.' But we're not in that age of literate film scripts. I don't have Robert Riskin or Jules Furthman or Waldo Salt or Robert Towne, and if they're around they're working for television, they're not doing movies. Movies suck. American movies in general suck except those done by writer-directors nowadays. We don't have screenwriters writing for the movies. Like the big overdone, overwritten *A Beautiful Mind* kind of crap, we don't even have that anymore, we don't even have like *A Beautiful Mind* anymore. We have nothing in general, so I've got to write it myself. And I've never gotten one from my agent. They've never sent me one fucking script (he wanted to direct) in twenty three years of being out of film school, not one. The ones I've done which have come from outside of me: *Election*, unpublished manuscript. *Sideways*, unpublished manuscript. *Nebraska*, from some ass hole out of Snohomish, Washington. *The Descendants* was on its way to being published. I think we had the galleys."

(An audience member asked if there are exceptions to this dearth of quality scripts coming his way)

AP: "I hope there are exceptions, I want there to be exceptions, but in my experience in almost a quarter century it's dismal. Or they're not getting to me. But then again I look and see what is made and I think, What's been made that God I wish I had had that script. Nothing. Oh, a Charlie Kaufman script would have been fun to direct but he's in with Spike Jonze."

(Another audience member asked what's broken about that system then?)

AP: "We're in an age of shit for movies but we're in a golden age for television. Everything is TV now. *Breaking Bad, Homeland, Mad Men*. That's where all the quality is. But it's a different thing. And then that form develops its own amazing virtues – an infinite time with characters. They're not two hour movies they're like fables now. A character in a movie gets two hours whereas a character in a TV show gets fifty hours. But I still believe in movies. I'm not working in TV.

"Joe Morgenstern of the *Wall Street Journal* came over to my house over the weekend and wants to write an article, Why should we still believe in movies when we have great television? And I said, 'Movies changed my life, TV hasn't, and also what do you want to do, go to Chartres Cathedral or stay at home and watch Mass for Shut-Ins? The quality is in movies. We spend two months mixing the sound. TV does it in two days. Even the greatest TV is mostly plot and character revealed through talking heads. Wonderful actors and all that but it's dialogue basically. It's theater versus the juxtaposition of images, how music cuts in, the lighting, the instruments of cinema. Shooting two pages a day versus shooting seven pages a day. I still believe in the movies."

8

Downsizing

Downsizing (The Reader)

Introduction

The fact that Alexander Payne's seventh feature turned out to be *Downsizing* came as no real surprise since he and Jim Taylor labored over the script ten years. They nearly got it made twice, which is why Google searches bring up links and references to earlier incarnations of the project, including stars and studios formerly attached who dropped away in the intervening years. As Payne puts it, the time was finally right for the project to happen.

Payne reportedly had an all-star cast attached to the project when it first gained steam nearly a decade ago. Though the actors have changed, the final cast of *Downsizing* constitutes the greatest collective star power and depth of talent yet seen in one of his films. The names include Oscar winners and box office draws of the first order and only one has previously worked with Payne. That who's-who roster includes: Matt Damon, Kristen Wiig, Jason Sudeikis, Neal Patrick Harris, Alec Baldwin, Christoph Waltz, Udo Kier, Paul Mabon, Warren Bell, and Hong Chau. Their ranks include an Oscar winner, a major box office draw, several critical darlings, and some international players. None has previously worked with Payne. Years back, when Payne spoke about the film in only cryptic terms, he referred to it as being in the spirit of an episodic Robert Altmanesque ensemble piece, Some of if does play that way on the page, although Payne and Taylor tend to be more narratively disciplined than Altman was.

In some interesting casting notes, just days before the April 1 shoot start it was announced that Reese Witherspoon, long slated to play Damon's wife, was no longer attached to the project and that Kristen Wiig had replaced her. I cannot recall anything like that happening so late in the process on any of Payne's previous films. Damon and Wiig both appeared in the acclaimed *The Martians*. Wiig represents the second *Saturday Night Live* alumnus, after Will Forte, to grace one of Payne's films. And with the casting of Paul Mabon and Warren Belle, there will finally be black actors in speaking parts in a Payne film. The absence of people of color in his films had not gone unnoticed. There are even some well-known actors of color from Omaha who have expressed dismay or disappointment at that lack.

The basic hook has been public knowledge for some time. The IMDB (Internet Movie Data Base) log line read: "A social satire in which a guy realizes he would have a better life if he were to shrink himself." Not much to go on. But the idea of miniaturized human life does set the mind to conjuring all sorts of scenarios. Something not left to the imagination but rather always known about the project is its reliance on visual effects in order to make believable the conceit of science giving human beings the option to be radically reduced in size. Effects are the only way to realize that on screen. It follows then that *Downsizing* is a science fiction flick, though Payne does not come right out and call it that. But clearly it resides somewhere in the sci-fi genre.

I do not mean to suggest Payne in any way distances himself from science fiction, In an interview with me he actually referenced a quote he attributed to the great author Ray Bradbury, who when asked something to the effect, you are such a great writer but why do you write science fiction, which of course implied that the genre is somehow inferior to or less important than other literature. Payne remembered Bradbury's answer as something like—Well, science fiction is the most realistic genre. While I could not find that quotation from Bradbury, I did find these quotations attributed to him that seem to make the same point:

"Science fiction is the most important literature in the history of the world because it's the history of ideas, the history of our civilization birthing itself. Science fiction is central to everything we've ever done . . ." and "Science fiction is not just the art of the possible, but of the obvious."

Any number of other great sci-fi authors, from Robert Heinlein to Isaac Asimov to Frank Herbert, have said similar things; the common sentiment being that the genre draws on humankind's oldest, deepest, and unfolding yearnings and imaginings and therefore it resides in the very nature of what it means to be alive from moment to moment.

Up until early 2016, all one could glean about the project is that after previous tries to get it financed the film finally found a home at Paramount, the studio that also produced Payne's *Nebraska*. All the trade press had to go on was that tease of a premise about miniaturization. Everything else was pure conjecture. Even with that bare thread it was not hard to conceive what fertile territory such a set up provided Payne and Taylor. Still, unless you read the script, saying anything more about *Downsizing* was supposition since Payne was protective about the story he and Taylor so long nurtured. Principal cast and crew were similarly reticent in giving anything away.

I actually ended up being the first journalist to report on the plot of *Downsizing* after Payne let me read the script and interview him about it. It is a practice we have long held. He shares his final drafts with me on a for-my-eyes-only basis and I am then able to mine depths not afforded other writers. Breaking that worldwide exclusive was extremely satisfying. That story, which follows this introduction, was the first to quote Patne extensively about the project. The story offers what I hope is a tantalizing preview of what should be one of the most talked about features of 2017. In this introduction I reveal a bit more than I could at the time about the film since the project is now finished and the publicity apparatus behind it is gearing up.

All scripts go through some evolutionary process but *Downsizing*'s lasted longer than most. Earlier versions contained more characters and scenes that stretched the budget necessary to create on screen miniaturized human life set against the backdrop of vast global events.

"It's the same basic strange story we've been working on for these many years but finally in 2014, right after I finished *Nebraska*, Jim and I returned to the script and we finally had the courage to jettison certain aspects of the script, which we still miss," Payne explained.

The script cuts were mandated "to compact the script into a decent form and length" that correlated to the budget the project could afford on the open market of film financing. Making things more complicated, as my article references, were the detours or digressions that Payne and Taylor take with their scripts.

"Jim and I tend not to write screenplays which conform to

traditional contemporary screenplay structure," Payne said. "Maybe they do after the fact, but while we're writing and while we're in the midst of it were writing what feels to us like a shaggy dog story." *Downsizing* was shaping up to be an unwieldy shaggy dog story until getting pruned into its shooting script form.

As my article also alludes to, there is naturally a tendency to assume that because of *Downsizing*'s subject matter and sci-fi contours, it must be a major departure from the artist's previous work. Payne disagrees. I concur that it in fact conforms quite neatly into the examination of minutiae running through all his work. In this case the minutiae just happens to coincide with miniaturization. So, where will *Downsizing* fit in the Payne canon? That cannot be known with any certainty until the film is released and reviewed. But I can surmise some things based on what I have read and on what Payne and his collaborators have told me about his vision for committing the story to the screen.

With this project, he digs even deeper than before to expose universal human fears, resentments, prejudices, and desires. There is great portent in the context for why people choose to be miniaturized in the first place. Payne and Taylor set the key events of the story in some near future when Earth is on the brink of disaster due to worsening natural resource depletion and global warming events. Therefore, the film explores the consequences of scarcity thinking run amok.

The story connects with the zeitgeist of impending doom in the air fueled by the threat of melting ice caps and global terrorism and the fear that some contagion will precipitate a zombie plague apocalypse.

"Well, you read it in the paper every day," Payne told me. "Everyone's talking about it. People have a genuine sense of finality these days. A hundred years, two hundred years, whatever it might be, that we have left. People have for millennia, well at least centuries—'Oh, the end of the world is coming,' and usually in some bogus religious context. But now it's occurring in a scientific and empirical context. So, I don't know, we thought it'd be fun to make a comedy about it."

He also plays with the notion that faced with such dire circumstances people will respond in very different ways. Some will choose to do nothing, either out of denial or despair, while others will engage in hedonism and exploitation. A few brave souls will be pioneers who undergo reduction and with it downsize their consumption footprint. But as our protagonist Paul. played by Matt Damon, discovers, that transformation unalterably separates him from his previous life. Additionally, instead of downsizing eliminating the problems of the big world that baggage follows him to the small world, where he encounters a whole new set of issues on top of the old ones. The small and normal worlds coexist in uneasy tension. The bigs look down, literally and figuratively, on the smalls. The smalls resent being marginalized and patronized by the bigs. All of it serves as rich metaphor for the bigotry and discrimination that historically attend The Other and that result in segregation and isolation.

Paul finds the same avarice, conflict, and inequity of the outside world present in the contrived new world he enters. He is a good-hearted, dutiful worker bee who just wants to do the right thing as a husband, as a son, as a neighbor, as a friend, as a citizen. In the big world he is an occupational therapist who tries hard to please his wife (played by Kristen Wiig), care for his mother, and help people with their physical ailments. Then, after a betrayal, he is thrust into the small world bereft of everything he held dear. Instead of the promised utopia, he finds a cold, artificial construct under glass called Leisureland Estates that sucks the life right out of him.

The aforementioned betrayal happens when his wife, who has talked Paul into the two of them being miniaturized, backs out of the downsizing process at the last minute. He only learns about her change of heart when it is too late and his own miniaturization is complete. He is stuck and there is no going back. Talk about a bummer.

Payne once had Paul Giamatti lined up to play Paul, but that was years ago. Matt Damon brings the same kind of ordinariness to bear with the advantage of being a bankable leading man.

"Among contemporary leading men he is the closest thing we have to an Everyman," Payne said. "We saw it in *The Martian* particularly. More and more he is assuming the role that say James Stewart and more recently Tom Hanks used to play. At least you can relate to the guy and you can project some of your own fears, yearnings, aspirations onto his face. You understand him. There are many contemporary American stars with whom I don't have that relationship. I can't project any of my vulnerabilities or fears or aspirations onto their faces. But on Matt Damon's, I can, and he's kind of the only one we have at that upper level. We don't have Dustin Hoffman as a young man any more, or Al Pacino or Jack Lemmon or James Stewart. Other people can disagree with me and say what about this one or what about that one but really among the upper echelon of contemporary American movie stars Matt Damon comes the closest to being our Everyman."

Two actors expert at incisive comedy, Alec Baldwin and Neil

Patrick Harris, play a real estate magnate and a salesman, respectively, who make fodder of the downsizing phenomenon. In this odd new existence, uprooted from all he knew, Paul struggles finding his bearings and thus his identity. He keeps running up against systems and persons predisposed to take advantage of the naive, the weak, the powerless, the dispossessed.

There is much here that makes subtle barbed reference to the false American Dream sold to the masses in real life. The fabricated small world set aside for the miniaturized population is suggestive of the internment-refugee camps, ghettos, and other confined areas that minorities have traditionally been relegated to by the majority population. Payne and Taylor also imply that the word "downsizing" refers to the ever narrow-minded views and declining values so prevalent today among nations and leaders.

Far from being only a bleak take on things, Payne and Taylor also portray this social experiment as a full-blooded experience where people are still passionate and where desire still rules the human heart. Paul eventually finds his way but in a most unexpected series of events that introduces him to people caught up in social-political-criminal intrigue. As with any fable where the protagonist is adrift in a strange new environment – think *Alice in Wonderland, The Wizard of Oz, The Hobbit* and *Star Wars* for starters – Paul partners with fellow travelers navigating the surreal landscape. One is a female Vietnamese dissident played by Hong Chau and the other is a crooked Serbian entrepreneur played by Christoph Waltz.

"You've got the guy who's on his journey, you've got the love interest who helps him do so and then you've got the reluctant, self-absorbed helper," is how Payne described this troika "As American a place as Leisureland Estates is in New Mexico we still wanted to have a sense of the global impact of downsizing – of the miniaturization process – and that in any small city around the world you might meet very diverse people, and Paul does."

All of it leads Paul to unknowingly assume a key role in a great shift about to occur in human history. In the process this meek man discovers he is stronger than he thinks. The plot-line makes *Downsizing* a Passage story of epic, mythic, even heroic dimensions

The story moves across great swaths of time and space. It opens in a setting that could be a prehistoric cave but that turns out to be a haven somewhere and sometime else altogether. In what is the most physically ambitious of Payne's films to date, we are taken to locations as diverse as South Omaha, the small world enclosure known as Leisureland, the fjords of Norway and a Middle Earth. Payne and the largest crew he ever worked with went to Los Angeles, Omaha, Toronto, and Norway to capture actual locales. They created imaginary locales on sound stages and in effects suites in Toronto.

The film ended up being based in Toronto for practical reasons, namely the generous tax credits offered by that country and American money stretching even farther there due to the soft Canadian dollar. The presence of Toronto's extensive, state of the art Pinewood Studios also helped sway Paramount to cross borders. For years now California state officials have railed against U.S. productions leaving the historical base of the American film industry, Hollywood, to shoot elsewhere but it is particularly galling when projects leave the country altogether to go north of the border. Incentives go a long way toward enticing filmmakers and their studios to shoot somewhere. It is an incredibly competitive environment, too, as states and countries vie for slices of the Hollywood pie. Norway sweetened the pot for *Downsizing* by giving it backing from the Norwegian Film Institute's new incentive scheme for international and local films and series. The picture, which makes great use of Norway's coastal and fjord areas, reportedly got four and a half million in Norwegian krones (equal to about $685,000).

In all his films, but most concretely starting with *About Schmidt*, Payne lays out a literal journey of self-discovery for his protagonists, each of whom is driven by crisis. When Warren Schmidt loses his career and wife he hits the road in search of himself only to learn it is an inside job. Screw-ups Jack and Miles lay waste to wine country in a dissolute attempt to avoid growing up before coming to terms with reality and love. After learning his comatose wife cheated on him, Matt's chase for revenge leads to reconciliation with the past. Woody and David set out on a seemingly silly quest only to have key revelations and truths revealed. Paul's self-worth shrinks with his body until he finds new resolve and purpose in the emerging new world he is catapulted into.

Thus, *Downsizing* is the latest in an unfolding narrative Payne posits about the human condition. All of life is a journey, he is telling us. We are both observers and participants, so buckle up and try to enjoy the ride because it is all we get in our finite lifetime. If we pay attention, we may just learn something about ourselves along the way and perhaps grow from the experience.

By way of explanation: Oscar-winner Waltz and several other prominent actors in the cast are not mentioned in the following piece because their casting had not yet been announced. Reese Witherspoon is mentioned because she was still attached to the project. Damon, Wiig, Walz, Baldwin, Harris, Sudeikis are the latest in a growing number of prominent actors who have signed to work with Payne in recent years. With any Payne watch. it is fun to speculate with whom he might next work. One of the anticipatory joys of *Downsizing* will be how the impressive ensemble he worked with mesh together. Given Payne's meticulous casting and outstanding record of working with actors, it is a good bet the results will be entertaining and perhaps even provide some of these artists' most memorable performances.

As for me, I will continue reporting and writing about *Downsizing* and whatever next Payne project emerges after it.

Payne's film about miniaturized human life tackles big themes: *Downsizing* to finally go before the cameras this spring

Published March, 2016 in *The Reader*

The high concept behind Alexander Payne's soon to shoot new feature, *Downsizing*, unfolds in a near future world where humans can opt to be miniaturized. Everything about the story, from the title to the characters to the plot-lines, gives Payne and co-scriptwriter Jim Taylor ample metaphorical opportunities.

The $76 million budgeted Paramount picture starring Matt Damon, Reese Witherspoon, Neil Patrick Harris, Jason Sudeikis, Alec Baldwin and Hong Chau endured a long gestation. A different cast was attached in 2008-2009 before the road to financing collapsed with the economy. The pieces almost came together again in 2014. All the while, the script, begun in 2006, got reworked and pared down to meet the budget cap Hollywood placed on this risky project marking Payne's first foray into science fiction and visual effects.

The production is based at Pinewood Studios in Toronto, Ontario, Canada, where Payne will work for the first time on sound stages and with green screens, CGI and motion capture. Little or no forced perspective will be used.

The sprawling, three-month shoot rolls out April 1 for a week in Los Angeles, then comes to Omaha for a few days. The whole works heads off to Norway for more shooting but the bulk will occur across the border in Canada, where some post-production will occur, but the bulk of the post production will happen in Los Angeles.

Arch satirists Payne and Taylor use the downsizing premise to skewer the small-mindedness of persons, policies. constructs. In this new work the veteran scenarists, whose previous credits together include the Payne-directed *Citizen Ruth*, *Election*, *About Schmidt* and *Sideways*, suggest not only are Earth's physical resources at risk but its intellectual-moral capital, too.

Downsizing's all too real musings on diminishing returns and bankrupt values posits a redemptive protagonist in Paul, a South

Omaha Everyman whom Matt Damon will play. Although the story has a fatalistic, end-of-world backdrop, it dangles hope that humankind, in whatever size survives, will muddle through somehow.

That Payne should use science fiction's expansive prism to consider world crisis issues and explore the nature of humanity may seem at odds with his intimate dramedies about neurosis, infidelity, promiscuity, loneliness, yearning. Then again, all his work has churned the existential wheel with mundane characters bogged down by the weight of their own mess. Just think of the angst that Ruth (*Citizen Ruth*), Jim (*Election*), Warren (*Schmidt*), Miles and Jack (*Sideways*), Matt (*The Descendants*) and Woody (*Nebraska*) confront. For all its fantastic elements this new narrative is anchored in that same morass of folks dealing with adult dilemmas, conflicts and flaws. Problems dog them wherever they go, even in the would-be miniature haven, Leisureland.

And why shouldn't Payne dip his toes in the sci-fi pool when filmmakers equally identified with humanistic storytelling have done the same? John Sayles (*The Brother from Another Planet*) and Barry Levinson (*Sphere*) come to mind.

Besides, sci-fi is a liberating and therefore attractive gateway for artists to tackle large, serious subjects free of constraints. The genre invites storytellers to ponder endless what ifs. In that spirit Payne and Taylor lay out an imagined scenario and burrow down that rabbit hole of speculation to follow what they deem the inevitable consequences.

Downsizing hinges on a hero sensitively responding to a world around him transformed. The implications and stakes are deeply personal and global. At least on the page Payne and Taylor manage to make us care about the micro and macro. Paul's journey pulls us along this upheaval of life as he knew it. Expectations, definitions and limitations are threatened or overturned. Ultimately, everything is on the line.

Unavoidably, the story echoes other speculative tales, including any dealing with miniature humans. It also resonates with themes from such disparate sources as *Dr. Strangelove, 2001: A Space Odyssey, The Truman Show, Children of Men* and *The Hobbit*. Payne and Taylor concoct a fable-like framework to hold the narrative together.

The most obvious—if unintentional resonance to *The Incredible Shrinking Man*—happens at the end, when our hero-pioneer once more enters the great unknown. As with Payne's previous films, the story concludes with a feeling more than an event or a resolution.

Payne, now married to a native of Greece and coming off his stark tone poem *Nebraska*, recently spoke about *Downsizing* with *The Reader*. "We always knew it would take a while, first to get the script right, then to secure the financing, and ten years is a long time. Fortunately I was able to squeeze in two other features and a pilot during that time. But it feels right now. You know, it's interesting that in life, not just film, you try to do something and you run into obstacles. You try again and you run into more obstacles, and you think, This is never going to happen. And then finally when it does it unfolds elegantly and without obstructions and you say, Wow, I guess this was the time it was supposed to happen. That has been my experience with *Downsizing*."

As the one hundred twenty five page script sits now, he said, "the story hums along with a good filmic rhythm." Achieving that flow was challenging for the "big idea" at its core. "So big," he said, "It was difficult during our writing process to always discern where it breaks off because every idea you come up with for this idea has a very long series of chain reactions. So you just kind of drive yourself crazy with possibilities. The script goes in very unpredictable directions. I'm not saying they're good because they're unpredictable. They were unpredictable to us as we were writing. So to corral this story and to get it happening as efficiently and we hope elegantly from point to point to point took a while. Right now it looks good on paper. I hope it will lend itself to a good movie. I won't know that until I'm in post-production."

He said the big idea that propels the piece is rife with "social-political overtones" but that it's the "human aspects of the story that most interest us." Thus, he's not getting hung up on its sci-fi pedigree. He just enjoys the unlimited canvas he has to work on.

Payne also isn't stressing the visual effects world he's entered though he acknowledges he's a fish out of water. "It's a whole new focus for me and everything. I'm not worried but I'm curious to see how they're going to work. There'll be a certain amount of tedium involved because you have to shoot the same scene two, sometimes three times to get the different aspects and elements.

"I want to make sure the actors who are acting in a vacuum on a stage against green screen feel as comfortable and normal as possible. That's my job. The acting style should not suffer because of the means of production. But it'll be fine. You know, who cares, it's just a movie."

One whose $76 million budget is double any of his previous pics. "If they don't spend it on that, they're just going to spend it on something else." he said by way of classic Hollywood reasoning.

He feels in good hands with his visual effects supervisor, James Price, with whom he's been in discussions since 2008-2009. "He is my effects czar. He knows how to explain things to me to make things easy for me and how to teach me how these things are achieved—what I need to know, what I don't need to know. It's really exciting. The best thing those guys do is to free the director up to say, 'I want a shot like this, can we do this?' and they say, 'Yeah, we can do that,' and I say, 'How?' and they say, 'Don't worry about how, but we can do it.' Between the visual effects supervisor, the DP, the production designer, they have to trick the director as much as possible into thinking that he or she is just shooting a regular movie so that I don't censor my imagination, or what I have left of it."

Payne said Price is on the same page as he and cinematographer Phedon Papamichael in terms of the desired visual palette. "James knows the aesthetic we want and he's an avid film watcher and film guy and so that makes me feel good. What I aspire to from the visual effects for this movie is not how eye-popping they are but rather how banal they are. I don't want the seams to show."

Payne also hopes to keep the effects to a minimum and to "try to do things in camera as much as possible." In addition to Price and his visual effects team Payne is working with a new production designer, Stefania Cella. But he's mainly surrounded by trusted old friends and collaborators in producer Jim Burke, casting director John Jackson, Papamichael and costume designer Wendy Chuck. His longtime editor, Kevin Tent, is on board as well.

After the seven year gulf between *Sideways* and *Descendants*, Payne's happy to be making films in short order. His last, *Nebraska*, was received warmly in Greece, where he met his wife while vacationing with his mother (Payne's father passed away in 2014.).

"I showed the film in Greece a couple times and people were only too quick to tell me they thought it was a Greek film, which surprised me. I said, 'Why do you think it's a Greek film?' and they said, 'Well. it has the elements of going back to the village where your people are from.' 'Okay,' I said. And they connected with the part of dutifully 'taking care of the parents who drive you crazy,' and I said, 'Well, I'm sure that's not just Greek.' I think that's pretty universal."

On the eve of finally making *Downsizing* after so long a wait and "jettisoning" subplots he admittedly "misses," he's content. "A movie is a movie is a movie and we have enough to make this movie, so it'll be fine. And if the gods decree there might be a *Downsizing 2*, then we have other ideas that we've been collecting."

9
The Wrap

Author Leo Adam Biga (www.leoadambiga.com)

At the time this book originally went to press in August 2012, Alexander Payne finally got the go-ahead on *Nebraska*. For a variety of reasons the project went from apparent sure thing at one point to a question mark at another point. Paramount seemingly signed off on it, even bowing to Payne's insistence it be shot and released in black-and-white, but rumblings of studio interference and casting difficulties, combined with investors' reluctance over the production shooting in Nebraska where until recently there were no film industry tax incentives, caused Payne to put the project on hold. It is not as if he was without other options. For one thing, there was an adaptation of the Daniel Clowes' graphic novel, *Wilson*, which had only somewhat recently come into focus as a viable project. The log line for *Wilson* read a lot like that of Payne's previous films starting with *Election*. All of which is to say that like those stories *Wilson* had at its core a disaffected man of a certain age whose attempts at integrating himself into the mainstream prove problematic.

The vagaries of film financing being what they are and his dependence on studios helping him realize projects being what it is, even an established filmmaker like Payne can only pull the trigger when given the go-ahead. That means contracts with i's dotted and t's crossed. It is why he has sometimes gotten very far down the road on some project before hurdles put it off and he turned his attention to some entirely new project that emerged or that he held in reserve. So it goes.

I wrote back in 2012 that based on Payne's track record *Nebraska* will, at the very least, get a lot of attention and likely be entered in major film festivals before hitting the general theater circuit. I went on to suggest that how it may fare with general audiences will be anybody's guess until the project comes more into focus, but that history tells us that if anybody can take off-the-beaten-path subject matter and make it palatable for critics and fans it is Payne.

As my introduction to the *Nebraska* section in this new edition makes clear Payne more than lived up to his end of the bargain by making a film that by consensus was considered one of the year's best. But I believe Paramount did not do it any favors by treating it, to my way of thinking anyway, as some kind of niche oddity or off-brand project.

As this book came out in its first printing Payne found himself in a most fortuitous spot. He had the worldwide respect of his industry peers. Critics adored his work. Audiences have more and more responded warmly to his films. Even though by that point he had still only five completed films into his feature career, retrospectives of his work were already happening with some frequency. He was roughly where Elia Kazan found himself in the late 1950s and early 1960s, where Hal Ashby found himself in the late 1970s, and where James L. Brooks and Barry Levinson found themselves in the early 1990s as dynamic, seemingly can-do-no-wrong filmmaking pillars with long runs of nearly uninterrupted success. Until the runs stopped. Virtually every filmmaker, even those who have reached the very top, hits a rough patch or dry spell as a result of some project that, for whatever reasons, does not turn out well or simply crashes with audiences.

In the aftermath of such a fall the artist is knocked down a peg or two in terms of his/her esteemed position in the industry hierarchy. It even happened to New Hollywood icons and kings William Friedkin, Francis Ford Coppola, and Martin Scorsese. All of these directors eventually suffered some humbling failures. In some cases their careers never fully recovered. In other cases, their subsequent output became a series of hits and misses. For some artists, Sam Peckinpah and Hal Ashby in particular, personal travails derailed their work to such an extent that their work became compromised. Other artists abandoned the personal art films they made their names on for less intimate, larger scale projects that lacked any soul. I suggested that Payne seems far too sober and stable to suffer any personal upheaval or turmoil. I said it is hard to imagine him turning his back on the small personal art films he prefers for the big budget, commercial, popcorn fare he disdains. I further stated that I do not think money will ever matter to him enough to do that, which would be tantamount to selling his soul to the devil.

I wrote that the most likely thing that could push Payne out of favor was his making a couple films that simply do not grab critics and audiences and thus relegate him, at least temporarily, to the ranks of the irrelevant. Hollywood is the ultimate what-have-you-done-for-me-lately club and though he is not a part of that society he is a part of its mechanism, meaning that he is reliant on it to do his work and to get it seen. However inevitable I believe it is that he have some kind of fall, I think it would be relatively short-lived because the unerring arbiter in him will ultimately hone in on some story that resonates with enough of us to put him right back where he was before, which is to say right where he is today.

Of course, I said, it is always possible he may be the exception and not the rule by continuing his unbroken sequence of hit dramas that are really comedies or comedies that are really dramas. It all depends on how you take them. And in truth his films are a melange of humor and pathos, just as life is. If there were a mask depicting the demeanor or character of his movies it would be two sided, with humor on one side and pathos on the other, or better yet it would feature a single visage with one side of the mouth curled up in a smile and the other side of the mouth sagging in despair. One eye would be wide open, carefully discerning the landscape, perhaps with a glimmer of compassion in it. The other eye would be winking, a glint of mischief showing through. Payne always gives us permission to both laugh and cry when viewing his films. There is often a mix of emotions elicited in a single shot and scene, certainly in a given sequence.

During an on-stage conversation he had with Jane Fonda in mid-2012 the actress expressed admiration for his use of long takes that let moments, emotions, situations play out minus unnecessary interruption or cutting away too quickly. As she noted to him and to the audience, "you're one of the few" (filmmakers today who allows scenes to breathe and linger in the beautiful, ordinary, awkward ways that life unfolds). She didn't say it, but I believe she meant he is one of the few with the courage of his convictions to allow the words to take hold and to be absorbed. At his best, he immerses you in the scene so completely that all your filters are suspended as you inhabit the scene with the characters.

Like the best art, his work encompasses many sides of the human condition, thus evoking many responses. Because his work is rooted in the truth it is hard to find many false moments. That is not to say his movies are not full of manipulation and guile. They are. He is still first and foremost a satirist, after all, and therefore he consistently uses the incidents and plot points in his stories as fodder for poking fun at this or that. But he is also increasingly a dramatist concerned with moving us to some emotions and insights about our shared human experience. Whatever his films are or however you describe them, they represent a body of work that already places him among the finest filmmakers of the last quarter century. I know I speak for many when I say that I look forward to what he brings us in the future.

Four years since committing those words to print I would not change anything about my analysis. The relatively meager returns of *Nebraska* have in no way jeopardized Payne's standing as a cinema force. Oh, some myopic producers and studio executives are sure to be less in love with the prospect of working with him now that his string of three consecutive box office hits has been broken. Chances are those would be people he has no interest in working with anyway. But as I argue in my *Nebraska* section introduction the film actually did well given the lukewarm embrace Paramount gave it and the strange stigma that attends black and white films. From a critical-aesthetic standpoint *Nebraska* has only enhanced Payne's reputation as an artist fully committed to following his own path. The fact that *Nebraska* did not end up winning a single Academy Award among its six nominations means little when you consider it was up against stiff competition in a very good year in the major categories of Best Picture, Best Director, Best Original Screenplay, Best Cinematography, and Best Actor (June Squibb's nomination for Best Supporting Actress rounded out *Nebraska*'s Oscar contention).

If there is any truth to the notion that *Nebraska* did not resonate with general audiences it is because Payne did not deviate from the hard truth and quirkiness of the story. He remained true to the material's and his own idiosyncratic sensibilities and did not spoon-feed audiences anything to make it more palatable or marketable. I do not subscribe to the idea he did this to a fault. No, I think like most really good artists he was well out ahead of audiences with this one. It may take some time, but I am certain many millions more film lovers will catch up to *Nebraska* through the years than saw it in its theatrical release.

The accolades bestowed on *Nebraska* further confirmed Payne as belonging to the vanguard of the world's best filmmakers. There is now an expectation he and his films will be in the mix for major honors. The writer-director is still without a single miss or blemish through his film career. He continues to defy the odds in that way. In talking with him one gets the real sense he feels he is just coming into his own as a complete filmmaker, which is exactly the way I see it. He has much more to give us.

With *Nebraska* Payne's body of feature work reached six films. In terms of output, it is interesting to compare where he is at this juncture of his career with where some famous American filmmakers were at a similar stage in their careers. By the time he hit six features Francis Ford Coppola had completed both *Godfather* films. *The Conversation* and *Apocalypse Now* came in rather short order after that. Martin Scorsese had given us *Mean Streets* and *Taxi Driver*. His *Raging Bull* would soon follow. Stephen Spielberg had made *Jaws* and *Close Encounters of the Third Kind*. Just ahead were *Raiders of the Lost Ark* and *E.T.* Joel Coen had already made, with his brother Ethan, *Raising Arizona*, *Miller's Crossing*, and *Fargo* and they were about to make *The Big Lebowski* and *O Brother, Where Art Thou?*

Those are remarkable runs early in these screen artists' careers. I would argue Payne's run is no less impressive. Up to, and including *Nebraska,* all of his films that have caught the wave either critically or commercially speaking. *About Schmidt, Sideways*, and *The Descendants* found both wide critical and commercial success. *Citizen Ruth, Election*, and *Nebraska* scored well with most critics but struggled at the box office, though *Nebraska* has actually done well compared to its budget. Like his counterparts and their first half-dozen films, Payne's first six films earned their share of awards and accolades. Some of his films have been nominated for Best Picture. He has been nominated for Best Director. Then there are the two writing Oscars he has to his name.

The thing about comparisons is that they are so imprecise and unfair. Start with the fact that these filmmakers create personal movies that are singular, stand-alone works. Their films are markedly different from each other's. Each has his own individual stylistic flourishes and strengths. Then there is the whole taste thing. What you consider a great film may not jibe with my idea of a great film. There is no right or wrong. Only a rough consensus might be reached. About the only thing you can say is that these films were very influential works in their own time and continue to be today. I will concede that Payne has not yet had the kind of crossover success Coppola had with *The Godfather*, which became embedded into the collective cultural consciousness. That same kind of embedding occurred with Scorsese's *Taxi Driver* and *Raging Bull* (though neither performed very well at the box office) as well as with Spielberg's *Jaws* and *Close Encounters* and the Coen Bros. *Fargo* (another lackluster box office performer). Clearly, a film does not need to be a big earner to become a classic or an icon or a source for imitation and homage.

Would any of the films Payne has made thus far crack the American Film Institute's Top 100 U.S. films of all time if a survey of cinephiles and critics were conducted today? Probably not. However, I do contend a case could made for *Sideways*, *The Descendants*, and *Nebraska* as deserving that recognition. I do think one or two of those might make that kind of list in ten or fifteen years. Just not now.

The real question is what does the future hold for Payne as a filmmaker now that he is firmly established among the world's best. Will he sustain his track record for quality? Will he slump and misfire? Will he surpass everything he has done thus far? Will he finally break through with a Best Picture and Best Director Oscar win? I believe the answer to all of those questions is bound to be yes.

In the course of promoting this book I often state that I believe Payne's best work is ahead of him. I mean it. Interestingly, he has intimated the same thing himself in interviews and seminars, though of late he demurs when the subject gets broached. For example, when I asked him in early 2016 if he felt he had reached some new level of maturation as a film artist with his work on *Nebraska*, he said, "I have no idea and I don't think that would be for me to say – that might be for viewers to say. I'm just always where I am in that moment. I have no idea how far I've come, how much farther I have to go." That modesty is not coyness. He really is uncomfortable talking about his own work in qualitative terms. But I think off the record he must acknowledge his progressive growth. In a very real sense he is only just getting started.

His craft has only just caught up with his film knowledge. He is barely two full decades into his feature career. He could reasonably have another twenty or thirty, maybe even forty years of active filmmaking before he is done. That might equate to an additional dozen or so films he makes. That is a lot to look forward to, especially when you consider he has shown tremendous growth from film to film, particularly with his last three. If he stays on this evolutionary trajectory then the odds are he will give us a few films, if he has not already, that become a part of the cultural collective the way some of his contemporaries have.

At the time of this book's original release, Payne had not publicly committed to a new project. He only stated his intentions to someday revisit *Downsizing*, the sprawling project he abandoned in the wake of the economic collapse. He unequivocally said he will ultimately get it made. He also kept mentioning his interest in making historical films. He even seemed to circle back around to an idea he has for a partly Spanish-language film to be made in Nebraska about the large influx of Hispanics there and how that has changed the face and dynamic of life in many rural and some urban centers. Then there remains his long standing interest in making a Western in his home state. I like to think his work on *Nebraska* was a kind of preparation for any Western he would shoot there because that film's locations, rhythms, and visuals seem consistent with what he would deal with in a Western. He has also indicated an interest in making films outside of America. Shooting in Greece is a distinct possibility one day given his ancestral ties there, his many travels there, and the fact that Greece closely follows and courts him. Shooting in Spain, another country he feels a close affinity to and has traveled extensively in, would also be a good bet.

He previously came close to pulling the trigger on an adaptation of the graphic novel *Wilson*. He has been attached to other properties as well. His company actively sought and procured materials for it to produce and/or for him to direct. I suggested four years ago that when he does pull the trigger on something you can be assured it will be a project he is totally invested in. Whatever direction he ends up going, I wrote, it will be guided by the right intentions.

As I began updating things for this new edition in 2014 Payne indicated he was hard at work writing. For a long time I did not know exactly what he was working on because he would not confirm anything for the record or off the record. Writing is arguably the most time consuming and sensitive part of the filmmaking process. I was left to surmise whether he was developing something alone or in tandem, an original or an adaption, penning a new script or freshening up an old one. Whatever the case, I envisioned him busily toiling away at a task he says he despises. He says he only resorts to writing his own films because he generally cannot find scripts he wants to direct or at least they very seldom make their way to him. It is why he likes to say he opens every script sent to him with the prayer, "Oh, God, let me want to direct this one."

During that period when he was noncommittal about what he was writing I imagined him toiling away at a computer keyboard composing dialogue that fills the empty space of a text file. In that revery of when a movie is still only a concept the words are static, only gaining animation in his mind or when he speaks and acts them out during the creative fever that is screenplay writing. I conjectured that the words he strung together then might have life breathed into them on the set of a new movie he shot in 2014 or 2015. Or, I wrote, perhaps those words would have to wait longer before taking shape in the form of action committed to the camera. Whatever the case, I suggested, Payne is like any filmmaker in that he is always in one way or another gestating and exploring ideas, waiting, hoping, praying they come together in words and scenes that end up on the screen.

As it turned out, Payne and his old writing partner Jim Taylor were reworking *Downsizing* all along. My *Downsizing* chapter provides a good overview of what to expect with this much anticipated project that goes back a decade or more. As you will read, Payne tried making it twice before. That is to say he twice previously tested the waters with studios and investors. But each of those times the prevailing economic conditions combined with the vagaries of what size budget could be financed based on the stars attached to it then and the amount of visual effects called for in that iteration forced him to put the project on hold. Following each of those stalled efforts the screenplay got recalibrated and the lead actors changed out.

"2009 we floated a balloon and it came falling back to earth pretty quickly," he shared. "2014 was closer but there were too many unknowns happening—where we shoot the movie, what price tag to put on things, whatever cast we could quickly collect so as to meet Matt Damon's schedule. But this third attempt at putting my shoulder to the wall is working and it feels like it's the right time. And the good thing is, too, that visual effects technology keeps improving and I'll be able to do things now that I wouldn't have been able to do five years ago for the (same) price and facility."

My conversations and interviews with Payne rarely go into the finances behind his films but just weeks before commencing production on *Downsizing* he shared some thoughts along those lines.

"One of the elements of my film career is trying to keep my costs down as much as possible so I can maintain more creative control. I think movies are too expensive anyway. I don't think they should be as expensive as they are. A lot of times filmmakers – producers and directors – will say, 'Oh, we'll tell them we can make it for this much but of course once we're in it we'll go back and ask for more money and they'll have no choice but to agree because what are they going to do . . . ' I don't like to do that. I tell them I'm from Omaha and I don't like to maintain fictions. I like to be straight from the get go and so all my movies to date have been on time and under budget.

"And I like to run a tight ship. I'm in a little bit of new territory for me on this one because I have the unknown of the fiddle-factor of visual effects. But I have people around me who are great and trust worthy and giving it all their best guess as to what things will genuinely cost —of course always trying to keep it on the cheaper side. And the studio believes us and I know this particular studio, Paramount, believes us because I just made *Nebraska* with them and while that's a completely different movie in terms of its budget and commercial expectations they nevertheless saw that my team and I like to run a tight ship and do what we say we're going to do and not create problems."

By the time you read this *Downsizing* will have finished production and be well into the edit. It should start playing major film festivals by mid-2017 and hit widely in cineplexes by that fall.

Since this section is called The Wrap it is only fitting I try to wrap up a few loose ends. The Daniel Clowes graphic novel Payne once considered adapting himself through the now defunct Ad Hominem Enterprises Payne had in partnership with Jim Taylor, and Jim Burke was eventually adapted by Clowes himself and directed by Craig Johnson. Ad Hominem was set up in part to help procure and in some cases shepherd projects for Payne to direct. *The Descendants* and *Nebraska* both happened under the aegis of Ad Hominem. The company also helped produce projects for other directors, including the aforementioned *Wilson* as well as *Cedar Rapids* (Miguel Arteta) and *The Savages* (Tamara Jenkins).

He has an option on the short story *The Judge's Will* by the late Ruth Prawer Jhabvala, who wrote most of the later Merchant-Ivory films. In the story a male judge of a certain age suffers the latest in a string of heart attacks and while awaiting surgery and contemplating his mortality he informs his wife he has been having a multi-year affair with a woman. His lover comes from nothing and he has included her in his will so as to provide for her. The judge wants his wife to promise that should he die she not contest the will. "After that Lear-like declaration, it's about all the fallout," Payne told me. Someone at Ad Hominem read it and correctly guessed the filmmaker might like it. But Payne also added that the story is just one among others he has "in the hopper" that he may or may not do anything with. He is always looking for new material. It comes with the territory.

His career is typical of most directors in that the material for his films comes from various sources. A newspaper article inspired Payne and Taylor to write *Citizen Ruth*. *Election* grew out of a book. They adapted *About Schmidt* from a book. A then-unpublished manuscript served as the basis for *Sideways*. Kaui Hart Hemmings' novel *The Descendants* was closely adapted by Payne into the film of the same name. Bob Nelson's original screenplay *Nebraska* landed in Payne's hands like manna from heaven.

Downsizing is the second original screenplay by Payne and Taylor. The high concept originated from an idea posed by Taylor and his brother Doug. But some time went by before the idea resonated enough with Payne, who put a new spin on it, that he and Jim Taylor began developing a script around it. Payne explained how this ephemeral idea in the ethers became the basis for a multi-million dollar feature film he actually made.

"Jim and his brother Doug had been musing about the possibilities if you were a small human. Basically that you could have a large house on a large lot for not very much space and they had told me this seed for an idea, and I always said no, it doesn't strike a chord with me, until after the 2004 election when Bush supposedly was reelected. I was coming off of *Sideways* and I just thought, Well, how can we Americans who have the privilege of making films not somehow be making political films and at least as I can see them not literally political films but you know films with a metaphor. But the metaphor had escaped me. And then in early 2006 I recalled Jim and his brother Doug's idea about small people and I said, 'What if we put that in more of a social and political context?' And that's where the idea came from."

As with all his projects, Payne is one of the producers, He does more producing than you may know. He has often acted as a producer or as an advisor, encourager, and influencer who opens doors and helps make things happen for friends and associates and their movies. He has even aided some of these projects financially. Most recently, he has served a producing role for others on: *Crash Pad*, the feature directorial debut of his long-time editor Kevin Tent; a pair of shorts, *Run Fast* and *L Train*, written and directed by his personal assistant Anna Musso; and the producing-writing-directing debut of fellow Omahan Yolonda Ross, an actress and writer who also starred in her own short project *Breaking Night*.

There are many anecdotes by emerging and established filmmakers from Omaha who attest to Payne assisting in one fashion or another. "I like to help Omaha people," he said by way of explanation,

Payne is intensely private and I make it a point to never intrude or press on that boundary. From time to time he does volunteer certain aspects of his life away from the business. For example, after exchanging limited correspondence and phone messages in the aftermath of *Nebraska*'s release and his murky references to being busy writing, in 2014 he finally confirmed *Downsizing* was back in play and then in 2015 he indicated it was going to happen on this, its third pass. Then, in late 2015 I got an email from him that explained some of why he had been incommunicado, as is his practice once he releases a film to the world. He always takes time to escape and decompress following the rigors of the marketing campaign with all its interviews and the awards season with all its personal appearances.

He wrote: "I've been lying quite low . . . low . . . low . . . and then the new OWH (*Omaha World-Herald*) entertainment reporter wrote me the other day and I didn't want to respond until I got to you first. So— with your permission—I'm going to write him/her back and maybe say a few brief words, but yes, I think the time is all right now for a check-in interview, if you say so. We can do it over the phone sometime, or I'll be in Omaha in three or four weeks. Hope all's well in your world, and sorry for the long silence. And....I got married!"

That closing oh-by-the-way revelation about his marriage was, of course, the first I had heard about it. In my reply I offered congratulations without pursuing the matter. I did jump online, however, to see what I could find, if anything, and the only references to his matrimony were from Greek media, who follow him closely. In a subsequent interview Payne confirmed those reports. Long story short, he was vacationing in Greece with his mother when he happened to meet a young woman named Maria Kontos and in movie-movie whirlwind romance fashion they fell in love and wed.

Good for him. May he and his bride find much happiness. This is Payne's second marriage. His first, to actress Sandra Oh, ended in divorce. I have nothing to base this on other than gut instinct, but I fully expect he and his new wife will start a family in the near future. It would not surprise me if they make their permanent home in Omaha. He is all about family and friendship, community and connection. If you only know the filmmaker by his work, it is understandable you might assume he is without a hint of sentimentality or softness given the hurtful things his characters say and do and the total asses they make of themselves. But look again. His stories are all about lost people in the throes of emotional-psychic pain. The literal and figurative journeys he has them go on represent personal pilgrimages in search of meaning and healing. Look again, and you will see the terrible leavened by the tender, the despair couched in hope,

Each of his protagonists has the solace of a friend or loved one or family, biological or not, to lean on. As imperfect as the protagonists and their support networsk may be, there is still love or at least the hunger for love. This dynamic is less apparent in his first three films, where the protagonists end up estranged from everyone, but it is much more visible in his last three films, where despite the protagonists' misdeeds or misgivings or harsh feelings, they gravitate to love anyway. Paul in *Downsizing* is somewhere in between these two opposites— hurt by rejection and abandonment, he resists the possibility of new love only to give in. Like the great directors Payne admires, his comedies arise out of pathos, so that tears of laughter and joy flow in the same stream. On second glance, there is more empathy there than you think.

I feel privileged to follow Payne's filmmaking from a reporter's perspective and to transmit his critical self-analysis to readers. It is an opportunity and a responsibility I do not take lightly. At the risk of sounding presumptuous, I expect to cover Payne for as long as I continue working as a journalist and author. With any luck, there are many more articles to write and there is still that making-of book awaiting my attention. Yes, it is a little strange to think about following someone for decades, but there is also something gratifying about having that kind of a through-line as a directional heading to hone in on. My ongoing coverage of Payne, other filmmakers, and a wide variety of other arts and culture subjects is featured on—

www.leoadambiga.com
www.facebook.com/LeoAdamBiga

As I feel a kinship to Nebraskans who have made contributions to the film industry, where their impact far exceeds their numbers, I am at work on a book about Nebraska's Film Heritage. It will surprise many that Payne is not the first or the last filmmaker from Nebraska to do interesting things and when considering film artists behind the camera and in front of the camera he is one of many hundreds, past and present, with notable career credits. Indeed, as significant as his work is, I contend he is not even the most important filmmaker from the state. That distinction belongs to Joan Micklin Silver, a writer-director, who opened doors for women in film. It belongs as well to the late Darryl Zanuck, who as a studio head greenlit many classic movies during the Golden Age of Hollywood.

Even though I live far from the filmmaking capitals of the world I always look for opportunities to write about film and I get more chances to do that than you might think being in Omaha, Nebraska. Indeed, a Nebraska New Wave in cinema is underway and while Payne is the unqualified leader of this movement, there are other emerging voices and talents to be reckoned with. You may not know their names yet, but I predict you will within a decade.My professional brand is: "I write stories about people, their passions, and their magnificent obsessions." It expresses why I was drawn to Payne in the first place and it is ultimately why I am drawn to profiling the artists and creatives I write about. I have met and profiled many remarkable talents and like the best of them Payne is an artist of singular ability and vision. His high standards have made me work harder and better. Simply put, his work inspires me. My hope for this book is that you may feel an inkling of inspiration to revisit his work or to see it for the first time.

Wherever Alexander Payne is, whether in private or public, I like to think of him as a classic creative and critical thinker who is always a bit distracted by his inner eye and ear fixing on the irony-laced observations of his imagination and analysis. Always observing, listening, weighing, interpreting. Always testing scenarios out in his mind. Always on his game. I intend to be there whenever and wherever the alchemy of fact and fiction, truth and drama, results in his next explorations-examinations of the human condition. I intend to share my own alchemy with you, the reader, as I continue reporting on him and his work, building this understanding and appreciation as he goes.

A comprehensive guide to quotes and topics chronicling the twenty year career of filmmaker Alexander Payne

DISCUSSION GUIDE WITH INDEX

1. Getting Started and Family

"... after watching the show a few years ago she made me promise that if I ever won another Oscar I had to dedicate it to her just like Javier Bardem did with his mother (eliciting laughter). So, Mom, this one's for you. *Se agapao poly.* (Greek for "I love you very much.") And thanks for letting me skip nursery school so we could go to the movies. Thanks a lot." Payne's speech at the 2012 Academy Awards (p. 207)

Obsessed with cinema since childhood, Payne collected 8 millimeter prints of old movies and shot several short films with a used Super 8 camera. (p. 20)

Informing Payne's humanist world view, too, I suspect is the everseeking and compassionate Jesuit philosophies he was imbued with at Omaha Creighton Preparatory School, better known as Creighton Prep. (p. 7)

Despite harboring a dream to pursue filmmaking, he didn't take a single film class at Stanford because he looked upon his undergraduate years as a time "to get an education." (p. 20)

"I went to UCLA [for graduate studies], and found it much more wild there. It's a public school. It seemed like a place to be freer and just explore and do what you want. Most of their student films are pretty experimental and unwatchable, but there's the attitude that it's one person, one film." Payne (p. 20)

Payne's intense 50-minute UCLA thesis film, *The Passion of Martin*, played festivals and pegged him as a real "comer" in the industry. (p 21)

2. Sense of Place

Oddly enough, Payne said capturing Hawaii "all comes back to Omaha," adding, "It's an exciting, logical extension of my process begun here in Nebraska, of how do you tell a story in the foreground and have a place in the background?" (pp. 186–87)

Essential to that style is a sense of place. In his early work, of course, that place was Omaha and the sensibility was ineffably Midwestern—

stoic yet anxious city folk lost in the heartland and looking for a way out. *Citizen Ruth* bolting down that alley at film's end said it all. Payne too had an impulse to "light out for the Territory," in Twain's memorable phrase, and so we find his restless protagonists further and further West—Denver, then California, then Hawaii. But the Midwestern values persist as his characters are displaced, with family and community and the land itself growing more important in each of Payne's films. Thomas Schatz, *Foreword* (p. xviii)

"I think if *Sideways* is successful at all in terms of getting a sense of Santa Barbara, it's because I was armed with tools I had learned in finally starting to get it right in *About Schmidt*, which was made in Omaha." By proving he could apply the same precisely-honed satire and well-observed scrutiny to character and place in Santa Barbara as he did in Omaha, he's opened a universe of possibilities once denied him by the suits. (p. 113)

Sense of Place Index: xv, xviii, 13, 53–54, 112–13, 118, 186–87, 200, 203, 225–26, 237–38, 245, 263.

3. Realism and Humanism
"I feel so strongly about shooting in Omaha," he said.. . . There's an atmosphere I want to get and be faithful to—about how people are. I want it to be real, I want it to be where I'm comfortable and where deep buttons in me are pressed." Payne (p. 13)

"Where most filmmakers would run screaming from anything that reminds people of everyday life, he loves the fact you can film everyday life and have people take a look at themselves in a different context than what they're accustomed to. And I think it's really important and admirable. It's also a very humble skill. Instead of trying to imagine and exaggerate, it's really just observing. It's a more writerly craft and a more European sensibility. I think it's an underrated gift. I don't think people realize how difficult it is to create that kind of verisimilitude on screen. That's why he's always at war with all the conventions of the movie world aimed at glamorizing people."
Sideways Producer Michael London (p. 81)

Descendants resonates with Paynesian themes and motifs. "I'm just always drawn to material that remains human and devoid of contrivance, that stays on the credible human plane. I try to somehow explore, express and mock the human heart." He said a friend who saw the film "enjoyed having a constantly shifting relationship" to the coma-stricken Mrs. King, who is variously an object of love, hate, pity, and indifference—both for the other characters and the audience." (p. 192)

She said the sensibility she and Payne share derives from their cinema weaning. "Alexander and I both grew up on the humanist films from the '70s. In the '70s there was a blossoming of the auteurist view and in the very specific way directors worked with their actors to find a singular voice." Laura Dern, actor (p. 164)

"I like to get reality in film and to somehow take a documentary approach in fiction filmmaking, and yet I felt I needed to get it right first in Omaha— in the place I knew best—before I could move on." Payne (p. 113)

"Alexander Payne has single-handedly restored humanism as a force in American films." Todd McCarthy, *Variety* review (p. 103)

Realism and Humanism Index: 6–7, 9–11, 13, 18–19, 34, 65, 81, 84–5, 90. 103, 113-14, 163–64, 196-97.

4. Comic/Tragic

"Jim and I like to extract comedy from sadness and pain."
Payne (p. 17)

"I tend to make comedies based in painful human situations that are filled with ferocious emotions. I find ferocious emotions exciting. The actor and director have to trust the writer that the absurdity or the comedy is there in the writing. You all know it's there, but you don't play it. Sometimes, I think, in my films I've so not wanted to play the comedy of it that it gets too subtle, where then people don't get that it's funny. I mean, some do, like my friends. Like I think people took *About Schmidt* much too seriously sometimes, and I don't know if it's because they're Americans and Americans are literal and non-ironic, or what. Payne (p. 85)

"One thing I witness with audiences is what someone described as hairpin turns in tone. That within a scene you can be laughing one moment, crying the next, and then laughing again. A couple journalists asked me about that and how it's accomplished and of course I have to say, I don't really know, but I do think life is like that. Life has laughter and drama all going on at the same time. So I don't really see hairpin shift in tone but rather a thicker tone or fabric of life." Payne (p. 192)

Comic/Tragic Index: 16–17, 52–53, 85, 192.

5. Meaning and Morality

"For him it's not all about trying to capture something truthful and comedically grim about the American landscape but also something archetypal," says [*Nebraska*] producer Albert Berger. (p.226)

"I like my movies to tell stories. But films don't operate only on a story level. There's a quote I like that says, 'A story exists only as an excuse to enter into the realm of the cinema.' Films operate on emotions, moods, sub-themes and maybe even poetry, if you're lucky enough to have a bit of mystery and poetry in your film." Payne (p. 44)

Payne dislikes much of today's nouveau hip American cinema. "Holly-wood, in the last few years, has produced films which take the attitude, 'Oh, isn't this cool, we have amoral characters,'" he said. "But in completely unredeeming, nihilistic films that simply anticipate moments of violence, rather than being about people in complex ways. I don't get much out of nihilism." Payne (p. 16)

Payne's insistence on adhering to his vision fits squarely within his overarching concern for the state of American cinema today, which he feels is disconnected from the potent issues of our time. He awaits a film movement, akin to what evolved in the '70s, that closely reflects what's happening in society. (p. 113)

Payne resists any suggestion his comic sensibility is vulgar: "I think, for example, that *Citizen Ruth* has an amoral protagonist, yet it's a very moral film. The same thing now with *Election*. There's a lot of irresponsible and immoral behavior in the film, but I believe strongly that it's a very responsible and moral film." (p. 15)

"I think in general we Americans need to see Americans in our films but we kind of don't, we see cartoons largely. As Americans we make cartoons easily digestible for the rest of the world but we're not show-ing ourselves to ourselves." Payne (p. 263)

". . . people compromise themselves through really, really good inten-tions. They all think they're doing the right thing, and they end up getting very, very compromised morally." Payne (p. 17)

6. Characters

Payne captures in his "hysterically funny yet melancholy comedy . . . subtle undertones of the great character movies of the 1970s and a del-icate though strong finish that fills one with hope for its most forlorn characters." Kirk Honeycutt, *Hollywood Reporter* review (p. 103)

He's happy with the results. "I think it's my best film." [*Sideways*] Oth-ers are noticing too. "Some of the critics are saying it's the film that least seems to satirize its protagonist (Miles). It seems to accept him more and to be a little more tender toward him. And that might be true." Payne (p. 105)

"He's sympathetic to the characters, even when they do stupid things. He doesn't look down on the characters from some kind of higher moral ground. They're all very human. He doesn't categorize people. People aren't either perfect or evil, smart or stupid, they're all a mix of things." Matthew Broderick, actor in *Election* (p. 15)

"Even with now just four films to his credit, Alexander Payne has es-tablished himself as a major voice in contemporary American cinema. I can't think of another filmmaker working today who is able to create characters as complex, as contradictory and as richly human." Richard Pena, New York Film Festival Chairman and Film Society of Lincoln Center Program Director (p. 12)

There have been no female lead characters in Payne's subsequent works about middle-aged men stumbling through mid-life angst. But upon review the women in *About Schmidt*, *Sideways*, and *The Descendants* all figure prominently if secondarily in the throes of the meltdowns the male protagonists undergo. (p. 158)

Personal Films/Filmmaking

I love voice-over in films, and there's kind of a stigma against it." That stigma is an artificial one imposed by film executives and by "script experts" . . . Payne (p. 18)

Payne talks about his desire to stretch beyond borders and make movies around the world, including Greece and Spain, two nations he has strong ties to. His grandparents hailed from Greece and the former Spanish lit scholar studied in Spain: "I feel Spain in my heart." (p. 59)

Ask him what *Election* is all about and he sighs, wearily weighing your question with one of his own: "How to articulate it? I don't know . . . It's very human and it's very real, it's about life. It's like life—I can't sum it up. I hope always to make movies that can't be easily summed up." (pp. 14–15)

On the craft of filmmaking, he said, "Anyone can really learn how to make a film in about a week," and in response to laughter from the On the Set crowd, he added, "No, it's true. The principles of film are very simple, but it's a matter of what you're going to film, what story you want to tell, and what eye you want to cast on the world that's important." (p. 62)

"Filmmaking is a struggle. It's just kind of sticking with it and not having a backup plan—I've never had a backup plan—and looking at every obstacle as an opportunity to be more creative." Payne (pp. 61 –62)

He began writing his own scripts "just to get stuff to direct," he said, again eliciting laughter while being dead serious. "No, it's true," he said adding that he views writing as a basic element of his craft. "I regard the term filmmaking as a three-part process: writing, directing, and editing. And I've tried to become as proficient as possible with all three." Payne (p. 62)

"And maybe the fact I've seen so many movies informs the fact that I can know even unconsciously what would be new. I don't want to make derivative films. I want to do something new." Payne (p. 245)

Prior to the *Sideways* crush, he was thinking in terms of his next film being political and referring to some of America's disturbing actions and policies that make the nation a corporate-run caste system at home and a reactionary military-industrial pariah overseas. That still seems to be the general direction he's leaning, although there's no single core idea for a film that's coalesced yet with him and Taylor. (p. 114)

Personal Films/Filmmaking Index: xv–xviii, 5–8, 12–15, 18, 20–22, 48, 58–59, 61–62, 65, 72–73, 84–85, 107, 114–116, 195, 205, 219–22, 232, 239–42, 245.

8. Directing

Before the cast arrives on set, Payne often acts out the physical action himself for the benefit of Papamichael and crew. He checks cheat sheets, including his "sides," a printed copy of the script pages being shot each day, and his "shot list," a personal breakdown of what he's after in terms of camera, lighting, movement, motivation, and mood. Before filming, he often has actors run through scenes in rehearsals. Sometimes, surreptitiously, he has ADs and PAs shush the throng of crew and extras while signaling the cameras to roll, hoping to pick up more natural, unaffected performances that way. (p. 83)

"What stands out for me is how much he loves the actual day-to-day process of filmmaking," said *Sideways* producer Michael London . . . and how much he loves the camaraderie with people on the set." (p. 81)

"You're always holding two things in mind and on a few different planes. It's like in painting. You're here looking at the stroke and it's not just later but simultaneously that you're looking at its placement in the entire canvas. Even on the technical side, knowing what the sound is doing, what the film stock is doing, but also emotionally . . . storywise, what's going on at once in the many vivisected ways that a director has to think about, and also being surrounded by tons of people yet also remaining alone and watching the movie. Because my only job is to SEE the movie. I'm the only one who this entire time is sitting in the theater watching the movie or possible versions of it." Payne (pp. 89–90)

Directing Index: 30, 81–83, 80–90, 260–61, 136.

9. Editing and Sound

He and editor Kevin Tent, who has cut all of Payne's features, have been editing [*About Schmidt*] since June. They and a small staff work out of a converted house in back of a dentist's office on Larchmont Street in Los Angeles. Payne and Tent work ten-hour days, six days a week. (p. 43)

Indeed, Payne said, "Film is all about editing. Kurosawa used to say, 'The only reason I write and direct is to get things to edit.'" (pp. 46–47)

"One thing you do is cut out redundancies while editing. The most painful part of editing comes in not only taking out parts that don't work, but taking out parts that do work and work well. You have to be disciplined enough to go, 'No, the film is better without them.'" Payne (p. 47)

"Ask anybody who does a voiceover picture—voiceover adds a whole level of time to the editing of the film to calibrate, to get the voice over just right. It's a rather musical element really. Dramatic and musical." Payne (p. 242)

Rather than bury a scene in sharp camera moves or extreme angles, special effects, and draw-attention-to-itself editing, he's confident enough in his screenplay and in his direction to often let a scene play out, interrupted by few cutaways or inserts. (p. 87)

In keeping with the romantic vibe [of *Sideways*], Payne encouraged composer Rolfe Kent "to concoct a jazz-infused score. I thought jazz would go well with wine.". . . Its jazz music kind of washes over whole scenes. It doesn't really score or hit emotionally what's going on. It's just kind of there, and I thought that would be nice. And I think it (Kent's score) turned out really well." Payne (p. 104)

"We spend two months mixing the sound. TV does it in two days." Payne (pp. 271–72)

10. Writing

"I was pretty sure when the book got optioned that that particular quality would get lost. But amazingly these guys were able to do this very daring screenplay where they have the voice-overs of different characters that in a way mimics the structure of the book. I think they pulled off a pretty amazing technical feat . . . and were deeply faithful to the book." Tom Perrotta, author of *Election* (p. 18)

He says he only resorts to writing his own films because he generally cannot find scripts he wants to direct or at least they very seldom make their way to him. It is why he likes to say he opens every script sent to him with the prayer, "Oh, God, let me want to direct this one." (p. 292)

"Even as much as the shot and edited film is like a bastard child of the script, somewhat related but different and kind of maimed, once you see the film coming together, it reminds you of the initial impulses you had writing it and, in a way, the screenplay which has been on vacation comes back." Payne (pp. 43-44)

"You kind of cover yourself, unconsciously, in writing. That's why scripts are always longer and have more scenes than finished films. The visual medium just has a different language from a screenplay because of the images. So points which you had to make verbally become redundant and unnecessary." Payne (p. 47)

Payne conferred with Nelson [*Nebraska* screenwriter Robert Nelson] as he tweaked the writer's work. "Yeah, every time I'd do a pass on the script I'd send it to him and see what he thought, and he seemed to like it," Payne said. "Sometimes there were certain moments or a certain scene I'd want a little more information about." (p. 227)

11. Jim Taylor, Writing Partner

The pair's operated like this since their first gig, co-writing short films for cable's *Playboy: Inside Out* series. The friends and one-time roommates have been linked ever since. "It's pretty hard to extract the friendship from the partnership or vice versa." Jim Taylor (. 143)

"The nice thing about writing with a collaborator is it makes the process less hideous. You're always fighting against discipline problems. It's hard sticking to a routine and sitting your butt down every day. But if you know you have an appointment with someone (to write), it's harder to blow it off. You have someone around you to help you identify the one good idea you may have all day." Payne (pp. 62–63)

"For me, I didn't set out to be a screenwriter, I set out to be a filmmaker," said Taylor, a former Cannon Films grunt and assistant to director Ivan Passer (*Cutter's Way*). So did Alexander. And we kind of think of it all as one process, along with editing . . . . People say everything is writing. Editing is writing and in a strange way acting is writing, and all that. Filmmaking itself is a collaborative medium. People drawn to filmmaking are drawn to working with other people. Sure, a lot of screenwriters do hole up somewhere so they're not disturbed, but I'm not like that and Alexander's not like that. I don't like working on my own. I like to bounce ideas off people. Filmmaking demands it, as opposed to being a novelist or a painter, who work in forms that aren't necessarily collaborative." Jim Taylor (p. 142–43)

"We're like, Oh, that's funny . . . that's meaningful, whether looking at other people or at the pathetic aspects of our own lives. That's the type of stuff we talk about." Payne (p. 116)

Unlike collaborators who write separately and then fashion a screenplay via email or fax or phone, the pair "actually have to be together to write," which requires that either Payne, who lives in L.A., and Taylor, who lives in New York, travel to the other. "We have one monitor with two keyboards," Payne said of their writing setup. "I take the lead sometimes in the grunt work, putting it into some basic form on the page. We don't outline. We don't plan all that much what we're doing. We really try to get as firm an idea as we can . . . but it's always the process of writing that brings the ideas. Often times, when we have an idea, I'll write half a page or a page and then Jim will jump in. But weeks can go by and we don't write anything other than notes. We talk. What's it going to be? How are we going to do it? Who are the characters? It's a slow process." (p. 61)

12. Photography

Working with director of photography Phedon Papamichael for the first time [on *The Descendants*], Payne complained on the shoot his DP was making things look "too beautiful," prompting Papamichael to observe, "No, that's just a side of you you haven't embraced." "So, what the hell, it's another side of myself and I'm just going with it." Payne (p. 105)

Each has a propensity for stripped-down, naturalistic, location- driven shoots that are a function of their low-budget roots. "I didn't come through the system of operators and gaffers, it was always do-it- yourself, use natural light, move quickly, keep it as simple as possible, be as unobtrusive as possible, so it was a good fit," said Papamichael. (p. 196)

"... I like deep focus. I shoot with wide lenses ... not by design but I just start fishing around with lenses and asking, What would look good? And I rarely come up with long lenses. Typically, Hollywood movies shoot close-ups with a 75 millimeter lens; whereas, I typically shoot close-ups with about a 35, so the camera is closer to the actors, which is not always so good for the actors, but it's just ... I don't know ... a little bit funnier." ... Payne (p. 71)

"The circumstances characters find themselves in are always very important. The longer the lens, the more the surroundings tend to blur away, and I so very much like to get a sense of the set and surroundings and to fill the frame with jokes or meaningful things." Payne (p. 71)

In devising the visual style for his films Payne said that while he works closely with his cinematographer, James Glennon ... he personally "figures out every shot. I mean, there's never a time where I just sort of stage the action and turn to the cameraman and say, 'You shoot it.'" (p. 72)

To Payne's way of thinking, "There's no such thing as a second unit, even when I have two cameras going at once." (p. 72)

Aesthetically and technically speaking, Payne also stretched himself by lensing for the first time in black and white, wide screen and digital [*Nebraska*]. He said abandoning celluloid marks a concession to the new digital norm and to the fact today's black and white film stock options are limited. (p. 223)

"Digital means needing less light, so we can do tighter interiors, which is important on this show because we're entirely a location picture [*Nebraska*]. We don't have anything built. A lot of these interior spaces are very small and whatever space we can save in terms of lighting and camera equipment is helpful. Rather than having traditional bigger car rigs and following cars with camera cars we're able to just get in the car hand-held. Also, these newer cameras allow us to do good car work without lighting. It just helps the whole natural feel we're going for."
Phedon Papamichael, Director of Photography (p. 223)

"In a way we're learning the power of black and white as we go. We're really coming to appreciate and love the poetic power of the black and white in combination with these landscapes and, of course, the landscapes are playing a huge role in this story—just scaling the human drama and comedy. The black and white is becoming a very powerful character in this film [*Nebraska*] just in terms of setting the mood for this."
Payne (p. 225)

Photography Index: 71–2, 82–83, 105, 123, 193, 196, 223–26

13. Casting and Auditions

Jackson [John Jackson, Casting Director] said the cast immersed themselves in the story's "magnificent simplicity." He said his job is to "build the world" Payne envisions for the characters in the script. "We paint with people. We want it to be as authentic as possible." Payne's often praised for his casting and he always deflects credit to Jackson, whom he calls "my secret weapon." (p. 248)

Payne said of their relationship: "In honing our working method over dthe last eighteen years we just have developed a very similar aesthetic of what we want to see in a film, the type of reality we want. Also I think the two of us have developed a pretty good eye for spotting acting talent in nonactors." (p. 248)

He said Payne engenders loyalty by "building a rapport that ends up showing up in the work." Crew are encouraged to speak their mind. "If Alexander and I didn't have that commitment I would cave to the pressure of the producers who say to me, 'You need to convince Alexander these are the people he needs.' Instead, I'm like, 'That's not my job, my job is to to support, encourage and grow his vision."
John Jackson, Casting Directot (p. 249)

"I'm always happy to say that John and I rely on auditions, the old fashioned way. Even actors who are well known I still need them to come in and read the text, with all respect. I mean, even if it's ten words, say a few words, help me out, I have a pea brain, I don't want to screw it up, and I don't want to screw up and cast you in the wrong part and then it's not right. We all benefit if we're able to have a meeting. Well, what else are we going to talk about? Read the fucking script. And to good pros, the ones who won't audition, but they will deign to have a meeting, the good ones will either consciously or unconsciously find the time in the meeting to say, 'Oh, I loved the moment in your screenplay where he says . . .' and he'll do a little bit of it. That's the courteous thing to do, that's the polite thing to do because those actors who won't even do that don't get the job in my experience." Payne (p. 267)

14. Actors and Acting

Studio execs often express dismay at Payne's unsympathetic protagonists. "My response is always, 'It hasn't been cast yet.' I think it's the actor who brings the humanity and the sympathy to that part," he said. "Yeah, of course, how the film is directed and the tone contribute also, but that's the actor's job—to bring us a really full human person, and I'd like to think that truth is always sympathetic." (p. 163)

"As I was finishing my segment [*14e arrondissement* in *Paris, je'taime*], Wes Craven was about to shoot his and they needed someone to play Oscar Wilde," he said, "and I got the part the way most actors get parts, which is that three other actors passed. "They just saw me in the hall walking from the editing room to the bathroom and they saw my long hair . . . I didn't want to do it. I told them I'm a terrible actor, but they didn't care." Payne (p. 120)

He said, "There's always a bit of nerves between actors and directors, the first couple weeks as you're learning to trust one another." That was true at the start of *Schmidt*, as Nicholson felt Payne out, but in short time "he made it very easy to direct him. He put a lot of appreciated effort into breaking the ice with those around him. He was very professional and very cool and very kind." Payne (p. 63)

"Nicholson does a lot of work on his character before shooting. Now, a lot of actors do that, but he REALLY does it. To the point where, as he describes it, he's so in character and so relaxed that if he's in the middle of a take and one of the movie lights falls or a train goes through or anything, he'll react to it in character. He won't break." Payne said Nicholson doesn't like a lot of rehearsal "because he believes in cinema as the meeting of the spontaneous and the moment. His attitude is, 'What if something good happens and the camera wasn't on?'"
Payne (pp. 68–69)

"I've read recently about her [Laura Dern] performance in *Recount*. That she would do many scenes three ways—underplayed, over the top, and then kind of neutral, so that Jay Roach, the director, would have choices to calibrate her performance in the cutting room. And that's just like textbook Laura. She understands film to the nth degree. She knows it's about editing and she gives you choices in editing." Payne went on to have the same experience with Jack Nicholson on *Schmidt*. "Oh, yeah, that's the kind of actor you want. Everyone has to understand it's not about what happens on set, it's about what you harvest on set to get to the cutting room." Payne (p. 167)

Actors and Acting Index: 30–35, 37–41, 45–46, 67–69, 96, 120, 162–71,194–95, 214, 226–28, 250, 253–62, 274, 277–78.

15. Producers and Production Company

Payne's growing place in the industry, which avidly awaits his next film, was made tangible last fall when he, [Jim] Taylor, and producer Jim Burke formed the production-development company Ad Hominem Enterprises. In the process they struck a first-look deal with Fox Searchlight Pictures that gives the studio first dibs on any projects the filmmakers develop. A producer on *Election*, Burke was brought in to manage the Santa Monica–officed Hominem's small staff. Taylor also has a support person in New York, where he lives. Fox Searchlight did such a good job handling *Sideways* that Payne inked the studio pact, a move he'd avoided doing until now. (p. 118)

Payne respects London. "If we look to directors to influence our cinema and make less false and fraudulent films and more affective ones about people, you need other people doing that, too—studio heads, producers, financiers. I think he'll ultimately be known as a producer who helped change our cinema." (pp. 96–97)

The title "producer" has many variations and meanings. Someone in a full producing capacity pulls projects together, brokers deals, keeps productions on track, troubleshoots, et cetera. An executive producer pulls strings. Some producers are glorified consultants or go-betweens. (p. 121)

"You try to be the type of producer you yourself would want," Payne said. "The best producer though does nothing because the film has been set up so well you just let it go . . . you just let it run. The thing about producing is, it's like parenting—it's not even important what you do, it's just that you're there." Payne (p. 123)

Producers and Production Company Index: 80–81, 92–97, 118, 121–23, 233, 235.

16. Film Team

Once attached to the project [the *Hung* pilot for HBO] Payne gathered his core crew and went to work. "I then was able to use my line producer, my editor, my costume designer, my second-unit director, my assistant. I kind of got my team on board. It was like, let's just stretch our legs a little before getting back to a feature. And so it was fun." (p. 128)

There's an ebb and flow to a working movie crew. Everybody has a job to do, from the Teamsters grips and gaffers to the ADs and PAs to the personal assistants to the heads of wardrobe, makeup, et cetera. As a setup is prepared, a flurry of activity unfolds on top of each other, each department's crew attending to its duties at the same time, including dressing the set, rigging lights, changing lenses, loading film, laying track, moving the dolly. (p. 86)

"He's paying attention to every detail in every department and quite often directors don't bother . . . even all the way down to introducing himself to the background extras and discussing with them what the scene is about. It's a genuine pleasure, because then you feel like you're contributing and your contribution is appreciated." Cynthia Rebman, Set Dresser (pp. 88–89)

"I always think that when it's the middle of the night and everyone's exhausted, that's when filmmaking is distilled down to its essence," Boyd said. "All the periphery is removed away, and you're really just going for it. It's really quite elegant in a way, even though it's miserable to get there." Tracy Boyd, Second Unit Director (p. 90)

Like any experience bringing people together in a close, intense way, a film set is replete with affairs and alliances emerging from the shared toil and passion. Cliques form. Asides whispered. Inside jokes exchanged. (p. 88)

Film Team Index: 80–81, 86–90, 115–16, 128, 136, 188–89, 226–27, 254, 278–79, 284.

17. Audiences and Film Festivals

"I just make the films, I don't really know what they are until I watch them with an audience. It's just interesting to see how this one functions and what I think I can do better next time and what I think works pretty well this time around." Payne (p. 193)

After the Cannes screening Payne says many viewers commented, "We haven't seen these Americans in a long time. It's as though they're forgotten. We never see them in the cinema," referring to the average types that populate the pic. (p. 245)

After Toronto came the New York Film Festival, where *Sideways* was the official closing night selection on October 17. Payne said he was "very happy" with the prestigious NYFF closing night slot. A darling of the NYFF, where *About Schmidt* was accorded opening night honors in 2002, Payne is being feted like the star he is in the international film community. (p. 12)

"I always think an audience is smarter than I am, not dumber. So often, at least in recent American filmmaking, there's a pressure—however spoken or unspoken—to dilute the intelligence or the sophisticated references or the quality of the jokes or something for a more general audience, and I just don't like to do that." Payne (p. 103)

". . . every once in a while you have to stand back and look at it and go, 'Oh, that's not working over there.' So, you need to get an overview and that's where a preview can help. The only way you know what your film is is by showing it to an audience." Payne (p. 47)

18. Work fot Hire and Work for Friends

Payne has a theory why feature directors like himself are sought after for pilots: "They figure a feature director might be a little bit more adept at creating the world of the show, helping cast it, helping determine the look, helping pick some of the creative and then beginning to shape something out of nothing that can then be used as a template for the show henceforth." Not only is it a chance to shape a world but to work on a more intimate scale. "It's fun to work in miniature and one puts no less attention," he said. (p. 128)

He's helped produce two feature films due out next year. *The Savages* stars Philip Seymour Hoffman and Laura Linney. *King of California* stars Michael Douglas and Evan Rachel Wood. Payne's a close friend of the filmmakers. He's an executive producer on *Savages*, written-directed by Tamara Jenkins (*The Slums of Beverly Hills*), the wife of Payne's writing partner Jim Taylor. He's a full producer on *King*, whose writer-director Michael Cahill was a film school buddy of Payne's at UCLA. (p. 117)

As much as he enjoys helping friends, it's still a distraction from his own work. "I mean, all of this is fine, but I don't want to produce anymore. I didn't get into film to be a producer. That's the last thing I want to be. I'm happy to help my friends when I can. I've done it and I'll do it again, but I can't for a while. Not the way I did it this year, because I need to do my own scuba diving"—his metaphor for immersing himself in his writing-directing—"and be utterly free to do my own thing. Every day I'm not directing I feel like I die a little." Payne (p. 123)

19. Studios, Financing, Budgets

"One of the elements of my film career is trying to keep my costs down as much as possible so I can maintain more creative control. . . . I tell them I'm from Omaha and I don't like to maintain fictions. I like to be straight from the get go and so all my movies to date have been on time and under budget." Payne (p. 293)

"The movie [*Sideways*] had gotten bigger. When we were talking to Artisan we were going to make it for seven to ten million dollars. On a shoestring. *After Schmidt*, Alexander now had the power that we could actually get a healthy budget and do it on a larger scale," London said, "without compromising. It was budgeted at 16–17 million dollars for a fifty-day shoot, which by the standards of contemporary studio movies is a tiny, tiny movie, but by the standards of a movie about a couple guys running around in wine country, is plenty of money to do it well and plenty of time to do it well."
Michael London, Producer (pp. 96–97)

Norfolk director of economic development Courtney Klein-Faust says the total impact the project [*Nebraska*] had on the local economy has yet to be tabulated but that just in lodging alone the production spent more than a half-million dollars accommodating its 100 cast and crew members. She says the film bought local goods and services whenever possible. She feels the experience will serve as "a case study" for elected officials to assess the trickle down effect of mid-major features and will be used by supporters of tax credits to push for more film industry friendly measures. (p. 224)

Ever since he began talking about *Nebraska* he's described his vision for it as "austere," referring to the small budget ($12 million), tight shoot schedule (six weeks), short script (ninety five pages) and minimal camera set-ups. (p. 242)

"A first-look deal is where a studio just kind of pays for some overhead and you have people working for you in an office and in exchange they [Fox Searchlight] get first right of negotiation . . . first crack at anything we do. It doesn't necessarily mean they're going to make it, but they get a short window of time in which to decide if they want to do it and, if not, it's in effect a free ball. And it just kind of formalizes good will and relationship between filmmakers and studio. Besides . . . the company allows Jim and me to have extra eyes and ears out there reading books or accepting scripts, taking phone calls. Otherwise, we're doing it all ourselves and not getting our work done. It's just sort of there to facilitate us. (pp. 118-19)

How Fox positions it [*The Descendants*] is beyond his control. "The studio, I trust, is going to do a great job. I completely trust in their greed." Payne (p. 193)

In no uncertain terms Payne wanted to make *Nebraska* in black and white and just as adamantly the studio [Paramount] wanted no part of it. He pushed and they pushed back. (p. 211)

From all indications, Payne kept busy in the months and years after *Sideways*, but one project after another came undone as the independent sector went into free fall and Indiewood seriously retrenched. With the studios' tentpole beasts—*Harry Potter*, *Spider-Man*, *Shrek*, and the rest—ruling the global marketplace, the conglomerates could no longer rationalize their risky indie divisions.
Thomas Schatz *Foreword* (p. xvii)

20. Films and Filmmakers Payne Admires

"For me, I look at Italian films of the '60s and American films of the '70s." Payne (p. 114)

"I grew up in the '70s with all those great movies, and those movies, which were the commercial Hollywood movies, were also strongly authorial and humanistic and artistic and realistic. Then we hit the '80s and '90s, where a lot of American cinema was dominated by a lot of formula, grossly commercial concerns. And it's true I don't see many current American films. I continue to watch old movies and to go see foreign films. I nourish myself that way." Payne (p. 34)

He enjoys discussing the filmmaking art, his working process, his celluloid passions (It turns out he's a huge fan of Westerns and samurai films.) and even his life outside cinema. At once a scholar and a celebrity, he is at his core a filmaholic grateful to be working in the field he loves. (p. 61)

Filmography

Downsizing (**2017**)
Matt Damon, Reese Witherspoon, Jason Sudeikis

Nebraska (**2013**)
Bruce Dern, Will Forte, June Squibb

The Descendants (**2011**)
George Clooney, Shailene Woodley, Beau Bridges

Sideways (**2004**)
Paul Giamatti, Thomas Haden Church, Virginia Madsen

About Schmidt (**2002**)
Jack Nicholson, Hope Davis, Dermot Mulroney

Election (**1999**)
Matthew Broderick, Reese Withersoon, Chris Klein

Citizen Ruth (**1996**)
Laura Dern, Swoosie Kurtz, Mary Kay Place

Inside Out (**1991**)

The Passion of Martin (**1990**)

Carmen (short) (**1985**)

Writer

Downsizing, screenplay, 2017 *
The Descendants, screenplay, 2011
I Now Pronounce You Chuck & Larry, screenplay, 2007 *
Paris, je t'aime (segment *14e arrondissement*), 2006
Sideways, screenplay, 2004 *
About Schmidt, screenplay, 2002 *
Jurassic Park III, screenplay, 2001 *
Election, screenplay, 1999 *
Citizen Ruth, screenplay, 1996 *
The Passion of Martin, screenplay, 1990

* with Jim Taylor

Producer

Downsizing, producer
Wilson, producer, 2016
Hung, executive producer, 2009–2011
L Train (short), executive producer, 2011
The Descendants, producer, 2011
Cedar Rapids, producer, 2011
King of California, producer, 2007
The Savages, executive producer, 2007
The Assassination of Richard Nixon, executive producer, 2004
The Passion of Martin, producer, 1990

Alexander Payne Awards Won

Academy Awards, USA

2012   Best Writing, Adapted Screenplay, *The Descendants* (with Nat Faxon, Jim Rash)

2005   Best Writing, Adapted Screenplay, *Sideways* (with Jim Taylor)

AFI Awards

2012   AFI Movie of the Year, *The Descendants* (with Jim Taylor, Jim Burke)

Writers Guild of America

2012   Best Adapted Screenplay, *The Descendants* (with Nat Faxon, Jim Rash)

2005   Best Adapted Screenplay, *Sideways* (with Jim Taylor)

2000   Best Screenplay Based on Material Previously Published or Produced, *Election* (with Jim Taylor)

National Board of Review, USA

2011   Best Adapted Screenplay, *The Descendants* (with Nat Faxon, Jim Rash)

2004   Best Adapted Screenplay, *Sideways* (with Jim Taylor)

Golden Globes, US

2005   Best Screenplay—Motion Picture, *Sideways* (with Jim Taylor)

2003   Best Screenplay—Motion Picture, *About Schmidt* (with Jim Taylor)

National Society of Film Critics Awards, USA

2005   Best Screenplay, *Sideways* (with Jim Taylor)

Alexander Payne Awards Won

New York Film Critics Circle Awards

2004   Best Screenplay, *Sideways* (with Jim Taylor)
1999   Best Screenplay, *Election* (with Jim Taylor)

Los Angeles Film Critics Association Awards

2004   Best Screenplay, *Sideways* (with Jim Taylor)
2002   Best Screenplay, *About Schmidt* (with Jim Taylor)
1999   New Generation Awards, *Election* (with Jim Taylor)

Independent Spirit Awards

2012   Best Screenplay, *The Descendants* (with Nat Faxon and
        Jim Rash)
2005   Best Director, *Sideways*
        Best Screenplay, *Sideways* (with Jim Taylor)
2000   Best Director, *Election*
        Best Screenplay, *Election* (with Jim Taylor)

Acknowledgments

This book would not exist without the support of publishers and editors who recognized a good thing in Alexander Payne when they saw one and consequently gave me free rein to report on him. Their recognition of the filmmaker as a singular talent may have been slower than mine at the start, but they eventually came around to seeing him as a rare and rich subject that could be mined over and over without ever exhausting our fascination with him or his work.

The journalist most responsible for enabling my ongoing coverage of Payne is John Heaston. As the publisher of *The Reader*, then the *Omaha Weekly*, and *The Reader* again, he has consistently granted me the assignments that form the bulk of this book.

Thanks, too, go to the copy editors, graphic designers, and photographers who helped make my stories look great on the page. Though this is an independently published book, it would not have been realized the first time without the team at Concierge Marketing in Omaha providing their invaluable services in the areas of editing, networking, distribution, marketing, and fulfillment. Concierge president Lisa Pelto deserves special thanks for guiding me through the process. This second time around I appreciate all that publisher Kira Gale has done in reformatting the book and in creating the Discussion Guide with Index. I am pleased to have this 2nd edition published by her River Junction Press.

The project may have never come together if not for the encouragement of friends, acquaintances, associates, and peers who believed in me and in what I wanted to do with this body of work. My late life partner, Joslen (Johnson) Shaw, who died in 2012, kept the faith even when I lost faith in myself.

Special thanks to Thomas Schatz and Timothy Schaffert for their insightful takes on Payne as indie auteur and Nebraska impressionist. Thanks go as well to Anna Musso, Alexander Payne's assistant at Ad Hominem, who provided candid photos of her boss that she shot herself on the set of *Hung* and *The Descendants*. I appreciate photographer Bryce Bridges of Omaha for his splendid portraits of Payne.

Finally, the subject of this book must be acknowledged for the faith and trust he has put in me to revisit his creative process time and again.

At any point in the last decade and a half he could have pulled back or cut me off, but he has always remained open to my entreaties. He has never, not once, made me feel I was an imposition or an inconvenience. Thank you, Alexander.

About the Author

Leo Adam Biga is an author-journalist-blogger who shares his hometown of Omaha, Nebraska with Alexander Payne and other film notables. Biga's award-winning cultural journalism has appeared in numerous publications since the 1980s. His special interest in film writing-reporting is an extension of his lifelong enthusiasm for cinema. His Nebraska Film Heritage Project is a planned website, book, lecture tour, and curriculum focusing on the state's deep roster of film talent from the start of the industry through today. He is also planning a book on Omaha's Black Sports Legends. His other books include *Crossing Bridges: A Priest's Uplifting Life Among the Downtrodden.*

You can follow his work on his blog, Leo Adam Biga's My Inside Stories at leoadambiga.com and on his Facebook page, My Inside Stories, at www.facebook.com/LeoAdamBiga. Biga is available as a speaker, panelist, moderator, and expert source. For inquiries regarding the book, visit www.alexanderpaynethebook.com.

His email is: leo32158@cox.net

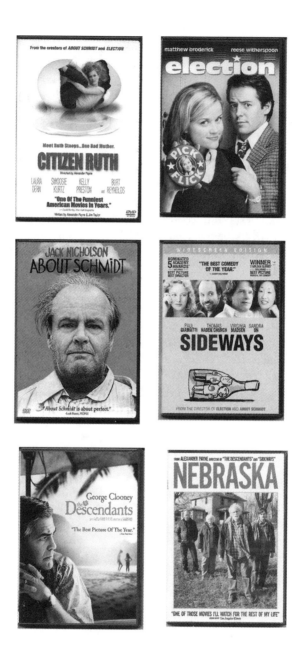

Rent or buy Alexander Payne's films on Amazon.com. *Paris Je T'aime* is also available. *Downsizing* will become available after its release. *The Descendants* and *Sideways* are also available as shooting scripts.